A Quest of Her Own

By Lori M. Campbell

*Portals of Power: Magical Agency and
Transformation in Literary Fantasy*
(Critical Explorations in Science Fiction
and Fantasy 19, McFarland, 2010)

A Quest of Her Own

Essays on the Female Hero in Modern Fantasy

Edited by
LORI M. CAMPBELL

McFarland & Company, Inc., Publishers
Jefferson, North Carolina

LIBRARY OF CONGRESS CATALOGUING-IN-PUBLICATION DATA

A quest of her own : essays on the female hero in modern fantasy /
    edited by Lori M. Campbell.
        p.   cm.
    Includes bibliographical references and index.

    ISBN 978-0-7864-7766-1 (softcover : acid free paper) ∞
    ISBN 978-1-4766-1763-3 (ebook)

    1. Fantasy fiction, English—20th century—History and criticism.
    2. Fantasy fiction, American—20th century—History and criticism.
    3. Women heroes in literature.   I. Campbell, Lori M., editor of
    compilation.

    PN3435.Q47 2014
    809.3'8766—dc23   2014019171

BRITISH LIBRARY CATALOGUING DATA ARE AVAILABLE

Printed in the United States of America

*McFarland & Company, Inc., Publishers
    Box 611, Jefferson, North Carolina 28640
    www.mcfarlandpub.com*

For Chuck and Colin,
for making the world less wobbly
and more magical every day

Acknowledgments

First and foremost, I would like to thank the contributors to *A Quest of Her Own* for making the editing process so smooth and painless, and more importantly, for your insightful explorations of the topic. Thanks to Gregory F. Tague for his helpful advice as I began to develop the idea for this book. I thank my research assistant, Colette Slagle, for being my second set of eyes on this project, and for being my superb teaching assistant for three semesters. And thanks also to my students—past, present, and future—for helping me to continue to love and appreciate my job even after more than a decade of teaching.

Table of Contents

Preface

One of my favorite things about working in academia is the exchange of ideas that occurs in the classroom between a teacher and her students. Particularly with fantasy, as I'm sure most teachers of the genre would agree, the multiple interpretations that are possible with each text mean that invariably a student will come up with an idea I hadn't thought of, or a fresh angle from which to look at a passage, character, or image. The idea for *A Quest of Her Own: Essays on the Female Hero in Modern Fantasy* was born out of discussions in my 2011 section of Fantasy and Romance, a literature course I have taught regularly at University of Pittsburgh virtually since I began there in 2001. Specifically, the discussions focused on *The Time of the Ghost* by Diana Wynne Jones, supplemented by her 1992 lecture "Heroes." At the time, my own research had not led me to think much about distinguishing female from male heroes. Though my first book, *Portals of Power: Magical Agency and Transformation in Literary Fantasy* (McFarland, 2010), primarily dealt with portrayals of women and children, I had not thought about female characters specifically in terms of archetypal heroism. In class, when my students wanted to talk more and more about the notion of a "female hero," I became increasingly intrigued as well. Several months later when McFarland asked if I might have an idea for a second book, the female hero immediately came to mind, and I had already done some investigation that revealed the topic had been practically untouched, apart from a few key texts that did not approach it in the way I had in mind.

One of these key texts was Donald Haase's excellent *Fairy Tales and Feminism: New Approaches* (2004), which I came across in my preliminary reading. Haase's work traces the history of criticism on the ways in which women and girls have been presented in fairy tales, but I found no noteworthy work providing literary analysis on the female hero in modern fantasy, and I envisioned *A Quest of Her Own* to fill that gap. Another early critical influence was Roberta Seelinger Trites' *Waking Sleeping Beauty* (1997), though her work more narrowly focuses on feminist books as influences on the female reader, and I was more interested in works that strive for what Miriam Polster calls "a balanced sense of heroic possibilities that draws from the best qualities of both" men and women (6). Polster's *Eve's Daughters: Forbidden Heroism of Women* (1992) was useful for its insights on real-world heroism at the time of its publication, though I wanted to organize *A Quest of Her Own* around more recent literary texts whose female heroes would challenge the idea that "the old heroic images are still in place albeit 'new and improved' versions, with modern packaging" (Polster 8). The book that probably comes nearest to my own work is Jennifer K. Stuller's *Ink-Stained Amazons and Cinematic Warriors: Superwomen in Modern Mythology* (2010). Stuller's premise, "superwomen have ... revolutionized depictions of collaboration in contemporary heroic narratives for women and men" (8), supports my assumption of the female hero as a site of influence, not solely for girl and women readers but for society as a whole. Beyond this, however, Stuller's work greatly contrasts *A Quest of Her Own*, primarily because she focuses on the notion of a "superwoman," which I resist for reasons explained in my introduction and because her subject texts are from film, television, and comics, rather than from literary fantasy.

Perhaps surprisingly (except to those who know me), the text that contributed the most to the development of my thinking on the female hero was J.R.R. Tolkien's *The Lord of the Rings*. Despite Tolkien's often being criticized for his lack of female characters, and for his conservative portrayals of the ones he does include, I find these characters to be more complex and their examples more progressive than some critics allow. Tolkien's personal attitudes toward women, presumably shaped by his time period and upbringing, are well known, having been explored in several volumes, including this one. Of course, these attitudes do find their way into his art, yet, I submit that his imperfectly realized female heroes—if they may be viewed as such—provide more to applaud than to complain about. The best known female heroes in a text that is accepted as having created modern fantasy—Galadriel, Arwen, and Éowyn—are invaluable for personifying a transition from the damsels in distress more typical of the myth and romance genres to the more nuanced, capable, and heroic women whose stories are explored in *A Quest of Her Own*. As a result, I decided early on that this study would benefit from having two essays dedicated to teasing out Tolkien's approach to gender as a way of providing a foundation for the rest of the book, in terms of establishing some tropes of modern fantasy as well as of female heroism.

The choice to include Tolkien was an easy one, as was the decision to do this book as a collection of essays rather than exploring the topic on my own. Like fantasy itself, the female hero exists in myriad forms with multiple layers of meaning, so having multiple perspectives seemed to be the most productive way to begin to define her. The volume is meant to instigate some rethinking of many of the premier texts of the last thirty years or so, but also to introduce some that have been largely overlooked, or that are very recent. In tracing the invention, construction, and actions of the female hero, together the diverse voices of the contributors assemble an archetype still in the process of becoming. While her story is only beginning to unfold, as the essays in this collection will illustrate, her presence is palpable and undeniable.

Lori M. Campbell
University of Pittsburgh

Introduction

Lori M. Campbell

As one of the most important ancestors of literary fantasy, the fairy tale has enjoyed a beloved and influential position in the tradition of storytelling from the earliest civilizations. Yet, feminist studies of the genre only began in earnest in the 1970s after Alison Lurie and Marcia R. Lieberman famously debated the extent to which classic tales depict strong females. Finding that in the "best-known stories ... most of the heroines are passive, submissive, and helpless" (Lieberman 190), Lieberman challenged Lurie's belief that fairy tales constitute "one of the few sorts of classic children's literature ... [to] suggest a society in which women are as competent and active as men, at every age and in every class" (Lurie).[1] While the Lurie-Lieberman debate was crucial for having instigated "the advent of modern fairy tale studies with its emphases on the genre's sociopolitical and sociohistorical contexts" (Haase 2), its central issue has yet to be fully applied to modern fantasy, the more expansive form of magical literature whose roots lie in the fairy tale, as well as in mythology and medieval romance.

This is not to say that feminism has ignored modern fantasy, only that a lack of strong female protagonists worth considering has postponed any in-depth panoramic studies of the female hero as an archetype in her own right. Critics interested in this topic have instead satisfied themselves with lamenting the few female protagonists populating such texts in their failures to live up to true hero status. With J.R.R. Tolkien's *The Lord of the Rings* as a prime example of this lack, "[u]ntil very recently, all heroes in the quest story have been male. Females in fantasy have been largely silent or invisible, and it used to be unthinkable that a woman would set out on a quest unprotected by a man to do battle" (Sprague and Keeling 113). Decades after Tolkien's success with *The Hobbit* (1937) and *The Lord of the Rings* (1954–5), however, the rapid expansion and increasing critical acceptance of modern fantasy—the genre that Tolkien is

4

widely known for having created—yielded a fortunate side effect: "the development of an increasingly nuanced view of the relation between gender and the fairy tale," both in the fiction and its analysis (Haase 2). Of course, this evolution in thinking about modern fantasy also coincided with and was inspired by the second wave women's movement in the early 1960s, but does not begin to impact the development of the female hero until about a decade or so later, around the same time as the Lurie-Lieberman fairy tale debate. More women were writing fantasy—not only in children's literature and low fantasy as they did in the nineteenth century, but in the previously male-dominated realm of high fantasy as well. Many of them, such as Marion Zimmer Bradley, Robin McKinley, and Tamora Pierce, recast "the typical male hero of the quest story with female heroes" (Sprague and Keeling 123), while others, including Angela Carter and Tanith Lee, chose to revise the classic fairy tales. Meanwhile, male authors such as Alan Garner, Terry Pratchett, Neil Gaiman, and Philip Pullman began writing about women and girls in more enlightened, less rigidly stereotypical ways. Out of these combined efforts rose a character type who could live up to the mantle of hero, one displaying bravery, assertiveness—and, at times, foolishness or arrogance—all familiar traits of her male counterpart, but also *human* traits shared by all.

This study contributes to the empowerment of the female hero as she carves out a permanent, independent position alongside—rather than in comparison or as subject to—the male version that has reigned for centuries. Our overarching goal is to tease out the ways in which literary fantasy writers following Tolkien uniquely define the female hero so that she "need not mimic the male hero's journey ... [she] may reject the established patterns, cast aside the old rules, and prevail on [her] own terms" (Barron 31). If, as Roberta Seelinger Trites argues, "a major goal of feminism is to support women's choices," then the prevalence and power of the female hero in the highly popular genre of literary fantasy becomes a way "to foster societal respect for those choices" (Trites 2). Based on the belief that, whether male or female, "heroes are agents of change ... [who] move other people—sometimes whole societies—forward with them" (Polster 49), *A Quest of Her Own* aims to identify some tropes of female heroism as it influences and is influenced by the culture out of which it is developed.

In doing preliminary research for this book, I was only slightly surprised to find very little substantive work had been done on the female hero. The most prominent exception is *The Female Hero in American and British Literature* (1981) in which Carol Pearson and Katherine Pope argue the need for women's heroism to be recognized for, as they put it,

> unless the heroism that women demonstrate in the world is reflected in the literature and myth of the culture, women and men are left with the impression that women are not heroic; that their heroism, when it occurs, is a reaction to

the moment and that they ultimately revert to dependence on a man; and that the woman who elects a life of courage, strength, and initiative on her own behalf is an exception, a deviant, and doomed to destruction [7].

Given the lack of examples of female heroes in literary fantasy at the time when Pearson and Pope were writing, it is unsurprising that they limit their subject texts mainly to realistic fiction, even though they use mythology and fairy tale as their lens for analysis. So, while their work remains important to this present study, it provides only a partial foundation for delineating female heroism in the genre where she comes to definitively exist and where she grows up.

With no clear sense of her attributes upon which to build, I wanted *A Quest of Her Own* to provide a study that sketches the female hero in modern fantasy by looking at some representative examples in well-known texts, as well as in some less familiar works that portray the character type in innovative and illuminating ways. Therefore I offer no definition of the female hero here in the introduction, but will draw conclusions about her in my closing remarks, after the contributors and I reveal some of her defining traits. Since it is not our specific goal to interrogate the notion of heroism itself but rather to consider how it operates in female form, we begin from a general understanding of "heroism" and "hero" in their long-established usage. With the hope that each contributor would resist being burdened by the baggage of the male hero (to the extent that this is possible), I provided a foundational hero definition and one of the most widely accepted, that of Joseph Campbell: "a hero or heroine ... has found or done something beyond the normal range of achievement and experience. A hero is someone who has given his or her life to something bigger than oneself" (*Power of Myth* 123). Acknowledging such a character to be "a hero or heroine," to his credit in *The Hero with a Thousand Faces* Campbell accepts the idea of a female being capable of heroism, though his collections of folktales and myths generally hold to a more conservative view of heroism. His "goddess" prefigures certain qualities of the modern female hero in her exercising of power, often over a hero figure, yet the goddess remains an element or test as part of the male hero's experience rather than a fully developed character with her own journey. Still, Campbell's understanding of a character "who has given his or her life to something bigger than oneself" allows for a range of applications to fully illustrate the scope of female heroism.

While I refrain from pinpointing the female hero here in the introduction, I need to say a few words about the book's terminology. Like Pearson and Pope in *The Female Hero in American and British Literature*, we purposefully refer to her as "female hero" rather than "heroine," and my reasoning for this choice requires some brief discussion. Since the female hero is only recently coming into her own, while the male version has been the standard and ideal for centuries, her representation of heroism must be considered in its own terms. While, as Pearson and Pope argue, "on the archetypal level the journey to self-discovery is the same for both the male and female hero" (vii-viii), the obstacles she must overcome for her journey to be recognized as heroic are different, and, like it or not, negotiating difference must be taken into account as inherent to her journey. Also, if as Susan J. Drucker and Gary Gumpert assert, "the hero exists in the eye of the beholder. Every hero must be a hero *to* someone" (20, emphasis in original), then a major trait of the female hero is the potential of her journey to inspire those with a similar need to prove themselves or rise above subjectivities of varying kinds. Supporting this, Miriam F. Polster makes the point that recognizing women as heroes based on their own unique traits results in "the concept of heroism [being] enlarged to include some previously overlooked heroic behavior by *men* as well as women" (42, emphasis in original).

Consequently, the use of the term "female hero" is helpful in that it reminds us of the challenges the character has faced and continues to face in her evolution toward true hero status. This is unfortunate to some extent; but besides being a practical way to differentiate her in the simplest way, "female hero" is a *positive* term in its ability to highlight and celebrate her femaleness in tandem with her heroism—and with heroism more broadly. We have yet to reach a point in our society where we might leave out "female," where "we could just discuss heroes and not have to focus specifically on gender[;] cultural ideas of sex and gender are present in our fictional stories, intended or not" (Stuller, "What Is" 19). With this in mind, this project uses "female hero" partly out of necessity and continuity, but more importantly as a way to signify a key transitional moment in her evolution. The term connotes both the remarkable strides the character has already taken and the distance she has yet to travel.

As I noted in the opening paragraphs of this introduction, although examples of female empowerment are visible in literature across the centuries, the female hero does not exist in any distinctive way until well into the second half of the twentieth century. Up until then (and even after with characters like Xena and Buffy), if she appears at all, she most often does so not as a hero in her own right but—in contrast to the characters discussed in *A Quest of Her Own*—as a *super-heroine*; a figment of masculine imagination whose major super power is sexuality, enlarged to *seem* like real power. Significant differences exist between literary fantasy and the comic book, yet many critics continue to conflate the female comic book super-heroine with the female hero in modern fantasy, as a representative for gauging fictional female empowerment as a whole. Perhaps the best example of this is Wonder Woman, who was introduced in *All Star Comics* #8 in 1941 by psychologist William Moulton Marston as a purposeful "counter reaction to the presence of prominent male super heroes" (*Comic Vine*). Assessing the character in terms of female power in 1943, Marston noted,

Not even girls want to be girls so long as our feminine archetype lacks force, strength, and power. Women's strong qualities have become despised because of their weakness. The obvious remedy is to create a feminine character with all the strength of Superman plus all the allure of a good and beautiful woman [*Comic Vine*].

Despite his possible good intentions, Marston's logic is troublesome: his comment here implies "weakness" as an inherent female trait and insists on beauty and goodness as necessary components of femininity, as well as of female power. To have "allure" in Marston's terms a female hero must not only demonstrate "force" but also the stereotypical qualities of femininity. I do not mean to suggest that the female hero as defined in *A Quest of Her Own* must be *un*attractive in order to *be* a hero. On the contrary, being attractive often buoys the female hero because being unattractive may be looked upon as an excuse for being strong and brave (i.e., "I'm nothing to look at so I have to rely on other qualities to get attention" or "I'm nothing to look at so I might as well forget about being a woman and emphasize my masculine side"). Yet, by making Wonder Woman so obviously sexualized—large breasts, tiny waist, minuscule costume, 1940s housewife hairdo, bracelets as armor—Marston and those who have reincarnated the character over time only reinforce the limitations of femininity as a product of the masculine imagination. In part, the problem results from the particular conventions of the comic book at the time, which I will not go into here as they lie outside the concern of *A Quest of Her Own*. Still, the comparison is useful for exposing the crucial and fundamental inequality that also troubles the female hero in her ongoing development in modern fantasy, as well as illustrating the skewed and limited critical attention female power in the genre has thus far received.

As opposed to the super-heroine, the female hero—Katniss Everdeen in Suzanne Collins' *The Hunger Games* being a prime twenty-first century example in my mind—can and often does possess attractiveness and femininity, but these qualities do not in themselves *define her*.[2] She does not concern herself much with how she looks because she has more important things to worry about; in Katniss' case, feeding her family, staying alive, and saving the world. Beauty does not become a valuable commodity for her until she arrives in the Capitol, and even then she has to be molded and taught how to access this side of herself by those for whom beauty is not only valued but constructed in highly artificial ways that Katniss has difficulty negotiating. As Katniss' example illustrates, female heroism—like heroism in general—is a work in progress and success is typically not realized without pain and hard work. *A Quest of Her Own* will focus on characters demonstrating a range of experiences meant to illustrate female heroism to its greatest and most admirable extent, while also pointing out the obstacles that plague them along the way.

To establish an historical and literary context for the topic, the book begins with "Pathfinders: Empowered Women from Romance and Folktale to the

Birth of Modern Fantasy," a section that acknowledges some early female characters from folk/fairy tale and medieval romance who demonstrate heroism as they endeavor to defy certain stereotypes. With a goal that "scholars of fantasy literature ... will look to folklore resources when researching the female hero," in "Strategic Silences: Voiceless Heroes in Fairy Tales," Jeana Jorgensen provides a thorough and informative look at the problems inherent in gender-based classifications of the tales. Jorgensen uses "ATU 451 (The Maiden Who Seeks Her Brothers)" as her master text to support her argument that silence may actually constitute a kind of heroism, as a "coded protest against patriarchal norms and constraints." Next, in "Neglected Yet Noble: Nyneve and Female Heroism in Thomas Malory's *Le Morte Darthur*," Kristin Bovaird-Abbo aims to rescue Nyneve, Merlin's famous consort from Arthurian legend, from the commonly-held view of the "archetypal maiden helper" and resituate her as "a powerful and independent force who becomes the rescuer of many male figures, including King Arthur himself."

"Pathfinders" closes with two essays on J.R.R. Tolkien, whose status as a medieval scholar as well as the premier architect of modern literary fantasy are well known, and whose treatment of female power in *The Hobbit* and *The Lord of the Rings* has been a subject of ongoing debate. In "'Radiant and terrible': Tolkien's Heroic Women as Correctives to the Romance and Epic Traditions" Jack M. Downs confirms Tolkien's work as a bridge between medieval and modern. While, as Downs acknowledges, "the popular perception that Middle-earth is a fantasy world mostly devoid of powerful women," in his own more nuanced interpretation of Tolkien's Guinevere, Lúthien, and Éowyn, Downs offers insight into the ways in which the author's "ongoing negotiation with the romance and epic genres" enables "the broader range of options available to later female heroes of contemporary fantasy literature." By "[r]eading against the grain of criticism that argues there are 'no women' in the text or arguments that 'hero' is synonymous with 'warrior,'" Sarah Workman furthers understanding of Tolkien's oeuvre in "Female Valor Without Renown: Memory, Mourning and Loss at the Center of Middle-earth." Workman starts from the premise that fantasy and elegy are at their core "performative" modes, convincingly arguing that "mourning in [Tolkien's] text becomes a gendered, cultural tool that centralizes the female characters and marks their contribution as heroes." Through their insightful readings, Downs and Workman contribute to the ongoing debate about Tolkien's (anti)feminism while also positioning Tolkien's women as precursors to the female heroes whose stories form the basis for the rest of the book.

From here we begin to explore the particular tropes of female heroism by organizing the representative examples according to categories, beginning with "Underestimated Overachievers: Unlikely and Unstoppable Female Heroes." In this section the contributors consider how being viewed as having less potential to succeed can be transformed into an asset rather than accepted as a liability. The male archetype deriving from mythology is an epic hero who typically demonstrates some fatal flaw that trips him up at inopportune moments and is best known for his ability to overcome these trials through super-human strength, courage, and virtue. This classical notion of heroism remains a standard by which all other variations are measured; however, the incarnation of the hero that has become most prevalent in modern fantasy derives more from folk and fairy tale. This hero, as W.H. Auden famously identifies, is "the one whom everybody would judge as least likely to succeed ... humble enough to take advice and kind enough to give assistance to strangers, who, like himself appear to be nobody in particular" (37). By virtue of their sex and the stereotypical qualities associated with it, female protagonists nearly always start out as unlikely heroes. In "'Weak as woman's magic': Empowering Care Work in Ursula Le Guin's *Tehanu*," Erin Wyble Newcomb finds that in this initially unplanned sequel to her *Earthsea* series, Le Guin "destabilizes the male monopoly of heroism and elevates ordinary women's work to the potentially extraordinary." Melissa Wehler similarly argues a transformation of the mundane into the remarkable in "'Be wise. Be brave. Be tricky': Neil Gaiman's Extraordinarily Ordinary Coraline." Identifying the title character as one who "consciously and creatively takes possession of her life and identity ... and brings fulfillment to herself and those around her," Wehler finds that Coraline "offer[s] young readers, both male and female, child and adult, a progressive model for heroism." In "Dancing with the Public: Alethea Kontis's *Enchanted*, Rachel Hartman's *Seraphina* and Marissa Meyer's *Cinder*," Casey A. Cothran traces hero journeys being carried out against "the dragon of public censure." In these three texts aimed at a young adult audience, Cothran argues that each female hero "must shatter the mirror, disregarding her desire to please others, and she must cultivate a self-confidence that is strong enough to withstand widespread public critique." Also focusing on works that assume a younger readership, in "'This huntress who delights in arrows': The Female Archer in Children's Fiction," Zoe Jaques demonstrates how texts including Suzanne Collins' *The Hunger Games* "navigate tensions concerning female identity, violence, childhood and survival."

Next, the section "Show-Stealers: Heroic Female Sidekicks and Helpers" highlights those women and girls who initially may be overlooked by virtue of their positions as the hero's companions or secondary characters. With important similarities to the unlikely hero, the sidekick begins from a place of even greater underestimation. Her initial subordination to the male protagonist is belied by the physical aid as well as the emotional and intellectual support she provides and without which he could not succeed. The female sidekick falls into the category of "donor" or "provider" to the hero in the terms established in Vladmir Propp's *Morphology of the Folktale* (39). Critics since Propp have commonly associated isolation with the hero archetype, including Max Luthi who sees this quality in the hero's helpers as well (143). For the female sidekick, this isolation engenders physical, and more importantly, emotional strength: the strength that is born out of being isolated, as well as the strength that isolates her in the first place for deviating from others of her sex and/or from social expectations based on sex. Combined with the extraordinary qualities (often manifested through a connection with magic), this strength becomes increasingly obvious through the help she provides to the male protagonist.

Ultimately, the heroic female sidekick becomes a vehicle for the author to mirror the motivations, actions, and consequences for real-world women and girls making a similar journey. In "Sublime Shape-Shifters and Uncanny Other-Selves: Identity and Multiplicity in Dianne Wynne Jones' Female Heroes," Apolline Lucyk explores how the author's "use of multiple character identities enables her to create complex, resourceful female heroes who are not simply shadows of male heroes, nor passive female heroines" in three key works. The identity of knighthood is at stake in John H. Cameron's " A New Kind of Hero: *A Song of Ice and Fire*'s Brienne of Tarth," a thoughtful repositioning of the character from an admirable if unconventional female knight into a "new kind of hero" for her representation of George R.R. Martin's nuanced treatment of gender identities and dynamics. My own essay, "And *Her* Will Be Done: The Girls Trump the Boys in *The Keys to the Kingdom* and *Abhorsen* Series by Garth Nix," rounds out this section by investigating Nix's tendency to "pai[r] his female heroes with weak, indecisive, and insecure male protagonists." While he offers a "more realistic, less stereotypical approach to gender," than is prevalent in the 1980s and '90s, Nix's work must be scrutinized for empowering the girls seemingly "at the expense of the boys."

The final section, "Unwilling Do-Gooders: Villains and Villain-Heroes," looks at darker manifestations of female power as a way of illuminating female heroism by contrast, and of locating the circumstances that turn good to evil (and back again). As Pearson and Pope assert, "Literature ... tends to portray the woman who demonstrates initiative, strength, wisdom and independent action—the ingredients of the heroic life—not as a hero but as a villain" (6). Particularly in recent years, more complex portrayals of villainy, which eschew good and evil as moral absolutes, have provided us with characters—both male and female—whose wrongdoing is not so always so easy to wholly condemn. In myth, medieval romance, and folk/fairy tales, a magical woman is nearly always an evil one, but more recent writers have overturned or at least complicated this association.

One popular way that writers in the last decade or so have found to do this involves repositioning magic, rescuing it from an assumption of evil. According to Marsha M. Sprague and Kara K. Keeling, such stories "are especially empowering when they feature girls who have supernatural powers that make girls equal, if not superior, to their male peers" (128). Such superiority carries with it an association with transgression that originally defines magic in a medieval or religious sense, but for modern readers this rule-breaking is a positive signifier of empowerment. Supporting this idea, scholars commonly take into account the evil as well as the good when measuring the extent of female power in a particular work. For example, in "From Sexist to (sort-of) Feminist Representations of Gender in the Harry Potter Series," Elizabeth E. Heilman and Trevor Donaldson tally Bellatrix LeStrange and Rita Skeeter alongside "good" wizarding women such as Hermione Granger, Molly Weasley, and Professor McGonagall in their estimation of the series' overall portrayal of female power. Evil continues to be both an inescapable and fascinating aspect of human nature, and, as Daniel Forbes argues, "the villain may be symbolic of the risk involved in reflecting on our beliefs—which may threaten established values but is also necessary for adventure and growth" (Forbes 19).

The contributors to this final section arguably explore female power to its most unexpected extent, starting with Amanda M. Greenwell in "The Problem of Mrs. Coulter: Vetting the Female Villain-Hero in Philip Pullman's *His Dark Materials*." Drawing upon the work of Simone de Beauvoir to "analyz[e] the way the narrative progression initially encourages the reader to dismiss Mrs. Coulter's mimetic qualities and label her as an archetypal villain," Greenwell "ultimately argues for [Mrs. Coulter's] late emerging heroics as key to the trilogy's attempt to reshape the authorial audience's—and therefore actual audience's—conceptions of the villainous and the heroic." In her study of a less well-known but equally thought-provoking example, in "'All little girls are terrible': Maud as Anti-Villain in Catherynne M. Valente's *The Girl Who Circumnavigated Fairyland in a Ship of Her Own Making*," Jill Marie Treftz demonstrates how the author "specifically deconstructs the ways in which children's fantasy has traditionally privileged little girlhood far above adult womanhood." Sarah Margaret Kniesler closes this final section with a fresh and unconventional reading of villainy in one of the most successful fantasy series of the twentieth century. In "'The Unbreakable Vow': Maternal Impulses and Narcissa Malfoy's Transformation from Villain to Hero in J. K. Rowling's *Harry Potter* Series," Kniesler surveys the various faces of motherhood—good and bad—throughout the series to support her argument that Narcissa's subtle "transformation from villain to hero" is the one "that most influences the outcome of the final conflict of the series."

At the heart of *A Quest of Her Own*, of course, is the issue of power, as it is claimed or used by the female hero, as well as in how it is represented by and around her, and the ways in which her stories reflect contemporary notions of power/powerlessness for both women and men in society. Whether she wields a bow, sword, superior magic, intelligence, or imagination as her weapon(s) of choice, the female heroes highlighted in *A Quest of Her Own* stand out for the fact of their very existence as well as for their courage, assertiveness, and willingness to self-sacrifice. Given such criteria, identifying more than a handful of female characters in modern literary fantasy who may be worthy of hero identification might seem to be a challenge, but the real purpose of this study is to bring awareness to this fact and to start—or re-ignite—that conversation. In the process, we celebrate those who will likely become the precursors for the further development of the female hero as an established convention, a true archetype of literary fantasy.

NOTES

1. For a more detailed analysis of the Lurie-Lieberman debate, see: Haase, Donald. "Feminist Fairy-Tale Scholarship." *Fairy Tales and Feminism: New Approaches.* Donald Haase, Ed. Detroit: Wayne State UP, 2004. 1–36.

2. Usually categorized as "dystopian fiction" *The Hunger Games* may seem to diverge from the fantasy genre, but in my view the series combines elements of fantasy and science fiction into a hybrid form that is part of an increasing trend in modern fantasy.

WORKS CITED

Auden, W.H. "The Quest Hero." *Understanding* The Lord of the Rings: *The Best of Tolkien Criticism.* Rose A. Zimbardo and Neil D. Isaacs, Eds. New York: Houghton Mifflin, 2004. 31–51.

Campbell, Joseph, with Bill Moyers. *The Power of Myth.* New York: Doubleday, 1988.

Comic Vine. "Wonder Woman." Accessed 1 August 2012. http://www.comicvine.com/wonder-woman/29-2048/.

Drucker, Susan J., and Gary Gumpert, eds. *Heroes in a Global World.* Cresskill, NJ: Hampton Press, 2008.

Forbes, Daniel. "The Aesthetic of Evil." Jamey Heit, ed. *Vader, Voldemort and Other Villains: Essays on Evil in Popular Media.* Jefferson, NC: McFarland, 2011. 13–27.

Haase, Donald. "Feminist Fairy-Tale Scholarship." *Fairy Tales and Feminism: New Approaches.* Donald Haase, ed. Detroit: Wayne State University Press, 2004. 1–36.

Heilman, Elizabeth E., and Trevor Donaldson. "From Sexist to (sort-of) Feminist Representations of Gender in the Harry Potter Series." *Critical Perspectives on Harry Potter,* 2d ed. Elizabeth H. Heilman, ed. New York: Routledge, 2009. 139–61.

Lieberman, Marcia K. "'Some Day My Prince Will Come': Female Acculturation through the Fairy Tale." *Don't Bet on the Prince: Contemporary Feminist Fairy Tales in North America and England.* Jack Zipes, ed. New York: Routledge, 1987. 185–200.

Lurie, Alison. "Fairy Tale Liberation." *The New York Review of Books* 15.11 (December 17, 1970). *The New York Review of Books Online.* Accessed July 10, 2012. http://www.nybooks.com/articles/archives/1970/dec/17/fairy-tale-liberation/?pagination=false.

Luthi, Max. *Once Upon a Time: On the Nature of Fairy Tales.* New York: Frederick Ungar, 1970.

Pearson, Carol, and Katherine Pope. *The Female Hero in American and British Literature.* New York: R.R. Bowker, 1981.

Propp, Vladmir. *The Morphology of the Fairy Tale.* Austin: University of Texas Press, 1968.

Sprague, Marsha M., and Kara K. Keeling. *Discovering Their Voices: Engaging Adolescent Girls with Young Adult Literature.* Newark, DE: International Reading Association, 2007.

Stuller, Jennifer K. *Ink-Stained Amazons and Cinematic Warriors: Superwomen in Modern Mythology.* New York: I.B. Tauris, 2010.

_____. "What Is a Female Superhero?" *What Is a Superhero?* Robin S. Rosenberg and Peter Coogan, eds. New York: Oxford University Press, 2013. 19–23.

Trites, Roberta Seelinger. *Waking Sleeping Beauty: Feminist Voices in Children's Novels.* Iowa City: University of Iowa Press, 1997.

I. Pathfinders: Empowered Women from Romance and Folktale to the Birth of Modern Fantasy

Strategic Silences:
Voiceless Heroes in Fairy Tales[1]

Jeana Jorgensen

In a number of international fairy tale types, such as ATU 451 ("The Maiden Who Seeks Her Brothers"), the female protagonist voluntarily stops speaking in order to attain the object of her quest. In ATU 451, found in the collected tales of the Grimms and Hans Christian Andersen as well as in oral tradition, the protagonist remains silent while weaving the shirts needed to disenchant her brothers from their birdlike forms. While this silence is undoubtedly disempowering in some ways as she cannot defend herself from persecution and accusations of wickedness, here I argue that the choice to remain silent is a coded form of protest. Drawing on feminist, queer, and folkloristic theories, I demonstrate that the fairy-tale female hero who chooses to remain silent does so strategically in a coded protest against patriarchal norms and constraints.

When studying female heroes in oral tradition, it is important to take into account the values and associations of silence in the cultures that transmit these tales.[2] Ruth Bottigheimer has studied the social context influencing the valuation of silence in the Grimms' fairy tales ("Silenced Women"; *Grimms' Bad Girls*). In her account, the voiceless heroines of the Grimms' tales reflect larger social norms that oppressively pressure women into silence as a matter of decorum. In contrast, Bethany Joy Bear's analysis of traditional versions and modern revisions of ATU 451 concentrates on the agency of the silent sister-saviors. She notes that the multiple versions of the tale in the Grimms' collection "illustrate various ways of empowering the heroine ... in 'The Twelve Brothers' and 'The Six Swans' her success requires redemptive silence" (45). How, then, should scholars read the silence of female heroes in fairy tales—as empowering or disempowering? Or must we move beyond simplistic binaries towards a more complex interpretation of silence? With an eye toward international folkloric

15

versions, I hope to illuminate how strategic silence and voicelessness create a different type of fairy-tale hero, one whose self-sacrificing nature is both coded protest and invitation to dialogue on the nature of gender, kinship, and life. By surveying scholarly approaches to the female hero, silence in various folktales and fairy tales, and the use of silence as coding specifically in ATU 451 texts, I establish how silent folktale and fairy-tale heroines act as pathfinders for the modern female hero, patterning possibilities of selfhood and heroism.

Folkloristic Approaches to Fairy Tales and the Female Hero

With its inception in the nineteenth century, while the Romantic Movement swept across Europe, the discipline of folkloristics offers a number of models for the study of fairy tales and their heroes, both male and female. The masculinist biases of the discipline, however, have produced a skewed model for understanding the unique circumstances and special contributions of the female hero. In this section, I will discuss key developments in folkloristics in the study of fairy tales, with special attention to how the female hero has been distinguished from the male hero (if at all).

There have always been female folklorists and those interested in women's folklore, though it has only been within the last few decades that feminist questions have come to the forefront of the discipline. The Women's Section of the American Folklore Society has been key in asking questions such as "Why does the expressive behavior of male members of a given 'folk' group receive more attention than that enacted by females in the same group—i.e., why are male performance genres so privileged in our discipline?" (Young and Turner 9). Among other reasons, such as the masculinist bent of university politics and the fact that male folklore collectors had an easier time accessing male informants, Jennifer Fox proposes that Johann Gottfried von Herder's Romantic Nationalist writings "helped form the basis for the study of folklore as a scholarly discipline" (33). In particular, Herder's emphasis on tradition, patriarchalism, and unity "elevates the masculine" (Fox 38) to the detriment of the feminine. These paradigms are built into folkloristics as a discipline, though it claims neutrality. Thus, much feminist folkloristic research has been devoted to exposing the biases at the root of our field, and pursuing more egalitarian models.[3]

Two of the discipline's most widely used tools of narrative study, the motif index and tale type index, also contain gender bias. The study of folklore is inherently comparative, with folklorists seeking to establish how widely an item of folklore, whether a ritual or charm, folktale or house type, is distributed. In narrative folklore—folklore that recounts a story, whether that story is in the form of a myth, legend, folktale, epic, ballad, or any number of minor narrative genres—one tool is Stith Thompson's six-volume *Motif-Index of Folk-Literature*

(1955–58). Motifs are narrative building blocks, those "specific recognized characters, themes, concepts, actions" (Conrad 644), which do not necessarily constitute full-fledged narratives in and of themselves, but in combination create a story. Motifs are classified under headings like A (Mythological Motifs), B (Animal Motifs), C (Motifs of Tabu), and D (Magic). A relevant example is motif D758, disenchantment by maintaining silence, which is found in the silent female hero tales under discussion here. Though the person doing the disenchanting is in many cases the tale's hero, and in many cases female, no mention of these facts appears in the index.

The tale type index similarly exists to help scholars search for commonalities in narrative folklore transmission, but at the level of plot rather than motif, and solely focused upon the genre of folktales. Folktales are fictional, formulaic narratives disseminated with variations through both written and oral traditions, and folklorists consider fairy tales to be a subset of the folktale genre (see Bascom for clarification). The first tale type index was written by Finnish folklorist Antti Aarne in 1910 in German, and translated into English in 1928. American folklorist Stith Thompson updated and revised the tale type index in 1960, and German folklorist Hans-Jörg Uther completed yet another revision in 2004 (the most recent to date). The common way of referring to tale types is according to which index one uses; so references to the Aarne-Thompson index of 1960 go by "AT types" (occasionally "AaTh") while references to Uther's updated numbers are known as "ATU types."[4] Thompson, who was an accomplished folk narrative scholar, defines a type as follows: "A type is a traditional tale that has an independent existence. It may be told as a complete narrative and does not depend for its meaning on any other tale. It may indeed happen to be told with another tale, but the fact that it may appear alone attests to its independence. It may consist of only one motif or of many" (415). The purpose of tale types in scholarly usage is to facilitate the comparative study of folklore, especially given that the titles and motifs of tales vary between different linguistic, regional, and ethnic groups (to take one example, "Cinderella" is not known by that title everywhere it is told, so referring to it as type 510A can be useful).[5]

While it is commonly agreed in folkloristics that the motif and type indexes are flawed but indispensable (Propp *The Russian Folktale*; Dundes), scholars interested in the female hero and women characters in folklore more generally will encounter special problems. As Torborg Lundell points out in her critique of gender-related biases in the tale type and motif indexes, neither index is as inclusive as it claims to be. The motif index, specifically, suffers from the following issues as it "(1) overlooks gender identity in its labeling of motifs, thus lumping male or female actions or characters under the same, male-identified heading or (2) disregards female activity or (3) focuses on male activity at the cost of female" (150). The tale type index suffers from many of the same issues, with passive constructions and selective labeling that obscure the real importance of female heroes and female characters in general (Lundell 152).

Fortunately, Uther's revision of the tale type index remedied many of the inconsistencies; for instance by retitling some of the tales that were mistakenly made out to be androcentric.[6] Neither are scholars to blame for this phenomenon; the folk frequently give male-oriented titles as well. ATU 451, the tale to be discussed in this essay, is a prime example of this phenomenon. While the tale type title ("The Maiden Who Seeks Her Brothers") reflects the sister's active role in the tale, the Grimms titled their versions "The Twelve Brothers," "The Seven Ravens," and "The Six Swans," while Andersen called his "The Wild Swans," and these iconic titles have endured. As Bethany Bear Joy notes, "Although these titles always focus on a group of brothers, the crucial figure in all literary incarnations of AT 451 is their sister, who redeems the brothers from exile, enchantment, or both" (45). Despite the titular emphasis on the brothers, ATU 451 is a female-centered tale.

Lundell raises another important issue: the question of whether fairy tales have only one hero. Using the example of tale type 313, in the AT index titled "The girl as helper in the hero's flight," Lundell points out, "The Type Index sees the boy of this tale as the hero and he is, in the sense that the tale initially focuses on him. However, the girl may be claimed as heroine considering the fact that she carries most of the action in the major portion of the tale" (153). She goes on to suggest instead titling the tale "Hero frees heroine, enabling them to escape from troll" (Lundell 153), which grants heroic status to both main characters.

In general, though, most fairy tales are classified as gendered: there are masculine tales and feminine tales. For the most part, the main character's gender is taken as the tale's gender, though scholars such as Kathleen Ragan have suggested alternative methods of calculating a tale's gender, such as counting the nominative nouns and pronouns of a given tale (231). The gendering of tales is played out in the tale type index, where we tend to find tales clustered together according to the protagonist's gender, starting with type 300, "The Dragonslayer," which has a male hero, as do many of the tales that immediately follow it in the type index. Bengt Holbek has noted that there are only a few exceptions to the gendering of fairy tales, and they tend to be children's tales (which end with the defeat of a monster rather than marriage).[7] Type 327A, perhaps best known in the form of the Grimms' version "Hansel and Gretel," is a good example of a tale that exhibits variation in terms of the gender of the protagonist. Most tales, however, tend to be more fixed: we see very few male Cinderellas or Sleeping Beauties, and inversely, few female heroes in the roles of traditionally male heroes such as the main characters of "Puss in Boots" or "The Frog King."

The gendering of tales also emerges on a structural level. Vladimir Propp's landmark structuralist study of fairy tales, *Morphology of the Folktale* (published in Russian in 1928 and translated into English in 1958), assumes that all protagonists of fairy tales are male. In his study he enumerated thirty-one plot points of fairy tales (which he calls "functions") that may be performed by any character who fulfills a given role. Not all thirty-one functions must be present in every fairy tale, and they may be repeated or trebled, in accordance with the stylistic laws of folk narrative. None of this is necessarily gendered, except that Propp's proposed prototype for the structure of all fairy tales follows most closely the plot of ATU 300, "The Dragonslayer," from the kidnapping of the princess (function 8, villainy/lack) to the (male) hero's wedding and ascension to the throne (function 31). Holbek confirms that "Propp's system seems to fit the masculine tale types in particular" (381). As a result, Proppian structural analysis often assumes that the "hero" is male. This leads Propp to distinguish between seeker heroes and victim heroes, the latter frequently being gendered as female:

> (1) if a young girl is kidnapped, and disappears from the horizon of her father ... and if Iván goes off in search of her, then the hero of the tale is Iván and not the kidnapped girl. Heroes of this type may be termed *seekers*. (2) If a young girl or boy is seized or driven out, and the thread of the narrative is linked to his or her fate and not to those who remain behind, then the hero of the tale is the seized or banished boy or girl. There are no seekers in such tales. Heroes of this variety may be called *victimized heroes* [*Morphology* 36, emphasis in original].

While there are some female heroes who are seekers—women who marry and must pursue fleeing beastly bridegrooms—the majority fall into Propp's category of victimized heroes, as they face persecution at home before either being ejected or rescued through marriage. Additionally, the sought-after princess often shares a tale role with her father in prompting the seeker hero's quest, further erasing her identity.

Other structural methods of studying the hero in folk narrative exhibit similar biases. Robert Segal's introduction to classical studies of the hero—those of Otto Rank, Lord Raglan, and Alan Dundes—gives an overview of these models, which can be considered structuralist in that they pay special attention to the syntagmatic (or sequential) structure of the hero's life story. Segal also mentions work on the hero by Carl Jung and Joseph Campbell, and then draws comparisons between the ways these writers all conceptualize the hero. The hero pattern, of course, assumes a male hero as the default.[8] Features such as the hero's relationship to his father and mother, his community, and to divine forces both male and female, are often commented upon. While the hero pattern does not necessarily provide a direct parallel to the plots found in folktales and fairy tales, it is still worth noting that much of the "heroic" behavior discussed by these scholars is framed solely in terms of masculine-gendered activities.

One solution to the gendering of folktales and fairy tales is to recognize that there are frequently tales that contain an active protagonist of each gender. Lundell's suggestion discussed above to label tales with both active protagonists, hence including both genders, is not entirely unique. Others, like Holbek, have suggested that complete fairy tales have two protagonists, one male and one female, and that only some forms of a given tale show each protagonist in the fullest extent of their roles. Holbek explains, "in a masculine tale, the two main characters are the low-born young male (LYM) and the high-born young female (HYF). Conversely, the two main characters of the feminine tale are the low-born young female (LYF) and the high-born young male (HYM)" (417). In some cases, a high-born character is cast into servitude or poverty, making them functionally low-class for most of the tale (as is the case in versions of ATU 451 where the female hero is a princess, but lives in rags due to disenchanting her brothers). This means of classifying characters according to their role in the tale's plot is a useful way of pinpointing the identity of the female protagonist (if there is one) in male-centered tales.

Given that fantasy literature has roots in fairy tales and narrative folklore in general (ranging from myths to medieval romances), it is my hope as a folklorist that scholars of fantasy literature and seekers of the female hero will look to folklore resources when researching the female hero. The tale type index and the motif index, though flawed, will help establish antecedents in oral (and sometimes written) folkloric traditions that persist in literary creations today, while an understanding of structuralism can similarly aid with evaluating the relationship of characters to plot. The move toward reevaluating sexist scholarly paradigms is an essential first step in these endeavors, from which a fuller comprehension of silent (and silenced) female heroes can emerge.

"The Maiden Who Seeks Her Brothers" (ATU 451)

Scholars have documented at least 600 variants of ATU 451 (Blécourt 283) and Christine Shojaei Kawan differentiates three main subtypes, the first of which

> focuses on the siblings' disenchantment through the sacrifice and cruel sufferings that are imposed on their sister, coinciding with the difficulties of the sister's noble marriage; the second tells of the girl's cohabitation with her brothers in a house in the woods where she is abused by an ogre figure, upon which follows the brothers' revenge and the dead ogre's counter-revenge; the third consists in a cosmic journey in the fairy-tale style, undertaken by a brave young girl who consecutively meets personifications of the sun and the moon, the stars and the winds [300].[9]

Interestingly, not every instance of this subtype contains the silence injunction. In the Basque tale "The Sister and Her Seven Brothers," the brothers choose to leave home before the sister is born. She finds them and keeps house for them until a witch's spell turns them all into cows. A king encounters the girl, who still has her powers of speech: "He speaks to her, and tells her that he wishes to marry her. The young girl says to him that she is very poor, and that cannot be" (Wentworth 189). The girl marries him on the condition that the cows will be cared for and will never be killed, but then the witch who had placed the spell on the brothers throws the girl over a cliff and orders the cows killed. Luckily the girl is rescued, and the king threatens the witch into removing the curse from the brothers. This version contains no instructions for how the girl can disenchant her brothers, and yet her powerlessness is coextensive with the silence to which protagonists in other forms of the tale are subjected. An Italian version similarly contains little magic, but continues the pattern of disempowering the heroine (Crane).

Holbek has the right idea in looking at the role of silence in fairy tales in terms of where it appears within the tales' structure. In many feminine tales (including versions of ATU 451), the silence occurs after the protagonist has married, but before her position in her new household is secure: "The heroine is usually incapacitated in some way or other: she has lost her hands, or she is mute, or she is under a vow not to speak for seven years while she is sewing the shirts for her enchanted brothers" (Holbek 430). Holbek then equates silence with vulnerability: "It is easy to understand the nature of her misfortune ... if one recalls how women were regarded in traditional rural communities: they were respected for their ability to bear children, primarily sons. By taking the children away, the mother-in-law hits her at her most vulnerable spot" (Holbek 430). The general trend of conflating silence with powerlessness is a persuasive one, and yet I will argue that if we reframe how we view silence, it becomes a powerful metaphor for women's experiences and thus a reflection of the unique sacrifices that are asked of the female hero in fairy tales.

The Voiceless Female Hero in Oral and Literary Fairy Tales

Before interpreting the meaning of silent female heroes, it is necessary to establish where and when they appear in folklore, and so in this section, I will discuss silence in both oral and written folktales and fairy tales. One of the main tools for this type of work is, of course, the tale type index, and fortunately Uther's updated 2004 index includes a thorough subject index. As we shall see, silence signals many meanings within European fairy tales, but it is predominantly associated with women and positions of disempowerment.

In many of the tales catalogued in the type index, silence appears as a motif, sometimes as a strategy, and more often as a punishment or limitation. As an example of silence being used strategically, in ATU 442, "The Old

Woman in the Forest," a girl disenchants a prince and his retinue by going inside the house of a witch, taking a plain ring, and not saying anything to the old woman/witch. In the Grimms' version of this tale, the prince (in the form of a dove) instructs the girl thus: "You are to go inside, where you'll find an old woman seated right next to the hearth. She'll say good day to you, but you're not to answer her, no matter what she does" (406). From there, the girl successfully disenchants the prince by finding the correct ring. The girl's voluntary silence—which the witch perceives as rude, but is unable to do anything about—is a key component in breaking the spell. However, this tale type is in the minority as more often than not women who do not speak in folktales are disadvantaged.

Where magic is not involved, however, silence does not seem to confer any advantages. In ATU 533, "The Speaking Horsehead" (better known as "The Goose Girl" from the Grimms' collection), the main character is a princess whose servant girl coerces her into swearing an oath of secrecy, never to reveal to a living soul that they have changed places. The princess does not literally lose her voice, but she is forced into silence on an issue that affects her life. Her secret is not revealed until she is maneuvered into a situation where the king can clandestinely observe her telling her woes to an inanimate object or animal (thereby not breaking her vow). Similarly, in ATU 898, "The Daughter of the Sun," the female character who marries a prince is represented as mute by choice. She will only speak to her new husband after he eavesdrops on a conversation and learns that he must address her properly (as the daughter of the sun, or whatever her title is in that variant). This tale is mentioned in R. Dawkins's early overview of folk narratives featuring silent women characters, fitting into the first category described here: "the three silent women are all silent and all break their silence for humanly comprehensible reasons the first from excessive pride" (Dawkins 138).

There are instances in folktales where a woman's silence is the cause of her misfortunes. Uther summarizes a tale found primarily in Mediterranean regions, ATU 705A*: "A prince grows tired of his wife because she cannot talk any more. He brings a new bride who insults the wife. The first wife starts to speak again. The prince rejects his new bride and lives with his first wife" (*The Types* Vol. 1, 378). ATU 710, "Our Lady's Child," dovetails closely with ATU 451 in that the female protagonist marries a king while mute and cannot speak to defend herself when her infant children are stolen from her. She is also accused of infanticide and condemned to die; however, her silence is the result of stubbornness, her unwillingness to admit that she had violated the interdiction of a supernatural figure, rather than a voluntary vow (Uther 385). Silence is thus equated with misfortune and oppression.

Other folktales touch on the connections between silence, gender, and power. ATU 1375, "Who Can Rule His Wife?" has among its variants a priest who instructs all the men who consider themselves the masters of their house to sing a song in church. All the men are silent, and only the women sing (Uther, *The Types* Vol. 2 180). Better known, perhaps, is ATU 1351, "The Silence Wager," which Uther summarizes as follows: "A man and his wife make a wager: Whoever speaks first must do certain work (close the door, wash the dishes, feed the animals, etc.). Strangers (robbers) enter their house and take or abuse their belongings (believe the couple are dead and share their estate). A man rapes the woman (a woman tries to rape the man). The husband (wife) protests (becomes jealous), cries out and thus loses the wager" (Uther 152). The ambiguity of the summary's phrasing is due to the fact that the tale is told both ways: either the man or the woman can be the one to lose the bet by speaking first.[10]

In the examples discussed above, silence tends to be imposed on women more than on men, with the exception of the husbands who stay silent because they know they cannot claim to be the masters of their households. When men choose silence, it is not automatically disempowering. For example, in ATU 1948, "Too Much Talk," three men withdraw from the world to pursue a monastic lifestyle. They have one conversation over the span of years, and the punchline is that the last one to chime in says, irritated, that he's leaving this place because there's too much talking. In contrast, tale types like ATU 945, "Luck and Intelligence," feature a mute princess who has been promised to anyone who can make her speak. Related thematically is the princess who is so melancholy that her father has promised her hand to anyone who can make her laugh, which appears as a motif in various tale types. The difference in agency between these situations is stark, setting up an opposition between speech and silence, subject and object.

Coding: Silence as Coded Speech

Female silence is also incorporated in fairy tales implicitly, during all those narrative moments when female characters are silenced while sleeping or dead. Sleeping and dead male heroes are rare in fairy tales, and when a hero dies and must be brought back to life (as in ATU 303, "The Twins or Blood-Brothers"), it is usually the hero's helpers or sibling, not his intended spouse, that resurrect him. Often, a sleeping (hence silenced) female hero is responsible for the social world she inhabits, as Kimberly Lau points out in the case of "Sleeping Beauty" (ATU 410): "So critical is her silence to upholding the social structure that in the Grimms' version the princess's falling asleep brings with it sleep for the entire community" (122). The foregrounding of women's silence in fairy tales is both structurally and socially coded differently than men's silence in fairy tales, and now I turn to the meaning of this silence.

Coding is a concept developed by feminist folklorists to describe the ways in which subaltern populations disguise their communicative messages so that dominant populations will not understand those messages (Radner and Lanser). Specifically, "coding may allow women to communicate feminist messages to other women of their community; to refuse, subvert, or transform conventional expectations; and to criticize male dominance in the face of male power" (Radner and Lanser 23). Along with coding, a queer reading of these tales emerges when we consider that the silent heroine must often make choices that negate her ability to live, or to live a whole life. In versions of ATU 451, the heroine seemingly chooses her brothers over her husband and children, and in some cases, over her own life. These tales thus engage questions of what makes a "livable life," to use Judith Butler's phrase referring to how "the very terms that confer 'humanness' on some individuals are those that deprive certain others of the possibility of achieving that status, producing a differential between the human and the less-than-human" (2). The female hero in these tales, by choosing the less-than-human, by choosing silence and an identification with the death drive, presents a very different type of hero than the happy-go-lucky youngest son or the bride who goes on a quest to recover her enchanted husband in other fairy tales. A discussion of coding in folk narrative, followed by an application of queer theory to this group of tales, will help illuminate the image of the female hero and what she can mean to different audiences.

The female hero in ATU 451 ("The Maiden Who Seeks Her Brothers") is daughter, sister, and finally, wife and mother. She is defined by her relationships to the men in her life—brothers and husband, and occasionally father—though it is often the women in her life who prove the most villainous. Most versions of ATU 451 have the female hero's mother-in-law condemning her to death, though some versions, such as the Grimms' "The Six Swans," begin with a female villain as well. A king who has children from a previous marriage gets lost in a forest, and must agree to marry a witch's daughter in order to find his way out. This maiden, too, is a witch, and, jealous of the attention the king gives his children, she tricks them: "she made small white silk shirts, and she used the witchcraft she had learned from her mother to sew a magic spell into them" (169). These shirts turn the boys into swans, so that their sister must quest after them.

The fact that the female villains in such tales are so loquacious, and that the modest female heroes are so voiceless, points to the social context informing silence as a female virtue. Bottigheimer connects the nineteenth-century German values and the prevalence of silent female heroes in the Grimms' tales: "In a society which prized silent retiring women one would expect female speech— which in conjuring potently bears women's will or intention—to be curtailed or even condemned in that society's literary productions, whether 'folk' or canonical, and that is precisely what happened in Germany" ("Silenced Women" 119). Similarly, Marina Warner demonstrates the suspicion directed at women's speech in seventeenth-century France, when Perrault and the various *conteuses* were authoring fairy tales. Warner notes, "The seduction of women's talk reflected the seduction of their bodies; it was considered as dangerous to Christian men.... The speaking woman also refuses subjection, and turns herself from a passive object of desire into a conspiring and conscious stimulation" (Warner 11–12). Many versions of ATU 451 reflect these ideas, with the female hero performing subservience and meekness, likely all the more beautiful in the eyes of the king precisely because she is mute. More importantly, however, the tale incorporates the idea of female perfection through silence—and then critiques it.

Viewing the tale with a queer lens helps to uncover this coded critique. As Kay Turner and Pauline Greenhill note in their introduction to *Transgressive Tales: Queering the Grimms*, "queer readings seem absent from feminist fairy-tale criticism" (3), and thus their project draws

> on queer theory to better understand the chaotic, fantastic, manipulated, and highly compressed fairy tale ... to understand further the complexities of that history—its multiple tellings and readings over time—as a source for solving problems pertaining to the individual, the social being in his or her own history [Turner and Greenhill 17].

Queer readings of fairy tales can help uncover coded critiques therein through their careful attention to lacunae, lapses, and excesses, which are often signals that the content under consideration is contested, conflicted, or otherwise ripe for an analysis that is open to non-dominant viewpoints.

Moments of silence in fairy tales are particularly multivalent. In the same collection, Kevin Goldstein writes, "No scholar would claim that silence has a single signification in the Grimms' tales. In fact, many kinds of silence inhabit the collection, with many significations" (61). Goldstein goes on to explore the "woeful quiet" (Goldstein 63) that characterizes "The Goose Girl at the Spring," which is the Grimms' version of ATU 923, "Love Like Salt." Similar to how the female hero of that tale cannot remain in quiet solitude, spinning and yet unmarried, the female hero of ATU 451 can only pass so much time unwed, spinning (or sewing), and silent. It is as though there is a social injunction to wed and be productively folded into a normative family unit in these tales that feature silent, spinning women—an injunction that is queerly resisted at the same time that it is explored.

The female hero of ATU 451 is a good sister, a poor wife, and a worse mother, thereby presenting a coded critique of the roles available to women. In my previous work on ATU 451, I focused on the three versions of ATU 451 in the Grimms' collection and the connections they might have to the brothers' life stories as well as issues of transbiological and non-normative kinship ("Queering Kinship"). However, I also touched on the way in which the tales critique gender roles, theorizing that "the heroine's disproportionate devotion to her brothers kills her chance at marriage and kills her children, which from a queer stance is a comment on the performativity of sexuality and gender" (Jorgensen 77). By drawing attention to the contradictions of normative femininity, the tale shows how constructed identities are rent with conflicting desires and drives. Further, the hero's silence prevents her from explaining her choices, which are rational to the tale's audience who knows her backstory, and irrational to those who encounter her only after she undertakes the period of silence. I consider her silence to be "the most positively portrayed female agency in this tale ... queer in the sense that it resists and unsettles; it acts while negating action, it endures while refusing to respond to life-threatening conditions" (Jorgensen 84). That statement was originally made about the Grimms' version of ATU 451, "The Six Swans," which contains a scheming witch and a wicked stepmother. An Irish version, "The Twelve Geese," also contains a wicked stepmother who disposes of the female hero's young children, but there is a fairy who helps the girl find out how to break the curse on her brothers. This fairy also appears to the wicked stepmother in the form of a wolf, causing her to throw each baby into the wolf's jaws. The fairy, of course, keeps the children safe until the hero's time of silence and persecution is ended, and may be seen as a coded comment on the resources required to successfully nurture children.

Tales of overextended mothers appear elsewhere in folklore, with coding suggested as one of the interpretive paradigms that can help make sense of them. As Janet Langlois discusses, folk narratives about unsupervised children maiming and killing each other date back at least to the 1812 publication of the Grimms' tales.[11] For all its grisliness, "the tale persists in oral tradition, usually told by mothers.... Its immediate context ... mirrors the tale's content—mothers with babies talking about mothers with babies" (91). The modern form depicts a girl castrating her brother, resulting in both of their deaths and possibly also a third sibling's death, while the distraught mother is helpless to stop any of these horrific events. Langlois views the female character as "an overburdened mother" (Langlois 92) whose ineptitude dramatizes the isolation and lack of support that can make the lives of mothers difficult or even unbearable. Here, then, is the coded protest: this tale can be used to subtly express ambivalence about and even hostility toward motherhood,[12] a role that is depicted as innately feminine and desirable for all women. In ATU 451, too, the inevitability of motherhood is questioned. This is an instance of what Barre Toelken, studying silence in ballads, calls "*metaphorical silence*, in which that which is articulated forces us to register figuratively what isn't being said" (italics in original, 93).[13]

The narrative use of silence can signal a coded message, a discontent that is diverted somewhere less noticeable than an outright protest, which is especially interesting given that fairy tales are a fictional genre that often contains fantastic elements. The very notion of coding contains at least a kernel of intentionality, and attributing intention in folk narrative can be tricky, not least because folklore is communally transmitted and performed. We can further distinguish between intentionality on the part of the (fictional) characters and the (real-world) narrators. There is also the issue of the fantastic content that specifically appears in folk narrative genres such as fairy tale, folktale more broadly, myth, and legend—how much should we interpret literally or symbolically? And how does this issue change when we are faced with characters and events that cannot exist in our world? Holbek addresses this issue of the marvelous or symbolic elements of fairy tales, from talking horses to enchanted sleep, concluding after a survey of existing interpretive tools: "*The symbolic elements of fairy tales convey emotional impressions of beings, phenomena and events in the real world, organized in the form of fictional narrative sequences which allow the narrator to speak of the problems, hopes and ideals of the community*" (435, emphasis in original). The problem with interpreting fairy-tale silence, however, is that frequently it is mundane and not magical; while it is undertaken in the context of magical elements such as the brothers' transformation into birds, the choice to stay silent is something that exists in the real world.

Further, as seen in the Basque version of ATU 451 discussed above, silence is not always a necessary component of the female hero's oppression in her marital home, though silence suggests an interesting relationship with trauma and oppression. It is with a queer eye toward the gaps and elisions of texts that I suggest that the spot that silence occupies in the structure of ATU 451 is a symptom of the female hero's oppression, and not its cause. Here I agree with Turner and Greenhill that "structural analysis ... still stands up as a way to unloose tales from their superficial, syntagmatic drive" (15). If we think back to Propp's structuralism and focus on the linear fairy-tale plot and where it demands silence from ATU 451's female hero, we see that silence is a means of liberation when paired with an interdiction, and a means of oppression when paired with the guidance of the hero into a new situation where a difficult task must be completed. This model, wherein silence is initially empowering but later disempowering, also corresponds to faith to the natal family in the first instance, and an inability to prioritize the marital family in the second instance. In a curious reversal of traumatized behavior, the female hero is victimized because she is silent, instead of being silent because she is victimized.

There is also a reversal in the meaning of silence that emerges in some versions of ATU 451, wherein the female hero's silence is interpreted as a sign of witchcraft. This happens in Asbjørnsen and Moe's version, "The Twelve Wild Ducks," where the king's mother says of the female hero: "Can't you see now, that this thing whom you have picked up, and whom you are going to marry, is a witch? Why, she can't either talk, or laugh, or weep!" (56). This tale, along with the Irish tale in Kennedy's collection, features a portrayal of women's speech as enchanting that conforms to the negative evaluation of women's speech discussed by Bottigheimer above: the mother of the female hero and her brothers wishes aloud to have a girl child, regardless of the consequences for her sons. In the Norse tale she says, "If only I had a daughter as white as snow and as red as blood, I shouldn't care what became of all my sons" (Asbjørnsen and Moe 51). A troll hag appears to grant the wish and claim the boys. In the Irish tale she says, "Oh ... if I had only a daughter with her skin as white as that snow, her cheeks as red as that blood, and her hair as black as that raven, I'd give away every one of my twelve sons for her" (Kennedy 14). An old woman chastises her for this wish, and the sons turn into geese when the girl is born. In a German version, the mother of six boys says, "Children, don't make me angry, or you shall become birds!" (Ranke 68). That is exactly what happens, and when the woman gives birth to a girl later on, the girl sets out to find her enchanted brothers. These tales seem to be saying in code: a woman cannot win whether she speaks or is silent; a woman's speech has negative consequences for others, and a woman's silence has negative consequences for herself.

Versions of ATU 451 that contain the silence motif provide a critique of the double standards applied to women's speech in society, and they also demonstrate a queer heroism. Her heroism is queer because it is perverse, contrary to social expectations, simultaneously excessive and self-negating. The sister is undoubtedly the hero of the tale, as she is the only one who can disenchant her brothers, and she bravely takes on this task. Her work is dangerous to her, even though it occurs in a domestic setting rather than as part of a quest that takes her elsewhere. To return briefly to a structural lens, a Scottish version of ATU 451 curiously combines both the disenchantment-through-silence form of the tale with the cosmic-journey form of the tale (found in the Grimms' "The Seven Ravens"). The female hero of the Scottish version, "The King's Children Under Enchantments," must first complete a quest with a repetitive structure in order to learn how to disenchant her brothers. Taking the advice of a seer, "her nurse bound the King's Daughter with crosses and with spells that she should neither marry nor flirt with any man until she had restored her brothers to their own proper forms" (Campbell 271). She encounters three giants, each of which helps her along the way to finding her brothers, who have been transformed into deer. They tell her to make shirts for them of bog-cotton down, and it is the seer who adds the injunction to not speak or laugh. A hunting king encounters the maiden, and, of course, falls in love and marries her. The result of the cosmic quest and the silent sewing events are the same: both are steps in the process of disenchanting the brothers. This tale contains both events, while most other versions of ATU 451 utilize just one. Structurally speaking, they are equivalent, thus proving that a female hero who chooses silence is performing the same kind of heroic action as a female hero who goes on a journey and encounters frightening, supernatural beings and manages to win them over to her side.[14] The benefit of this kind of structural analysis is that the symbolic equation of the two events is contained within the tales themselves, rather than being imposed by the interpreter.

As Warner suggests regarding ATU 451 in social contexts where it is told, "Women's capacity for love and action tragically exceeded the permitted boundaries of their lives—this self-immolatory heroism was one of the few chivalrous enterprises open to them" (*From the Beast*, 393). The female heroes in ATU 451 experience love on multiple fronts, as wives, mothers, and sisters, in what from a queer perspective resembles the excess seen in camp and drag performances. While some excessive women tend toward the grotesque (and thus villainous), our excessively-loving hero is fortunately redeemed and rescued before she can be punished for her monstrosity. Substituting silence for speech, her story is a coded protest of the social conditions that condemn her to illegibility.

Conclusion

Acting heroically though silently, the female protagonists of ATU 451 from oral and written traditions defy some gender norms (conflating femininity with motherhood) even as they conform to others (the image of the self-sacrificing "good" woman). Reading this tale with queer, feminist, folkloristic, and structural lenses helps to make sense of these contradictions, and also to illuminate the complex relationship between folk narrative and society. Even a psychoanalytic reading, attuned to unconscious drives, could help make sense of this tale. To Freudian scholar Otto Rank, "hero myths originate in and fulfill ... socially and personally unacceptable impulses. The fulfillment that myth provides is compensatory: it is a disguised, unconscious ... fantasized venting of impulses that cannot be vented directly" (Segal, "Introduction" xxvii). Ironically, Rank's statement—made originally about hero myths solely with male heroes—applies quite well to ATU 451, as it is socially unacceptable for women to criticize the chiasmic nature of femininity and motherhood, socially constructed though they both are. Coding allows for expression of this criticism, while the female hero's silence parallels the silencing effects of culture on various aspects of women's life experiences.

The question of how much and whether the female heroes in fairy tales should function as role models for girls and women in our era is relevant as well. Kay Stone conducted fieldwork in the 1980s with men and women of various ages, interested in how they conceive of gender roles in fairy tales. She found that both men and women "clearly view fairy tale heroines and heroes as providing different kinds of idealized behavior, and both males and females react to these differences in different ways" (143). Recognizing that the hero of ATU 451 only partially conforms to gendered expectations, and that her failure to conform is a coded protest against patriarchal constraints, heightens the relevance and impact of this tale.

Stone elaborates that for women, "the problem-creating aspect of the tales is the attempted identification with the ideal woman, or the guilt if one fails to identify with her, and the expectation that one's life will be transformed dramatically and all one's problems will be solved with the arrival of a man" (Stone 143). As noted above, in ATU 451, the arrival of men is often what causes more problems for the female protagonist; thus it is unlike the many canonical fairy tales (like "Cinderella," "Snow White," or "Sleeping Beauty") that Stone found to be important and relevant to her informants. The female hero of ATU 451 fulfills one male ideal, in that she is silent rather than loquacious, and her silence almost gets her killed. This is a poignant lesson for women who read and hear this tale, whether or not they are aware that there is a deeper critique of gendered expectations of women.

In 2009, Jonathan Gottschall wrote in response to Ragan's paper on heroines in folktales that there might be more male heroes than female heroes in folktales because the lives of men are simply more interesting than the lives of women: "The lives of a traditional culture's males—of its warriors, chieftains, big men, thugs, murderers, political usurpers, wooers, and hunters—may simply possess more dramatic wallop, *on average*, than can typically be generated from the more domestic activities of that culture's females" (441, emphasis in original). The silencing tactics of male-biased scholarship are unfortunately alive and well in the twenty-first century. Thus, it is all the more important to consider the female hero in folk narrative, what her contributions are, and what she might be saying to us even through her silence.

Notes

1. I would like to thank Linda Lee for her helpful comments on an early draft of this paper.

2. Silence occurs prominently in literary fairy tales, perhaps the most famous example of which is Hans Christian Andersen's "The Little Mermaid." In exchange for giving the little mermaid legs, the sea witch demands her voice: "You have the most beautiful voice of all those who live in the ocean. I suppose you have thought of using that to charm your prince; but that voice you will have to give to me. I want the most precious thing you have to pay for my potion" (69). When the little mermaid assents to this trade, the sea witch cuts out her tongue, highlighting the permanence of her voiceless state (in contrast to the Disney adaptation of the film, in which the voice-taking is neither graphic nor permanent). The witch's statement implies that the little mermaid's voice is precious because it is beautiful, and that its lack will be harmful. As we shall see, being voiceless presents unique challenges to the female hero in fairy tales.

3. See Jorgensen, "Political and Theoretical Feminisms in American Folkloristics: Definition Debates, Publication Histories, and the *Folklore Feminists Communication.*" *The Folklore Historian* 27 (2010): 43–73.

4. Most tale types retain the same numbers between the revisions, but it is common practice to use the most recent version of the tale type index where possible.

5. Uther describes the aim of tale type systems as "to ascertain the extent to which the sources and stylistic traits were connected as well as the degree of interdependency

between oral and literary traditions. In addition, the classifications served as scientific tools to promote access to certain folktales or collections" ("Tale Type," 939). There are both practical and scholarly applications of the system.

6. As in ATU 707, "The Three Golden Children," which had been previously titled "The Three Golden Sons" despite the fact that one of the children is usually a girl, and an active one in the tale at that. This tale also features, in some versions, a silence injunction in order to win an enchanted bird.

7. Examples include giant- and witch-killing tales, as Holbek demonstrates: "Thus, there are masculine as well as feminine versions of AT 328 (*The Boy Steals the Giant's Treasure* according to Aarne-Thompson—it might just as well have been a girl)" (*Interpretation* 422).

8. Segal notes, however: "Campbell later allows for female heroes, but in *Hero* he, like Rank, limits himself to male ones. More accurately, he presupposes male heroes even though some of his examples are female!" ("Introduction" xvii).

9. In *The Types of International Folktales*, Uther summarizes the tale's first form (with references to various motifs):

"A stepmother transforms her stepsons into swans [D161.1] (ravens [D151.5]). The sister looks for her brothers and finds out how to release them: She has to be silent for some years [D758] and has to make shirts out of cotton-grass for the brothers [D753.1].

"A king finds the young woman in the forest and marries her [N711]. In his absence she bears a child, but her mother-in-law takes it away and accuses her of eating the child [K2116.1.1] (having borne an animal). The young queen remains silent because of her brothers, even though she is to be executed. On her way to the funeral pyre her period of silence ends and her brothers are disenchanted. Everything is explained and the mother-in-law is punished." (Vol 1, 267)

10. Other folktales, classified as anecdotes and jokes, deal with silence in household disputes, adultery, and attempts to get food. These include ATU 1355A, 1355B, 1358C, 1360B, 1567E; see Uther, *The Types* Vol. 3, subject index under "Silence."

11. The tale was omitted from the text's second edition, as it was deemed too gruesome; the title, "How Children Played Butcher with Each Other," gives us some clue as to why.

12. While discussing unconscious motivations, it is worth mentioning that in certain psychological readings of ATU 451, the sister's silence symbolizes her transitional status as she matures. Marie-Louise von Franz lists the following associations: "During the time the heroine of the fairy tale is up the tree, she must not speak or laugh, which is often the rule during a state of incubation.... The words *mysticism* and *mystic* come from *myo*, keeping one's mouth shut.... So mystical silence is the conscious variation of something that is less positive when it happens to one unconsciously" (*The Feminine* 151). Von Franz's far-reaching associations are an example of how psychological interpretations of fairy tales often stray far from the text under consideration. Holbek on has this to say of psychological approaches to fairy tales: "What we must object to is that those notions do not result from studies of the *texts*. They are derived from different hypotheses about the unconscious processes of the *mind*, which are believed to be reflected in the tales" (*Interpretation* 1998, 316, italics in original). This does not invalidate them, but rather reminds us to be cautious of uncritically accepting psychological interpretations of folklore.

13. Many of Toelken's categories of silence in ballads apply in fairy tales as well (such as narrative ellipsis, where plot elements are omitted in a given performance, and grammatical silence, where the audience is forced to glean information from an incomplete or

ambiguous phrase or sentence). Toelken also eloquently explains how things that are unsaid can be understood to indicate meaning.

14. Within folkloristics, this type of analysis is commonly called allomotific analysis. Alan Dundes is credited with its invention. I utilize and explain it in greater depth in Jorgensen 2012.

WORKS CITED

Andersen, Hans Christian. *The Complete Fairy Tales and Stories.* Trans. Erik Christian Haugaard. New York: Anchor Books, 1983. Print.

Asbjørnsen, Peter Christen, and Jørgen Engebretsen Moe. *Popular Tales from the Norse,* 3d ed. Trans. Sir George Webbe Dasent. New York: G.P. Putnam's Sons, 1888. Print.

Bascom, William. "The Forms of Folklore: Prose Narratives." *The Journal of American Folklore* 78.307 (1965): 3–20. Print.

Bear, Bethany Joy. "Struggling Sisters and Failing Spells: Re-engendering Fairy Tale Heroism in Pegg Kerr's *The Wild Swans.*" *Fairy Tales Reimagined: Essays on New Retellings.* Ed. Susan Redington Bobby. Jefferson, NC: McFarland, 2009. 44–57. Print.

Blécourt, Willem de. "Metamorphosing Men and Transmogrified Texts: Some Thoughts on the Genealogy of Fairy Tales." *Fabula* 52 (2011): 280–296. Print.

Bottigheimer, Ruth. *Grimms' Bad Girls & Bold Boys: The Moral & Social Vision of the Tales.* New Haven: Yale University Press, 1987. Print.

_____. "Silenced Women in the Grimms' Tales: The 'Fit' Between Fairy Tales and Society in Their Historical Context." *Fairy Tales and Society: Illusion, Allusion, and Paradigm.* Ed. Ruth Bottigheimer. Philadelphia: University of Pennsylvania Press, 1986. 115–131. Print.

Butler, Judith. *Undoing Gender.* New York: Routledge, 2004. Print.

Campbell, John Francis. *More West Highland Tales,* Vol. 2. Trans. John G. McKay. Edinburgh: Published for the Scottish Anthropological and Folklore Society by Oliver and Boyd, 1960. Print.

Conrad, JoAnn. "Motif." *The Greenwood Encyclopedia of Folktales and Fairy Tales.* Ed. Donald Haase. Westport, CT: Greenwood Press. Volume 2: G-P, 643–645. Print.

Crane, Thomas. *Italian Popular Tales.* 1885. Ed. and introd. Jack Zipes. Santa Barbara: ABC-CLIO, 2001. Print.

Dawkins, R. M. "The Silent Princess." *Folklore* 63.3 (1952): 129–142. Print.

Dundes, Alan. "The Motif-Index and the Tale Type Index: A Critique." *Journal of Folklore Research* 34.3 (1997): 195–202. Print.

Fox, Jennifer. "The Creator Gods: Romantic Nationalism and the En-gendermentt of Women in Folklore." *Feminist Theory and the Study of Folklore.* Ed. Susan Tower Hollis, Linda Pershing, and M. Jane Young. Urbana: University of Illinois Press, 1993. 29–40. Print.

Goldstein, Kevin. "Nurtured in a Lonely Place: The Wise Woman as Type in 'The Goose Girl at the Spring.'" *Transgressive Tales: Queering the Grimms.* Ed. Kay Turner and Pauline Greenhill. Detroit: Wayne State University Press, 2012. 49–67. Print.

Gottschall, Jonathan. "Response to Kathleen Ragan's 'What Happened to the Heroines in Folktales?'" *Marvels & Tales* 23.2 (2009): 437–442. Print.

Grimm, Jacob, and Wilhelm Grimm. *The Complete Fairy Tales of the Brothers Grimm,* 3d ed. Trans. Jack Zipes. New York: Bantam, 2003. Print.

Holbek, Bengt. *Interpretation of Fairy Tales.* Helsinki: Academia Scientiarum Fennica, 1998. Print.

Jorgensen, Jeana. "Queering Kinship in 'The Maiden Who Seeks Her Brothers.'" *Transgressive Tales: Queering the Grimms.* Ed. Kay Turner and Pauline Greenhill. Detroit: Wayne State University Press, 2012. 69–89. Print.

Kennedy, Patrick. *The Fireside Stories of Ireland.* 1870. Norwood, PA: Norwood Editions, 1975. Print.

Langlois, Janet L. "Mothers' Double Talk." *Feminist Messages: Coding in Women's Folklore Culture.* Ed. Joan Newlon Radner. Urbana: University of Illinois Press, 1993. 80–97. Print.

Lau, Kimberly J. "A Desire for Death: The Grimms' Sleeping Beauty in *The Bloody Chamber.*" *Transgressive Tales: Queering the Grimms.* Ed. Kay Turner and Pauline Greenhill. Detroit: Wayne State University Press, 2012. 121–139. Print.

Lundell, Torborg. "Gender-Related Biases in the Type and Motif Indexes of Aarne and Thompson." *Fairy Tales and Society: Illusion, Allusion, and Paradigm.* Ed. Ruth Bottigheimer. Philadelphia: University of Pennsylvania Press, 1986. 149–163. Print.

Propp, Vladimir Yakolevich. *Morphology of the Folktale,* 2d ed. 1928. Trans. Laurence Scott. Austin: University of Texas Press, 1968. Print.

_____. *The Russian Folktale.* Ed. and trans. Sibelan Forrester. Foreword by Jack Zipes. Detroit: Wayne State University Press, 2012. Print.

Radner, Joan N., and Susan S. Lanser. "Strategies of Coding in Women's Cultures." *Feminist Messages: Coding in Women's Folk Culture.* Ed. Joan N. Radner. Urbana: University of Illinois Press, 1993. 1–29. Print.

Ragan, Kathleen. "What Happened to the Heroines in Folktales? An Analysis by Gender of a Multicultural Sample of Published Folktales Collected from Storytellers." *Marvels & Tales* 23.2 (2009): 227–247. Print.

Ranke, Kurt. *Folktales of Germany.* Trans. Lotte Bauman. Urbana: University of Illinois Press, 1966. Print.

Segal, Robert. "Introduction: In Quest of the Hero." *In Quest of the Hero.* Ed. Robert Segal. Princeton: Princeton University Press, 1990. vii–xli. Print.

Shojaei Kawan, Christine. "Fairy Tale Typology and the 'New' Genealogical Method: A Reply to Willem de Blécourt." *Fabula* 52 (2011): 297–301. Print.

Stone, Kay. "The Misuses of Enchantment: Controversies on the Significance of Fairy Tales." *Women's Folklore, Women's Culture.* Ed. Rosan A. Jordan and Susan J. Kalčik. Philadelphia: University of Pennsylvania Press, 1985. 125–145. Print.

Thompson, Stith. *The Folktale.* 1946. Berkeley: University of California Press. 1977. Print.

Toelken, Barre. "Silence, Ellipsis, and Camouflage in the English-Scottish Popular Ballad." *Western Folklore* 62.1/2 (2003): 83–96. Print.

Turner, Kay, and Pauline Greenhill. "Introduction: Once Upon a Queer Time." *Transgressive Tales: Queering the Grimms.* Ed. Kay Turner and Pauline Greenhill. Detroit: Wayne State University Press, 2012. 1–24. Print.

Uther, Hans-Jörg. "Tale Type." *The Greenwood Encyclopedia of Folktales and Fairy Tales.* Ed. Donald Haase. Westport, CT: Greenwood Press, 2008. Volume 3: Q-Z, 937–942. Print.

_____. *The Types of International Folktales: A Classification and Bibliography,* 3 vols. Helsinki: Academia Scientiarum Fennica, 2004. Print.

Von Franz, Marie-Louis. *The Feminine in Fairy Tales,* rev. ed. 1972. Boston: Shambhala, 1993. Print.

Warner, Marina. *From the Beast to the Blonde: On Fairy Tales and Their Tellers.* New York: Farrar, Straus and Giroux, 1994. Print.

_____. "Mother Goose Tales: Female Fiction, Female Fact?" *Folklore* 101.1 (1990): 3–25. Print.

Wentworth, Webster. *Basque Legends*. London: Griffith and Faran, 1879. Print.

Young, M. Jane, and Kay Turner. "Challenging the Canon: Folklore Theory Reconsidered from Feminist Perspectives." *Feminist Theory and the Study of Folklore*. Ed. Susan Tower Hollis, Linda Pershing, and M. Jane Young. Urbana: University of Illinois Press, 1993. 9–28. Print.

Neglected Yet Noble:
Nyneve and Female Heroism in
Thomas Malory's *Le Morte Darthur*[1]

Kristin Bovaird-Abbo

Given the male-dominated world of fifteenth-century England in which Sir Thomas Malory lived, it may be surprising to find an essay discussing *Le Morte Darthur* in a collection dedicated to the female hero. Malory was certainly no stranger to the notion of male heroism, having crusader kinsmen and personally serving "in the retinue of Richard Beauchamp Earl of Warwick at the siege of Calais in Henry V's time" (Field 54). Not surprisingly, Malory's *Morte Darthur* is littered with male heroes, including Sir Gawain, Sir Launcelot, and of course, King Arthur. The women who accompany the men of the *Morte Darthur* are often nameless, such as the various damsels who appear only to summon knights; these are largely passive figures, subject to seizure by the more active males while functioning primarily to inspire knights to greater deeds. Even the highest ranking females, Queens Igrayne and Guenevere, are not immune to such depredations on their persons.

Much of this female passivity is due to historical realities; as Maureen Fries notes, "there were very few heroic role models for females in medieval life: they were only infrequently rulers and forbidden to bear arms or enter the priesthood" (59). As the conventional routes to heroic status were closed off to women, we should not be surprised to find few female heroes in medieval literature. In addition, surviving documents from Malory's own life reflect a significant disregard for females. In May of 1450, for example, Malory was charged with sexual assault against the wife of a Hugh Smith, and a similar charge was brought forth in August of that same year (Field 97). To be fair, Malory was also frequently charged with incidents of violence against males. Still, given his love for chivalry as well as his creation of the Arthurian Pentecostal Oath within

35

the *Morte Darthur*, which specifically dictates knights "allwayes to do ladyes, damesels, and jantilwomen and wydowes [socour:] strengthe hem in hir ryghtes, and never to enforce them, uppon payne of dethe" (120:20–23),[2] we might expect a more reverent treatment of women within Malory's *Morte Darthur.*

Yet there are some female characters who insist on autonomy, defying expectations of passive female behavior; perhaps the most well-known, especially for readers of modern fantasy literature, is Morgan le Fay.[3] As Dorsey Armstrong notes, Morgan is unique in Malory's text in that she gains power both through her position as Arthur's kin and through her marriage to one of Arthur's kingly allies; no other female in the *Morte Darthur* concurrently holds these two positions (59). More importantly, she also obtains power through witchcraft, power she repeatedly uses to threaten Arthur's kingship. Ultimately, Morgan rejects her passive roles as wife, mother, and sister to pursue her own objectives independent of the chivalric community that attempts to contain her. Although modern authors have successfully recast Morgan in a heroic vein—beginning with Marion Zimmer Bradley's *The Mists of Avalon* in 1983— such sympathetic treatments are not to be found in medieval literature. Rather, such outspoken female characters are often ostracized and vilified by their medieval authors; for example, Malory depicts Morgan le Fay as perpetually attempting to destroy her brother merely out of hate.

That is not to say that the female hero cannot exist in the literature of this time period. She exists on the margins, emerging to interact with the more visible male heroes only to fade back into the shadows where the majority of her heroic journey continues. In the case of Morgan, recent scholarship has begun the process of rehabilitating her role in Malory's *Morte Darthur*; part of this rehabilitation is due to the success of modern retellings such as Marion Zimmer Bradley's *Mists of Avalon* (1982).[4] While acknowledging that Morgan's actions against Arthur are problematic, Jill M. Hebert argues that in *Morte Darthur*, Morgan has a more important purpose motivating her actions: "Morgan's concern over the political consequences to Arthur of both private betrayal and public revelation is demonstrated as she repeatedly attempts to unmask the flawed ideologies of knights while she also dons the mantle of political advisor to Arthur" (70). Perhaps the attention that Morgan le Fay receives is due to the character's own insistence; that is, one cannot ignore Morgan; to do so is to court peril. She demands to be seen, to be heard, and whereas earlier scholarship on women in Malory dismisses their political impact, scholarship by Hebert and others shows that female characters in *Morte Darthur* are actively involved in the establishment and maintenance of the political systems.[5] Yet there are other female figures who function in similar roles, albeit in less intrusive ways. In this essay, I argue that Nyneve, one of Malory's Ladies of the Lake, is such a figure. While she first appears as a passive female in need of rescue, she quickly transforms into a powerful and independent force who becomes the rescuer of many male figures, including King Arthur himself. Ultimately, her journey leads her to bring renewal to the Arthurian world, although in an unexpected way.

Nyneve may not be a protagonist in Malory's *Morte Darthur*, but she is a hero in the Campbellian sense, experiencing the separation, initiation, and return stages that allow her to resurface, in Joseph Campbell's words, "from this mysterious adventure with the power to bestow boons on [her] fellow man" (30). There are many gaps in the medieval female hero's journey—largely due to male medieval authors' focus elsewhere—but at the same time, such gaps open up their stories for modern authors who rediscover the Nyneves, Gueneveres, and Morgans of Arthurian legend. Although Campbell's work on the hero's archetypal journey, outlined most explicitly in his 1949 *The Hero with a Thousand Faces*, postdates the *Morte Darthur* by several centuries, Campbell found the seeds of the monomyth within the works of Malory (in addition to other classical and medieval texts). As Mildred Leake Day notes, Campbell wrote his master's thesis specifically on *Morte Darthur*, and he viewed "the Arthurian legend and the Holy Grail [as] a re-telling of the ancient Hero's Journey by authors sensitive to the mythic power of the material" (80, 81). While Campbell limits himself to masculine heroes, his notion of the hero and the heroic journey can be applied to both genders with some adjustments. As Fries notes in her discussion of medieval female characters, "'Female hero' may seem at first a paradoxical term, since we are accustomed by long literary tradition to think of the word 'hero' as masculine and the word 'heroine' as feminine" (60). Part of this is due to the nature of the Arthurian legend, which, as Lee Ann Tobin notes, "pays little attention to female experience" in both medieval as well as modern Arthuriana (148). Yet Fries acknowledges the possibility for female heroes, women who "assume the usual male role of exploring the unknown beyond their assigned place in society; and reject to various degrees the usual female role of preserving order (principally by forgoing adventure to stay at home)" (60). Nyneve, I argue, follows this prescription.

Despite the applicability of Campbell's hero's journey to the Arthurian legend, no scholars to date have viewed Nyneve as a female hero.[6] Notwithstanding Nyneve's frequent assistance to the Knights of the Round Table, Fries hesitates to acknowledge her as a hero, choosing instead to view Nyneve as lacking the aspect of sacrifice essential to Campbell's hero: "she deprives the male Arthurians of their counselor and reveals her own cunning ambition" (71). Anne Berthelot also views Nyneve negatively, describing her as "Merlin's bane, the traditional embodiment of 'the woman who conquers the wisest man in the world'" (99). As I will discuss below, close readings of Nyneve's appearances contradict the selfish ambition that Fries and Berthelot ascribe to her. Although Geraldine Heng is willing to acknowledge Nyneve as "beneficent" (104), like Fries, she does not see Nyneve as fulfilling the role of the female hero, noting that Nyneve "does not, unlike Merlin, interfere in the purely human struggle of social destiny" (105), a claim that I will oppose below. Sue Ellen Holbrook sees Nyneve as a positive force, but limits her to a "role of benign helper" to Arthur's knights (172). Catherine Batt follows a similar path, designating Nyneve as a "guardian angel" set in opposition to Morgan le Fay's malicious intent (66). I argue that Nyneve is much more than the archetypal maiden helper; she is not bound by the strictures of society's expectations for female behavior, and her actions suggest not a lack of interest in the larger political scheme but rather a fixed interest. Nyneve acts not for her own needs and desires, but rather for the good of the realm. In essence, she provides an entry into the role for the modern female hero.

Not all scholars are content to assign Nyneve a passive or side role. Kenneth Hodges, for example, argues that she redefines "crucial elements of political and romantic chivalry, demonstrating that women can participate in chivalry as agents instead of objects" (78). In fact, Hodges even argues that Nyneve's "career, defeating a lustful sorcerer, rescuing the king, and then winning a spouse, is suitable for a knight" (90); however, Hodges does not go so far as to label Nyneve a "hero," merely a "chivalric character" (93). I would go that extra step, though, because Nyneve removes herself from the court and passive female domesticity to dedicate her life to helping Arthur. While her actions may at times evoke those of a knight, as Hodges suggests, Nyneve has two weapons that the male heroes of the *Morte Darthur* lack: her feminine nature and her ability to use language, and she uses both in her service to Arthur and the larger vision of chivalric society. Although not recognized by the medieval narrator, who has eyes only for the masculine exploits, the roots—even the blossoming tree—of female heroism are visible in Nyneve's narrative.

Malory is not the first to incorporate Nyneve into the Arthurian legend, for she has a long history in Arthurian romance, variously appearing as Viviane, Éviène, Niviene, or Nimuë. Yet in the texts predating the *Morte Darthur*, Nyneve's role is minor. In the thirteenth-century French text familiarly known as the Prose *Merlin*, she entraps Merlin after learning his magic; in the Post-Vulgate *Suite du Merlin*, also thirteenth century, she bestows the magic sword Excalibur upon Arthur. While Malory retains both of these episodes, he alters them significantly; for example, Nyneve is not the Lady of the Lake who gives Arthur his magical sword. Ann Howey, writing on modern fantasy, notes that "Arthurian rewritings that use female protagonists go beyond this tradition to create new roles for their protagonists, often by emphasizing the nation-building aspects of the story rather than the courtly love aspects" (64). This idea is applicable to Nyneve's appearance in Malory, for he also expands her role to involve her more actively within the construction and maintenance of the Arthurian court; although she does have a love interest, he is not central to her role.

Campbell's monomyth begins with a departure from the everyday world, initiated by a "call to adventure." A herald typically signals this shift, and at first glance, Nyneve could be mistaken as the herald, for by requesting the return of her stolen hound during Arthur's wedding festivities, she provides opportunities for the newly knighted Sir Gawain and Sir Torre, as well as the more experienced Sir Pellinor, to go questing. In addition, the Campbellian hero frequently ignores the call—and Arthur's response to Nyneve's request is simply, "'I may nat do therewith'" (103.8), followed by inaction when a strange knight seizes Nyneve. Initially, then, Arthur may appear to be positioned as the reluctant hero whom Merlin must then push to call for Nyneve's rescue.

At the same time, however, Nyneve is being initiated into another world of sorts, for she is not as passive as might be expected. Whereas damsels are typically introduced by a third party as objects in need of rescue, Nyneve has had something taken from her and she takes immediate and direct steps to have it returned. Her behavior when she first arrives in Arthur's court is aggressive with its use of the imperative mood: "'Sir, suffir me nat to have thys despite, for the brachet ys myne that the knight lath ladde away'" (103.5–7). These words contrast sharply with those of other female petitioners; for example, the sword-bearing damsel in the *Balin le Sauvage* episode allows Arthur to speak first before presenting her request (for a knight capable of drawing the sword from her sheath) in a polite tone using the subjunctive mood (61–62). Likewise, Lynet in the *Sir Gareth of Orkney* episode "prayde hym [the king] of succoure" (296.18), a self-effacing linguistic move. Nyneve, by entering into the Arthurian realm, must learn to readjust her demeanor and language in order to obtain success. Her first foray is, in a sense, a failure, for not only does Arthur deny aid, but also she is seized by a strange knight. Arthur, meanwhile, remains unmoved: "whan she was gone the kynge was gladde, for she made such a noyse" (103.11–12).

The "refusal of the call to adventure" has the potential to render the hero passive; as Campbell notes, "Walled in boredom, hard work, or 'culture,' the subject loses the power of significant affirmative action and becomes a victim to be saved" (59). In this case, Nyneve gives no indication of ennui or dedication to her former life; culture, however, proves to be her bane, for Arthur's society does not tolerate outspoken females, particularly ones who loudly interrupt his proceedings. When the hero is female, then, the "call to adventure" is perhaps elided; after all, we do not know what has prompted Nyneve to enter Arthur's court, much less from where she has come. The "refusal of the call" lies outside of Nyneve's power, for by entering into Arthur's court and loudly making demands of him, she signals her willingness to act against her gender norms. Thus begins Nyneve's "road of trials," to use Campbell's term, for to be a woman in Arthur's world is to be passive and more often than not, silent.

The events that next unfold seem to do little to suggest Nyneve's heroic nature; however, we must remember that the medieval female is ever on the margins. Having been commanded by Arthur to recover the abducted maiden,

Pellinor follows after the maiden and her abductor, only to find that another knight has challenged the abducting knight for the lady. Pellinor interrupts the fight to battle the abductor knight, and subsequently kills him. We might at this point expect Nyneve to assume a domestic position; after all, during Campbell's discussion of the "refusal of the call," he invokes the Norse warrior maiden Brynhild only to comment that she "was preserved for her proper hero" (63), and other knights within the Arthurian legend often marry the damsels that they rescue. But Pellinor is not in search of a bride—only the fulfillment of his liege's commands. In addition, Nyneve is watching and learning, waiting for a chance to embark on her own adventure. Passivity at this stage of the hero's journey is not unusual, especially when the "call to adventure" is frustrated by an external force.

Another aspect of the departure is significant. As Campbell notes, the hero must be removed from the familiar world—that is, the family. Even masculine heroes experience well-meaning family members who are reluctant to release them into the world; for example, Percival's mother attempts to keep him ignorant of chivalry after the passing of his father. Although Nyneve is standing quietly by—Pellinor does address her directly, but only to issue an order: "'Fayre lady, ye muste go with me unto the courte of kynge Arthure'" (115.8–9)—she remains an object rather than a subject in his eyes: she is being held back by her family. When Pellinor inquires of a laborer as to Nyneve's whereabouts, he is told of the two knights fighting for her that "'one seyde he wolde have hir by force, and that other seyde he wold have the rule of her, for he was hir kynnesman and wolde lede hir to hir kynne'" (114.32–35). Nyneve is objectified and thus caught between two men who would rule her—either by force or by kinship ties. Her passivity in this situation, then, may be viewed as calculating; she does not wish to interrupt Pellinor's quest to retrieve her and thus remove her from such an imprisoning situation. To voice an opinion at this point may be interpreted as preferring one knight over another—and Nyneve desires autonomy, which neither can provide. Accompanying Pellinor allows Nyneve to begin upon her hero's journey.

Perhaps it is fateful that Nyneve begins her departure by exchanging her place within the prison of expected feminine behavior with the more masculine role of counselor when she entraps Merlin, Arthur's chief advisor. Merlin becomes enamored of Nyneve and follows her everywhere; eventually, she entombs him in a rock using magic to escape his advances (126.23–27). This action earns (wrongfully, I would argue) Nyneve much negative critique from twentieth-century Arthurian scholars. Beginning in the late nineties, however, other scholars have begun to reassess Nyneve's actions in a more positive light. For example, Holbrook, in comparing Malory's treatment with those of his predecessors, notes that "Malory's Nymue is more acceptable than the *Suite*'s Niviene, who secretly hates and plots against Merlin all along" (181). Hodges views her actions as self-defensive rather than malicious: "Instead of a knight showing up to protect Nyneve, she protects herself [from Merlin] by permanently entombing [Merlin] beneath a stone" (83). When we view this incident as part of the hero's journey, Nyneve's actions become necessary, for to act otherwise would be to jeopardize the quest.

Traditionally, the male hero requires "supernatural aid" to proceed on the quest, and this is certainly true for the female hero as well. Merlin most clearly fulfills this role in the *Morte Darthur*, for not only does he initiate Nyneve's rescue following her abduction at Arthur's wedding; he then instructs her in the ways of magic, which Nyneve eagerly absorbs: "And ever she made Merlion good chere tulle sche had lerned of hym all maner of thynge that sche desired" (125.6–8). Of course, he does this not to aid her on her quest, but rather to fulfill his own sexual needs. This is yet another way in which the female hero's experience may differ from that of the male hero. Mentors such as Professor Albus Dumbledore in J. K. Rowling's *Harry Potter* series or Gandalf in J. R. R. Tolkien's *The Hobbit* and *The Lord of the Rings* who interact with heroes of the same gender do not pose the same threat as they may when dealing with female heroes[7]; they may possess love for the younger male heroes, but it is typically not a romantic or sexual love. Nor is it simply a matter of mixed genders, for male heroes often have female mentors; as Campbell notes, "[t]he helpful crone and fairy godmother is a familiar feature of European fairy lore; in Christian saints' legends the role is commonly played by the Virgin" (71). These female mentors are mother-figures, often separated from the hero by age, and combined with their gendered passivity and nurturing natures, do not pose sexual threats to the hero. The male mentor, however, does not experience such restrictions, and often must be incapacitated in some other way so as to not jeopardize the female hero's quest. For example, in Suzanne Collins's 2008 young adult science fiction novel *The Hunger Games*, Katniss Everdeen's mentor Haymitch Abernathy appears in a perpetually intoxicated state. In other instances where the female hero's mentor is male, he is often related to her—often as a grandfather; thus, the taboo against incest prevents any problems of a sexual nature within the mentoring relationship. In the case of Merlin, however, when confronted with a beautiful and socially unattached female whom society attempts to render inert, he proves unable to control himself.

Holbrook argues that Nyneve's "motives for incarcerating [Merlin] are that she is tired of his sexual interest and also that she is afraid of him" (180). While I agree with Holbrook to an extent, I believe that she underestimates Merlin's role here, for when we examine his actions more closely, it becomes clear that Nyneve is not merely trying to rid herself of an unwanted lover. Their relationship may start out innocently enough; Merlin's feelings towards her are initially described by Malory as *dotage* (125.2), a word which, according to the *Middle English Dictionary*, denotes "foolish behavior" (def. 1a); initially Merlin is annoying but not dangerous. Yet Merlin quickly becomes much more threatening, and Malory repeatedly draws attention to Merlin's obsession with Nyneve in such a way as to condemn Merlin while excusing Nyneve. Although she may seem to invite Merlin's attentions in a predatory manner, offering him "good chere" so that she may learn his magic (125.7), when we look at the larger context of the passage, we see that these actions are a direct result of Merlin's actions: "Merlion wolde nat lette her have no reste, but allwayes he wolde be wyth her" (125.5–6). His parasitical behavior becomes even more menacing with time, for during their time in Cornwall, he is depicted as a thief waiting to ambush her: "allwayes he lay aboute to have hir maydynhode" (126.17–18).

We might even read Nyneve's encounter with Merlin as evidence of the "crossing of the first threshold" in Campbellian terms—that is, while he initially serves as a mentor figure, Merlin quickly transforms into a threshold guardian. In the traditional male hero's journey, the "road of trials" involves a transitional state, variously described as the descent to the underworld or the "belly of the whale." As Campbell notes, "the passage of the magical threshold is a transit into a sphere of rebirth ... the hero, instead of conquering or conciliating the power of the threshold, is swallowed into the unknown, and would appear to have died" (90). Merlin now becomes fearful and dangerous, threatening to consume (sexually) Nyneve; if he were to be successful in his attempts to gain Nyneve's maidenhood, she would be returned to her initial passive role. Yet because of the magical knowledge gained from the mentor, Nyneve is able to escape Merlin to continue upon the "road of trials." Interestingly, Malory suggests that Nyneve's entrapment of Merlin is unavoidable, for immediately after Merlin falls in love with Nyneve, he tells Arthur of his impending fate: "he tolde to kynge Arthure that he scholde nat endure longe, but for all his craftes he scholde be putte into the erthe quyk" (125.10–12). That the word "craftes" is then replaced by "subtyle worchyng" to describe Nyneve's entrapment of Merlin suggests that the mentee has surpassed the mentor (126.24). The idea that the mentor may pose a danger to the hero is not novel; as Campbell points out, the mentor of Johann Wolfgang von Goethe's nineteenth-century *Faust* is none other than Mephistopheles (73); however, typically the innocence of the hero is not complicated at this early stage of the hero's journey. For the female hero, then, the movement beyond the mentor, once he or she has fulfilled the role, is fraught with peril that may leave the female hero stained by the guile that she must employ in order to proceed.

Typically, the narrator follows the male hero through the descent to the underworld; for example, we are privy to Aeneas's conversations with his father in Virgil's *Aeneid*, and we follow Pwyll's adventures in the Otherworld in the Welsh *Mabinogion*. In Malory's *Morte Darthur*, however, once Nyneve entombs Merlin, we are told only that "she departed and leffte Merlyon" (126.27). Nyneve then travels alone, presumably through the wilderness. When she resurfaces, she continues to be alone and outside of civilization, but we are not given any indication of where she goes or what she accomplishes. As with Campbell's "call to adventure," this portion of Nyneve's journey is elided, and this again may be due to the narrator's interests—he does not follow female characters, unless they are, like Morgan after the theft of Arthur's scabbard, being pursued by a significant male figure; as a result, any "rebirth" that Nyneve may have experienced following her entombment of Merlin is unknown. At the very least, she is "swallowed" by the narrative.

When she next emerges, Nyneve has changed, both in terms of her abilities and her demeanor; however, modern critics continue to underestimate her heroic character. For example, Heng acknowledges that Nyneve replaces Merlin as Arthur's magical advisor; and I would add that like Merlin, Nyneve does not remain at the court but rather comes and goes at her pleasure. Heng then argues, "We are given to feel, however, that [the court] is far less central to her interests than it was to Merlin, whose preoccupation with its concerns was obsessive" (105). Amy Kaufman makes a similar observation, noting Nyneve "can be beneficent, but she can also be selfish, ruthless, desiring, and capricious" (56)—behaviors equally attributable to male heroes. Because Nyneve does not interfere every time there is a problem at Arthur's court, scholars quickly denounce her. Yet Merlin frequently fails to solve problems; for example, Merlin arrives at Arthur's court during the *Balin le Sauvage* episode too late to save either the previous Lady of the Lake or Balin. He also reveals the true identity of Morgause, Arthur's sister, after Arthur has begotten Mordred upon her (44.16–19). Merlin is partly human, after all, and thus subject to human errors. Launcelot, too, cannot save everyone; a woman under his protection is beheaded when Launcelot is tricked to look away (285.7–14). Balin cannot save a knight from the malicious knight who rides under the cover of invisibility (80.8–18). Nyneve, then, should not be held to an impossible standard. After all, she repeatedly saves Arthur's life, and the lives of several of his knights. More importantly, though, she neutralizes malicious females; because of the Pentecostal Oath, the knights are essentially rendered impotent when dealing with aggressive and malevolent females. Nyneve, however, has no such restrictions, and can neutralize such figures effectively, and this is due largely to the tools acquired from Merlin, her supernatural mentor, as well as her gender and her innate ability to learn from previous mistakes. Her actions are calculated, not capricious, and her next action within the Arthurian realm indicates that as the female hero, she continues to serve the needs of the larger realm.

Nyneve next appears within the narrative as Arthur fights for his life against Accolon. Morgan le Fay has stolen Excalibur and its magical scabbard and given them to her lover, Accolon, arranging the circumstances to allow Accolon to kill Arthur in battle. Nyneve appears suddenly, and the narrator signals her purpose: "she com thidir for the love of kynge Arthur, for she knew how Morgan le Fay had ordained for Arthur shold have bene slayne that day, and therefore she com to save his lyff" (142.21–24). As Fries notes, "Romance females are patriarchally predicated by passive verbs; to romance males belong the active ones" (63). Here, though, Nyneve clearly possesses agency. In addition, she now possesses the foreknowledge that previously had been Merlin's specialty. At first, she appears passive, standing by while watching two men fight; however, the wheels are turning in her head, and she waits for the right moment to act. When that time comes, she effectively uses the magic taught her by Merlin: "by the damsels inchauntemente the swerde Excaliber fell oute of Accalons honde to the erthe, and therewithal sir Arthure lyghtly lepe to hit and gate hit in his honde" (144.24–27). Further, as Hodges notes, Nyneve carefully evaluates the fight: "Only after hearing Arthur and Accolon speak does she act.... Nyneve's standards, an appreciation of prowess and worship and an abhorrence of treason, provide the lens through which the announced principles of the Round Table code will be judged" (84). Nyneve has come a long way from when we first meet her at Arthur's wedding; when demanding the return of her hound, the emphasis is firmly on herself and her desires when she tells Arthur, "suffir *me* nat to have thys despite, for the brachet ys *myne*" (103.5–6, my emphasis). Now, however, Nyneve not only desires to save the life of a man whom she esteems; she is also concerned with the social code, which affects all who dwell within Arthur's realm.

What is significant about a female hero's actions here, as opposed to a male hero's actions, is the silence that accompanies her deeds. While her behavior at Arthur's wedding is loud and abrasive, Nyneve draws no attention to her intervention in the fight between Arthur and Accolon; only the narrator is aware of her presence, and Arthur at no point wonders why Accolon drops the sword at such an opportune moment. This is not an exception to Campbell's monomyth—as he notes, "Frequently [the hero] is honored by his society, frequently unrecognized or disdained" (37)—but the lack of recognition is unusual in the Arthurian world. Even when knights attempt to hide their good deeds, eventually they are found out, as in the case when Sir Launcelot saves Sir Kay from several knights (273.25–27). Because women are largely treated as objects of exchange between men, however, they are not deemed as capable of heroic deeds. For Nyneve to trumpet Arthur's debt to her would be to undermine society's underpinnings. Arthur must appear to defeat his opponent through his own prowess, not via the skills of a woman. As the hero must sacrifice himself or herself for the greater good, so too must Nyneve remain unacknowledged.

This is also one of the major traits that distinguishes Nyneve from Morgan le Fay. Some scholars view Morgan and Nyneve as two sides of a single coin; for example, Kaufman points out the similarity in their romantic relationships (64), and Heng notes their isolation from the larger society (104). Yet a major distinction between them lies in their motivations. Morgan is largely self-serving, and all of her attempts to capture Arthur's knights are geared towards serving her own ends. After learning of Accolon's death, Morgan frees a knight accused of fornication simply because he is related to Accolon, and then enlists the rescued knight to send a message to Arthur: "'Telle hym ... that I rescewed the nat for the love of hym, but for the love of Accolon, and tell hym I feare hym nat whyle I can make me and myne in lyknesses of stonys, and lette hym wete I can do much more what I se my tyme'" (152.25–28). In one breath, Morgan publically signals her opposition to Arthur, professes her magical prowess, and challenges Arthur to future conflicts.

Nyneve, on the other hand, remains on the margins. When she next comes to Arthur's aid, following the arrival of a magical mantle sent from Morgan to Arthur as false front of reconciliation, she effectively uses language in such a way as to not aggravate or undermine Arthur. As with the Accolon episode, Nyneve is observant; she sees Arthur fall under the visual enchantment of the richly adorned mantle, and then acts accordingly: "Whan the kyng behelde this mantell hit pleased hym much. He seyde but lytyll. With that come the Damesell of the Lake unto the kynge" (157.20–22). This episode occurs the day after Arthur's return from his near fatal encounter with Accolon and the delivery of Morgan's challenge. Resentment towards Morgan is abundant within the court—yet no one, prior to Nyneve's intervention, thinks to question Morgan's sudden change of heart. When it is clear that no one else will speak up, Nyneve must act, but she does so carefully. While she still adopts a firm tone with Arthur, she no longer uses the imperative tone and there are no narrative indications of her previous loud volume with Arthur. Our female hero has learned how to interact with powerful men in such a way that they do not dismiss her. Rather than initially announce her warning to all within hearing, Nyneve acts discretely: "'Sir, I muste speke with you in prevyté'" (157.23). Although Arthur then commands her to speak in the hearing of all, she has publically deferred to him in order to allow him to maintain control of the situation. Once she has warned Arthur of the danger inherent in wearing the mantle, and provided him with a way to confirm the truth of her words without danger to his person, she vanishes from the narrative yet once more. As she does not require recognition for her deeds, she has no cause to remain at court.

It is difficult to assess whether or not Nyneve experiences Campbell's "atonement with the father," which involves the "abandonment of the attachment to ego itself" (130). However, if we play with the gender assignments somewhat, Nyneve's actions against Morgan suggest the moment to be a type of "atonement with the father" that occurs simultaneously with the "meeting with the goddess." This is not unusual in the traditional monomyth, for as Campbell notes, "the father and mother reflect each other, and are in essence the same" (131). The Goddess personifies "the feminine attributes of the first, nourishing and protecting presence" (Campbell 113), and in Geoffrey of Monmouth's twelfth-century *Vita Merlini*, Morgan is known primarily for her healing abilities; in the fourteenth-century anonymous *Sir Gawain and the Green Knight*, she is explicitly called "Morgne þe goddes" (2451). While much pejorated by the time of Malory's fifteenth-century romance, she still retains traces of the Universal Mother; however, Morgan now emerges as a perverse mother who threatens to destroy her family; in addition to her numerous attempts to bring about Arthur's death, she also attempts to kill her husband, King Uriens.

Because the meeting with the father is "a reflex of the victim's own ego" (Campbell 129), for a female hero, it is really a meeting and atonement with the mother rather than the father. Nyneve sees Morgan's attempts to gain power and to destroy her brother—these are the temptations of the power Nyneve now holds from Merlin.[8] Not surprisingly, any time that Morgan speaks, she uses multiple first-person pronouns to signal her selfish purposes—much as Nyneve does in her first appearance in the *Morte Darthur*. Yet once she has crossed the threshold and gains supernatural aid, Nyneve thinks about the greater good each time that she rescues Arthur, and purposes to bring life instead of the death that Morgan threatens. Nyneve essentially neutralizes Morgan, for the latter withdraws to her castle, rarely interfering with Arthur or his knights. More importantly, Morgan as a threat dissipates much like the father-figure in the guise of the ogre, for when Morgan does try to disrupt the Round Table following the failure of her enchanted mantle, other figures—often nameless damsels with no evident magical abilities—successfully undermine her attempts. The father, or in this case, the mother, is no longer a threatening figure; "at-one-ment" has been achieved.[9]

The hero, male or female, who survives the encounter with the Goddess gains "the boon of love (charity: *amor fati*), which is life itself enjoyed as the encasement of eternity" (Campbell 118), and this is demonstrated in Nyneve's next appearance as her life-preserving deeds significantly expand to knights other than Arthur. However, there is yet another way in which the female hero's journey diverges from the traditional monomyth. According to Campbell, "when the adventurer, in this context, is not a youth but a maid, she is the one who, by her qualities, her beauty, or her yearning, is fit to become the consort of an immortal" (119). Nyneve rejects this role—"consort" suggests passivity, or at the very least, a lower status, particularly since the spouse is immortal. Instead, Nyneve is very active in choosing and gaining her husband—and more importantly, becoming married does not keep her at home.

Morgan's malicious actions against Arthur lead him to temporally exile Morgan's son, Sir Ywain, and accompanied by Gawain, he embarks on a series of quests. When Gawain meets Sir Pelleas, a knight desperately in love with the Lady Ettarde, Pelleas trusts Gawain to woo Ettarde on his behalf. When Gawain proves false, Pelleas despairs and seeks only to die. Nyneve, wandering as usual through the forest, comes across one of Pelleas's retinue and learns of his plight.

At this point in the narrative, Pelleas has no connection to Arthur; he is not one of the Round Table knights. Nyneve is not obligated to intervene, but she does. While Malory does not invent the Pelleas and Ettarde interlude, he alters its conclusion, for Ettarde is punished (she falls deeply in love with Pelleas, who then rejects her) and Pelleas is saved—and married to one who returns his love (172.16–18). The agent, for Malory's *Morte Darthur*, is Nyneve; as Holbrook notes, "Malory creates a role ... that she has nowhere else in literature—the savior and beloved wife of Sir Pelleas" (181).

Nyneve's behavior in the Pelleas episode may be described as her most masculine, for as Kaufman notes, "In a complete reversal of the usual gendering of power, Nynyve marries the knight she rescues and protects him for the rest of his life. Pelleas becomes her subject, and she his sovereign" (63). Yet all of her prior actions have led her to this moment. Because she has gained Merlin's foreknowledge and developed her own patience and judgment—all resulting from her hero's journey—Nyneve is not only able to confidently command Pelleas's knight, she can also guarantee that the knight will live and that the offending lady be punished: "Brynge me to hym ... and y woll waraunte his lyfe ... hit is no joy of suche a proude lady that woll nat have no mercy of suche a valyaunte knyght" (171.23–27). This is similar to what the male heroes of the *Morte Darthur* do; Launcelot, for example, when sought after by a damsel distressed by a false knight, offers his compliance: "All youre entente, damsell, and desyre I woll fulfylle, so ye woll brynge me unto this knyght" (264.34–35). Yet rather than argue for a reversal of gender, I argue that this is simply the next stage in the hero's journey: Nyneve has achieved "apotheosis."[10]

When Nyneve saves the life of Pelleas, she makes it clear that no power higher than herself is owed his thanks; when Pelleas comments that "now suche grace God hath sente me that I hate hir as much as I have loved hir,'" Nyneve responds, "'Thanke me therefore'" (172.22–24, 25). She has assumed the position of the father (or in this case, the mother). As a result, Pelleas proves very receptive to Nyneve's commands: "Anone sir Pelleas armed hym and toke his horse and commaunded his men to brynge aftir his pavylyons and his stuffe where the Lady of the Lake wolde assyngne them" (172.26–28). Nyneve is firmly in control of the situation, and this continues when she returns to Arthur's court. The narrator's description of her arrival is significant because Nyneve is clearly in the subject position: "agayne the feste of Pentecoste cam the Damesell of the Laake and brought with hir sir Pelleas" (179.25–27).

We may be tempted to consider Nyneve's actions here as evidence of the hero's return with what Campbell calls a "life-transmuting trophy" (193), but she has not yet reached that stage of the hero's journey. Her own life, certainly, has changed through marriage to Pelleas, for several of her next textual appearances are augmented by the narrator's reminders of her marriage. We might also view Pelleas as the trophy, for he is welcomed into the Round Table and performs worthily; he is even described as "one of the foure that encheved the Sankgreal" (although Malory seems to have forgotten this detail by the time he narrates the Grail Quest) (180.9–10). Pelleas all but disappears from the *Morte Darthur*, and he does not stand out as one who significantly changes life at Camelot.

Nyneve, however, continues to wield her influence, ensuring that Pelleas never meets Launcelot on the tournament field (180.10–14). Her scope also continues to broaden, though, for in *The Healing of Sir Urry*, Nyneve is mentioned twice. When a knight bearing an enchanted wound appears at Arthur's court seeking healing, every knight proceeds to lay their hands on the knight. Not surprisingly, Pelleas is one of the knights to make the attempt, and Nyneve is invoked as his wife and savior. Yet she also appears independently of Pelleas, for when Sir Severause le Brewse is named, the narrator inserts a brief aside about how "the chyff lady of the Lady off the Lake fested sir Launcelot and sir Severause le Brewse, and whan she had fested them both at sundry tymes, she prayde hem to gyff her a done, and anone they graunted her" (1148.21–25). The request that she makes of them individually is to never fight with one another. The implication is that if these two knights were to meet in battle or tournament, one of them would certainly be killed, and both knights (especially Launcelot) are vital to Arthur's Round Table.

Another indication that Nyneve's journey is not over yet is that Arthur's life is still threatened, and Nyneve continues to intervene to save his life as demonstrated by two subsequent episodes. She has achieved the "boon" through her full acquisition of Merlin's foreknowledge and development of her own judgment; however, she refuses the true return because she is not yet ready to allow Arthur to be removed from kingship despite his increasing lapses from justice. She continues to place her personal needs—her love of Arthur—above the needs of the nation; however, two incidents take place that change her mind. First, the sorceress Aunowre captures Arthur, and when he refuses to sleep with her, sends him into the forest to be killed by her knights. What follows is similar to the Accolon episode; Nyneve learns of the threat to Arthur's life, and acts (490.25–28); however, rather than using her magic to free Arthur, she seeks either Launcelot or Tristram to intervene. Second, when Queen Guenevere is accused of poisoning a knight at a feast, Nyneve again uses her foreknowledge, clears the queen's name, and reveals the true culprit. In this second instance, Arthur's life is not directly endangered, and Launcelot has already proved Guenevere's innocence through trial by combat; however, as Holbrook notes, "without Nymue's confirmation [of Guenevere's innocence], the knights ... might have continued to mistrust the Queen despite their necessary acquiescence to the verdict achieved through trial by combat, and so it is indeed for the good of Arthur's court that Nymue makes the truth known" (186). Yet these actions do not renew the court; they only guarantee that life continues on as the subjects under Arthur have always known. At the same time, Nyneve also signals the importance of judgment. Although Guenevere has been cleared by Launcelot, prior to Nyneve's arrival, the true instigator of the knight's death is unknown; in fact, the court's behavior suggests the truth is not even important, for "there was made grete joy, and may merthys there was made in that courte" (1059.8–9). Such destructive behavior cannot, in Nyneve's mind, be allowed to remain in the shadows, and Arthur's failure to seek out the root of the poison must weigh heavily on Nyneve's mind.

Although Nyneve's magic may indirectly result in death, as it does in the case of Ettarde, she does not kill directly, nor does she order anyone else to kill on her behalf; I would also note that Ettarde dies "for sorow" after judgment has been passed upon her (172.29). Yet when Nyneve brings Tristram to save Arthur from the sorceress Aunowre, Arthur performs a violent action, one that, like his inaction in the Poisoned Apple episode noted above, has resounding consequences. As Tristram kills the two knights attacking Arthur, Nyneve quickly commands Arthur regarding Aunowre, "'Lat nat that false lady ascape!'" (491.28). The implication, given Nyneve's pattern of saving, rather than destroying life, is that she intends Arthur to seize the sorceress so that she may be brought to a proper judgment, but Arthur beheads the false sorceress. Nyneve's response following this exploit is significant: "the Lady of the Lake toke up hir hede and hynge hit at hir sadill-bowe by the heyre" (491.30–31). Interestingly, Kaufman connects Nyneve's action here to classical mythology, specifically the legend of Medusa, noting that both Nyneve and Athena mount the heads of slain females as trophies (65). At the very least, this parallel with Athena is more evidence that Nyneve attains "apotheosis."

But at the same time, the placement of the head upon the saddle carries symbolic weight in the *Morte Darthur*, for in the other notable times when this action is performed, it is a punishment to the bearer. For example, Gawain accidently beheads a woman during his first quest; his penance is to then "bere the dede lady with hym on thys maner: the hede of her was hanged aboute hys necke, and the hole body of hir before hym on hys horse mane" (108.22–24). Launcelot also orders a knight to bear the head of a slain lady (285.29–32). Thus Nyneve's actions indicate that the sorceress's head is a burden, not a trophy. Arthur has killed a defenseless woman (magical defenses aside), thus violating the tenants of the Pentecostal Oath. Nyneve carries the weight of the action, however, because she is ultimately responsible for Arthur's actions, having saved him from near death time and again.

It is in Nyneve's final appearance in the *Morte Darthur* that the female hero's journey is concluded, and the "life-transmuting trophy" is brought back to the mortal world. As Campbell explains, this final action "may rebound to the renewing of the community, the nation, the planet, or the ten thousand worlds" (193). Through the process of "apotheosis," the hero, male or female, becomes more aware of the larger picture—particularly regarding the cyclical nature of life. As noted earlier, Heng does not consider Nyneve to be a hero because she does not seem to affect the destiny of Arthur's civilization (105); however, it is through Nyneve's inaction that the fate of Arthur's kingdom is irrevocably changed. Arthur and Mordred have concluded their mortal battle, and Bedivere has returned Excalibur to the waters from whence it came. As Arthur lies dying, a barge bearing four women appears to take Arthur to "'the vale of Avylyon to hele [Arthur] of [his] grevous wounde'" (1240.33–34). The next day, Bedivere comes across the newly dug grave of Arthur.

In yet another contribution original to Malory, Nyneve is one of the women standing on the barge, but unlike her previous appearances, she now engages in traditionally female behavior as the four women twice "wepte and shryked" in unison (1240.16; 1241.1). It may be that Arthur is beyond help, for Morgan, the only woman on the barge who speaks, notes of Arthur that "'thys wounde on youre hede hath caught overmuch coulde!'" (1240.24–25). However, given the pattern of last-minute rescue of Arthur by Nyneve that Malory has established throughout the *Morte Darthur*, we may question why Nyneve does not intervene in the final battle with Mordred. In fact, when the narrator identifies the four women in the barge—the Queen of North Gaul and the Queen of the Waste Lands accompanies Morgan and Nyneve—Nyneve is the character who receives the most narrative attention, and her protective acts are highlighted: "thys lady had done much fo[r] kynge Arthure. (And thys dame Nynyve wolde never suffir sir Pe[ll]eas to be in no place where he shulde be in daungere of hys lyff...)" (1242.11–13). Given Arthur's actions in the previous episode concerning Aunowre, however, the answer may be that Nyneve recognizes that Arthur's time is truly at an end. Arthur's lack of interest in finding the true killer in the Poisoned Apple episode, coupled with the rash beheading of Aunowre, reveals to Nyneve that he is no longer dedicated to justice, and thus not a king still fit to rule. The kingdom must be renewed—not restored under Arthur—and Malory indicates that Constantine, Arthur's successor, surpasses him: "he was a ful noble knyght, and worshypfully he rulyd this royame" (1259.28–29). We have no reason to suspect Nyneve's tears at Arthur's death—he has lived a long and productive life, and the loss of life is to be mourned—but her silence here speaks volumes. She must sacrifice a man she respects in favor of upholding the greater good, as the world cannot continue to prosper under Arthur's rule.

Ultimately, then, although Campbell (and many following in his footsteps) focuses on the male hero to the exclusion of the female (beyond the interventions of female deities and helper maidens), the path she finds herself upon remains remarkably similar to that of the male hero. She too requires supernatural aid and faces temptations, some of which may be sexual in nature—and which is certainly not limited only to female heroes—and she is equally capable of the transformation of the male hero, and the subsequent renewal of the world. At the same time, the nature of the female hero requires some modification of the traditional monomyth, for given the environment in which the female hero is likely to be raised, traditional weapons such as swords are often beyond her reach. Instead, she more frequently must use language to pass through the "road of trials." In addition, the male hero typically advances through deeds of destruction, most frequently the killing a dragon or a giant, or some other monstrous obstacle. Launcelot must kill Sir Tarquin, and King Arthur must kill Sir Mordred. By the end of the journey, however, the male hero must embrace the feminine—either within or without—in order to bring healing to the land; in other words, he must allow the feminine side of himself to emerge in order to become a whole person. Likewise the female hero undergoes a similar conversion, but she must learn to kill rather than to heal. Thus when she knows his reign should end, Nyneve must deny healing to Arthur. Although he is lamented by many, including Nyneve herself, significant events subsequently occur that could not happen had Arthur survived. After all, it is only through Arthur's death that Guenevere is able to truly repent her infidelity to him, with the result that Launcelot follows her example.

Robert Frost once wrote of two paths diverging in a yellow wood in "The Road Not Taken," noting of the two that "the passing there / Had worn them really about the same" (9–10). So too are the male and female hero journeys; both are equally traversed; however, the path of the male hero appears to the human eye to be the one more frequently navigated. The human eye is tricked; as Nyneve's narrative demonstrates, her path weaves in and out of the more visible male hero's journey. Because Nyneve in her role as the female hero must destroy in order to renew—behavior often viewed as antithetical to the medieval social expectation of the female as healer—the loss of a king as beloved as Arthur would not endear Nyneve to her fellow characters, and so it is appropriate that Nyneve as the female hero remains ever in the shadows; just as her earliest deeds go unacknowledged by the Arthurian society, so too must her final (in)action, which has the greatest and lasting impact. Although one must peer closely, as I have attempted to do throughout this essay, in order to see Nyneve's influence on the course of events, the trace remains.

As the majority of romance writers from this time period are male, many gaps exist in the narrative of the female hero in medieval literature. Such oversight actually proves useful for modern writers such as Marion Zimmer Bradley, Mary Stewart, Gillian Bradshaw, and Nancy McKenzie, just to name a few, providing a space in which they can interrogate medieval texts and ponder the offscreen lives of female characters. Although medieval authors such as Malory may not have been interested in the trials and adventures of women such as Nyneve, modern authors and audiences alike are, and the legend is continually renewed. What is surprising, however, is the paucity of positive depictions of

Nyneve in modern Arthurian fantasy. In *The Mists of Avalon*, Nimue's sole purpose is to trap Merlin so that he may be brought to the judgment of Morgaine, the Lady of the Lake; however, Nimue then kills herself out of grief, having fallen in love with Merlin. T. A. Barron recreates Nyneve as Merlin's antagonist in his *Lost Years of Merlin* series, and the BBC television series, *Merlin*, takes a similar route in the first season (although this modern Merlin manages to defeat Nimue). Fay Sampson reduces Nyneve to Merlin's lover. Mary Stewart's depiction is the most positive; as in the *Morte Darthur*, Niniane is Merlin's willing student and eventually takes his place as Arthur's advisor, but Merlin's withdrawal from the Arthurian court is voluntary, rather than forced upon him.

What is striking in all of these modern depictions is that Nyneve exists only as part of Merlin's story, which is surprising given her various exploits following Merlin's entrapment in Malory's narrative. Brynhild may exist solely for Sigurd in Campbell's eyes, but as Malory's *Morte Darthur* demonstrates, Nyneve is so much more than a tangent to Merlin's adventure, and Malory downplayed her relationship to Merlin while significantly increasing her role in Arthur's kingdom. King Arthur may be the *rex quondam rexque futurus* ["The Once and Future King"], but it is through the potential agency and quests of heroic females such as Nyneve that the legend continues to be rediscovered. To follow the path of the female hero may prove, as the narrator of Frost's poem discovers, to "[make] all the difference" (20). Nyneve's path is waiting to be followed.

NOTES

1. I am most grateful to Susan Dunn-Hensley, Matthew Candelaria, and Lori Campbell who commented and improved earlier versions of this article.

2. Malory, Thomas. *The Works of Sir Thomas Malory*. Ed. Eugène Vinaver, rev. P.J.C. Field. 3rd edn. 3 vols. Oxford: Oxford UP, 1990. All future references to this work come from this edition and will be noted parenthetically by page and line numbers.

3. Several books and articles are dedicated to exploring Morgan le Fay in modern fantasy; see, for example, Carolyne Larrington's *King Arthur's Enchantresses: Morgan and Her Sisters in Arthurian Tradition* (London: I.B. Tauris, 2006), Jill M. Hebert's *Morgan Le Fay, Shapeshifter* (New York: Palgrave Macmillan, 2013), and Ann F. Howey's *Rewriting the Women of Camelot: Arthurian Popular Fiction and Feminism* (Westport: Greenwood P, 2001).

4. *Mists of Avalon* has been hailed by some as a feminist retelling; for example, Lee Ann Tobin notes that Bradley's text "seeks to reinscribe power for female characters" in the article "Why Change the Arthur Story? Marion Zimmer Bradley's *The Mists of Avalon*." *Extrapolation* 34.2 (1993): 147–157. 147. However, as Hebert notes, although Bradley shows how Morgan le Fay is a complex character, '[a] positive reading of that complexity is undercut ... by Bradley's inability to move Morgan's characterization beyond the limiting influence of her sources and perhaps her society" (128).

5. Two other scholars who explore the roles of women in political matters in Malory's *Morte Darthur* include Dorsey Armstrong, in *Gender and the Chivalric Community in Malory's* Morte Darthur (Gainesville: University Press of Florida, 2003), and Kenneth

Hodges, in *Forging Chivalric Communities in Malory's* Le Morte Darthur (New York: Palgrave Macmillan, 2005).

6. Micheal Crafton, in "Joseph Campbell and Teaching Arthuriana," discusses some of the drawbacks of applying Campbell's theory of the monomyth to Arthurian texts—largely centering on Campbell's insistence on universalizing myths, thus reducing them to one basic pattern. *Studies in Medieval and Renaissance Teaching* 12.1 (Spring 2005): 33–51. While I agree with Crafton that the Arthurian legend cannot and should not be limited in such a fashion, I do believe that Campbell's Hero's Journey is a useful way of teasing out Nyneve's role in the *Morte Darthur*, as I hope to demonstrate in this essay.

7. Of course, there are no female heroes in *The Hobbit*, with the result that all of the mentor-mentee relationships are of the same gender. Heroic females do appear in *The Lord of the Rings*. In addition to the two essays in this collection on Tolkien, see Leslie A. Donovan's "The Valkyrie Reflex in J. R. R. Tolkien's *The Lord of the Rings:* Galadriel, Shelob, Éowyn, and Arwen" in *Tolkien the Medievalist*. Ed. Jane Chance (London: Routledge; 2003): 106–32.

8. Although in the *Morte*, Morgan's powers are acquired while she is at put to school in a nunnery, in several other medieval accounts, including *Sir Gawain and the Green Knight*, Morgan learns her magic from Merlin. This is yet another way in which Morgan and Nyneve appear as almost interchangeable.

9. I am not trying to suggest that Morgan is evil, for as Heng notes, "Morgan's impact is not as destructive as it might superficially seem. The trials she provides Arthur's knights serve to increase their abilities and reputations with successful endurance" (107). Just as the Goddess or the Father must test would-be heroes, Morgan too pushes Arthur's knights—and Nyneve—to their limits. Hebert comes to a similar conclusion regarding Morgan: "Morgan often functions as Arthur's backbone in her attempts to expose the private issues that Arthur refuses to face publically, such as Lancelot and Guenevere's treasonous love affair and the potential disloyalty of his knights" (72).

10. As Campbell points out, the Bodhisattva can be depicted as male or female; also, "Male-female gods are not uncommon in the world of myth" (152).

Works Cited

Armstrong, Dorsey. *Gender and the Chivalric Community in Malory's* Morte d'Arthur. Gainesville: University Press of Florida, 2003. Print.

Batt, Catherine. *Malory's* Morte Darthur: *Remaking Arthurian Tradition*. New York: Palgrave, 2002. Print.

Berthelot, Anne. "From Niniane to Nimüe: Demonizing the Lady of the Lake." In *On Arthurian Women: Essays in Memory of Maureen Fries*. Ed. Bonnie Wheeler, Fiona Tolhurst. Dallas: Scriptorium Press, 2001. 89–101. Print.

Campbell, Joseph. *The Hero with a Thousand Faces*. New York: MJF Books, 1949. Print.

Day, Mildred Leake. "Joseph Campbell and the Power of Arthurian Myth." In *Popular Arthurian* Traditions. Ed. Sally K. Slocum. Bowling Green: Bowling Green State University Press, 1992. 80–84. Print.

"dotage, n." Def. 1a. *Middle English Dictionary*. April 2013. *Middle English Compendium*. Web. 16 July 2013.

Field, P. J. C. *The Life and Times of Sir Thomas Malory*. Woodbridge: D. S. Brewer, 1993. Print.

Fries, Maureen. "Female Heroes, Heroines, and Counter-Heroes: Images of Women in

Arthurian Tradition." In *Arthurian Women*. Ed. Thelma S. Fenster. New York: Routledge, 1996. 59–73. Print.

Frost, Robert. "The Road Not Taken." *The Poetry Foundation*. Web. 18 July 2013. http://www.poetryfoundation.org/poem/173536.

Hebert, Jill M. *Morgan Le Fay, Shapeshifter*. New York: Palgrave Macmillan, 2013.

Heng, Geraldine. "Enchanted Ground: The Feminine Subtext in Malory." In *Arthurian Women*. Ed. Thelma S. Fenster. New York: Routledge, 1996. 97–113. Print.

Hodges, Kenneth. "The Chivalry of Malory's Nyneve." *Arthuriana* 12.2 (Summer 2002): 78–96. Print.

Holbrook, Sue Ellen. "Nymue, the Chief Lady of the Lake, in Malory's *Le Morte Darthur*." In *Arthurian Women*. Ed. Thelma S. Fenster. New York: Routledge, 1996. 171–190. Print.

Howey, Ann. *Rewriting the Women of Camelot: Arthurian Popular Fiction and Feminism*. Westport, CT: Greenwood Press, 2001. Print.

Kaufman, Amy S. "The Law of the Lake: Malory's Sovereign Lady." *Arthuriana* 17.3 (2007): 56–73. Print.

Malory, Thomas. *The Works of Sir Thomas Malory*, 3d ed., 3 vols. Ed. Eugène Vinaver, rev. P.J.C. Field. Oxford: Oxford University Press, 1990. Print.

Sir Gawain and the Green Knight. Ed. J.R.R. Tolkien and E.V. Gordon. 2d ed. Ed. Norman Davis. Oxford: Oxford University Press, 1967. Print.

Tobin, Lee Ann. "Why Change the Arthur Story? Marion Zimmer Bradley's *The Mists of Avalon*." *Extrapolation* 34.2 (1993): 147–157. Print.

"Radiant and terrible": Tolkien's Heroic Women as Correctives to the Romance and Epic Traditions

Jack M. Downs

Where Are the Women in Middle-earth?

The question of heroic women in J.R.R. Tolkien's fantasy fiction is a difficult one, at least on the surface. Critics and reviewers often hone in on a perceived dearth of female characters as a failing in Tolkien's conceptualization of Middle-earth. The perceived absence of women in Tolkien's work is only exacerbated by the massive popularity of Peter Jackson's film versions of *The Lord of the Rings* and *The Hobbit*, which frequently attract criticism of the sort offered by *Time* magazine Ideas editor Ruth Davis Konigsburg, who, upon viewing Jackson's 2012 *The Hobbit: An Unexpected Journey*, condemns Tolkien's entire secondary world by announcing, "Tolkien seems to have wiped women off the face of Middle-earth" ("Why are there no women" n. pag.). Setting aside Konigsburg's unfortunate conflation of Jackson's film interpretations with their original source material, such criticisms seem to have some merit: in *The Hobbit* and *The Lord of the Rings* Tolkien assigns the bulk of the action to male characters, and women are primarily present in secondary and background roles. But a careful analysis of Tolkien's entire mythos reveals that women are neither absent, nor entirely confined to secondary roles within Middle-earth.

In this essay, I will recover the lost or overlooked representations of female heroes in Tolkien's Middle-earth. This effort at recovery will rest primarily on an application of Joseph Campbell's familiar construction of the mythic hero in two close readings of prominent female characters from Tolkien's mythos, Lúthien and Éowyn. In *The Hero with a Thousand Faces*, Campbell describes the mythic hero as "the man or woman who has been able to battle past his personal and local historical limitations" and who after completing the heroic quest "is to return to us, transfigured, and teach the lesson ... learned of life renewed (Campbell, *HwaTF* 19–20). Furthermore, Campbell's construction of the hero is predicated on submission (*HwaTF* 16) and sacrifice (*PoM* 123). As these readings will demonstrate, Lúthien and Éowyn both battle personal and historical limitations, and both are asked to submit and sacrifice for the greater good, though the end result of their achievements is called into question when they reintegrate into their respective cultures' gender-based expectations for female roles.

These readings of Lúthien and Éowyn will be further contextualized through an examination of Tolkien's attempt to revise the romance and epic traditions in an effort to create a new, authentically English mythology. While it is well-known that Tolkien, as a scholar of Anglo-Saxon and Norse literatures and languages, drew heavily upon these cultures and literary traditions in his creation of Middle-earth, he was also intentionally inventing a "new" mythology for England, one which corrected what he saw as the corrupt medieval romance tradition embodied in the Arthurian corpus. Tolkien was wary of Arthurian romance for a number of reasons, and while he admits the attractiveness of the Arthurian world, he felt that most romance was "too lavish and fantastical, incoherent and repetitive" (Tolkien, *Letters* 144). This desire to correct what he saw as the failure of Arthurian romance extends into every facet of his conceptualization of the Middle-earth mythos, and is a crucial concept in understanding Tolkien's portrayal of female heroes. While Tolkien consistently draws upon romance and epic conventions in developing social and cultural contexts for his heroic female characters, those characters consistently defy, subvert, and discard those same conventions through the deployment of their hard-won individual agencies. Rather than delving into the popular perception that Middle-earth is a fantasy world mostly devoid of powerful women, this essay will focus on Lúthien and Éowyn in an effort to explore how Tolkien's intention to create a new mythology for England led to the creation of empowered female characters whose instinctive, innate heroism created a framework for future iterations of female heroes in fantasy literature.

Yet characterizing Tolkien's fiction as a bastion of male-dominated escapism in which women are sidelined or entirely absent is an easy generalization for two reasons. First, despite the presence of strong female characters throughout the mythos of Middle-earth, there are actually very few female characters— strong or otherwise—in Tolkien's work. Second, most of Tolkien's powerful female characters are active primarily in Middle-earth's mythic past, portrayed at some length in the posthumously-published *Silmarillion*,[1] but largely absent or unknown to readers familiar only with the hobbit-centric perspective presented in the much more widely read *Hobbit* and *Lord of the Rings*.

Casual readers whose knowledge of Middle-earth is limited to these works are to be forgiven for assuming women have little or no place in Middle-earth: of the several heroic female characters introduced in *The Silmarillion*, only Galadriel is present, and she appears as a secondary and largely passive character in *Lord of the Rings*. Varda, the angelic creator of the stars revered by the elves, appears obliquely in two renderings of the elvish song "A Elbereth Gilthoniel" found in *Lord of the Rings* (*FotR* 312; *TT* 430), but these references are so obscure that the younger hobbits[2]—and thus, the readers—do not know that the Elbereth of the song is the angelic being credited with creating and brightening the stars. Likewise, Lúthien is referenced only through a fragment of song sung by Aragorn at the camp on Weathertop (*FotR* 258–260). So while women are *not* absent from Middle-earth, they are also not present in the most familiar and widely-read presentations of Middle-earth found in *The Hobbit* and *The Lord of the Rings*. Examining Tolkien's engagement with the romance and epic traditions reveals crucial, though subtle, complexities in his portrayals of women, and while women might not be as present as men in Middle-earth, Tolkien creates space in which women can make their presences felt.

Tolkien and Arthurian Romance

Any attempt to understand Tolkien's portrayals of women requires understanding his work within the context of the literary traditions from and against which he was working. One of these literary traditions was Arthurian Romance. Tolkien was, of course, familiar with the late–Victorian revival of Arthurian literature, and as the translator of a well-regarded version of *Sir Gawain and the Green Knight*, he was professionally engaged with the medieval Arthurian corpus. But Tolkien's respect for the romance tradition—and particularly, Arthurian romance—was outweighed by a professional and personal rejection of the aesthetic excesses of the genre. In a 1951 letter, Tolkien describes a clear disappointment with the Arthurian legends as the focal narratives of England's mythic past. He felt "grieved" that England had no genuinely English mythology, that "it had no stories of its own ... not of the quality that I sought, and found ... in legends of other lands" (Tolkien, *Letters* 144). Regarding the Arthurian mythos, Tolkien conceded its power, but as an English mythology, he asserted, "it is imperfectly naturalized, associated with the soil of Britain but not with English" (*Letters* 144). Tolkien betrays his abiding interest in the relationship between linguistics and literature, but he goes on to argue that the Arthurian corpus falters aesthetically as well as linguistically. Tolkien's criticism is consistent with his well-known approach to sub-creation; specifically that successful fantasy literature (what Tolkien would describe as "fairy-stories") depends upon portraying the secondary, created world as largely consistent with itself. Inconsistent or extravagant deviation from the reality of the secondary world damages the impact of a fairy-story on its readers (Tolkien, "On Fairy-Stories" 126; 146).

In this regard, Tolkien found Arthurian stories entirely deficient. He described the failure of Arthurian romance as deriving from too great a deviation from its own internal consistency (Tolkien, *Letters* 144). The romance tradition, in Tolkien's view, was not only divided from England historically and linguistically; it was also aesthetically flawed, presenting a shallow, underdeveloped secondary world possessed of little internal consistency, prone to fantastical flights of fancy that extravagantly and capriciously flaunted the realities of the secondary world of the Arthurian romance. In short, the romance tradition was entirely unsuitable as a vehicle for a mythic English history fit to stand with the Celtic, Germanic, Scandinavian, and Finnish mythologies Tolkien loved so well.

Yet none of this prevented Tolkien from attempting to revise and recover the romance tradition. His translation, with E.V. Gordon, of *Sir Gawain and the Green Knight*, was instrumental in placing the poem within the canon of English literature. Tolkien's attitude toward the romance tradition was not, then, an outright rejection of the genre and its subject matter. Instead of rejection, Tom Shippey describes Tolkien's entire oeuvre as "engaged in deep negotiation with the ancient genres of epic and romance" (311). The concept of negotiation is perhaps the most useful lens for examining Tolkien's engagement with the romance and epic traditions and the portrayal of women in his own work.

Guinevere, *The Fall of Arthur*, and the Failed Female Hero

Nowhere is Tolkien's negotiation with romance more directly portrayed than in his recently-published (2013) alliterative poem, *The Fall of Arthur*. The poem's 954 lines provide an extended, tantalizing, and unfortunately unfinished rendering of the Arthurian legend, and offer an invaluable glimpse of Tolkien's intellectual and artistic engagement with the Arthurian mythos and the romance genre. Christopher Tolkien dates the poem's primary composition during the 1930s, beginning perhaps in 1931, with editing and revision continuing at least until 1937 (C. Tolkien 10–11; 155).[3] As Christopher Tolkien observes, these dates place the composition of the poem immediately after Tolkien ceased work on verse renderings of several early Middle-earth myths and during his work on *The Hobbit*, which was published in 1937. *The Fall of Arthur* was thus written while Tolkien was actively conceptualizing and composing some of the major elements of his own still-forming mythos. While the poem possesses a number of features that make it worthy of extended critical attention, for our purposes, a brief summary and contextualization of Guinevere's portrayal must suffice.

Tolkien's Arthurian legend begins *in media res*, with Arthur campaigning on the European continent. As Arthur and his host arrive at the edge of a vast, ancient forest,[4] a messenger arrives from Britain, informing Arthur of Mordred's treason. Arthur immediately turns back and considers requesting aid from Lancelot, who has been banished to Benwick for his affair with Guinevere. As Arthur's fleet makes landfall on the shores of Britain, the landing is opposed by Mordred's allies. Gawain leads an assault on the enemy ships and routs Mordred's forces. The poem breaks off as Arthur takes council with Gawain, wondering if they should sail to another landing point to avoid the massed opposition of Mordred and his confederates.

Woven throughout this narrative are references to Guinevere: the reader sees her through the eyes of Arthur, Lancelot, and Mordred. The poem only briefly adopts Guinevere's perspective as she considers how to escape Mordred's less-than-honorable designs. The momentary attention paid to the queen, though, is telling. The characterization of Guinevere is clearly a site of Tolkien's negotiation with romance as described by Shippey. Christopher Tolkien asserts that *The Fall of Arthur* draws heavily from Malory's *Morte d'Arthur*, and to a lesser extent, the anonymous alliterative *Morte Arthure* and the French *Mort Artu* (C. Tolkien, "Preface," 71–122), and with these sources in mind, we can draw some useful generalizations about women in medieval romance and Tolkien's attempts to revise and negotiate with the romance tradition. In the medieval Arthurian corpus, women are at the center of virtually all conflict. As passive characters, they are prizes to be won, damsels to be saved or defended, and political tools to be exchanged between men. In these roles, Sheila Fisher argues, "[w]omen figure significantly not so much for their own sakes, but in order to become involved in the construction ... of men's chivalric identities" (152). When women demonstrate any sense of personal agency, though, they become threatening, mysterious, and unpredictable. Fisher points to Bertilak's wife in *Sir Gawain and the Green Knight* as paradigmatic in this regard, demonstrating the dangers that emerge when women assert themselves in any meaningful way within the power structure of medieval romance (153). In the Arthurian romance tradition as written by the *Gawain* poet, Malory, and the anonymous authors of the alliterative *Morte Arthure* and the French *Mort Artu*, women most often function either as plot devices that allow men to establish their chivalric masculinities, or as agents of chaos, intent on disrupting the chivalric identity of Arthur's court.

Tolkien's Guinevere is caught between these two stereotypical romance roles: she is both a central agent in the dissolution of Arthur's court and a passive commodity. Although Guinevere is at the center of the controversy that dissolves Arthur's court, Tolkien is unwilling to lay the blame for the affair with Lancelot and its consequences solely at Guinevere's feet. Yet although the reader is told "Strong oaths *they* broke" (Tolkien, *FoA* III.62, my emphasis), Guinevere's attempt to assert her own agency in the affair with Lancelot produces disastrous results, since the affair becomes the catalyst for the death of Arthur's best knights, the breaking of the fellowship of the Round Table, and the pretext for Mordred's attempt to usurp the throne.

Once Mordred moves openly against Arthur, Guinevere's status as commodity is reasserted. As Arthur's wife, she is a symbol of the king's authority, and as such, Mordred's move to force her to marry him is an attempt to legitimize his usurpation of the throne. Guinevere's commodification is unmistakable: after Mordred's secret malice breaks into open rebellion, he first greets Guinevere as the "Lady of Britain" (Tolkien, *FoA* II.125). After Guinevere challenges his right to the crown, however, Mordred sets aside any pretext of respect and declares his intent to take the queen, both as a symbol of royal authority and as an object of sexual desire in saying,

> Thou at my side shall lie,   slave or lady,
> as thou wilt or wilt not,   wife or captive.
> This treasure take I,   ere towers crumble,
> and thrones are o'erturned,   thirst first will I slake.
> I will be king after   and crowned with gold' [Tolkien, *FoA* II.151–158].

Mordred reduces the queen to a commodity and mocks the idea that she might exercise any choice in the matter as he conflates her possible roles as "slave or lady."

Faced with such a choice, Guinevere dissembles, asking Mordred for time to consider his request. Mordred mocks the queen again, asking,

> What proof of power   shall prisoner seek,
> captive of captor?   Be I king or earl,
> 'twixt bride and bond   brief be the choosing! [Tolkien, *FoA* II.171–173].

Guinevere chooses the only option left to her: withdrawal from the male-dominated world in which she is caught among her vows to Arthur, her love for Lancelot, and her fear of Mordred. Tolkien's description of her escape, however, allows the possibility that Guinevere's choices are not quite so limited. Although she is fleeing from Mordred into an uncertain life as a fugitive, she grimly considers a possible reunion with Lancelot if Mordred conquers Arthur:

> Then from ruin haply
> were gladness wrested.   Guinevere the fair,
> not Mordred only,   should master chance
> and the tides of time   turn to her purpose [II.210–213].

Whatever Tolkien's intentions may have been for Guinevere, the poem breaks off before he returns to her fate. The reader is left with a poignant final image of the queen, riding alone on a dark night into an uncertain life as a fugitive, with no companions, and no certainty that Arthur will prevail over Mordred, or that Lancelot will come to her aid. With this stark image of the fugitive queen, Tolkien provides a final glimpse into the strength of her character: Guinevere determines that she will not allow men to control her fate, and she promises herself that she will find a way to master her own destiny.

Tolkien's negotiation with the romance tradition is on display throughout his treatment of Guinevere, yet the negotiation ends in something of an impasse. Guinevere is not a hapless damsel, nor is she demonized as the destroyer of Camelot. Contrary to medieval portrayals of women as "weak, vain, lustful, and needful of the guidance ... of men" (Fries 59), Guinevere challenges her status as a commodity and refuses to accept her fate as a pawn in the war between Mordred and Arthur, choosing instead a flight into the unknown, embracing her own agency regardless of the difficulties such a decision entails. Throughout Tolkien's narrative, Guinevere's most salient characteristic is a heroic strength of will. Lancelot's remembrance of the queen provides a succinct encomium:

> From war she shrank not,   might her will conquer,
> life both and love   with delight keeping
> to wield as she wished   while the world lasted [Tolkien, *FoA* III.97–99].

Guinevere is caught in an untenable situation: possessed of a strong will, married to a man she does not love, in love with a man she cannot have, the queen exudes frustration and despair. Tolkien presents Guinevere in a mostly sympathetic light, but he does not deviate far from his source material in Malory and *Mort Artu*. When Campbell's construction of the hero is applied to Tolkien's Guinevere, she falls well short: she certainly "battles past ... personal and local historical limitations" (Campbell, *HwaTF* 19), yet there is no return, no "lesson ... learned of life renewed" (*HwaTF* 20). In Guinevere, there is no heroic submission, no heroic sacrifice. Yet in *The Fall of Arthur*, Tolkien provides a blueprint for the female heroes found in *The Silmarillion* and *The Lord of the Rings*. His Guinevere attempts—mostly unsuccessfully—to elude the constraints of the gender conventions associated with the romance tradition; however, when Tolkien transports similar gender conventions to Middle-earth, the results are far different for Lúthien and Éowyn.

Lúthien and the Inversion of Romance

The story of Lúthien and Beren occupies the central position in *The Silmarillion*, and in a 1972 letter to his son Christopher, Tolkien describes the story as "the chief part of the *Silmarillion*" (420). Furthermore, in relating the genesis of the Lúthien myth, Tolkien reveals that he first began conceptualizing the story in 1917, long before he began thinking about hobbits or the One Ring.

Tolkien felt the story communicated truths about his relationship with his wife, Edith, which could only be expressed in "tales and myths" (Tolkien, *Letters* 421), and is perhaps the most deeply personal story Tolkien ever wrote.[5] The tale of Lúthien and Beren is in a sense the ur-myth of Middle-earth, and so it is significant that this story inverts and reverses the conventions of the romance tradition concerning women's roles.

At first, though, the story is driven by romance conventions. Tolkien introduces the reader to Beren, a mighty human warrior who has been singled out by Morgoth, the great enemy of men and elves in Middle-earth's mythic past. Beren's companions have all been hunted down and killed by agents of Morgoth, but Beren escapes, passes through unspeakable perils, and arrives at the border of Doriath, the hidden kingdom ruled by Thingol, a powerful elf lord, and Melian, a demi-goddess. For centuries, Melian has used her powers to enchant the borders of Doriath, creating an impenetrable maze that prevents intruders from entering the kingdom, but Beren's destiny is so strong that he passes through the border of Doriath unharmed (Tolkien, *Silmarillion* 164–165). He wanders alone in the forest until one day when he encounters Lúthien, the daughter of Thingol and Melian, dancing in a forest glade.

In true romance fashion, Beren falls into an enchantment at the sight of her, "for Lúthien was the most beautiful of all the [elves]" (Tolkien, *Silmarillion* 165). Lúthien departs the glade and Beren wanders for some time searching for her; when he again encounters her, he cries out "Tinúviel!" (elvish for "Nightingale") and she allows Beren to approach. Lúthien also falls in love at first sight and for a time, Beren and Lúthien roam the woods of Doriath together, and Tolkien tells the reader that "no others ... have had joy so great, though the time was brief" (*Silmarillion* 166). Throughout the opening pages of the story, romance conventions abound as Lúthien and Beren meet. He is a great warrior who is enchanted at the sight and sound of a maiden dancing and singing in a magical forest glade and they fall in love almost immediately, a consequence of what seems to be a pre-determined "fate" or "doom" (165).

The tale continues to follow a romance script as Lúthien and Beren are observed by Daeron, King Thingol's minstrel, who is himself in love with Lúthien. Like Mordred in the Arthurian tradition, Daeron's jealousy and bitterness toward the illicit relationship[6] leads him to betray the couple to Thingol and Melian. When Beren is conducted to the court of Thingol and Melian, the reader is confronted with yet another romance convention. Arthurian stories are often structured around the presentation of Arthur's court, whole and at peace, disrupted by the presence of an outsider who brings a challenge to the king and his assembled knights. In *Gawain and the Green Knight*, for example, Arthur's New Year celebration is interrupted when the Green Knight rides into the banquet and challenges Arthur or any of his knights to an exchange of blows. The challenge disrupts the equilibrium of Arthur's court: the knights

are all reluctant to accept the challenge and Arthur himself is about to participate in the Green Knight's game when Gawain interposes and accepts on
Arthur's behalf. The disruption of the court is only solved after Gawain satisfactorily completes the quest and proves the chivalry of Arthur's knights
(Tolkien, *SGGK* 26–37; 87–88).

Beren's presence at Thingol's court in Doriath similarly disrupts the equilibrium of the court as Beren and Thingol negotiate the price of Lúthien's hand
in marriage. When challenged concerning his presence in Doriath, Beren's
answer might be perfectly at home in a medieval romance:

> [H]ere I have found what I sought not indeed, but finding I would possess for
> ever. For it is above all gold and silver, and beyond all jewels. Neither rock, nor
> steel, nor the fires of Morgoth, nor all the powers of the Elf-kingdoms, shall
> keep from me the treasure that I desire. For Lúthien your daughter is the fairest
> of all the Children of the World [Tolkien, *Silmarillion* 166].

Beren's language commodifies Lúthien, using the pronoun "it" (rather than
"she") to refer to Lúthien, while comparing her to gold, silver, and jewels, and
calling her a "treasure" before finally granting personhood by mentioning
Lúthien's name. Her father tacitly agrees to the reduction of Lúthien to the status of a commodity in his answer to Beren. Thingol pronounces the price of
Lúthien's hand in language echoing that of Beren:

> I too desire a treasure that is withheld. For rock and steel and the fires of
> Morgoth keep the jewel that I would possess against all the powers of the Elf-
> kingdoms. Yet I hear you say that bonds such as these do not daunt you. Go
> your way, therefore! Bring to me in your hand a Silmaril from Morgoth's crown;
> and then, if she will, Lúthien may set her hand in yours. Then you shall have my
> jewel [*Silmarillion* 167].

Thingol's pronouncement, much like that of Beren, dismisses Lúthien's personhood, comparing her with treasure, and with a specific jewel—a Silmaril. Thingol and Beren both refer to prices and to selling Lúthien (*Silmarillion* 168);
and throughout this exchange, Lúthien is entirely silent, standing by while two
powerful men discuss her fate. Thus far in the narrative, Lúthien fulfills a female
medieval romance role earlier described by Fisher: Lúthien does not exist for
her own sake; rather, she is a plot device that allows Beren and Thingol to assert
their competing masculinities (Fisher 152). Though at this point in the narrative
Lúthien has exhibited no evidence of her heroic nature, she soon exchanges
passivity and silence for agency and action.

Lúthien's passive acceptance of being commodified ends as soon as Beren
departs Doriath on his quest. Beren is almost immediately imprisoned by
Sauron; Lúthien senses Beren's plight and resolves to come to his aid. Once
again, she is betrayed by Daeron, the king's minstrel. To prevent Lúthien from
following Beren, King Thingol orders a house built high in the branches of the

tallest tree in Doriath where she is imprisoned. At last, Lúthien begins to assert her personal agency, using her innate powers escape the treehouse prison:

> [S]he put forth her arts of enchantment, and caused her hair to grow to great length, and of it she wove a dark robe that wrapped her beauty like a shadow.... Of the strands that remained she twined a rope, and she let it down from her window.... Then Lúthien climbed from her prison, and shrouded in her shadowy cloak she escaped from all eyes [Tolkien, *Silmarillion* 172].

Lúthien's escape from Doriath echoes Guinevere's flight from Mordred in *The Fall of Arthur*, as Guinevere flees into voluntary exile, shrouded in shadow, unobserved by Mordred's agents.[7] But while Guinevere is escaping into an uncertain fate in which the best possible outcome seems to be that her husband and her captor batter each other to pieces so that she can reunite with her lover, Lúthien demonstrates her heroism by escaping to *save* Beren from the terror and despair of Sauron's prison.

In a complete inversion of the romance tradition, it is Lúthien who consistently rescues Beren from the various perils they encounter in their attempt to seize a Silmaril from Morgoth's crown. When Lúthien rescues Beren from Sauron's prison pits, she banishes Sauron from his physical body, "his ghost ... sent quaking back to Morgoth" (175). After banishing Sauron, Lúthien demonstrates her full power:

> Lúthien took the mastery of the isle [Sauron's island-fortress] ... stood upon the bridge, and declared her power: and the spell was loosed that bound stone to stone, and the gates were thrown down, and the wall opened, and the pits laid bare; and many thralls and captives came forth in wonder and dismay [175].

Throughout the narrative, such demonstrations of power by Lúthien seem to indicate that she is innately, inherently powerful—so powerful that she can banish Sauron, destroy his fortress, and cleanse the isle from his taint. Sauron, who in *The Lord of the Rings* is the incarnate representation of evil in Middle-earth, is completely helpless and his fortress crumbles in the face of Lúthien's heroic deployment of her power.

With Lúthien operating as the hero of the tale, it is Beren who occupies a traditional female role. Despite his very real prowess as a warrior, Beren is constantly in need of Lúthien's assistance. After escaping Sauron's pits, Beren is mortally wounded when he steps in front of an arrow intended for Lúthien, and Lúthien, "by her arts and her love ... healed him" (Tolkien, *Silmarillion* 178). As Beren and Lúthien approach Morgoth's fortress, Lúthien once again uses her power, this time to disguise Beren as a werewolf and herself as a vampire in bat form. When Beren and Lúthien discover Carcharoth, the great wolf of Morgoth, guarding the gates of Morgoth's fortress, Lúthien instinctively sheds her disguise and enchants Carcharoth: "[C]asting back her foul raiment she stood forth, small before the might of Carcharoth, but radiant and terrible.

Lifting up her hand she commanded him to sleep.... And Carcharoth was felled, as though lightning had smitten him" (Tolkien, *Silmarillion* 180). Throughout these episodes, Beren is often a bystander in his own quest while Lúthien manages to overcome every obstacle virtually on her own, with very little assistance from Beren. Beren's heroism is the externalized male heroism traditionally associated with the romance tradition, with his martial prowess, warrior's reputation, and attendant sense of masculine identity (Cartlidge 1–5). Yet it is Lúthien who is the true hero of the tale, and whose heroism is primarily internal and inherent.

Lúthien's use of her own beauty and grace also thoroughly inverts an important romance convention. In the romance tradition, the beauty and allure of female characters is rarely represented in an entirely positive light. Beautiful women are, at best, distractions to be avoided by Arthur's virtuous knights; at worst, they are destructive, scheming temptresses who use their feminine attractions to orchestrate the downfall of chivalric knights (Fisher 151–160). Lúthien's beauty and grace, however, are entirely positive attributes that only adversely affect men who already possess evil intentions. Daeron, Thingol's minstrel who twice betrays Lúthien to her father, is prone to jealousy and envy before he falls in love with Lúthien. Lúthien's beauty and grace are not the cause of Daeron's jealousy; instead, Lúthien is the focus for Daeron's innate character flaws. Celegorm and Curufin, the renegade elvish princes who attempt to kidnap and then murder Lúthien, fall from grace long before they meet her, and Lúthien's goodness and beauty simply provides a foil to their dark intentions. Unlike the women of the Arthurian tradition—Morgan Le Fay, Nimue, Bertilak's wife, Elaine of Corbenic, and of course, Guinevere—Lúthien's virtue is unquestionable and her motives pure, bringing out the best in virtuous characters, and the downfall of un-virtuous characters when they act out on their worst impulses.

Nowhere is this concept more evident than in the confrontation with Morgoth. When Lúthien and Beren reach Morgoth's throne room, Morgoth immediately sees through Lúthien's disguise. She is undaunted and instead exhibits an astonishing level of courage and bravado: "She was not daunted by his eyes; and she named her own name, and offered her service to sing before him, after the manner of a minstrel" (Tolkien, *Silmarillion* 180). Morgoth accepts her offer, and "looking upon her beauty conceived in his thought an evil lust" (180). Morgoth fails to achieve his dark purpose, however, because he is "beguiled by his own malice" (Tolkien, *Silmarillion* 180) and Lúthien's power overmatches the dark lord of Middle-earth. Lúthien sings a song of such unspeakable beauty that Morgoth is blinded and soon he and his entire court fall into a deep, enchanted slumber cast by Lúthien's voice.

Lúthien's song resonates with the Silmarils set in Morgoth's crown. These ancient and holy jewels, crafted centuries earlier and containing the first light of the world, respond to Lúthien's purity and goodness. The jewels begin blazing of their own accord and their radiance has a stupefying effect which overcomes even Morgoth's mighty will. Morgoth falls asleep under the power of the jewels, allowing an opportunity for Lúthien and Beren to escape: "[s]uddenly he fell, as a hill sliding in avalanche, and hurled like thunder from his throne lay prone upon the floors of hell. The iron crown rolled echoing from his head. All things were still" (Tolkien, *Silmarillion* 181).

Lúthien's exhibition in Morgoth's throne room provides critical insight into the operation of her power, which is predicated on her own inherent goodness, grace, purity, and beauty. Her power inspires virtue in characters like Beren or the mighty wolf hound Huan, and disarms the intentions of wicked characters, rendering fearsome opponents from Sauron to Carcharoth to Morgoth and his entire court powerless. Lúthien's power, in fact, causes evil to founder on its own intentions: as Tolkien informs the reader, Morgoth failed to stop Lúthien and Beren from taking a Silmaril because "he [Morgoth] was beguiled by his own malice" (180).

Lúthien's heroism continues as she and Beren make their escape from Morgoth's fortress. She uses her healing powers once again when Beren loses his hand to the poisoned bite of Carcharoth, and "he was drawn back to life by the love of Lúthien" (183). Later, after Lúthien and Beren return to Thingol's court and tell their tale, Beren is once more grievously injured, again by Carcharoth, who has penetrated the boundary of Doriath. Beren's injury is severe and he dies of his wounds. Lúthien saves him once again, though the mode of his deliverance is problematic. After his death, Beren's spirit lingers in a half-life across the sea in the Halls of Mandos, the god-like immortal keeper of the dead, who lives across the western sea in Valinor, separated from Middle-earth though still present in the world. Lúthien's sadness at Beren's death causes her body to sicken, and her spirit soon joins Beren in the Halls of Mandos. There, before Mandos, Lúthien demonstrates the full extent of her power and heroism: she sings a song of such exquisite beauty and strength that Mandos releases the spirits of Lúthien and Beren to return to Middle-earth for a short time (Tolkien, *Silmarillion* 187). Lúthien's plea is answered at a price, however: restoring Beren to life in Middle-earth requires Lúthien to give up her immortality and power as an elf and take up the life of a human mortal. In so doing, she divests herself of all the power she commanded as an immortal elf.

What begins as a standard romance narrative, with a mighty warrior attempting to win the hand of a fair maiden through the completion of an impossible quest, ends as something else entirely. Beren, the mighty warrior, plays a secondary and mostly passive role in the quest, and frequently finds himself in need of rescue or salvation by the fair maiden, Lúthien, whose courage, loyalty, power, and innate goodness place her as the central hero of the central myth of Middle-earth's ancient past. Lúthien fulfills Campbell's construction of the hero: she confronts the gendered limitations of her culture, sacrifices herself for the good of others, and returns—literally—as a living example of "life renewed" (Campbell *HwaTF* 19–20; *PoM* 123). The tale of Lúthien and Beren, and its centrality in the Middle-earth mythos, as well as its deep personal significance to Tolkien, should be enough on its own to banish any questions about the presence of powerful, heroic women in Tolkien's work.

But Lúthien inhabits a mythic past that serves as the mostly-unseen backdrop for the more familiar narratives found in *The Hobbit* and *The Lord of the Rings*; as such, she is in many ways unapproachable, both for readers *and* the fictional inhabitants of Middle-earth who live in the centuries following Lúthien's life and death. Lúthien is, perhaps, too perfect: her virtue, power, and heroism are all so great that nothing can withstand her, not the pits of Sauron, not the might of Morgoth, and not the hold of death in the Halls of Mandos. She is the paradigmatic hero of ancient Middle-earth, but Lúthien is an unattainable vision from Middle-earth's mythic past. For a more approachable, realistic, and thoroughly human version of a female hero, we must move from the legends of the First Age to the War of the Ring in the Third Age, and from the immortal and flawless perfection of Lúthien to the desperate choices of Éowyn and a confrontation with the King of the Nazgûl at the Battle of Pelennor Fields.

Éowyn and the Female Epic Hero

The Lord of the Rings has no central female hero like Lúthien in *The Silmarillion*, as it is unquestionably a story primarily concerned with male-male relationships: the friendship of Frodo and Sam is the most obvious, but others include the friendship of Legolas and Gimli, as well as the power dynamic between Aragorn and Boromir, and the father-son relationship between Denethor and Faramir. In *The Silmarillion*, several female characters play prominent roles and demonstrate a certain capacity for decisive and independent action. Yet during the intervening three thousand years between the tale of Lúthien and Beren and the events of *The Lord of the Rings*, Middle-earth seems to have become a decidedly male-centric world in which female characters are consistently sidelined. Of the powerful female characters from *The Silmarillion*, only Galadriel is still present, and her role is primarily passive and oracular, rather than active and heroic. Galadriel's most significant act in *The Lord of the Rings* is, in fact, an act of abstention: she refuses to take the One Ring from Frodo, correctly fearing the Ring's corruptive influence. Tolkien does introduce new female characters in *The Lord of the Rings*: Goldberry, the enigmatic wife of the equally enigmatic Tom Bombadil, and Arwen,[8] the daughter of Elrond whose choice to marry Aragorn and give up her Elvish immortality echoes the choice of her great-great-great-grandmother, Lúthien.[9]

Neither Goldberry nor Arwen figure significantly in the narrative and neither rises to even the level of secondary characters. But in *The Two Towers*, Tolkien introduces Éowyn, a female character who plays a substantial, if not central role in the narrative of *The Lord of the Rings*. Like Lúthien, Éowyn's first appearance places her firmly within gender conventions and expectations from another well-known literary tradition: the epic. Éowyn is introduced simply enough, and her role is clear: she is the king's niece, fulfilling the role of nurse and cup-bearer. As King Théoden prepares to ride out to gather his army, he summons Éowyn to fulfill a singularly feminine role: "The king now rose, and at once Éowyn came forward bearing wine ... 'Receive now this cup and drink in happy hour'.... Théoden drank from the cup, and she then proffered it to the guests" (Tolkien, *TT* 162). The queen-as-cup-bearer is an ancient image from the epic genre, familiar to Tolkien as a scholar of Anglo-Saxon literature. In *Beowulf*, for example, Queen Wealhtheow serves wine to the members of the king's retinue and to Beowulf, passing among the assembled warriors and reminding the court that peace should reign in the king's hall. In R.K. Gordon's prose translation of *Beowulf*, the description of Queen Wealhtheow's role in Hrothgar's court mirrors Tolkien's rendering of Éowyn's place in Meduseld:

> [Queen Wealhtheow] greeted the warriors in the hall; and ... first offered the goblet to [King Hrothgar] ... he gladly took part in the banquet and received the hall-goblet.... Then the [queen] went about everywhere among old and young warriors, proffered the precious cup, till the time came that she ... bore the mead-flagon to Beowulf [*Beowulf* 12].

Like Lúthien, Éowyn is first presented to the reader in a familiar gender role—Lúthien as the fair damsel from the romance tradition, and Éowyn as a cup-bearer from an Anglo-Saxon epic. But as with Lúthien's tale, Éowyn does not remain in that familiar gender role for long.

Unlike Queen Wealhtheow, Éowyn is granted an active role in the kingdom's governance out of respect for her courage and capabilities apart from her role as the king's cup-bearer. As Théoden prepares to leave Meduseld, he asks his court who should act as his regent during his absence. The immediate answer is Éowyn. Háma, one of King Théoden's best warriors and chief advisors, offers unequivocal praise for Éowyn: "She is fearless and high-hearted. All love her. Let her be as lord ... while we are gone.' (Tolkien, *TT* 163). Théoden then reinforces Éowyn's status as his regent by presenting her with a sword and corslet. Théoden's people acknowledge Éowyn's abilities and willingly elevate her to be their leader while the king is off to war, but even this level of respect is not enough for Éowyn.

Throughout the initial introductions to Éowyn, Tolkien shows that she has fallen in love with Aragorn. Éowyn watches him as he interacts with Théoden and she trembles when his hand touches hers at the presentation of the guest cup (Tolkien, *TT* 162). Éowyn later chides the king for intimating that he may not return, claiming that each day will be like a year to her until the warriors return. Tolkien, though, is sure to inform the reader that "as she spoke her eyes went to Aragorn" (163). Such an infatuation places Éowyn in an impossible situation. Aragorn is committed to Arwen, and is intent on winning her hand. He senses Éowyn's affection for him and deflects it at every turn, to no avail. When the warriors return from the Battle of Helm's Deep, Éowyn greets them all, but "on Aragorn most of all her eyes rested" (Tolkien, *RotK* 65).

As Éowyn continues to seek Aragorn's affection, her deep dissatisfaction with her gender-derived social role begins to show. When Aragorn and his companions speak of the recent battle, Éowyn's true interest is unmistakable: "when she heard of the battle in Helm's Deep and the great slaughter of their foes, and of the charge of Théoden and his knights, then her eyes shone" (Tolkien, *RotK* 65). Éowyn is far from content to stay behind and rule in Théoden's stead. When Aragorn denies her request to accompany him on his ride through the Paths of the Dead, Éowyn's frustration boils over. Aragorn reminds her that she has accepted a charge to rule on Théoden's behalf, but Éowyn refuses to listen, saying: "Too often have I heard of duty.... I have waited on faltering feet long enough.... Shall I always be left behind when the Riders depart, to mind the house while they win renown, and find food and beds when they return? (*RotK* 67). Éowyn's desperation to claim a place among her male relatives as a warrior and hero is clearly evident, and while she was content to dutifully care for Théoden during his illness, she demands equality with the men now that her obligation as her uncle's nurse is fulfilled.

As Aragorn attempts to dissuade Éowyn from her intent to ride to battle in Gondor, she delivers a clear and direct rejection of the gender roles expected of women, both within the narrative, and within the larger gender-based conventions of the epic and romance traditions:

> All your words are but to say: you are a woman, and your part is in the house. But when the men have died in battle and honour, you have leave to be burned in the house, for the men will need it no more. But ... I can ride and wield blade, and I do not fear either pain or death [*RotK* 68].

Éowyn drives her point home, telling Aragorn that she fears only "[a] cage.... To stay behind bars until use and old age accept them, and all chance of doing great deeds is gone beyond recall or desire" (68). Éowyn's explicit rejection of the cultural expectations for her gender brings to mind Elrond's selection of members of the Fellowship from among "the free peoples of the world" (Tolkien, *FotR* 361). While Elrond includes Elves, Dwarves, Humans, and Hobbits, no thought is given to the inclusion of women from any of the races of Middle-earth. Éowyn's bitter complaint asks the question left unspoken in Rivendell: why are women left out of the great events of the War of the Ring?

The answer is complex and somewhat speculative. Multiple scholars have argued that Tolkien's artistic vision in *The Lord of the Rings* was driven, at least in part, by his experiences on the front during World War I. As John Garth observes, Tolkien explained that the relationship between Frodo and Sam mirrored the relationship between World War I British army officers and their servants (Garth 310). Tolkien was also deeply affected by the death of his closest school friends during the war, and the camaraderie of his school days and army service stayed with Tolkien throughout his life (Tolkien, *Letters* 9–10). Reading *The Lord of the Rings* through the lens of Tolkien's battlefield experiences is a useful exercise for a number of reasons, but for our purposes, such a reading has a very specific application: there were no women on the battlefields of the First World War. Such an explanation is entirely too simplistic to satisfactorily explain the remarkable dearth of female characters in *The Lord of the Rings*, but it does contribute to our understanding of Éowyn's bitterness. Éowyn interprets Aragorn's words as a gender-based dismissal of her desire to achieve something beyond maintaining the hearth while the men are at war, and her response reverberates far past the confines of Middle-earth.

But Éowyn goes beyond merely voicing her rejection of a prescribed gender role. When the Riders of Rohan set out for Gondor, Éowyn disguises herself and rides with them. Aware that Aragorn will never return her romantic feelings, and overcome by the ennui of staying behind as the men ride to war, Éowyn's decision to ride to Gondor is driven by desperation. This desperation is plainly visible: when Merry catches sight of the disguised Éowyn, he does not recognize her, but describes the rider as "one without hope who goes in search of death" (Tolkien, *RotK* 91). After the Battle of Pelennor Fields, as Éowyn recovers from her ordeal with the King of the Nazgûl, Gandalf explains her despair to her brother, Éomer, in no uncertain terms:

> "[Y]ou had horses, and deeds of arms ... but she, born in the body of a maid, had a spirit and courage at least the match of yours. Yet she was doomed to wait upon an old man ... and her part seemed to her more ignoble than that of the staff that he leaned on.... [W]ho knows what she spoke to the darkness, alone, in the bitter watches of the night, when all her life seemed shrinking" [*RotK* 174–175].

Éowyn's heroism is, in a sense, an expression of her desperation and she determines to stay near the king during the battle. When Théoden is unhorsed by the King of the Nazgûl, Éowyn is the only warrior of Rohan who remains by the king's side. Rather than collapse under the terror borne by the King of the Nazgûl, Éowyn opposes him, first killing the great winged beast he rides, then dispatching the fearsome King of the Nazgûl (*RotK* 140–143).

Éowyn's actions at the Battle of Pelennor Fields are especially significant because she accomplishes the deeds, not *in spite* of her gender, but *because* of it. When she stands between the King of the Nazgûl and the dying Théoden, the King of the Nazgûl warns her with a taunt, telling Éowyn—still disguised as a young male warrior—that "[n]o living man may hinder" the Nazgûl (*RotK* 141). Éowyn's response, though, shows her confidence not only as a warrior, but as a woman: "But no living man am I! You look upon a woman. Éowyn I am, Éomund's daughter. You stand between my lord and kin. Begone, if you be not deathless. For living or dark undead, I will smite you, if you touch him" (*RotK* 141). Éowyn's presence on the battlefield, as a woman wholly unafraid in the face of a terror that has sent men and horses running from Théoden's side, is a disruptive revelation. Merry, who rode to the battle with the disguised Éowyn, does not realize she is a woman until she reveals herself. The King of the Nazgûl, who has never before shown a moment of hesitation or lack of confidence, is stunned by Éowyn's presence: "[t]he Ringwraith made no answer, and was silent, as in in sudden doubt" (Tolkien, *RotK* 142). The presence of a woman on the battlefield provides Merry an opportunity to stab the King of the Nazgûl, crippling him. Éowyn then destroys the King of the Nazgûl, driving her sword into the space between his crown and mantle, sending his disembodied spirit shrieking into the wind, "never heard again in that age of this world" (*RotK* 143). Éowyn's heroism at the Battle of Pelennor Fields is unmistakable. The aftermath of the battle, though, complicates Éowyn's character.

Éowyn's decision to disguise herself and fight at Pelennor Fields is compelled only in part by her rejection of the constrictive gender expectations dictating that she should manage the King's household while he is away at war. As Tolkien emphasizes throughout his descriptions of Éowyn, she is infatuated with Aragorn, and her choice to join the Riders of Rohan in battle is at least partially due to her despair over Aragorn's gentle rejection of her romantic advances. Likewise, Éowyn's recovery from the injuries and mental distress she suffers in her confrontation with the King of the Nazgûl is predicated on her romantic involvement with Faramir, the son of the Steward of Gondor. Faramir perceives that Éowyn's lingering malady is psychological and understands the despair that colors her thoughts as she doubts that she will ever know hope again (*RotK* 177). As she recovers physically, her continuing bitterness is apparent: she would rather die in battle than be healed and left waiting for the warriors again (*RotK* 292) and tells Faramir as much at their first meeting (*RotK* 293). When Faramir tells her that she is beautiful, Éowyn recoils, telling the Steward, "[N]ot me, lord! ... Shadow lies on me still.... I am a shieldmaiden and my hand is ungentle" (Tolkien, *RotK* 294).

Yet after only a few days in the company of Faramir, Éowyn's recovery is complete when Faramir proclaims his love for her and asks if she loves him in return. Like Lúthien, Éowyn voluntarily surrenders her identity as a hero—in Éowyn's case, setting aside her role as a shieldmaiden—so that she can accept Faramir's love: "'[T]he shadow has departed! I will be a shieldmaiden no longer…. I will be a healer, and love all things that grow and are not barren'" (*RotK* 300). The language Tolkien uses to describe the betrothal of Faramir and Éowyn is equally telling. Éowyn herself, after accepting Faramir's marriage proposal, characterizes their courtship as Faramir "tam[ing] a wild shield-maiden" (*RotK* 300); later, as Aragorn blesses the union of Faramir and Éowyn, he tells Éomer that in granting Éowyn's hand in marriage to Faramir, he has given "the fairest thing" in the realm of Rohan.

Éowyn voluntarily returns to her previously prescribed female gender roles as, once again, she fulfills the role of cup-bearer (*RotK* 315). Furthermore, she steps into another female role from the Anglo-Saxon epic tradition: Éowyn is offered in marriage as a peace-weaver. The peace-weaver is an Anglo-Saxon concept also found in *Beowulf* when the tale of Hildeburh is briefly mentioned. Hildeburh was a Danish princess who was married to a Frisian king in order to insure peace between the two peoples (*Beowulf* 19–20). There is no mistaking the peace-weaver symbolism in Éowyn's marriage to Faramir: as they are betrothed, Éomer pronounces that with their marriage, "the friendship of the Mark [Rohan] and of Gondor [is] bound with a new bond" (Tolkien, *RotK* 315). Éowyn's desire for a heroic life of action is contained, in the end, within the conventional bounds of marriage and traditional womanly duties. While Éowyn has become a hero in the Campbellian sense, confronting societal and cultural limitations and sacrificing herself in spectacular fashion on the battle-field, her return to gender-specific cultural roles provides an ambiguous coda to her heroic escapades.

Tolkien, Middle-earth, and the Female Hero

Does Tolkien offer any sustainable framework for portraying female heroes in the fantasy fiction that follows in his considerable wake? Lúthien and Éowyn are undoubtedly heroes, their self-sacrificial deeds frequently outshining the actions of their male companions. But their heroism is eventually constrained within the bounds of marriage and both women accept traditional roles as wives, mothers, healers, and nurturers. These are admirable roles, and there is certainly no shame in a woman fulfilling such obligations. In Middle-earth, though, female domestic expectations seem to be mutually exclusive of heroic female action. Lúthien and Éowyn must choose: life as a powerful immortal elf or indomitable shieldmaiden versus more traditional roles as wives and moth-ers—and in Éowyn's case, as political capital. Still, Lúthien and Éowyn demon-strate the possibility for women to step into roles traditionally filled by men in the romance and epic traditions, and each in her turn exhibits personal char-acteristics—faithfulness, courage, determination, and strength of will—which resonate far beyond questions of gender and heroism.

Tolkien was not, of course, intentionally addressing questions of feminism or gender roles, but his ongoing negotiation with the romance and epic genres naturally encompassed a revision of the roles of women within such stories. And while it is impossible to deny that Tolkien's fantasy fiction is overwhelmingly male-centric, it is equally true that women are vitally important to his vision of Middle-earth. In *The Silmarillion*, the creation of Middle-earth is a joint and equal effort between the male and female Valar, the angelic guardians and keepers of Middle-earth (Tolkien, *Silmarillion* 13–42). After Morgoth's rebellion, he fears Varda (the angelic female creator of the stars) more than any other of the Valar, male or female (Tolkien, *Silmarillion* 26). As I point out at the beginning of this chapter, Lúthien is the central hero in the central tale of Middle-earth's mythic past. Galadriel (with Elrond and Gandalf), is responsible for keeping Sauron at bay during the long years after the Last Alliance of Elves and Men until the destruction of the Ring; and Éowyn pushes aside the gender restrictions of her culture to ride to war with her uncle and brother, achieving immortality in her heroic defeat of the King of the Nazgûl.

The place of female heroes within the configuration of gender and power in Middle-earth remains somewhat unsettled. Tolkien's decision to write female characters who so clearly and intentionally deviate from the conventional gender expectations of the romance and epic traditions render irrelevant criticisms that claim Tolkien's mythos has no place for strong women. Yet the women of Middle-earth—heroic or not—are eventually confined to conventional gender roles as wives, peacemakers, mothers, and protectors, and the bursts of heroism demonstrated by Lúthien and Éowyn seem unsustainable. Tolkien's attempt to correct the failure of the romance tradition and provide a new mythology for England included a revised and expanded range of possibilities for female characters within the traditionally male-dominated literary territory of the heroic quest. Yet heroic women in Middle-earth occupy an uneasy position between the prescribed gender roles of the romance and epic traditions and the broader range of options available to later female heroes of contemporary fantasy literature.

NOTES

1. The extensive publication of Tolkien's unreleased material by his son, Christopher Tolkien, is a treasure-trove for researchers and readers interested in the development of Tolkien's Middle-earth mythos. Much of this material offers alternative and competing versions of familiar stories from Middle-earth. For the purposes of clarity, in this chapter I will only reference the "canon" of Middle-earth texts: *The Silmarillion, The Hobbit*, and *The Lord of the Rings*.

2. Bilbo's long experience with Elves and Elvish languages allows him to explain, obliquely, that the song is dedicated to "Elbereth" and that it is a song of "the Blessed Realm" (313). Frodo, like Bilbo, is somewhat familiar with Elvish lore. But the casual reader has no context for understanding the obscure references to Elvish language, culture, and history.

3. In a 1955 letter written to Tolkien's American publisher, Houghton Mifflin, Tolkien

mentions *The Fall of Arthur*, saying that he still hoped to finish the poem. The letter, though, gives no indication that Tolkien was actively working on the poem at this date (Tolkien, *Letters* 219).

4. The forest is referred to, interestingly enough, as Mirkwood (Tolkien, *FoA* 19).

5. In a poignant testimony to how deeply personal the Lúthien and Beren story was to Tolkien, he requested that "Lúthien" be inscribed on Edith Tolkien's headstone and "Beren" on his own.

6. Unlike Lancelot and Guinevere, though, Beren and Lúthien's relationship is forbidden because Beren is a mortal man and Lúthien is an immortal half elf, half goddess. Beren and Lúthien's relationship possesses none of the sexual transgression present in the Lancelot and Guinevere affair.

7. Luthien's escape from the treehouse recalls another familiar tale from another literary genre: the fairy tale story of Rapunzel. Rapunzel, of course, is waiting for a hero to save her, while Luthien is the agent of her own escape. Tolkien explains his relationship to the fairy tale tradition at some length in his well-known 1964 essay, "On Fairy Stories" which I only briefly touch on in this chapter.

8. Peter Jackson's cinematic interpretation of *The Lord of the Rings* provides a much-expanded role for Arwen. For example, in Tolkien's *FotR*, an elf lord named Glorfindel assists Frodo in escaping the Black Riders across the Ford of Bruinen; in Jackson's film version, Arwen replaces Glorfindel, challenges all nine riders, and uses her power to cause the Bruinen to flood, allowing Frodo to escape.

9. For the sake of perspective, it should be noted that while Lúthien is Arwen's great-great-great-grandmother, almost 3,000 years pass between the tale of Lúthien and Beren told in *The Silmarillion* and the events recounted in *The Lord of the Rings*.

Works Cited

Campbell, Joseph. *The Hero with a Thousand Faces*, 2d ed. Princeton: Princeton University Press, 1968.

_____. *The Power of Myth*. New York: Doubleday, 1988.

Cartlidge, Neil. Introduction. *Heroes and Anti-Heroes in Medieval Romance*. Neil Cartlidge, ed. Rochester: D.S. Brewer, 2012.

Fisher, Sheila. "Women and Men in Late Medieval English Romance." *The Cambridge Companion to Medieval Romance*. Roberta L. Krueger, ed. Cambridge: Cambridge University Press, 2000.

Fries, Maureen. "Female Heroes, Heroines, and Counter-Heroes: Images of Women in the Arthurian Tradition." *Arthurian Women*. Thelma S. Fenster, ed. New York: Routledge, 1996.

Garth, John. *Tolkien and the Great War: The Threshold of Middle-Earth*. New York: Houghton Mifflin, 2003.

Gordon, R. K., trans. *Beowulf*. Mineola, NY: Dover, 1992.

Konigsberg, Ruth Davis. "'The Hobbit': Why Are There No Women in Tolkien's World?" *Time* 31 Dec. 2012: n. pag. Web. 22 July 2013.

Merwin, W.S., trans. *Sir Gawain and the Green Knight*. New York: Knoph, 2004.

Shippey, Tom. *J.R.R. Tolkien: Author of the Century*. New York: Houghton Mifflin, 2001.

Tolkien, Christopher. "Preface." *The Fall of Arthur*. New York: Houghton Mifflin, 2013.

Tolkien, J.R.R. *The Fall of Arthur*. Christopher Tolkien, ed. New York: Houghton Mifflin, 2013.

_____. *The Fellowship of the Ring*. New York: Ballantine, 1973.

_____. *The Letters of J.R.R. Tolkien*. Humphrey Carpenter, ed. New York: Houghton Mifflin, 2000.

_____. "On Fairy Stories." 1964. *Poems and Stories*. New York: Houghton Mifflin, 1994.

_____. *The Return of the King*. New York: Ballantine, 1973.

_____. *The Silmarillion*. Christopher Tolkien, ed. New York: Houghton Mifflin, 1977.

_____. *The Two Towers*. New York: Ballantine, 1973.

_____, trans. *Sir Gawain and the Green Knight, Pearl, Sir Orfeo*. New York: Houghton Mifflin, 1978.

Female Valor Without Renown: Memory, Mourning and Loss at the Center of Middle-earth

Sarah Workman

In a 1955 letter to Houghton Mifflin published in the *New York Times*, J.R.R. Tolkien voiced his complaints over the recent critiques of *The Lord of the Rings*: "The only criticism ... that annoyed me was one that it 'contained no religion' (and 'no Women,' but that does not matter, and is not true anyway)" (*Letters* 220). In part, Tolkien was reacting to complaints that his lifestyle as a member of the all-male group of academics at Oxford, the Inklings, influenced the predominantly male make-up of Middle-earth. Even today, more than fifty years after the first publication of *The Lord of the Rings*, critics continue to lament the lack of women within the text. Candace Fredrick and Sam McBride recently voiced one such critique in *Women Among the Inklings* by asking how the actual lived experience of the Inklings in terms of male-male and male-female relationships translates and is translated by their work (xi). Like the majority of scholars working at the crossroads of gender studies and fantasy literature, Fredrick and McBride's project concludes that "there is no female presence whatsoever" among the work of the Inklings, where plot "focuses on the adventures of like-minded males" (108). In his work on fantasy more generally, Brian Attebery notes the tendency of the genre to reflect gender dynamics of cultures past, which is especially prominent in *The Lord of the Rings* given Tolkien's reliance on Anglo-Saxon and Norse mythology. As Attebery indicates, "a willingness to return to the narrative structures of the past can entail as well an unquestioning acceptance of its social structures" (87). Tolkien's personal views unfortunately fuel the criticism waged against his work and against fantasy in general; misogyny reigns throughout Tolkien's personal letters. In writing to his son Michael in March 1941 on the subject of marriage and relationships,

Tolkien expresses his disdainful views on female intelligence. Without men, Tolkien writes, women are fundamentally lacking, as "she" should always be taught to see "his" point (*Letters* 49). Women, he notes, "can go no further, when they leave his hand, or when they cease to take a personal interest in him" (*Letters* 49). Tolkien continues along this line of thought, positioning women as passive receivers of all things male: "It is their gift to be receptive, stimulated, fertilized (in many other matters than the physical) by the male" (*Letters* 49).

Despite Tolkien's personal misogyny and the heaping criticism against a strong feminine presence in *The Lord of the Rings*, I argue here that Tolkien's female characters mourn their way to the narrative's core. In Tolkien's most well-known work, and the one that essentially gives birth to modern fantasy, mourning becomes an heroic, explicitly feminine act. Questioning the extant approaches to women in *The Lord of the Rings*, this essay relies on the formal elements of elegy and the gendered politics of memory and mourning to move the women from the margin to the center of Tolkien's major work. What follows is a look into the ways that the elegiac and fantastic structures of the narrative re-position the women as central mourners of the loss in the text and world of which they are part. These female characters reject established patterns of heroism that are often limited by gender stereotypes and prevail on their own terms. As Carol S. Pearson has observed, "what we imagine immediately when we think of the hero really is only one heroic archetype: the Warrior" (1). Because the women's work within *LotR* is performative in nature, their heroism is shaped by language and narrative form rather than the traditional and gendered-male stereotype of the "warrior." Tolkien's female heroes defy stereotypes of passivity within what is often considered the primary text of modern fantasy, and thus have the potential to help critics better understand how the female hero has evolved from the foundation *LotR* establishes. Reading against the grain of criticism that argues there are "no women" in the text or arguments that "hero" is synonymous with "warrior," my approach to *LotR* enables readers to better understand the trajectory of the female hero as it has evolved from Tolkien's foundational text.

Fantasy and Elegy as Performance: The Context of Mourning in *LotR*

Moving women to the center of *The Lord of the Rings* first requires understanding how fantasy appeals to its readership; that is, to show how fantasy as a genre is performative. In J.L. Austin's important work on how language *acts*, he argues that language does not just "say" but "does": "the uttering of the sentence is, or is a part of, the doing of an action, which again would not *normally* be described as, or as 'just,' saying something" (5). Each utterance, Austin continues, "is not to *describe* my doing of what I should be said in so uttering to be doing or to state that I am doing it: it is to do it" (6). As a genre, fantasy does not just "say," but *does*. By relying on Austin's work, I suggest that fantasy restores the enchantment of language and supernatural forces in an otherwise disenchanted world. When I refer to disenchantment, I am referencing the hypothesis developed by Max Weber in his 1917 lecture at the University of Munich. In this speech, Weber contemplates the loss of these "mysterious incalculable forces" through their ability to be mastered and known: "One need no longer have recourse to magical means in order to master or implore the spirits, as did the savage, for whom such mysterious powers existed. Technical means and calculations perform the service. This above all is what intellectualization means" (524–5). Fantasy in general, and Tolkien in particular as the primary architect of the genre, aim to transport the reader to a world where mysterious, incalculable forces dominate. Relying upon performative language (words that open doors), or performative objects (phials that magically transmit light), fantasy as a genre itself is performative. Applying this concept to Tolkien's text, the enchanted world of Middle-earth also embodies what is lost in the reader's departure from the text to the "real world." Through enchantment, fantasy provides the reader with a sense of wholeness otherwise impossible in the *dis*enchanted world outside the text.[1]

Both in structure and content, the elegiac quality of *LotR* further illustrates its performative nature. Performed by the female characters, mourning in the text becomes a gendered, cultural tool that centralizes the female characters and marks their contribution as heroes. As a philologist and Professor of Anglo-Saxon Language and Literature at Oxford, Tolkien would have been intimately familiar with the elegiac tradition of Anglo-Saxon literature. The elegiac mood of *LotR* reveals Tolkien's scholarly interests, and indeed, Tolkien was writing and editing *LotR* during his tenure at Oxford. In both the classical and British traditions, elegy was performative as it served as a means of working through of grief for the author. In fact, the notion of mourning itself is performative; in the statement "I mourn" one does not "just" say, but also emotes lament. In *LotR,* the poetics of grief resonate with the gendered markings of the Anglo-Saxon laments. Medievalist Bonnie Wheeler explains that mourning in early vernacular literatures, in particular Welsh and Old English, brings readers close to brief moments of absorption in death as they expose "their cultures' bones in their searing, plangent laments for the dead" (65). In this way, the cultural work of mourning distinguishes these female heroes from the traditional tropes of the journey or quest narrative that mark male heroism in fantasy literature. In "Archetypes, Stereotypes, and The Female Hero," Terri Frontgia contests Joseph Campbell's claim in *The Power of Myth* that without a "journey" women lack the requisite choices, trials, and cultural rite of passage into maturity (16). Frontgia points out that even as Campbell advocates for the female hero paradigm, his model is hampered by gendered stereotypes and biological determinism as "mother" delimits the female paradigm in Campbell's work (Frontgia 16). On the contrary, Frontgia notes the profound shift in the heroic paradigm that moves beyond gendered readings of the hero in recent speculative fiction (here she means science fiction and fantasy literatures). This new conception of the female hero is based on human needs, abilities, and achievements (Frontgia 18). Accordingly, it is no longer necessary to emphasize the heroic journey as a singular or atypical event, but rather this event "may now more significantly take its place as an aspect inherent in the larger journey of life itself" (Frontgia 18). Frontgia continues, "Heroic being and action, outside the restrictions of gender, may finally express not just the integration of the individual's self, but also the unique contributions of that self to the larger community of humanity" (18). Frontgia's framework has significant implications for the so-called "inaction" of women in *LotR*. While women may not share in the central action of the text—they are not privy to battle nor the camaraderie of the fellowship—they mourn and mark the departures of both text and world. Much like Wheeler's description of the poetics of grief for Welsh and Old English, the mourning work of women such as Arwen, Eowyn, Galadriel, and Goldberry is "a crucial cultural tool, gender-expressive and imbricated in its cultural moment" (66). The female characters perform memory and mourning key to the text on multiple narrative levels.

Structurally, in the way that the enchanted secondary world is already removed from the reader's disenchanted primary world, there already exists a sense of loss between reader and text. Further, within the text these feminine laments almost always revolve around physical departures: Galadriel mourns the loss of Lórien and the travelers' leave-taking; Éowyn mourns the loss of Aragorn; Arwen mourns Aragon at his deathbed and thereafter; and Goldberry too mourns her last moments with the Hobbits (*LotR* 376, 785, 1058, 135). As conscious markers of these double departures, the women of *LotR* literally and figuratively ground the text; fantasy and elegy prove mutually illuminating in order to reposition the women as not only central to the text, but also heroes who prevail on their own terms.

Like fantasy texts, elegy too is a genre with performance at its core. Looking at the literary history of elegy, taking into account both its form and content, allows me to underscore the performative nature of the genre before I turn to how it functions specifically in *LotR*. In *Elegy*, David Kennedy explains that the term "elegy" itself derives from the Greek *elogos*, meaning "mournful song," but he notes that the earliest surviving elegies are not funereal (11). Written by seventh-century BC poets such as Arhchilochus, Callinus, and Tyrtaeus, these classical poems take the form of Greek elegiac couplets that alternate dactylic hexameters and pentameters (Kennedy 11).[2] The concept of the personal elegy championed by Samuel Taylor Coleridge and his fellow Romantics started to appear at the end of the Middle Ages in five main groupings: laments for monarchs, poems about the fall of the mighty, political poems, warnings from the dead, and allegorical dream visions (Kennedy 15). As Coleridge writes, "It *may* treat of any subject, but it must treat of no subject for *itself*; but always and exclusively with reference to the poet" (qtd. in Kennedy 4, emphasis in original). By stressing the "authority and authenticity of individual feeling," Coleridge introduces the psychic component that underlies elegy, thus linking the performative to the elegiac mode. In this definition, elegy subsumes the expression of the writer's feelings and "acting out" of loss.[3] Particularly with the work of Edmund Spenser, John Donne, and John Milton, a definition of elegy as "a poem of mortal loss and consolation" took hold in the sixteenth century (Kennedy 11–15).[4]

As John Hollander articulates, even within this formal method, elegy in English poetry has always been "a mood rather than a formal mode" (qtd. in Kennedy 2). I would suggest that this "mood" substantiates the performative nature of elegy. Kennedy underscores the notion of transformation at work that also contributes to this performative sensibility: "the elegist starts from a negative position. Positives, made into negatives by death, must somehow be made into positives again or have that transformation compensated for" (Kennedy 21). It is important to note that the performative nature of the elegy is ascribed to the writer, rather than the reader. "His love, or, perhaps, more properly, his desire for the deceased, must be narrated as loss, as dispossession," Kennedy continues (21). Sacks's work also elucidates this psychic "acting out" that occurs between writer and elegy, where elegy should be seen as a "working through of experience and as a symbolic action" (1). Relying on psychoanalytic theory, Sacks refines the belief that compensatory mourning is the psychic basis of elegy.[5] He writes:

> The elegy, as a poem of mourning and consolation, has its roots in a dense matrix of rites and ceremonies, in the light of which many elegiac conventions should be recognized as being not only aesthetically interesting forms but also the literary versions of specific social and psychological practices [2].

As "the literary versions of specific social and psychological practices," and "acting out" of such practices, Sacks's characterization of elegy is performative at heart.

Over time, elegy has moved farther away from its formal origins in dactylic hexameter; it is with this contemporary understanding of elegy that this essay is primarily concerned. In a diary entry for June 27, 1925, Virginia Woolf begins to develop the concept of elegy in the contemporary sense: "I have no idea that I will invent a new name for my books to supplant 'novel.' A new—by Virginia Woolf. But what? Elegy?" (qtd. in Kennedy 1). As Kennedy attests, "the possibility that a novel might be an elegy exemplifies the particular difficulties in giving an account of elegy written in the last hundred years or so. If a novel can be an elegy then we have already travelled some considerable distance from elegy as a sub-genre of poetry" (1). In these new discursive understandings championed by Woolf, critics divorce elegy from its origins as a poetic mode; elegy as a performative mood leads to contemporary interpretations. It is here that Kennedy develops an understanding of elegy at the center of my analysis: "Following the implications of Woolf's 'new name,' then, elegy is as likely to be a distinctive idiom, mode of enquiry or species of self-description as a distinctive form" (2). Initially a poetic form, elegy in contemporary criticism revolves around its performative potentiality.

It is with this contemporary understanding of elegy as a performative mode that I approach *The Lord of the Rings*. As mythopoeia, fantasy texts naturally lend themselves to the elegiac function. Mythopoeia originates from the Greek term meaning "the creation of a myth or myths" to describe the practice of the ancients (OED). Adopted by Tolkien as the name of his 1931 poem addressed to C.S. Lewis, "Mythopoeia" was Tolkien's response to "a man who described myth and fairy-stories as 'lies'" and deemed fairy-story-making "breathing a lie through silver" (Tolkien, *Tree and Leaf* 97). The poem distills the process of mourning and lament at the core of the mythopoeia genre with which it shares its name. Philomythus (Tolkien as myth-lover), addresses Misomythus (C.S. Lewis as myth-hater) and laments the system of classification of the natural sciences; Philomythus bemoans the "technical means," to borrow from Weber, that constrain the essence of language's meaning (Tolkien, *Tree and Leaf* 97). In "Mythopoeia," time marches on to usher in the natural sciences at the expense of language's romantic sensibility. As "time unrolls from dark beginnings to uncertain goals," trees and stars, the would-be fabric of Romanticism are constrained by their labeling: "You look at trees and label them just so, / (for trees are 'trees,' and growing is 'to grow')" (Tolkien, *Tree and Leaf* 97). Philomythus continues, "a star's a star, some matter in a ball / compelled to courses mathematical / amid the regimented, cold, inane, / where destined atoms are each moment slain" (*Tree and Leaf* 97). As "some matter in a ball," the guiding light (pun intended) of Romantic poetry loses its magical luster, and it is this luster that Tolkien aims to reinvigorate in *LotR*. Just before Frodo leaves Lothlórien, Galadriel gives Frodo a small crystal phial miraculously lit by the light of Eärendil's star (Tolkien, *LotR* 376). Galadrial tells Frodo, "It will shine still brighter when night is about you. May it be a light to you in dark places, when all other lights go out. Remember Galadriel and her Mirror!" (Tolkien, *LotR* 376). The light that springs from Galadriel's phial restores "that matter in a ball" to its mystical, glittering state before technological calculation (Tolkien, *LotR* 376). While Frodo sets forth on a typical, gendered-male heroic quest, her cry, "Remember Galadriel and her Mirror!" emphasizes Galadriel's centrality to Tolkien's larger project of enchantment. Galadriel becomes a hero not through extant models of the "quest" narrative, but for ways in which she arrests that narrative and calls attention to the larger project of fantasy literature itself—the meaning *behind* Frodo's journey. Tolkien enchants language with a mythopoetic and performative sensibility, and does so by revaluing Galadriel's gift. Thus, the hero is not simply Frodo, but the women who literally enchant (or light) the quest's possibility in the first place.

Heroes Who Mourn: Performing Loss in Middle-earth

As I have illustrated, loss functions at the level of language in *LotR* to reveal what language cannot do outside the text: enchant. As I will go on to show, the content and framing of *LotR* also situate the text as a performance of mourning the Third Age of Middle-earth, which emphasizes the exigency of the gendered-female lament throughout the text. Frodo's story begins at the end of the Third Age, or "the fading years of the Eldar" (Tolkien, *LotR* 1084). In Appendix B, Tolkien explains, "the *Third Age* came to its end in the War of the Ring; but the *Fourth Age* was not held to have begun until Master Elrond departed, and the time was come for the dominion of Men and the decline of all other 'speaking peoples' in Middle-earth" (Tolkien, *LotR* 1082). Neither can Men escape a certain degeneracy: "The wisdom and the life-span of the Númenórians also waned as they became mingled with lesser Men" (Tolkien, *LotR* 1084). Against the waning, declining spirit of the Third Age, Gandalf emphasizes a need "to preserve" (Tolkien, *LotR* 971). In his final speech to Aragorn, he cautions that the Elder Kindred will fade under the Dominion of Men, and "it is your task to order its beginning and to preserve what may be preserved," Gandalf says to Aragorn" (Tolkien, *LotR* 971). While Gandalf tasks Aragorn with the "ordering" and "preserving," I argue that it is the women of the story who ultimately become heroes by carrying the burden of the past throughout the text. Given this context of fading, female mourning embodies a heroic, critical role in preserving the text and the world to which Frodo's journey is part. Here I will define female heroism not through the archetypal (male) hero's journey, but rather, I will extend Frontgia's project that looks outside the boundaries of gender where "heroic being and action ... may finally express not just the integration of the individual's self, but also the unique contributions of that self to the larger community of humanity" (18). The idea of moving beyond the self will be central to my conception of female mourning as heroic throughout *LotR* as the work of cultural mourning embodies the female hero's contribution to the larger community.

Having underscored the central importance of memory as a framing narrative for the text, I will return to the gendered politics of grief in early elegy to illustrate how the female heroes in *The Lord of the Rings* carry the burden of mourning throughout. This cultural work not only makes a distinct contribution to the project of enchantment that I have previously mentioned, but also opens the possibilities for female heroism in the long tradition of Anglo-Saxon lament. As I discussed in my introduction, much of the extant criticism on gender in *The Lord of the Rings* focuses on the marginalization of the women in Middle-earth due to their ancillary roles in propelling the action of the narrative. Unlike their male counterparts at the heart of both *The Lord of the Rings* and fantasy novels in general, the female characters neither come-of-age in the text nor further the central action of the plot (Atterbury 88). One way, however, of re-casting the role of the feminine is through the gendered-female work of mourning in Anglo-Saxon tradition. Scholars such as Patricia Ingham have argued that the female "voiced" Anglo-Saxon elegiac poems *Wulf and Eadwacer* and *The Wife's Lament* suggest the relevance of gender and agency to the grief and loss of the larger elegy tradition (17).[6] Nowhere is this more apparent than in the character of Galadriel, especially as more than any other beings in the text, the Elves in and of themselves reflect a preoccupation with "fading" and loss. The natural state of being for Elves is to occupy living memory. As Gimli remarks upon the state of the Elves, "for them memory is more like to the waking world than to a dream" (Tolkien, *LotR* 379). In a note to the publisher, Tolkien explicates this Elvish preoccupation with memory and the past:

> Thus they became obsessed with "fading," the mode in which the changes of time (the law of the world under the sun) was perceived by them. They became sad, and their art (shall we say) antiquarian, and their efforts all really a kind of embalming—even though they also retained the old motive of their kind, the adornment of earth, and the healing of its hurts [*Letters* 151–2].

In Tolkien's terms, Elves embalm and heal the past to resist future change; Elves immerse themselves in their own nostalgia. Svetlana Boym's definition of nostalgia helps here: "Nostalgia (from *nostos*—return home, and *algia*—longing) is a longing for a home that no longer exists or has never existed. Nostalgia is a sentiment of loss and displacement, but is also a romance with one's fantasy" (xiii). The way that nostalgia is "a romance with one's fantasy" apprehends Galadriel's unwillingness "to face change."

While Tolkien locates Galadriel's powers of embalming and preservation in Elvish weakness, re-positioning the text as elegy centers Galadriel's heroic power as essential to the narrative's existence. Her presence certainly impacts the text more than that of her male counterpart, Celeborn. When the Fellowship enters Lothlórien, Haldir says to Frodo and Sam, "You feel the power of the Lady [not the Lord] of the Galadrim" (Tolkien, *LotR* 351). As one of the three Elven ring-bearers, Galadriel uses her power for healing, not domination. In this way, she directly rejects the archetypal mode of the male hero. In *The Female Hero in American and British Literature*, Carol Pearson and Katherine

Pope argue that looking at female heroes on their own terms makes it clear that the "archetypal hero masters the world by understanding it, not by dominating, controlling, or owning the world or other people" (4–5). In the masculine modes of war and conquest in Anglo-Saxon poetry, valor often leads to a death that negates heroic deeds, which fails to serve the dead or their people (Forrest-Hill 85). As Lynn Forrest-Hill explains, "many aspects of *The Lord of the Rings* belong to the traditions of Anglo-Saxon elegiac verse with its emphasis on the fate of the 'doomed man'" (85). Part redemptive, Galadriel's heroic power is that of memory and commemoration, not domination or control. Nenya, the Ring of Adamant, rests on Galadriel's finger to bestow her with this power. As Elrond says to Gimli:

> The Three [rings] were not made by Sauron, nor did he ever touch them.... They are not idle. But they were not made as weapons of war or conquest: that is not their power. Those who made them did not desire strength or domination or hoarded wealth, but understanding, making, and healing, to preserve all things unstained [Tolkien, *LotR* 268].

Preservation of "all things unstained" is key to Galadriel's prowess; her valor is rooted in what is antithetical to the corruptible nature of strength, wealth, "weapons of war or conquest," all symptoms of the world changing for the worse (Tolkien, *LotR* 268). As Galadriel tells Frodo, if he succeeds "then our power is diminished, and Lothlórien will fade, and the tides of Time will sweep it away. We must depart into the West, or dwindle to a rustic folk of dell and cave, slowly to forget and to be forgotten" (Tolkien, *LotR* 365). Read through the impending loss of Lothlórien to Time, the heroism of Galadriel's power of preservation becomes multiple: to resist the loss that comes with forgetting in Frodo's story, to preserve against Time as change for the worse, and to resist the fate of the "doomed man." But as Galadriel expresses to Frodo, "For the fate of Lothlórien you are not answerable, but only for the doing of your own task" (Tolkien, *LotR* 365). Here Frodo's "task" recalls not only the action of the plot and return of the One Ring, but the framing narrative and intent of Frodo's written story to serve as "the last living memory of the Elder Days" (Tolkien, *LotR* 16). If the light of Eärendil's star literally guides Frodo's physical path, here Galadrial's advice dictates the way in which Frodo must remember; the "doing of your own task" is also Galadriel's reminder for Frodo to "preserve all things unstained" in his story (Tolkien, *LotR* 268).

After Galadriel passes the test her power quickly diminishes. Framed in terms of Galadriel's loss of power, her presence self-consciously preserves and is preserved in the text. As the Fellowship prepares to leave Lórien, the sound of Galadriel's song from the Elven Swan-ship permeates the ethereal environment. Lamenting the passing of Lórien, Galadriel's voice recollects the classical origins of elegy as mourning song:

There [in Eldamar] long the golden leaves have grown upon the branching years,
while here beyond the Sundering Seas now fall the Elven-tears.
O Lórien! The Winter comes, the bare and leafless Day;
The leaves are falling in the stream, the river flows away
O Lórien! Too long I have dwelt upon this Hither Shore
And in a fading crown have twined the golden elanor [Tolkien, *LotR* 373].

Galadriel's voice acts out her loss and performs the passing away of *Lórien*, the loss of a physical world and the materiality of its leaves, tears and days all swept away by the river. Here the repetition of "*O Lórien!*" directly invokes elegiac roots; according to Sacks, repetition is one of the central conventions English Elegy. Repetition "creates a sense of continuity, of an unbroken pattern such as one may oppose to the discontinuity of death" (Sacks 23). Galadriel repeats a similar mourning song as the Fellowship departs, "but now she sang in the ancient tongue of the Elves beyond the sea" and Frodo did not understand the words (Tolkien, *LotR* 377). As Sacks explains, the purpose of repetition in elegy often has to do with its relation to time: "Time itself is thereby structured to appear as a familiar, filled-in medium rather than as an open-ended source of possible catastrophe" (23). The continuity of the song, this time in Elvish, exemplifies the elegiac mode: "the repetition of words and refrains and the creation of a certain rhythm of lament have the effect of controlling the expression of grief while also keeping that expression in motion" (Sacks 23). In listening to the song, Frodo becomes self-consciously aware, even agitated: "fair was the music, but it did not comfort him" (Tolkien, *LotR* 377). The narrative continues, "yet as is the way of Elvish words, they remained graven in his memory, and long afterwards he interpreted them, as well as he could: the language was that of Elven-song and spoke of things little known on Middle-earth" (Tolkien, *LotR* 377). As Galadriel's mourning song "remained graven in his [Frodo's] memory" a moment of textual self-consciousness arises; it is not until "long afterwards" that Frodo interprets and thus transcribes this memory of the elven-world. Galadriel's expression of grief makes possible Frodo's own transcription of the elven-world. As the action of the text progresses, Galadriel's nostalgia allows Frodo to preserve the memory at the core of her own mourning songs: Lórien. Frodo's last image of Galadriel as the Swan-boat floats away arrests Galadriel in time is of one who has already lost her power. Galadriel is already a memory of herself: "She seemed no longer perilous or terrible, nor filled with hidden power. Already she seemed to him, as by men of later days Elves still at times are seen: present and yet remote, a living vision of that which has already been left far behind by the flowing streams of Time" (Tolkien, *LotR* 377). In the action of the lived experience of the story, Galadriel's is already figured as living memory. She grounds the purpose of the metanarrative itself as she arrests the action of the text to suspend mourning in the present of the forever fading Elven-years. As Galadriel extends the female tradition of Anglo-Saxon lament, the power of her heroic, healing mourning song reaches across narrative traditions and contributes to the larger projects of preservation and enchantment in the textual world of *LotR*.

It is important to underscore that Galadriel performs the work of mourning the Eldar days and not her male counterpart Celeborn; in this way Tolkien incorporates the tradition of female lament in Anglo-Saxon literature into the realm of fantasy. In turn, this critical cultural tool in the world of Middle-earth marks Galadriel's heroic contributions to the community of which she is part (Wheeler 66). As Leigh Smith argues, the elements of Lórien that imitate and evoke *Beowulf*, especially the parallels between Galadriel and Wealhtheow, are intended to "create the same elegiac tone that makes *Beowulf* so emotionally powerful, leaving the reader with the same noble sorrow Gimli feels at looking 'the last on that which was fairest'" (44). At the center of the nostalgia for *Beowulf*, Smith suggests, are Galadriel's songs, as well as Galadriel's control of the mead cup and gift giving (44). Smith argues, "the traditions and manners of Lothlórien, including the cup-passing and gift-giving, are among the 'ancient things' that Frodo senses 'lived on in the waking world'" (44). If, as Smith argues, an intertextual elegiac quality between *Beowulf* and Lothlórien arises through Galadriel, and in turn this quality allows Frodo to memorialize these ancient qualities of the past, then the performance of mourning in Middle-earth is simultaneously linked to an Anglo-Saxon tradition of female laments. Traditionally in Anglo-Saxon poetry, "female-voiced poems offer emotional expression, while male-voiced poems offer an emotional restraint" (Kinch 125). Thus, the emotional resonance of the departing scene in Lothlórien attests to an heroic and emotive female presence. In Middle-earth, Tolkien creates a "public and cultural female power" that is simultaneously heroic, as women arrest the text at moments of departure, both in leave-taking and death, to mark the loss of the story's core and reinforce the reader's intent to recall an enchanted possibility (Ingham 19). In contrast to a tradition that believed mourning is the opposite of agency and activity, Ingham argues that *Wulf and Eadwacer* and *The Wife's Lament* offer evidence that Anglo-Saxon culture "deployed representations of female grief and public and cultural power" with important (though not necessarily self-evident) consequences for the position of actual women (18). While the mourning process in *The Lord of the Rings* may not provide a self-evident position of Galadriel within the action of the narrative, the emotive quality of her songs, as well as the traces of Anglo-Saxon lament embodied in her character, enable Galadriel to actively preserve and mourn for Lothlórien as she is in turn preserved in Frodo's memory. In contradistinction to the leave-taking of the male characters, Galadriel's mourning songs privilege the memory of Lothlórien above the self and transmit the otherwise ephemeral memories of the Elven-world to Frodo.

If Galadriel is the most nostalgic of the female characters, Éowyn's characterization most actively defines memory as an heroic female trait in the text. Through Éowyn's conversation with Aragorn, the story reveals a gendered ideal of "renown" that differs across male and female spaces. For men, "renown" is tied up with the valor of battle and of bravery. Aragorn declares that he must go to fight Sauron via the paths of the dead, and Éowyn responds: "You are a stern lord and resolute ... and thus do men win renown" (Tolkien, *LotR* 784). When Éowyn persists, begging to accompany Aragorn to battle, he responds: "Your duty is with your people" (Tolkien, *LotR* 784). "Duty" here refers not specifically to Éowyn but to all women. Éowyn attempts to draw upon a traditional sign of male power—lineage—in order to sway Aragorn: "But am I not of the House of Eorl, a shieldmaiden and not a dry-nurse? I have waited on faltering feet long enough" (Tolkien, *LotR* 784). However, Aragorn refuses this appeal to a gendered-male logic. Positioned in terms of sacrifice, Éowyn's role has been "chosen": she is to guard and govern the people so that a marshal or captain may be free to ride. While Galadriel embodies the memory of Lothlórien before it has fully slipped away, Éowyn too figures as a type of preemptive memorial to the Riders of Rohan. Aragorn refuses to allow Éowyn's role to reach the male-centered action of battle; however, scripted to remember, Éowyn's heroism is tied to the metanarrative project of living memory. "A time may come soon," declares Aragorn, "when none will return. Then there will be need of valor without renown, for none shall remember the deeds that are done in the last defense of your homes" (Tolkien, *LotR* 784). Aragorn leaves Éowyn behind not for her inability to perform as "shieldmaiden," but for her potentiality to outlive, and thus remember when "the men have died in battle and honour" (Tolkien, *LotR* 784). While Galadriel already exists as living memory of the lost age of Eldar, Éowyn already memorializes the Riders of Rohan expected never to return. Éowyn, too, is memorialized as the company rides off into battle: "But Éowyn stood still as a figure carven in stone, her hands clenched at her sides, and she watched them until they passed into the shadows under the black Dwimorberg, the Haunted Mountain, which was the Door of the Dead" (Tolkien, *LotR* 785). While the Riders are in motion, propelling the story forward, Éowyn is left behind as the "chosen" caretaker and one who shall remember. "Still as stone," Éowyn *already* embodies the memory of the departed; Éowyn's stone-still passivity turns to active presence when couched in terms of a performance of elegy at the story's core. Éowyn's female heroism, like Galadriel's, is rooted in the transmission of the story itself, without which the reader would have no way of marking the importance of the narrative action.

The idea of an enduring female presence where women outlive men resurfaces through Arwen and Aragorn's relationship. Although Tolkien relays the story of Arwen and Aragorn's coupling in the Appendix, this does not subordinate its importance. Tolkien writes in his letters that he is "only concerned with Death [in *LotR*] as part of the nature, physical and spiritual, of Man, and with Hope without guarantees" (*Letters* 237). Tolkien continues, "That is why I regard the tale of Arwen and Aragorn as the most important of the Appendices; it is part of the essential story, and is only placed so, because it could not be worked into the main narrative without destroying its structure: which is planned to be 'hobbit-centric'" (*Letters* 237). Just as Tolkien introduces Celeborn and Galadriel in terms of Galadriel's powerful presence, Elrond and Aragorn remark on Aragorn's inferiority as compared to Arwen. In intelligence, wisdom and lineage, she far outranks him. Elrond tells Aragorn as much when he says, "But as for Arwen the Fair, Lady of Imladris and of Lórien, Evenstar of her people ... she has lived in the world already so long that to her you are but as a yearling shoot beside a young birch of many summers. She is too far above you" (Tolkien, *LotR* 1058). Aragorn expresses that the traditional sign of male power—lineage—feels slight in the presence of Arwen. In their meeting for the first time he says, "'Estel I was called ... but I am Aragorn, Arathorn's son, Isildur's Heir, Lord of the Dúnedain'; yet even in the saying he felt that this high lineage, in which his heart had rejoiced, was now of little worth, and as nothing compared to her dignity and loveliness" (Tolkien, *LotR* 1058). Tolkien describes this loveliness in terms of Aragorn's sense that Arwen is not only beautiful, but also wise: 'Then Aragorn was abashed, for he saw the elven-light in her eyes and the wisdom of many days" (Tolkien, *LotR* 1058). In the wisdom of many days that is the "elven-light in her eyes," Arwen's beauty is not only physical but also internal, in part the wisdom of her immortality. While Arwen's knowledge is innate, Aragorn's largely comes from having journeyed in the wild for thirty years and from his own experience of being a Ranger. Only through this lived experience, and especially through his friendship with Gandalf the Wise, did he acquire wisdom through Gandalf's teaching.

These elements elevate Arwen to a position socially and culturally above Aragorn; they also aid the elegiac quality of the text. In marrying Aragorn, Arwen abdicates her lineage and renounces her immortality, but still outlives Aragorn. Her selfless, heroic decision privileges the gendered-female work of mourning above her own life. Unlike Tolkien's other female mourners, Arwen chooses her mortal fate; out of love for Aragorn, *she chooses* the path that *Aragorn decides* for Éowyn. In so doing, Arwen reveals the significance of mortality over immortality, the way that death naturally bestows meaning upon life. Peter Brooks argues that there exists an analogous relationship in narrative itself. Interrogating narrative in terms of Sigmund Freud's work in *Beyond the Pleasure Principle*, Brooks argues, "the beginning [of the narrative] in fact presupposes the end. The very possibility of meaning plotted through time depends on the anticipated structuring force of the ending: the interminable would be the meaningless" (283). Arwen ultimately chooses mortality, mourns Aragorn's death, and thus overcomes the interminable nature ("meaningless" in Brooks's terms) of immortality. Brooks goes on to conclude, "all narration is obituary in that life acquires definable meaning only at, and through, death" (284). It is through Brooks's conception of narration-as-obituary that Tolkien ascribes a value to Arwen's mortal fate: "But Arwen became as a mortal woman, and yet it was not her lot to die until all that she had gained was lost" (Tolkien, *LotR* 1062). The free indirect discourse of Arwen's gaze frames the reader's last impression of Aragorn: "And long there he lay, an image of the splendour of the Kings of Men in glory undimmed before the breaking of the world" (Tolkien, *LotR* 1062). While not herself a stone-still image, Arwen suspends Aragorn's image in time through effigy, and it is her mourning gaze that allows for the transmission of Aragorn's memory.

While Goldberry's role is minor compared to the other women (she does not reoccur outside Book One of *The Fellowship of the Ring*), Goldberry is equally heroic as she mourns the changing Middle-earth. Furthermore, her status begs equal attention to that of her male counterpart, Tom Bombadil. Goldberry and Bombadil share domestic duties and neither seems to overshadow the other. When they welcome the hobbits into their home for the evening meal, the narrator describes that "in some fashion they seemed to weave a single dance, neither hindering the other, in and out of the room, and round about the table; and with great speed food and vessels and lights were set in order" (Tolkien, *LotR* 132). Like the hobbits' departure from Lothlórien, Goldberry's female presence creates a moment of textual arrest. When the hobbits leave Bombadil, the description is one of uplift: "Tom came out of the house and waved his hat and danced upon the doorstep, bidding the hobbits to get up and be off and go with good speed" (135). In contrast, Goldberry, like her female counterparts previously discussed, momentarily pauses time:

> Turning back, when they reached the bottom of the green hollow, they saw Goldberry, now small and slender like a sunlit flower against the sky: she was standing still watching them and her hands were stretched out towards them. As they looked she gave a clear call, and lifting up her hand she turned and vanished behind the hill [Tolkien, *LotR* 135].

"Standing still watching them ... like a small sunlit flower against the sky," Goldberry's description in part memorializes her within the text at the same time that she mourns the action of the departure and the progression of the story. The women may be repeatedly left behind, however, as mourning the passage of the story and already memorialized within the text, their roles are not as marginal as the action of the plot dictates. In fact, by directly rejecting the tropes of male hero as those characters who move the action of the plot forward, Goldberry and her heroic female counterparts contribute to the memorial practice that makes them heroes on their own terms.

As I have indicated, the women of *The Lord of the Rings* carry the weight of mourning in the text. The emotive capacity for female mourning in Anglo-

Saxon laments and elegy more generally is especially drawn out in this mythopoetic secondary-world. The repetition of the female mourners throughout *LotR*
echoes Sacks's characterization of elegy and becomes a central method of drawing readers into this story world, a process I will refer to in terms of Simon
Spiegel's "naturalization" (369–85). Spiegel's project takes off from that of Vic-
tor Shklovsky and Bertolt Brecht's work on estrangement, or what he argues
these scholars use as a "stylistic device that describes *how* fiction is being communicated" (371). If estrangement in fiction constantly makes the mundane
feel strange, then it "it would mean that *sf* [science fiction] and fantasy are constantly making their *marvelous* elements appear strange" (Spiegel 371, emphasis
in original). But in fantastic literature the reverse is true: on a formal level, "*sf
does not estrange the familiar, but rather makes the strange familiar*" (371–2,
emphasis in original). Spiegel continues:

> Although "unrealistic" characters populate fairy tales, they are not "strange" in
> the sense of Shklovsky or Brecht. They are not constructed to surprise—on the
> contrary, witches and fairies and the like are expected—and hence they do not
> serve to de-automatize or to make strange whatever is happening in the story
> [371].

The repetition of fantasy characters both within a text and across various texts
in the genre serves this naturalization function; naturalization, as Spiegel suggests is in part due to a type of canonization (371–2). In *The Lord of the Rings*,
qualities of elegy and fantasy simultaneously naturalize the reader into the text's
secondary world. As Sacks argues, one of the characterizations of elegy resides
in its performance and potential for working out of grief: "through a kind of
repetitive dialogue the bereaved is forced to accept a reality that he might otherwise refuse" (36). Because of the shock and trauma of grief, there is a conscious, imposed suspension of disbelief necessary for the mourner that also
exists, for different reasons, in the fantastic. Sacks writes, "the griever must be
convinced of the actual fact of loss" (36). This reading of elegy invokes Galadriel's lamentations of Lothlórien as well as the idea that the fantastic naturally
requires the reader to accept a reality she might otherwise refuse. Here I would
like to highlight a principle way that fantasy and elegy are well suited for each
other: their texts rely on repetition to make familiar grief or the unnatural.
Both genres render the strange familiar, either by way of "working through"
grief or customizing reader expectations around particular foreign phenomena.

Gendered-feminine mourning may entail moments of arrest within
Tolkien's text, but these stone-still pauses in time do not exemplify female passivity. While the men of the fellowship propel the action of the story forward,
the moments of female arrest self-consciously attune the reader to the inevitability of the story's end, both in Middle-earth itself and the end of the reading
process. This is the inevitability of departure both fantasy and elegy embody.

In the former, the reader departs from the secondary world (when the story ends) into her lived reality, while in the latter the author suspends reality to create a space of mourning. In Tolkien's Middle-earth, however, the loss is *both* of the primary world for the reader and the inevitability of the end of the Eldar days, where female lament momentarily stops the progression of this fading world to literally hold the reader in place. Narrative, Peter Brooks reminds his reader, is always in some way a desire for the "end": "If beginning is desire, and is ultimately desire for the end, between lies a process we feel to be necessary (plots, Aristotle tells us, must be of a 'certain length') but whose relation to originating desire and to end remains problematic" (Brooks 284). In this formulation, "plot is a kind of arabesque or squiggle toward the end" (Brooks 292). In the textual moments where action suspends and women reign, readers are suspended in the text along the journey to the end of Middle-earth. In these moments of arrest, the female heroes guide readers to the narrative core: of mourning and of the fantastic world itself. In fiction, Brooks writes: "The desire of the text is ultimately the desire for the end, for that recognition which is the moment of the death of the reader in the text. Yet recognition cannot abolish textuality, does not annul the middle which, in its oscillation between blindness and recognition, between origin and endings, is the truth of the narrative text" (296). While the fellowship leads the reader to that end by furthering the plot, the female heroes most intimately suspend readers in the secondary world, the "truth of the narrative," as they momentarily deflect the "squiggle" of plot away from a straight path towards the end. Mourning the multiplicity of departures at *The Lord of the Rings*'s end, the reader has no choice but to seek solace and compulsively re-enter the fantastic realm.

NOTES

1. In the introduction to *A Secular Age*, Charles Taylor writes, "Somewhere, in some activity or condition, lies a fullness, a richness; that is, in that place (activity or condition), life is fuller, richer, deeper, more worthwhile, more admirable, more what it should be" (5). According to Taylor, secularity defines the state in which we search for this sense of "fullness." In a pre-secular age of enchantment, fullness existed in the external presence of God or through the affirmation of the supernatural. Key to this argument is the way that we currently live in a disenchanted world marked by this sense of loss: "we experience above all a distance, an absence, an exile, a seemingly irremediable incapacity ever to reach this place..." (6).

2. As Peter Sacks explains, traditionally, the flute, or the oboe-like pipe *aulos* accompanied these early poems (3).

3. In his work on trauma, Dominick LaCapra differentiates between "acting out" and "working through" trauma. In acting out, "tensions implode, and it is as if one were back there in the past reliving the traumatic scene.... In this sense, the aporia and the double bind might be seen as marking a trauma that has not been worked through" (21). However, in "working through," one participates in an articulatory practice: "to the extent one works

through trauma (as well as transferential relations in general), one is able to distinguish between past and present and to recall in memory that something happened to one (or one's people) back then while realizing that one is living here and now with openings to the future" (21–2).

4. Sacks explains that before elegies were elegies, they were a mode of expression; not melancholy, these elegies covered a wide range of topics including "exhortatory martial epigrams, political philosophy, commemorative lines, or amatory complaints." This does not mean there were no early associations between elegy and mourning. As Margaret Alexiou has written, it was possible that there was a school of Dorian elegists who used the form as a kind of lament around 578 BC (qtd. in Sacks 3).

5. Sacks refines this psychoanalytic approach through Ovid's *Metamorphisis* vis-à-vis Freud (7–8). Freud's healthy work of mourning "requires a withdrawal of affection from the lost object and a subsequent reattachment of affection to some substitute for that object" (8). In Sacks's reading, "Ovid presents a condensed version of this process, a metamorphosis in which the lost object seems to enter or become inscribed in the substitute, in this case the found sign or art" (6).

6. Citing the tendency of scholars to ignore the cultural import of grief and mourning in Anglo-Saxon society, Ingham discusses the history of looking at women in a warrior society in terms of the passive, "non-roles" of peaceweaver and mourner that occur in the private domain (18). These scholars, such as Helen T. Bennett and Alexandra Hennessey Olsen, share in the belief that mourning is the opposite of agency and activity. It seems that in this view, the mourner somehow comes to embody the literal loss as figurative place in society.

Works Cited

Attebery, Brian. *Strategies of Fantasy*. Bloomington: Indiana University Press, 1992. Print.

Austin, J.L. *How to Do Things with Words*, 2d ed. Edited by J. O. Urmson and Marina Sbisà. Cambridge: Harvard University Press, 1975. Print.

Boym, Svetlana. *The Future of Nostalgia*. New York: Basic Books, 2001. Print.

Brooks, Peter. "Freud's Masterplot." *Yale French Studies* 55/56 (1977): 280–300. *JSTOR*. Web. 8 May 2013.

Forest-Hill, Lynn. "Boromir, Byrhtnoth, and Bayard: Finding a Language for Grief in J.R.R. Tolkien's *The Lord of the Rings*." *Tolkien Studies* 5.1 (2008): 73–97. *Project MUSE*. Web. 20 Jul. 2013.

Fredrick, Candace, and Sam McBride, eds. *Women Among the Inklings: Gender, C.S. Lewis, J.R.R. Tolkien, and Charles Williams*. Westport, CT: Greenwood Press, 2001. Print.

Frontgia, Terri. "Archetypes, Stereotypes, and The Female Hero: Transformations in Contemporary Perspectives." *Mythlore* 67 (1991): 15–18. *Print*.

Ingham, Patricia. "From Kinship to Kingship: Mourning, Gender and Anglo-Saxon Community." In *Grief and Gender: 700–1700*. 17–33. Edited by Jennifer C. Vaught. New York: Palgrave Macmillan, 2003. Print.

Kennedy, David. *Elegy*. New York: Routledge, 2007. Print.

Kinch, Ashby. "The Ethical Agency of the Female Lyric Voice: 'The Wife's Lament' and Catallus 64." *Studies in Philology* 3, no. 2 (2006): 121–152. Print.

LaCapra, Dominick. *Writing History, Writing Trauma*. Baltimore: Johns Hopkins University Press, 2001. Print.

"mythopoeia, n." OED Online. November 2010. Oxford University Press.http://www. oed.com/view/Entry/235084?redirectedFrom=mythopoeia.

Pearson, Carol. *The Hero Within: Six Archetypes We Live By.* New York: Harper & Row, 1989. Print.

Pearson, Carol, and Katherine Pope. *The Female Hero in American and British Literature.* New York: R. R. Bowker, 1981.

Sacks, Peter. *The English Elegy: Studies in the Genre, from Spenser to Yeats.* Baltimore: Johns Hopkins University Press, 1985. Print.

Smith, Leigh. "'I have looked the last on that which is fairest': Elegy in Beowulf and Tolkien's Lothlorien." *Mallorn: The Journal of the Tolkien Society* 44 (2006): 43–46. Print.

Spiegel, Simon. "Things Made Strange: On the Concept of 'Estrangement' in Science Fiction Theory." *Science Fiction Studies* 35, no. 3 (2008): 369–385. Print.

Starck, Lindsay. "Re-enchanting language through Fantasy or: The True Story of How I Learned to Stop Crying and Spin My Own Gold." Unpublished manuscript, last modified December 9, 2010. Microsoft Word file.

Strand, Mark. "A Poet's Alphabet." In *The Weather of Words: Poetic Invention.* New York: Alfred A. Knopf, 2000, 4–5. Print.

Taylor, Charles. *A Secular Age.* Cambridge: Harvard University Press, 2007. Print.

Tolkien, J.R.R. *The Letters of J.R.R. Tolkien.* Ed. Humphrey Carpenter. New York: Houghton Mifflin, 2000. Print.

_____. *The Lord of Rings.* 1954–5. New York: Houghton Mifflin, 2004. Print.

_____. *Tree and Leaf: Including the Poem Mythopoeia.* London: Unwin Hyman, 1964. Print.

Weber, Max. "Science as a Vocation." In *Collected Essays on Education*, 524–55. Munich: Duncker Humboldt, 1919. Web. 15 September 2010.http://tems.umn.edu/pdf/Weber ScienceVocation.pdf.

II. Underestimated Overachievers: Unlikely and Unstoppable Female Heroes

"Weak as woman's magic": Empowering Care Work in Ursula Le Guin's *Tehanu*

Erin Wyble Newcomb

Ursula Le Guin published *Tehanu* in 1990, eighteen years after most readers considered the Earthsea series concluded. Critical consensus cites Le Guin's burgeoning feminist consciousness as the reason for her return to Earthsea, and *Tehanu* supports those claims. As Holly Littlefield states, "this book deals with the importance of female experience and knowledge" (254). Laura Comoletti and Michael Drout claim that Le Guin "is undertaking a feminist intervention into her secondary world" (113), while Alice Mills sees the author's (unsuccessful, according to the critic) mission as being to "redress the balance in a fourth book" by emphasizing female characters (2). Many critics share Mills' opinion that placing Tenar at the center of the story is itself an act of feminist revision. Perry Nodelman explicitly ties the tale as "revisionist act" to the fact that the "protagonist is Tenar as a middle-aged woman, someone more like Le Guin herself than like her intended audience" (198). Len Hatfield agrees, emphasizing Tenar's age and gender to indicate "that patriarchal adult males ignore or repress children in virtually the same ways they do women" (54). Placing Tenar as a middle-aged woman at the center of the story changes the plot as well; Amy Clarke deals with this issue in depth, describing the book as "woman's writing" defined as "stories about women, told in non-linear fashion, about non-heroic people, and using what Le Guin calls the 'mother tongue,' the language of the household" (7). Discussing *Tehanu* specifically, Clarke asserts, "[w]e are fully aware of Tenar as the tender of the hearth; whether this is her own kind of magic or power is a question central to the narrative" (117). I concur with these critics, and, in addition, I argue that *Tehanu* is not just a feminist revision of the *Earthsea* series but a reconsideration of the fantasy genre and the definition of the hero. Using theories of feminist ethics of care, I will demonstrate that the prominence of Tenar and her care work in *Tehanu* simultaneously destabilizes the male monopoly of heroism and elevates ordinary women's work to the potentially extraordinary. Tenar is a female hero, however seemingly unlikely, precisely because of her commitment to care and her efforts to achieve justice through care. Care work is not merely the back-story or invisible support of the hero, but it is work that can define a female hero and transform her world.

Defining Care

Le Guin has much to say about the exclusion of women from the hero-tale (and thus about the moniker "hero"). She writes, "the experience of women as women ... is what civilization has left out, what culture excludes" (*Dancing* 163), leaving women "in relation to heroes" but not as heroes themselves (*Earthsea Revisioned* 5). The hero-tale genre "has concerned the establishment or validation of manhood" (Le Guin, *Earthsea Revisioned* 5) and ignores the contributions of women as possible content for a heroic quest. In this sense, Tenar at first seems to be a "non-hero" simply by virtue of being female; in *Tehanu*, Le Guin seems eager to challenge the hero-tale as well as the hero, ironically stating in *Earthsea Revisioned*,

> [w]omen's work, as usual, is the maintenance of order and cleanliness, housekeeping, feeding and clothing people, childbearing, care of babies and children, nursing and healing of animals and people, care of the dying, funeral rites— those unimportant matters of life and death, not part of history, or of story. What women do is invisible [15–16].

Le Guin's frustration particularly shines through in the line "those unimportant matters of life and death," and her examples establish the centrality of care work to every stage of life. Yet instead of orienting *Tehanu* around care work as important support for a hero, she puts care work and a care worker at the heart of an atypical hero's tale. Tenar's story unfolds in the domestic sphere and revolves around housekeeping chores; she travels in *Tehanu* to care for the sick or the home, and she always brings a child in tow to care for as well. Her heroism consists not of singular events and powerful figures but of the everyday work that maintains life.

Le Guin's reorientation of the genre and her own fantasy world to legitimize females and care workers as heroic parallels the work of Carol Gilligan, whose landmark text *In a Different Voice* critiques the once-dominant perception that males attained higher levels of moral development than females. It is not, Gilligan reasons, that males are morally superior, but that females discuss their morality in different terms—terms unrecognized and unvalidated by the male-centered rubric. As Gilligan explains, "[t]he reinterpretation of women's experience in terms of their own imagery ... provides a nonhierarchical vision of human connection." Instead of a hierarchy, Gilligan offers "the image of web," which "changes an order of inequality into a structure of interconnection" (62). Just as Gilligan requires a different metaphor to conceptualize women's morality, Le Guin requires a different kind of story to manifest a female hero. That story, like the definition Gilligan provides, is one of relationship and interconnection, and, ultimately of care.

Other feminist ethicists build upon Gilligan's initial work. Diemut Grace Bubeck defines "care as an activity or practice aimed at the meeting of needs in others" (160). Nel Noddings also emphasizes the active nature of care work, explaining that "[t]o act as one-caring, then, is to act with special regard for the particular person in a concrete situation" (24). Both Bubeck and Noddings regard care work not as passive, accidental, or incidental, but as meaningful labor central to individual and communal well-being. Bernice Fisher and Joan Tronto assert the social centrality of care work as well, "because caring efforts speak ultimately to our survival as a species rather than as isolated individuals" (39–40). Fisher and Tronto also caution against conflating care work with an essential femininity, declaring that their characterization of care work "does not assume that certain people (women rather than men) have a special ability to sustain our world or that some efforts (healing rather than house-building) make a more important contribution to sustaining life on earth" (40). Valuing care work, these authors suggest, does not mean that it is (or ought to be) the only meaningful work for women, or that such work somehow excludes men; their statements align with a persistent concern within feminist ethics that the validation of care work can circularly contribute to women's oppression or a reductionist vision of femininity. Marilyn Friedman counters that perspective, articulating that "[c]are ethics is inspired and engaged by a respect for women's traditional domestic and familial care-giving labor. Any system of thought that shows such esteem combats the aspect of women's oppression that has to do with the cultural devaluation of women's work" (149). Virginia Held takes a different strategy, deconstructing the dichotomy between care and justice that Gilligan originally wrote against. Held writes: "Care is probably the most deeply fundamental value.... There can be no justice without care, however, for without care no child would survive and there would be no persons to respect" (17). Reading *Tehanu* through the lens of feminist ethics of care highlights the tensions within the novel and the *Earthsea* quartet; in *Tehanu*, Le Guin makes Tenar's care work visible and promotes both care work and care workers as material worthy of heroic stories. At the same time, the characters within the text do not necessarily witness the same feminist revelations as Le Guin's readers do, and Tenar's care work renders her vulnerable and ignored in her own society. The easy dismissal of Tenar's status and work mirror the typical real-world disregard for care, but Le Guin's decision to authenticate care work through story asks the reader to respect the considerable contributions of care workers like Tenar, elevating her efforts—and care work itself—to a kind of heroism.

Defined by Care

Only one other critic addresses the particular role of care in *Tehanu*. Susan McLean alludes to care as "an alternative 'woman's power'" (110) and explicitly states, "Tenar embodies the power of caring" (112). On that subject (one of many she addresses in an essay on power in the novel), McLean concludes, "Le Guin captures the essence of 'women's power,' in small ways affirming life in the face of death and trying to increase the number of good things in the world" (117). McLean discusses power where I discuss care work, but I question the essential nature of "women's power" as something that is both shifting and deceptive. Tenar defines herself and is defined by others through her care work, but she also reflects on her status in multiple ways, sometimes using her matronly appearance to mask her power and sometimes feeling frustrated that others disregard her because of that same appearance. When the king's messengers come searching for Ged, Tenar protects the former archmage's privacy, pondering how "she used the defense of her appearance, her seeming to be a mere goodwife, a middle-aged housekeeper—but was it seeming? It was also truth, and these matters were more subtle even than the guises and shape-changes of wizards" (Le Guin, *Tehanu* 112–3). Tenar cannot represent the essence of female power, because there is no essential female power—only multiple and shifting subjectivities contingent on the context of Tenar's personal history and Earthsea's values. Feminist ethics of care illustrate the complexity of care work as gendered and socially situated while also acknowledging that "small ways of affirming life in the face of death" are not small at all, but the very stuff of heroism. Within Earthsea (and often beyond its boundaries into the real world), power is defined by how much one can control while care work is defined by how much one can serve; power tends to be visible, hierarchical, and exclusive but care work references community and inclusivity while remaining largely invisible. *Tehanu* expands the definition of power to incorporate care work but extends its heroism beyond Tenar to all of Earthsea, female and male alike.

As critics Susan Bernardo and Graham Murphy write, "Tenar's idea of multiple kinds of power aligns with feminist thought that emphasizes multiplicity and circulation of thought. Sharing power and recognizing the gifts and abilities of others in this line of thinking does not weaken the individual, but strengthens society" (141). Care work defines Tenar and her efforts to fortify Earthsea; her giftedness exists within the realm of care work, yet it is by no means a simple contribution to her world. At the novel's opening, Tenar is unnamed, referred to only as "the widow," her existence defined tangentially to her deceased husband Farmer Flint and her former teacher, the mage Ogion. She is further identified by her foreignness and the use-name given to her by her husband: "Goha, which is what they call a little white web-spinning spider on Gont. That name fit well enough, she being white-skinned and small and a good spinner of goat's wool and sheep fleece" (Le Guin, *Tehanu* 1). These initial descriptions characterize Tenar as dependent on others for her identity. Indeed, in "Heroes or Sheroes," Christine Mains, Brad J. Ricca, Holly Hassel, and Lynda Rucker explain, "female characters have been restricted to roles defined in relation to the male hero.... Even female protagonists are often passive heroines rather than active heroes." They continue, "[e]ven Ursula K. Le Guin, in *The Tombs of Atuan* (1972) resolves Tenar's coming-of-age story with the conventional plot of marriage and motherhood—a situation later addressed by her return to Tenar's story in *Tehanu*" (Mains 180). The initial depiction of Tenar seems to belie this claim, but the novel's opening scene sets up the tension of the story, its fictional world, and even the ambivalent nature of care work. In each instance, we may see only "the widow" to whom we are introduced; yet the matron whose name reveals her domestic prowess also weaves a web of relationships established through care work, and those largely-feminine connections can unravel the misogynistic and oppressive hierarchies that dominate Earthsea. Her allies include a female cast of characters she describes as "this fine household—a witch, a widow, a cripple, and a half-wit," all of whom work together "to do what must be done" in taking care of Therru as both a vulnerable child and the future archmage (Le Guin, *Tehanu* 54). Appearances can be both deceptive and accurate, just as Tenar and her care work can be both matronly and heroic. In *Tehanu*, care work does not preclude Tenar from heroism but establishes her as a female hero who cooperates with other female heroes (mostly children, mothers, and witches), in spite of their collective lack of social recognition or appreciation.

Throughout the novel, Tenar reflects upon her own shifting subjectivities, which change depending on her stage of life and the company she keeps. Her antagonist, the mage Aspen, knows her former glory as "the White Lady, who had worn the Ring of Erreth-Akbe on her wrist, who had made whole the Rune of Peace" (Le Guin, *Tehanu* 75), yet Tenar also recognizes that her power is inconsequential to Aspen's opinion of her: "[h]e could not hate her more. To be a woman was her fault. Nothing could worsen or amend it, in his eyes; no punishment was enough" (143). Femaleness is the one unifying thread in Tenar's web of subjectivities, and it is what makes her offensive to Aspen and the abusive patriarchy he represents, regardless of what contributions she makes to Earthsea, through care work or otherwise. Tenar understands the depths of Aspen's misogyny, and she also understands the complexities of female existence. At one point in the novel, she reminisces:

There was the widow who had carried a burned child here, who sat by the side of the dying, who waited for a man to return. Like all women, any woman, doing what women do. But it was not by the names of the servant or the wife or the widow that Ogion had called her. Nor had Ged, in the darkness of the Tombs. Nor—longer ago, farther away than all—had her mother, the mother she remembered only as the warmth and lion-color of firelight, the mother who had given her her name [24].

This passage reveals Tenar's ordinariness, the stereotypically-feminine practices that mark her time and connect her to "all women, any woman, doing what women do." The passage also highlights Tenar's extraordinariness: her choice to rescue and adopt Therru, a severely-abused child whose future includes becoming the first female Archmage; her childhood as a priestess in the Tombs of Atuan; her adventures with Ged, her tutelage with Ogion. Those experiences are framed by motherhood, her own care work for Therru, and her remembrance of being cared for by her own mother. Tenar's care work gives her power, just as Aspen's magery gives him power, but she uses hers to heal where he uses his to harm. The difference is not one of masculine and feminine, because Ged and Ogion engage in care work just as Tenar does, but between care and neglect—or in Aspen's case, outright violence. Aspen comes to represent the abuse of power in Earthsea, power-as-violence in direct opposition to care. Unlike the men who initially burn Therru, Aspen bears the status and concomitant power of mage, and he abuses that power to torture Ged and Tenar; Therru recognizes Aspen "whose name was Erisen, and whom she saw as a forked and writhing darkness" (Le Guin, *Tehanu* 272). Therru knows Aspen's true name, thus pitting her unschooled power against his magery and allowing her to call upon the dragon for help—where only a dragon is powerful enough to thwart the misuse of violence and power by Earthsea's own wizards.

Their culture affords Aspen status and power, but Tenar's carework epitomizes actual heroism, work that rectifies injustices in her world, raises up another (eventual) female hero, and moves the story forward through continual acts of care. Tenar is summoned to heal Therru (Le Guin, *Tehanu* 3), to help Ogion die in peace (7), and to care for Ged in his infirmity (54). She sings Therru to sleep (82), and manages Flint's farm and Ogion's home. She recognizes the gendered implications of her care work, "pondering the indifference of a man towards the exigencies that ruled a woman: that someone must be not far from a sleeping child, that one's freedom meant another's unfreedom" (84). Tenar sacrifices some level of freedom to ensure Therru's safety, in this specific instance of slumber and in the larger role of adopting the abused child. But Tenar also recognizes her care work as justice—defending and protecting Therru from those who want to harm her again, offering the child hope and a life beyond hatred and cruelty. When even Ged tells Tenar it would have been better to let Therru die, she dismisses him and holds to her belief in the justice and rightness of care work. Tenar sidles into bed next to Therru and muses, "What wrong could she be? Wronged, wronged beyond all repair, but not wrong. Not lost, not lost, not lost" (92). That Therru is "not lost" is only because of the care work of Tenar and women like her, those who care in spite of the invisibility and degradation of care work and those who practice it. Therru's own biological parents subject their child to neglect and brutality; the death of her pregnant mother Senini (229) illustrates the fate that would have awaited Therru if Tenar and the other women had not intervened. The blatant lack of care where care ought to be primary casts into relief the heroism of Tenar's care work—care that extends to the vulnerable like Therru as much as to the powerful like Ogion. As a middle-aged widow, mother, and housekeeper, Tenar does not embody the traditional young, male hero whose exploits take place in the public sphere, yet Tenar's life's work and her care for Therru do embody the self-sacrifice common to heroism.

As Rita Manning writes in *Speaking from the Heart*, "[a]n ethic of care is open to need; it acknowledges that we all have needs.... We are all needy; our relationships are based on a recognition of need and the commitment to fill need" (97). Theorizing an ethic of care destabilizes the myths of independence and autonomy. By highlighting the inherent neediness of the human condition, an ethic of care challenges the perception that only femininity is relational. Life requires care, and thus care workers. Certain privileges may allow some members of society to choose what kinds of care and what kinds of care workers, but care remains a condition of living. Bubeck describes care as "a response to a particular subset of basic human needs, in other words, those that make us dependent on others" (165). While she identifies the beginning and end of life as times that tend to necessitate care, she sees care and dependency (at least at some level) not as feminine or masculine but as human.

Care work may be perceived as feminine and care workers may be predominantly female, but the essence of care is human—and any gendering is social construction. To say that care is human does not alleviate the potential to exploit care work and care workers in the real world or in Earthsea, but works like *Tehanu* draw attention to the significance of care to life itself. As Daryl Koehn asserts, "The desire to care appears to be identical with a desire to alleviate human suffering and pain and to meet the material needs of all concerned parties, including the caring agent herself" (29). Koehn's words affirm the relational necessity of both life and care, namely, that care workers need care too. Within the context of *Tehanu*, Tenar's web of relationships strengthens her; unlike the wizards (who shun social connections and adhere to celibacy), Tenar's care work allows her to see the real conditions of life in Earthsea, and to respond to inequalities, injustices, and needs with acts of care that amount to heroism.

Recognizing Care

By choosing Tenar for her protagonist, Le Guin centers the novel's experience on care work and declares through her artistry that care work and care workers are worthy of attention, but Tenar remains an unlikely hero. She is not the titular character; that honor belongs to Therru, whose true name—Tehanu—is revealed by the dragon Kalessin (Le Guin, *Tehanu* 277). Instead, the novel seems to assert that there are kinds of power that are marginalized, lacking in visibility. Le Guin's attention to Tenar's story reorients fantasy literature by asserting the merits of care workers and care work for a heroic tale, and within the book, Tenar must also come to terms with herself as a female hero. For instance, when warily receiving visitors from the king, Tenar "used the defense of her appearance, her seeming to be a mere goodwife, a middle-aged housekeeper—but was it seeming? It was also truth, and these matters were more subtle even than the guises and shape-changes of wizards" (112–113). Tenar also reflects on her past opportunities and her choices to reject the kinds of power offered to her by men: "Priestess of the Tombs of Atuan or foreign ward of the Mage of Gont, she was set apart, set above. Men had given her power, men had shared their power with her" (37). In these two passages, Tenar identifies the ways that subjectivities nurture or obstruct intimacy: the same visage of "a mere goodwife" that distances her from the king's messengers gives her access to the local women and witches, and vice versa. The powers offered to her by men feel exclusionary to Tenar, perhaps because her gender means she can never really belong in that echelon—not in an Earthsea where only men are mages and the expression "*Weak as woman's magic, wicked as woman's magic*" (39, emphasis in original) is commonplace. Tenar rejects the phallocentric subjectivities that seem at odds with her gender and chooses "the other side, the other room, where the women lived, to be one of them" (Le Guin, *Tehanu* 37). In so choosing, Tenar defines herself as a "wife, a farmer's wife, a mother, a householder, undertaking the power that a woman was born to, the authority allotted her by the arrangements of mankind" (Le Guin, *Tehanu* 37). The wording "allotted her by the arrangements of mankind" indicates the social-constructedness of these roles, each of which is defined in relation to another person or a domestic space.

Tenar likely enjoys more options than most women of Earthsea, but her decisions remain circumscribed within a context that values strictly-prescribed gender roles and assigns power (and punishment) according to the fulfillment of those roles. As feminist ethicist Marilyn Friedman points out, "care is simultaneously a perilous project for women, requiring the sacrifice of other important values, its very nobility part of its sometimes dangerously seductive allure. An ethic of care, to be fully liberatory for women, must not fail to explore and reflect this deep complexity" (183). Tenar chooses care work and executes her work admirably, but her devotion and giftedness do not change the reality that her decision makes her less lonely at a cost. Nor does her care work protect her even in an environment that expects women to care, no matter the cost; the problem in Earthsea is not (or not just) the gendering of care work but insidious and ubiquitous misogyny. That misogyny is writ large in the devaluation of care work in Earthsea as well as in the violence directed toward Tenar and Therru throughout the novel. A novel about care work asserts the heroism of care workers, however unlikely their heroics may seem within their cultural context. Even Tenar frets "her wiving and mothering were done. There was nothing in her, no power, for anybody to recognize" (Le Guin, *Tehanu* 76). The problem is not one of impotence but of recognition, and as the novel progresses, Tenar begins to appreciate the importance of power that cares. That kind of power stands in stark contrast to the magery that positions itself alone at the top of Earthsea's hierarchy. For example, Tenar gives the visiting mages instructions for Ogion's burial and reveals the deceased wizard's true name, but they ignore and overlook her (Le Guin, *Tehanu* 31–2). Frustrated, Tenar speaks more assertively: "[t]his is a bad time—a time when even such a name can go unheard, can fall like a stone! Is listening not power? Listen, then: his name was Aihal.... I've lost my father, and dear friend" (Le Guin, *Tehanu* 33). The visiting wizards are not relationally bound to Ogion; because they bear an equal status as mages, they assume the right to hear Ogion's true name and organize his funeral to bolster their own reputations. Tenar, meanwhile, is triply bound to Ogion as daughter, friend, and student. The deceased wizard called specifically for her to care for him at the end of his life and chose to reveal his true name to her alone—a mark of Tenar's importance that the mages interpret as insult instead of care. They do not see Tenar as a person worthy of their attention, and Ogion's relationship with Tenar offends them and makes them hate her rather than listen to her. These mages conflate power with status, and protect their reputations more than their communities, suggesting that typical heroism might be more show than substance. Their neglect also illustrates her culture's disregard for women and women's work, all while Tenar successfully uses care work to thwart the systemic misogyny that permeates Earthsea; she sacrifices herself for the good of Therru and the good of the community as a whole.

Daryl Koehn addresses the issue of attention and the care ethic in *Rethinking Feminist Ethics: Care, Trust, and Empathy*. She writes,

> The care ethic contends that we will not be able to identify the conditions under which individuals can co-exist satisfactorily within a community if we fail to create a space in which we can hear from individuals in their own voices.... We cannot have identified conditions of satisfying living for all members of the relevant community because our mode of proceeding has prevented some members' concern from being present to us [27].

Koehn emphasizes listening, relationships, and recognizing the needs of all members of a community; her description of the ethic of care reiterates what feminist ethicists continually claim—that care is not a passive feeling but an active force that seeks to alter social conditions for the better. Yet in *Tehanu*, even male characters who want to improve Earthsea and reform its corrupt abuses of magic struggle to truly hear Tenar. When the king sets sail seeking "A Woman on Gont" (unidentified, but assumed to be Tenar), he and the mage aboard ship do not know how to listen to her. Of the mage, Tenar muses, "it did not make him hear her. How could he, who had never listened to a woman since his mother sang him his last cradle song, hear her? ... It was no use; he could not hear her" (Le Guin, *Tehanu* 180). In her estimation of the mage's shortcomings, Tenar refers to the absence of a feminine presence in his life; as a mage, he is so divorced from the world of women and women's work that he cannot recognize her voice. The irony, of course, is that a mother's care work sustained even the great mage in his early years of life. Of the king, Tenar admits "[h]e listened. He was not deaf. But he frowned, intent, as if trying to understand a foreign language. And he said only, under his breath, 'It may be'" (Le Guin, *Tehanu* 181).

Tenar is and is not "The Woman on Gont." That prophecy refers to Therru, but the king and his messengers still seek Tenar, even as they fail to heed her advice for their quest. Her words are like "a foreign language," but this time Tenar's foreignness is not her ethnicity but her gender—femaleness as foreignness. Despite their mutual concern for Earthsea, this trio of powerful people cannot connect because their worldviews are so differently oriented; as readers, we see Tenar's ethic of care and understand its significance even when other characters suffer from selective hearing.

In his critique of the series, Christopher Robinson describes the "literal anonymity of the witch—and of the boy's mother, for that matter" in Earthsea's male naming ceremonies. Robinson highlights the witches' namelessness "because it reflects the general anonymity (in the broader sense of the term) of women and witches, not only in the original Earthsea trilogy, but in traditional fantasy and romance literature as a whole" (393). As Robinson's title, "The Violence of the Name: Patronymy in Earthsea," suggests, masculine coming-of-age rites that erase witches and mothers (and, I add, the influence and labor of their care work) perpetuate misogyny. Tenar faces that misogyny, implicitly and explicitly, throughout *Tehanu*. Neither a trained witch nor a "mere goodwife," Tenar presents interpretive difficulties for a culture that would prefer easy categorization; her failure to fit in elicits hostility and endangers her. On the road to visit her dying teacher, Tenar invokes Ogion's name as she passes a group of suspicious male travelers: "The men, mistaking effrontery for witchery, stood still. Ogion's name perhaps still held power. Or perhaps there was a power in Goha, or in the child." As she walks on, one man spits and says "[w]itch and her monster brat" (Le Guin, *Tehanu* 20). Aspen calls Tenar a witch, too just before he curses her:

> "Slander's cheap, and a woman's tongue worse than any thief. You come up here to make bad blood among the field hands, casting calumny and lies, the dragon-seed every witch sows behind her. Did you think I did not know you for a witch? When I saw that foul imp that clings to you, do you think I did not know how it was begotten, and for what purposes?" [Le Guin, *Tehanu* 141].

This passage contains Aspen's defense for the worker who raped and abused (or at least aided the rapist and abuser of) Therru. His statement illustrates Aspen's ignorance of care work; he cannot conceive of a relationship between Tenar and Therru that is not based on using the child. He refuses to consider that her speech might be true and fair because she is female, so instead of failing to listen well he twists her words. It does not matter to the men on the road or to Aspen that Tenar is not an officially trained or practicing witch, that her work is care work (mostly) without magical intervention. A powerful care worker seems an oxymoron in Earthsea, yet Tenar embodies power and care— or, rather, the power of care that ultimately upsets the power structure of Earthsea by positioning Therru as Archmage.

　　That kind of power is inherently threatening to mages like Aspen and the oppressive patriarchy he represents and sustains. It also subverts conventions of fantasy literature by redefining the hero and the heroic quest. As Lara Saguisag writes, "We have a protagonist, but she is no power-wielding hero; there is conflict, but it is not one of combat. *Tehanu* is populated by a community of women, and the book largely focuses on their concerns, their domesticities—women's work" (75). Saguisag's comment echoes Le Guin's own words about the writing process: "[m]odernist manuals of writing often conflate story with conflict. This reductionism reflects a culture that inflates aggression and competition while cultivating ignorance of other behavioral options" (Le Guin, *Steering the Craft* 146). *Earthsea's* author seems here to censure the generic conventions of fantasy literature as well, which relates to her motivations to revisit and revise Earthsea through *Tehanu*. Moving beyond a limited interpretation of conflict, Le Guin asserts other opportunities for growth within stories and life, like "relating, finding, losing, bearing, discovering, parting, changing. Change is the universal aspect of all these sources of story. Story is something moving, something happening, something or somebody changing" (Le Guin, *Steering the Craft* 146). Tenar's care work is not combative, but it is nonetheless threatening, as it establishes her as a person of power who cares for Therru, whose power is even greater. Their power thrives in a relational context, not a hierarchy but a reciprocal and predominantly feminine community that threatens wizards like Aspen by its very existence. As Sandra Lindlow writes of Earthsea, "when wizards describe women as unclean it may be a projection of blame due to *their own* unclean work, work that blurs the clear line between life and death" (emphasis in original 36). Yet Tenar's work also straddles the boundary between life and death; she and the other women and witches are ever-present at scenes of birth, death, and sickness, and their everyday work revolves around the sustenance of life. It is care work that makes the difference—care that separates Tenar's power from Aspen's representative cruelty.

Revising Care

Tehanu subverts the male-oriented hero tale through Tenar's care work, which redefines power through the lens of care and revises the kinds of power available to both women and men in Earthsea. The sought-after "woman on Gont" turns out to be both Tenar and Therru: Tenar because the king and his messengers seek her council and Therru because she is the future archmage. Yet it takes most of the novel to reveal Therru's true name and her destiny, in part because she deconstructs the hierarchies of power in Earthsea. As even Ged says,

> "A woman on Gont" can't become archmage. No woman can be archmage. She'd unmake what she became in becoming it. The Mages of Roke are men— their power is the power of men, their knowledge is the knowledge of men. Both manhood and magery are built on one rock: power belongs to men. If women had power, what would men be but women who can't bear children? And what would women be but men who can? [Le Guin, *Tehanu* 245].

Ged describes power here as something to own, a possession, a metaphor that relates to the social divisions between those who possess power and those who do not; the system Ged depicts here is dichotomous—masculinity, magery, and power in opposition to femininity, witchcraft, and weakness (as well as wickedness, as they say in Earthsea). Without those binaries, Ged sees only biology, but his questions also seem strange coming from a former mage who sacrificed all of his power to save Earthsea from evil and addressed to a powerful woman who can no longer bear children. Both of them sacrifice themselves in heroic acts that counter their culture's expectations of those who wield power. What, then, is the difference between Ged and Tenar if both hold power without magery or the ability to bear children? Tenar counters that "[r]eal power, real freedom, would lie in trust, not force" (Le Guin, Tehanu 247), asserting once again the primacy of relationships and care. Though Ged doesn't quite understand in this conversation, he adapts to Tenar's redefinition. As Yoshida Junko writes, by the end of *Tehanu*, Ged marries Tenar and adopts Therru, learning that "by nurturing and loving others he can reconcile his masculine identity with the feminine aspects buried within himself, such as the nurturing, intimate, and emotional, and thereby can heal his wound" (Junko 193). I would say that Ged's ability to be both "masculine" and "feminine" (to use Junko's words) illustrates the falseness of those binaries. Care work need not be an exclusively female realm, and it holds the potential to heal the care workers, those cared for, and Earthsea itself—as even a former archmage realizes.

Ged's choice to adopt Therru helps groom the child for her future as archmage, a major upheaval to the structures of power in Earthsea. Susan Bernardo and Graham Murphy write that "*Tehanu* creates the groundwork for women's progress in Earthsea by challenging the ideas and hatreds that have so long hemmed them in. Each of the first three Earthsea novels brings change, but the fourth brings that change to the domestic, political, and wizardly aspects of the world all at once" (142). Laura Comolettti and Michael Drout agree about the significance of *Tehanu's* conclusion, claiming "Tenar begins to bring about a revision or revolution in the gender order, through one act of caring and nurturing" (128). While these authors cite Tenar's rescue of Therru as the "one act," I maintain that it is many acts, along with the reorientation of the *Earthsea* series and the fantastic hero-tale as a genre, that bring about that revolution; it is a transformation ignited by bringing care work to the forefront of the genre and the novel. Comoletti and Drout explain the effects of such a revolution: "[n]ot content with merely incremental change in gender roles, or the promise of some far-off day when equality will be achieved, Le Guin modifies her social order right at the top" (129). Nearly every critic of *Tehanu* agrees that the book alters the world of Earthsea, not only in the fourth novel but by changing the readers' perspective on the entire series. *Tehanu's* tone, content, and protagonist shift the center of Earthsea away from Ged and magery to Tenar and care work, and Le Guin expresses the revision of her work as parallel to feminist movements. The author says, "thanks to the revisioning of gender called feminism, we can see the myth as a myth; a construct, which may be changed; an idea which may be rethought, made more true, more honest" (Le Guin, *Earthsea Revisioned* 17). Part of deconstructing gender myths includes destabilizing supposedly-static character(istics): Tenar as caretaker and wielder of power; Ged as depleted wizard and helpful husband; Therru/Tehanu as abused child and future archmage. Reframing the novel, the series, and the genre through the feminist ethic of care reveals the characters' complexity, their existence within a network of relationships founded on care and perpetuating care as an alternative and antidote to oppression.

Early in *Tehanu*, Tenar recognizes a "new thing," a change she muses upon: "[s]o she was a woman dragons would talk to. Was that the new thing, the folded knowledge, the light seed, that she felt in herself, waking beneath the small window that looked west?" (76). Tenar talks to dragons—the embodiment of power and magic in Earthsea—when she rescues Ged, just as Therru later talks to the same dragon when she saves her adoptive parents from Aspen's abuse (272). Kalessin, the dragon, frees Tenar and Ged and promises to return for Tehanu, saying to Tenar, "I give you my child, as you will give me yours" (278). The dragon's involvement in the plot could easily be viewed as a *deus ex machina*, but Kalessin's appearance also always coincides with acts of care, suggesting the link between true magic, true power, and the commitment to care work. Len Hatfield depicts *Tehanu* as a movement "from an ethics of rights to an ethics of responsibility" where, "[f]inally, in Earthsea, the marginalized speak, and men can become brothers (not masters) by learning to listen to and participate in the 'ordinary' community with their mothers and sisters" (61). While Hatfield's essay deals primarily with the subjugation of women and children and not specifically with an ethic of care, he too notices how the shifting focus of the novel alters the definition of heroism to include listening and community. *Tehanu* works toward an Earthsea that values care work without achieving full resolution of the gendered power imbalances. For instance, Tenar's relationship with her biological son Spark sharply contrasts her relationship with Therru. Tenar maintains the farmstead while her son works as a sailor: "A widow's tenure of her husband's property was contingent on there being no male heir or claimant. Flint's son the seaman was the heir, and Flint's widow was merely holding the farm for him. If she died, it would go to Clearbrook to hold for the heir; if Spark never claimed it, it would go to a distant cousin of Flint's" (Le Guin, *Tehanu* 237). When Spark returns, he never thanks his mother or acknowledges her work (indeed, he attributes it to the male farmhands 253–8), and he refuses to participate in "women's work" even though Ged does it (259). The irony of Spark's seafaring profession is, of course, the absence of women—a similarity to magery—so it seems likely that men on ship do care work too, when there aren't (or aren't allowed to be) women present. Care work only becomes "women's work" within a context of oppression, when it can be denigrated along with those who partake in it. There is nothing inherently gendered about many kinds of care work; so while care work defines Tenar's heroism and shifts the focus of the heroic tale in a specifically gendered way, it opens up the possibility of a male hero who cares, too, an alternative to the cruel bastions of patriarchy in Earthsea and beyond.

As feminist ethicist Margaret McLaren states, "[r]eclaiming care as a feminist virtue recognizes the value of care in a world that desperately needs individuals to perform more than the moral minimum" (112). Earthsea is undoubtedly such a world, just as it reflects and revises the places of care work and care workers in our own world. Reading *Tehanu* through the lens of the feminist ethic of care helps readers to imagine a transformed Earthsea with its Tenar as its unlikely hero who steadfastly cares simply because it is the good and right thing to do. McLaren further asserts "that care ought to be a *feminist* virtue. It is essential to helping us envision morally desirable alternatives that promote equality and emancipation" (112–3). Here McLaren, like Le Guin, moves beyond the false binary of masculine and feminine, relying instead upon the feminist deconstruction of care as "women's work." *Tehanu* affirms "women's work" as important without decontextualizing it and losing its potential to exploit and oppress. Care work makes Tenar vulnerable, but both her work and her vulnerability are inextricably intertwined with her femaleness. Failure to care would not protect Tenar, nor did it protect Therru; it would only inflict further damage, further suffering for the individuals and communities of Earthsea. Rita Manning, in her essay "Just Caring," poses the question "What are caring persons to do?" She responds, "[c]aring persons should try to respond to need by caring for, but they must pay attention to their own needs for care. They must navigate through an uncaring world without falling into total caring burnout" (52). Tenar can care because she participates in a community of care and care workers, most of whom are devalued, ignored, or likewise mistreated by the powerful people in Earthsea. Yet those relationships support Tenar and ultimately help her and Therru overthrow Aspen and the regime he represents. It is no coincidence that the king's messengers look for an anonymous "woman on Gont," since so many of the women on Gont support the protagonist of *Tehanu* and so few of them get any credit. *Tehanu* pays attention to the women of Gont, revealing their care work, like their hero Tenar, as both ordinary and extraordinary—care that can change the world.

WORKS CITED

Bernardo, Susan M., and Graham J. Murphy. *Ursula K. Le Guin: A Critical Companion.* Westport, CT: Greenwood Press, 2006. Print.

Bubeck, Diemut Grace. "Justice and the Labor of Care." *The Subject of Care: Feminist Perspectives on Dependency.* Eds. Eva Feder Kittay and Ellen K. Feder. New York: Rowman & Littlefield, 2002. 160–85. Print.

Clarke, Amy M. *Ursula K. Le Guin's Journey to Post-Feminism.* Jefferson, NC: McFarland, 2010. Print.

Comoletti, Laura B., and Michael DC Drout. "How They Do Things with Words: Language, Power, Gender, and the Priestly Wizards of Ursula K. Le Guin's Earthsea Books." *Children's Literature* 29.1 (2001): 113–41. *ProQuest.* Web.

Fisher, Bernice, and Joan Tronto. "Toward a Feminist Theory of Caring." *Circles of Care: Work and Identity in Women's Lives.* Eds. Emily K. Abel and Margaret K. Nelson. Albany: State University of New York Press, 1990. 35–62. Print.

Friedman, Marilyn. *What Are Friends For? Feminist Perspectives on Personal Relationships and Moral Theory.* Ithaca: Cornell University Press, 1993. Print.

Gilligan, Carol. *In a Different Voice: Psychological Theory and Women's Development.* Cambridge: Harvard University Press, 1982. Print.

Hatfield, Len. "From Master to Brother: Shifting the Balance of Authority in Ursula K. Le Guin's Farthest Shore and Tehanu." *Children's Literature* 21.1 (1993): 43–65. *Project MUSE.* Web.

Held, Virginia. *The Ethics of Care: Personal, Political, and Global.* New York: Oxford University Press, 2006. Print.

Junko, Yoshida. "The 'Masculine Mystique' Revisioned in *The Earthsea Quartet*." *The Presence of the Past in Children's Literature*. Ed. Ann Lawson Lucas. Westport, CT: Praeger, 2003. 187–93. Print.

Koehn, Daryl. *Rethinking Feminist Ethics: Care, Trust, and Empathy*. New York, Routledge, 1998. Print.

Le Guin, Ursula K. *Dancing at the Edge of the World: Thoughts on Words, Women, Places*. New York: Grove Press, 1997. Print.

_____. *Earthsea Revisioned*. Cambridge: Children's Literature New England, 1993. Print.

_____. *Steering the Craft: Exercises and Discussions on Story Writing for the Lone Navigator or the Mutinous Crew*. Portland, OR: The Eighth Mountain Press, 1998. Print.

_____. *Tehanu*. New York: Aladdin Paperbacks, 2001. Print.

Lindow, Sandra J. "Becoming Dragon: The Transcendence of the Damaged Child in the Fiction of Ursula K. Le Guin." *Extrapolation* 44.1 (2003): 32–44. *ProQuest*. Web.

Littlefield, Holly. "Unlearning Patriarchy: Ursula Le Guin's Feminist Consciousness in The Tombs of Atuan and Tehanu." *Extrapolation* 36.3 (1995): 244–58. *Humanities International Complete*. Web.

Mains, Christine, Brad J. Ricca, Holly Hassel, and Lynda Rucker. "Heroes or Sheroes." *Women in Science Fiction and Fantasy*. Vol. 1. Ed. Robin Anne Reid. Westport, CT: Greenwood Press, 2009. 179–201. Print.

Manning, Rita. "Just Caring." *Explorations in Feminist Ethics: Theory and Practice*. Eds. Eve Browning Cole and Susan Coultrap-McQuin. Bloomington: Indiana University Press, 1992. 45–54. Print.

Manning, Rita C. *Speaking from the Heart: A Feminist Perspective on Ethics*. Lanham, MD: Rowman & Littlefield, 1992.

McLaren, Margaret A. "Feminist Ethics: Care as a Virtue." *Feminist Doing Ethics*. Eds. Peggy DesAutels and Joanne Waugh. New York: Rowman & Littlefield, 2001. 101–117. Print.

McLean, Susan. "The Power of Women in Ursula K. Le Guin's Tehanu." *Extrapolation* 38.2 (1997): 110–118. *Humanities International Complete*. Web.

Mills, Alice. "Burning Women in Ursula K. Le Guin's Tehanu, the Last Book of Earthsea." *New York Review of Science Fiction* 7 (1995): 2–7.

Noddings, Nel. *Caring: A Feminine Approach to Ethics & Moral Education*. Berkeley: University of California Press, 1984. Print.

Nodelman, Perry. "Reinventing the Past: Gender in Ursula K. Le Guin's Tehanu and the Earthsea 'Trilogy.'" *Children's Literature* 23.1 (1995): 179–201. *Project Muse*. Web.

Robinson, Christopher L. "The Violence of the Name: Patronymy in Earthsea." *Extrapolation* 49.3 (2008): 385–409. *ProQuest Research Library*. Web.

Saguisag, Lara Q. "Outside Authority: Reflections on Gender and Education in Tehanu." *Journal of English Studies and Comparative Literature* 7.1 (2004): 74–88. Web.

"Be wise. Be brave. Be tricky": Neil Gaiman's Extraordinarily Ordinary Coraline

Melissa Wehler

Coraline, Neil Gaiman's female hero in the dark fantasy novel by the same name, unlocks a mysterious door in her new flat's drawing room and discovers an alternate world where a beldam called "other mother" has taken on her real mother's likeness. The other mother plots to trap Coraline in an uncanny world where she will slowly devour the young protagonist body and soul. As she prepares for battle with other mother, Coraline reminds herself: "when you're scared but you still do it anyway, *that's* brave" (59). As her self-affirming conviction suggests, Coraline becomes powerful enough to defeat other mother not because she is different from everyone else but because, like everyone else, she is afraid. By acknowledging the normalcy of her fear, Coraline is also able to acknowledge her extraordinary strength: "*I will be brave*, thought Coraline. *No, I* am *brave*" (Gaiman emphasis in original, 61). Her inner-strength allows her to outwit the cunning other mother and save herself, her parents, and several other children whom the beldam has captured. She rejects the "sick and evil and weird" (Gaiman 78) agency of archetypes like other mother and the pantheon of fantasy's negative female characters—the greedy stepmothers, jealous sisters and stepsisters, and wicked witches—in favor of a power that derives not from supernatural gifts but from being extraordinarily ordinary. She also does not find power through princes, knights, or fairy godmothers, but through a journey of self-discovery and affirmation. Trial by trial, she consciously and creatively takes possession of her life and identity, comes to feel safe, accepted, and loved, and brings fulfillment to herself and those around her, offering young readers, both male and female, child and adult, a progressive model for heroism.

Because it deals with a story populated with an other mother and an other father, an oddly named protagonist, and absent parental figures, *Coraline* scholarship has mostly trended toward psychoanalytic readings of Gaiman's young female hero. Richard Gooding, Vivienne Muller, and David Rudd, for instance, examine Coraline's psychological development as she does battle with the tricks and challenges of other mother's world, grounding their readings in the concept of the uncanny and Freud's theorization of otherness that is certainly applicable to other mother's world.[1] Likewise, Elizabeth Parsons, Naarah Sawers, and Kate McInally use a psychoanalytic approach to describe the ways Coraline's maturation is circumscribed in the novel and how this negatively impacts her ability to create a fully realized identity (372–3). Kara K. Keeling and Scott Pollard also examine Coraline's identity vis-à-vis discussions of maturity and adulthood. Using Lacan's oral-sadistic theorization, Keeling and Pollard examine how Coraline's relationships to food and orality allow her to navigate the problematic adult landscape of other mother's realm (3). Certainly, such psychoanalytic readings make sense given that themes of identity, maturation, and development underpin *Coraline* and many other such *bildungsroman* fantasy works.

Coraline scholarship, however, has been almost universally dependent on psychoanalysis in its discussions, and as result, has tended to focus on similar reference points in the text. This focus has left much of the complicated narrative unexplored. By using close reading and literary analysis to fill in some of the critical gaps, this essay most notably argues that Coraline develops into a self-affirming female hero who serves as a model not only for Gaiman's readers but for the literary fantasy genre.

"Be wise": The Female Hero's Extraordinary Creativity

Gaiman positions Coraline as a conduit through which the reader comes to understand the surprising characteristics of her or his own imaginative capabilities. For the author's part, he views Coraline as "a bit [my daughter], a bit me, but mostly herself" ("Neil Gaiman"). In another interview, he explores Coraline's character further, saying:

> She's a smart kid and she doesn't have magic powers. She's not the chosen one. There's nothing cool and magical going on. She's just like you, and she's going to fight this thing and she's going to win. That, for me, is the important thing [Gaiman, "Interview"].

As Coraline learns to become the protagonist of her story, she passes along crucial heroic philosophies centered on the importance of personal affirmation. One of the ghost children Coraline eventually saves gives her the narrative's defining mantra: "Be wise. Be brave. Be tricky" (145). These words fittingly serve to create the three basic tenants of what eventually becomes her heroic philosophy.

When scholars consider the role of wisdom in children's fantasy literature, emphasis is usually placed on the maturation of the character from child to adult or from innocence to experience. For some *Coraline* critics, however, the character's maturation is informed—and complicated—by Gaiman's seeming insistence that she learns and subscribes to stereotypical gender roles.[2] Christine Wilkie-Stibbs, for instance, describes how the "wisdom" Coraline gains is how to operate within a patriarchal system and how in the end, she "has been metaphorically put back into her box and firmly (re)placed in the role of domesticated, nurturing female in the grip of male power" (50). For such critics, Coraline's learned wisdom becomes a matter of learning to navigate the complex adult world of circumscribed gender identity and then successfully perform that identity through domesticity. I would argue, however, that for Coraline, wisdom means learning how to creatively overcome life's challenges even (and especially) if that means acting like a child.

Towards the beginning of the twentieth century, British writers began rethinking the role of imagination in the development of children, creating a paradigmatic shift that Rebecca Knuth's survey of over two hundred and fifty years of British children's literature suggests reflects the social attitudes concerning children and childhood. According to Knuth, children's literature from the period shows how "some adults began to wonder whether childhood, with its special access to the imagination and play, was not in fact a better way of being; for adulthood, with its curtailment of imagination and renunciation of play, left humans undeniably diminished" (111). The idea that children have "special" access to imagination is exactly the issue at stake in the novel. Like her young readers, Coraline does not see her access to imagination and play as particularly "special." Instead, she uses it as a lens to navigate obstacles and solve problems much like the adults in the novel use computers and car keys. However, like the adults that Knuth describes, adult readers view the kind of creativity in the novel as "special" precisely because adulthood has "diminished" their capacity for creativity. Gaiman unflinchingly writes with both audiences as his book interviews attests, and using Coraline's "double audience" (Gooding 391), Gaiman exploits the seemingly paradoxical position of the imagination as extraordinary in its ordinariness.[3]

For most of the narrative, Coraline's enactment of "being wise" is marked as much by her failures as it is by her successes. Throughout the narrative, she often discounts the warnings of other characters such as Mr. Bobo's mice, the black cat, and Misses Spink and Forcible. Instead of learning from these missteps, she wallows in her failure: "Now she felt nothing but cold loss. She had failed the ghost children. She had failed her parents. She had failed herself, failed everything" (122). Narratively, these episodes function as benchmarks for Coraline's individual maturation and her developing identity. They demonstrate that seeking wisdom is not a linear processes towards maturation, but rather a circuitous path punctuated by success and failure. To beat the beldam, Coraline must learn to accept the assistance of other others and harness her power—in this case, her imagination—in order to continue her progress towards self-actualization and fulfillment.

Driven by the banalities of everyday life, the perceived neglect of her parents, and her anxieties about a new home and new school, Coraline seeks adventure and transformation through imagination. The reader first meets a protagonist who longs to be different. As she shops with her mother for school clothes, Coraline insists that she must have the "Day-Glo green gloves" because "'everybody at school's got gray blouses and everything. Nobody's got green gloves. I could be the only one'" (23). When this simple rebellion fails to persuade her mother and win her the coveted gloves, she determines to save the outing with a leap into the extraordinary. Coraline wanders off while her mother picks out the abhorrent gray blouses only to return with a fantastic story about adventure: "'I was kidnapped by aliens,' said Coraline. 'They came down from outer space with ray guns, but I fooled them by wearing a wig and laughing in a foreign accent, and I escaped'" (24). Of course, this wild story receives no reaction, as her mother is much too busy with the particular issue of hair clips to entertain such nonsense. Her mother, however, is not the real audience for this story: the reader is. This seemingly simplistic interchange between imaginative daughter and distracted mother provides a lighthearted yet poignant example of Coraline's ability to turn the monotony of everyday errands into an extraordinary adventure where she saves the world from extraterrestrial invaders. In the shopping scene, Coraline learns her most valuable lesson as an author-ity figure: see your ordinary world as extraordinary, and it becomes extraordinary.

Coraline's ability to manipulate her reality vis-à-vis her imagination begins as a delightful distraction that becomes increasingly dangerous not only for her, but also for the other characters. For instance, once she discovers that her parents have been "grown-up-napped" (54) by other mother, Coraline must find a way to translate her imaginative abilities that she had been using for entertainment towards a singular, humanitarian purpose. She is certainly more than capable of growing and adapting, which is perhaps best represented by her story about learning to ride a bicycle: "back then, in with all the cuts and scrapes (her knees had scab on top of scabs) she had had a feeling of achievement. She was learning something, doing something, she had not known how to do" (122). The story of Coraline's many ill-fated attempts at learning to control her bicycle symbolizes the very same evolution of her imaginative wisdom: she learns about it, uses it, and then teaches it to do something it had not previously known how to do.

As Coraline's imagination becomes more powerful, her creative abilities transcend the immaterial world of storytelling and begin transforming her physical reality. The reader watches as Coraline transforms several seemingly mundane items into powerful, supernatural totems including her mother's old, black key and the dead-end drawing room door. In the hands and perspectives of others in the story, these items remain nothing more than simple utilitarian objects, and several, including the key and the door, have even ceased to serve their intended function. Coraline's mother demonstrates this line of thinking entirely as she begrudgingly selects "the oldest, biggest, blackest, rustiest key" from her string and proceeds to unlock the door in the drawing room, which has been completely bricked up (8). Gaiman's superlative description of the key—"oldest, biggest, blackest, rustiest"—draws the reader's attention to how discarded and disregarded these objects actually are. Coraline's mother's complete indifference to these useless objects is further emphasized as she forgets to re-lock the door, saying, "Why should I lock it? [...] It doesn't go anywhere" (9). These items, like all tools, cease having value as soon as they cease serving a purpose. In Coraline's hands, however, these (seemingly) broken tools become the two most powerful objects in the world, capable of creating, destroying, trapping, and freeing beings from another realm. Like Coraline, these items have been discarded by the adult world. She feels a unique kinship with these so-called useless trinkets and sees the value in them much as she wishes the adult world, and more specifically her mother, would see the value in her. Thus, while other mother certainly plays a part in creating the alternate world, it is Coraline's imaginative ability that transforms these useless objects into these extraordinary totems capable of unleashing the only other creature in the story whose creativity rivals her own.

As Coraline begins to harness the agency of her creativity, Gaiman forces her to confront the beldam and her imposing imagination. Like Coraline, other mother is a storyteller and attempts to use her linguistic prowess to gain control over Coraline. For instance, the beldam takes her to the other world's hallway mirror and shows the protagonist a scene that is supposedly taking place in her "real-world" home. Coraline's real parents appear to be happily coming back from a "fine holiday" expounding how they can now "do all the things we always wanted to do, like go abroad, but were prevented from doing by having a little daughter" (62). Coraline rejects the story, but not because she disagrees with the premise. Indeed, Gaiman describes how this story produces "tiny doubt inside her, like a maggot in an apple core" (63). Rather, Coraline rejects the story in the mirror because she does not "see" what the beldam hopes to show her (63). Unlike Coraline, the beldam cannot successfully create reality through storytelling, and just like her other world, she only creates enough to give the impression of substance and purpose in an effort to deceive Coraline. Coraline's rejection of the story—and of other mother—is vindicated just a few pages later when the beldam accidentally slips and says, "Mirrors [...] are never to be trusted" (77). When Coraline looks into the mirror, she does not "see" the scene the way the beldam wants her to because her story features flat characters, sophomoric dialogue, and a contrived plot that are so egregious that a child, especially one as inventive as Coraline, can see through them. Gaiman uses this un-seeable story to demonstrate other mother's rather limited imagination, and by extension, the circumscribed agency that comes from manipulation rather than creation.

Gaiman often reminds the reader that the beldam uses her power by manipulating her environment rather than by creating or transforming it as Coraline does. For instance, other father tells her, "There isn't anywhere but here. This is all she made: the house, the grounds, and the people in the house" (71). When Coraline explores the other world, she learns that this is precisely the case. After walking only a little way from the house, she discovers: "The world she was walking through was a pale nothing-ness, like a blank sheet of paper or an enormous, empty white room. It had no temperature, no smell, no texture, and no taste" (73). When Coraline asks if the beldam has created this world, the black cat responds coldly: "Made it, found it—what's the difference?" (75). Despite the black cat's flippant comment, the difference between making it and finding it is exactly the difference between Coraline and other mother. Coraline's imagination has the power to transform and invent while the beldam's creativity is limited solely to copying and recopying. After Coraline untangles the beldam's rather childish tricks, she comes to the same conclusion: "Other mother could not create. She could only transform, and twist, and change" (124). Coraline's imagination allows her to see through the beldam's inventions and strengthens her resilience against such deceits. In this scene, Coraline recognizes that other mother's supernatural powers are her greatest weakness because unlike her own transformative imagination, the beldam can only distort what is already there.

However, of all of the examples of Coraline's imaginative prowess, it is the so-called "stone with a hole in it" that becomes the most potent metaphor for Coraline's ability to transform the ordinary into the extraordinary (Gaiman 21). Coraline receives this seemingly valueless item when she visits her eccentric neighbors, Misses Spink and Forcible. These two retired starlets, who still entertain grandiose illusions of themselves, their careers, and their possible return to the stage, read Coraline's tea leaves, and upon determining that she is in mortal danger, want to provide her with a protective totem. Gaiman describes their treasure trove of useless items as including "a tiny china duck, a thimble, a strange little brass coin, two paper clips and a stone with a hole in it" (21). It is this final object that Miss Spink hands to Coraline, which she accepts. In the world of bricked-up doorways and rusted keys, this amulet remains nothing more than "a stone with a hole in it." In Coraline's world of doorways as portals and black keys as traps, however, the stone becomes not only powerful protection against the tricks of other mother, but more importantly, it allows Coraline to see through the so-called mist of the other world to what may be called—albeit vaguely—"the truth" about other mother and herself.

In this other world, "a stone with a hole in it" again becomes the medium through which Coraline ultimately transforms her imaginative abilities into the true wisdom of her self-affirming philosophy: the ordinary *is* extraordinary. After other mother leaves her alone to find her parents and the souls of the trapped children, Coraline—for the first time in the narrative—must rely solely on her ingenuity to solve the very crisis her inquisitive imagination has created. She feels in her pocket for the "reassuring shape of the stone with a hole in it," and having thus been reassured by this seemingly ordinary object, she holds it in front of her "as if she were holding a gun" (95). The first transformation of the stone is from a "reassuring shape" that calms and protects Coraline into the "gun," which she holds in front of her as if to dare other mother to cross her or betray their agreement. The initially surprising imagery of this naïve and thoughtful protagonist engaging in what can only be categorized as modern-day swordplay is at its surface rather alarming and appears to disrupt Coraline's ethos as a wise, rather than violent, champion.

Gaiman has not established Coraline as a hero who accomplishes her goals through violence nor has he established the stone as a medium through which Coraline might undertake such violent action. Yet, the reader understands Coraline's interpretation (or rather misinterpretation) of the stone's power. She is, after all, an unlikely champion in an unlikely world: an ordinary girl battling a beldam in a quest to save not only herself, but also her parents and a trio of lost souls. Her world has taught her that in such cases the hero pulls a gun, shoots the "bad guys," and wins the day. In this case, however, the hero is a protagonist alone and afraid, and fighting to save herself and the very people who are supposed to be protecting her. In this way, the image of Coraline with a gun demonstrates the problematic way that children are often called upon to "act" like adults both in literature and in life. The image quickly melts away—the other mother's world is not the "real world," the "stone with a hole in it" is not a gun, and Coraline is not that kind of hero—but the real violence and danger it symbolizes never really disappears.

When the stone-turned-gun fails to reassure Coraline in the same way the "stone with a hole in it" had, Coraline allows the stone to transform yet again, only this time, because she has understood the stone's real power—the power of reassurance—she is able to harness and use it to her advantage. After looking in the mirror, Coraline notices that the stone is emitting a powerful green light. Disbelieving, she looks back down at her hand "surprised" and thinks: "it is just a stone with a hole in it, a nondescript brown pebble" (95). This scene is particularly poignant because as Coraline examines this pebble in her hands, she is also examining herself in the mirror, asking the audience to draw the parallels between the stone's transformation into a powerful totem and her continued maturation. In Coraline's hands, the "nondescript brown pebble" becomes a bright beacon of light and hope in a world that is "gray and colorless, like a pencil drawing" (97). For the other missing and trapped characters, Coraline and her incredible imagination are also beacons of light—and not just any light, a Day-Glo green light, the same color of the gloves at the department store where Coraline unknowingly begins her journey. Coraline's ability to transform the stone into the lens through which she discovers the souls of the missing children becomes a powerful testament to the agency of imagination and Coraline's own wisdom to see the extraordinary in the ordinary.

"Be brave": The Female Hero's Ordinary Empathy

While Coraline's imaginative wisdom allows her to think her way into and out of the beldam's various traps, it is her empathy that pushes her to accept her unlikely place as that narrative's hero. The reader is told many times throughout the story how unlikely it is that Coraline should discover herself in the position to be brave. The narrator describes Coraline as "small for her age" in a way that sounds, at best, a way to differentiate her from the novel's adult worlds, and at worst, a marked disadvantage in said worlds (Gaiman 95, 121). The narrator also emphasizes that Coraline is not particularly brave in a conventional hero sense. She is often frightened even as she is telling herself she is not: "[Coraline] hugged herself, and told herself that she was brave, and she almost believed herself," and then only a few pages later, Gaiman has her repeat it: "*I'm not frightened*, she told herself, and she thought it she knew that it was true" (114, 117 emphasis in original). Yet, despite all of the various internal foibles and external setbacks, Coraline perseveres—not because she is frightened or fears she will fail, but because she is frightened to fail herself and others.

Empathy, as a specifically heroic attribute, is perhaps not as well explored in children's literature as other qualities such as courage or physical prowess because it requires both the hero and the reader to understand and respond to the needs of others in complicated ways. That is not to say, however, that this concept has been completely unexplored in children's literature. Scholars have often discussed J. K. Rowling's Hermione Granger as a character that exhibits an extraordinary capacity for empathy. Describing the concept of "ethics of caring" (231) in relationship to Hermione, Eliza T. Dresang uses the work of Carol Gilligan to explain that for female characters,

> the concept of morality is concerned with the activity of care and that moral development centers around understanding of responsibility and relationships. Men, on the other hand, understand the morality of fairness and tie moral development to the understanding of rights and rules. In essence this boils down to care versus justice and a focus on other versus structures [232].

Like Rowling's Hermione, Coraline exhibits a sense of maturity far beyond what writers and readers typically expect from these young heroes, and it is this maturity that gives these two female heroes the capacity to understand the perspective and position of others. The ethics of caring is omnipresent in Coraline precisely because she feels a unique sense of responsibility to those around her including the ghost children, the black cat, and even her neglectful parents. Indeed, the utter lack of supervision and attention from her parents only helps to throw Coraline's maturity and empathy into ever-sharper relief. Coraline's ethics of caring means that she acts like an adult even (and perhaps especially) when the adults have lost all sense of understanding and compassion.

Perhaps the most persuasive examples of Coraline's empathetic bravery are her various interactions with the ghost children. Trapped by other mother in the hallway mirror, these children have been consumed by the greedy beldam into near extinction. Indeed, when Coraline first meets them, she is immediately moved by their impoverished circumstances: "The voice sounded so sad that Coraline put out a hand to the place where the voice was coming from, and she found a cold hand, and she squeezed it tightly" (83). This simple, empathetic gesture comforts the ghost child and gives him the strength to "[glow] a little more brightly in the darkness" (84). These children have lost not only their substance, but the very markers of their identities: their names. Seeing these nameless, hollow children moves Coraline to propose several plans for their escape, but each one is met with sad dejection. The only possible solution is that Coraline must discover their "secret hearts," which the beldam has hidden (85). Despite her own apprehensions about challenging other mother, Coraline draws bravery from seeing the plight of these forgotten children. The ghost children, however, are not the only lost, forgotten, and discarded characters in the novel from which she draws her empathetic bravery.

Coraline also exemplifies the power of empathy when she comes across the inhuman wreckage that once was her other father. After some prodding by other mother, Coraline goes into the empty flat of her multi-family home and down into the basement. While Coraline is fairly convinced that this is nothing more than a trap, she feels compelled to go, and as she enters the basement, Coraline sees something lurking in the corner: "The thing was white, and huge, and swollen. *Monstrous*, thought Coraline, *but also miserable*" (111). She learns that the "thing" is the discarded other father. As her description suggests, the "thing" obviously scares her, but she does not allow those feelings to distract her from its clear and utter suffering. She is able to easily, yet forcefully, dissect the difference between something that is monstrous and something that is miserable. In the world of fantasy, many "things" that are monstrous are inherently dangerous. In Coraline's world, however, the monstrous body of the other father symbolizes brutality, inhumanity, and misuse: "You're just a thing she made and then threw away" (111). Coraline uniquely understands other father's fate because like him, she will be thrown away once other mother has finished with her. In this way, Coraline's empathy is the antithesis of other mother's callousness. Even as the other father urges her to run away, Coraline refuses to leave what was once something like her father, and what is now a miserable copy. She tells him to fight other mother's influence: "'You *can*,' said Coraline. 'Be brave'" (112 emphasis in original). While the other father cannot be brave, Coraline is able to draw strength from seeing the thing's misery and not wanting to share its fate: "Either she could scream and try to run away, and be chased around a badly lit cellar by the huge grub thing, be chased until it caught her. Or she could do something else. So she did something else" (112). By taking his initial advice to run, Coraline's decision to "do something else" is the most empathetic act she can do on behalf of the creature that was once her other father. Her empathy cannot save him, but meeting the other father and seeing his misery does push her to continue her quest to save the others, no matter how terrified she may be.

As a testament to the power of Coraline's empathetic bravery, she does ultimately triumph over other mother, but only with the help of those very characters she tries to save. After winning her exploring game by locating the "secret hearts" of the ghost children as well as the essence of her "grown-up-napped" parents, Coraline travels back through the portal with the treacherous beldam swiftly on her heels. When the moment of her escape seems imminent, Coraline discovers that she is exhausted by the other world's trials and challenges and lacks the strength to shut the drawing room door and trap other mother permanently. Coraline cries out to her spectral allies who she senses floating around her: "'Help me, please,' she said. 'All of you'" (133) and promises once more, "We're going to go home[...]. We are. Help me" (134). Through repetition and urgency, Gaiman here emphasizes the importance of "we." Like empathy, Gaiman suggests that bravery can only be accomplished with the help of others.[4] The word "help" here is also reinforced through repetition, demonstrating Coraline's needful reliance on the very people she is attempting to save. Like Rowling's Heromine, Coraline's vulnerability and dependency lend her particular brand of heroism a literary ethos meant to appeal to a readership for which larger-than-life gestures are anathema to their everyday struggles.

In order to defeat the beldam, Coraline must be willing to accept that she is—as we all are—a small part of a larger "we." The "we" here is important because it shows how the assistance of these spectral allies only multiplies Coraline's inherent convictions: "The other people in the corridor—three children, two adults—were somehow too insubstantial to touch the door. But their hands closed about hers, as she pulled on the big iron door handle, and suddenly she felt strong" (133–4). Here, Coraline "suddenly feels strong" because she has the power of the family she has created in the other world—the other children—putting their hands around hers. Again, the reader sees Gaiman defining Coraline's bravery not as the effort of an extraordinary *individual* but of an extraordinarily ordinary *community*. Of course, this community only exists because of Coraline and her extraordinary capacity for empathy. She gives the ghost children the strength to "glow a little more brightly in the darkness" (84); she saves her parents through her creative, impromptu problem-solving; and she brings all of her allies together by promising that with their help, "we" will go home (134).

Ultimately, Coraline's empathy allows her to become a conduit for her own salvation. Coraline's exploring game with other mother allows her not just to collect the "secret hearts" of the ghost children and the essences of her parents; the exploring game also allows her to collect people. It is fair to say that Coraline touches many characters throughout the novel, some of whom she cannot save (the other father); some of whom she saves and who save her (the ghost children, her parents, and the black cat.) As other mother threateningly moves toward her in the corridor between the worlds, Coraline is able to call upon these characters for help, and in a particularly emotive scene, the narrator describes how "They moved through her, then: ghost hands lent her strength that she no longer possessed" (134). Here the narrator offers a tangible description of empathy in action. She literally senses the ghosts moving through her, feeling their touch as they all grab her hand simultaneously and pull in the same direction. Coraline gives herself over to the power of these others as she herself reaches her physical nadir and demonstrates for her audience an act of incredible bravery.

The scene itself symbolizes how the hero's journey towards self-actualization is not a selfish act, but one that requires and benefits from the assistance of others. Coraline's use of "we" as she battles the beldam also suggests that in this other world, she has momentarily turned away from the adamancy of her individuality that she had in the "real world." Taking a hostile and defensive tone, Coraline was constantly forced to assert identity to the adults in the novel: "'It's Coraline. Not Caroline. Coraline'" (4). As often happens in the "real world," Coraline's name is her identity. In the tunnel between the other world and the "real world," her identity merges with her spectral allies and becomes a literal "we": a body inhabited by multiple beings simultaneous. In so doing, Coraline sacrifices her selfhood—and her previously held conceptions about her identity—for the salvation of those she loves. When she emerges from the tunnel, she does so as a Coraline who asserts her*self* to the adult world instead of just her name, which is extraordinary brave.

"Be tricky": The Cunning Female Hero

The final tenant of Coraline's heroic mantra, "be tricky," suggests that whenever wisdom and bravery fail—and they both ultimately do—a hero must rely on cunning. Trickery is perhaps a characteristic more often assigned to the villain than the hero. With its connotations of dishonesty, fraudulence, and deception, Gaiman's encouragement of Coraline and her young readers to "be tricky" appears to be an instigation to be destructive. However, in the world of the other mother, Coraline faces a foe that is not only willing to use trickery, but revels in any opportunity to do so. Like the reader's own world, the world of the other mother is not always a fair place, and sometimes even heroes must use a trick to survive.

Throughout the exploration game, Coraline constantly reminds the beldam to "play fair" (98) just as the other characters warn Coraline that she will not (65, 124). Other mother tricks Coraline into the basement trap where the other father waits to attack her, and even after Coraline appears to defeat her, other mother's right hand—the one she swears by—comes to steal the drawing room door's big, black key, in order to let herself out. Muller argues that Gaiman's description of other mother's trickery upholds many of the common stereotypes associated with women particularly in the fantasy genre, "includ-[ing] the wicked stepmother, the childless hag, the pre–Oedipal mother, the non-biological mother, the spinster, the 'monstrous feminine' (Creed) mother and the powerful Medusa figure" ("Same Old"). Other mother's problematic villainy does indeed warrant such critics, but her traditional characterization substantiates her as a powerful and dangerous enemy. Coraline lacks the super-natural advantages of her villainous foil, and therefore, must defeat her using nothing more than her own strengths and abilities, which she does by using other mother's best weapon—her cunning—against her.

Coraline's dealings with other mother, the only other character to match her in terms of inventiveness and guile, demonstrate the continuing develop-ment and progressive maturation of her inner strength. For instance, when Coraline challenges other mother to a game, the beldam inquires, "But what kind of game shall it be? A riddle game? A test of knowledge or of skill?" to which Coraline replies, "an exploring game [...] a finding-things game" (92). While Coraline immediately second-guesses this decision as the beldam reacts enthusiastically, the decision itself demonstrates Coraline's cleverness. First, the exploring game obviously plays toward Coraline's strength as an explorer, which the narrator introduces in the opening pages of the novel: "that was how she spent her first two weeks in the house—exploring the garden and the grounds" (6–7). Second, since it is her game, Coraline gets to decide the rules and the rewards, which she does to her own advantage as Danya David describes: "Through her ability to negotiate language, Coraline is ultimately able to manipulate her captor" ("Extraordinary Navigators"). Third, by choosing the exploring game, Coraline rejects the "riddle game" or the "test of knowledge" that play to other mother's sphinxlike abilities. Much like deciding her own rules, this maneuver allows Coraline to reclaim agency from other mother.

Finally, just as the exploring game plays to her strengths, Coraline's rejection of the other games demonstrates her understanding of her own limitations. She does not choose a "test of skill" not only because she is "small for her age," but because Coraline's heroic bravery is less physical than it is intellectual in her ability to find her inner strength to save those she loves. Thus, when she finds that her other skills fail her, Coraline exhibits enough wisdom and bravery to rely upon her cunning.

It is important to note here that Coraline progressively matures as a hero, and thus, is not always quite the match for the beldam, especially as it comes to trickery. For instance, when Coraline determines the parameter of their game, she demands that the beldam swear that she will not cheat. Other mother invokes an everyday oath perhaps more typical of a schoolyard pact: "'I swear it on my own mother's grave" (93). Coraline then asks, "'Does she have a grave?'" to which the beldam sincerely responds, "'Oh, yes,' said other mother, 'I put her in there myself. And when I found her trying to crawl out, I put her back'" (93). Other mother weaves her words very carefully here in order to set a linguistic trap for Coraline. Coraline, however, rejects the proposed oath because it sounds so near to cheating. Other mother's second proposal—to swear by her right hand—ends up being a much more dangerous proposition than the one that Coraline rejects since it is her right hand that later escapes through the portal with Coraline and attacks her. The beldam proves more cunning than Coraline when they seal the terms of the game precisely because Coraline's trickery is grounded in creative invention, unlike other mother, whose trickery is more aptly categorized as artful deception.

Certainly, Coraline's rejection of other mother's deceitfulness and her desire to set her own rules and boundaries demonstrate the progress of her "be tricky" mantra, but it is her use of "protective coloration" that cements her position as the novel's real trickster figure. The reader is initially introduced to the concept of "protective coloration" through what appears to be an interesting, though unnecessary, aside. In the opening pages, the narrator describes how the bored Coraline happens upon a nature television program: "Eventually, she found something to watch: it was the last half of a natural history program about something called protective coloration. She watched animals, birds, and insects which disguised themselves as leaves or twig or other animals to escape from things that could hurt them" (7). Perhaps, for the particularly astute reader, these lines act as foreshadowing, but mostly they are a part of series of everyday nothings that Coraline uses to fill her rainy day. Like many random occurrences in the narrative, Gaiman shows Coraline fashioning this happenstance into something extraordinary. Here Gaiman positions trickery, even more than bravery and wisdom, as something that anyone can learn—as Coraline does—through the everyday activities, including flipping through the television channels. Thus, for Coraline, even ordinary knowledge must be applied in extraordinary ways.

The next reference to "protective coloration" is when Coraline grapples with other mother's escaped right hand in its desperate attempt to recapture the big, black key that has locked the beldam on the other side of the drawing room door. Coraline devises a particularly cunning plan where she will set up a doll's tea party over a dangerous and conveniently deep abandoned well. When her mother inquires as to her sudden interest in her previously discarded dolls, Coraline simply replies "protective coloration" (153), which, of course, means so little to her mother that she does not inquire further. For Coraline, however, this small memory of a natural survival tactic may mean the difference between victory and defeat, or perhaps even life and some kind of living death. When other mother's hand goes for the key strategically placed in the middle of a seemingly innocent, ordinary tablecloth, the hand falls down into the abandoned well—ultimately fooled and defeated by Coraline's cunning use of "protective coloration" (158–159).

Coraline's use of "protective coloration" is also particularly important to her maturation into the narrative's a hero. Much of her becoming a hero is the result of heeding the advice of others: she learns bravery through the example of her father, accepts the protective stone from Misses Spink and Forcible, gladly heeds the advice of the ghost children, and openly asks for the physical assistance of the souls in the tunnel between worlds. In the final test of wills between her and other mother's right hand, however, Coraline is most decidedly alone. Her parents show no signs of remembering their time trapped in the beldam's snow globe, the ghost children have all moved on, and even her confidante, the black cat, has disappeared. Coraline, armed only with the knowledge and skills she has acquired to this point, must turn her ordinary abilities into extraordinary ones and fend off an enemy that is both powerful and supernatural. Thus, while wisdom and bravery feature prominently in Coraline's ultimate defeat of the beldam, it is trickery more than anything that finally frees her from other mother's literal and figurative grasp.

Finally, it should be noted that Coraline's heroic mantra—"Be wise. Be brave. Be tricky"—directly contrasts with the narrative's other predominant philosophy: other mother's "sick and evil and weird" agency (Gaiman 78). From early on, readers realize there is something quite rotten about other mother and her host of supernatural powers, and at every narrative turn, Coraline's sensibility is tested against the beldam's own extraordinary abilities. Gaiman teases the reader about the similarities between the young hero and other mother, suggesting that by taking any wrong direction during her hero's journey, Coraline might fall prey to the beldam, or worse, become her. Gaiman is careful to show these two characters as near parallels, differentiated only by the application of their abilities rather than the abilities themselves. If anything, he tips the scales in favor of other mother who is not only magical, but also far older and more experienced. By pitting the characters in tests of wisdom, will, and wit,

Gaiman demonstrates how Coraline's audacious normality overcomes the supernatural obstacles of other mother and her world. To do so, Gaiman provides other mother with a sick, evil, and weird arsenal inversely proportional to Coraline's extraordinarily ordinary capacity for wisdom, bravery, and trickery. Where Coraline uses creativity, other mother uses "sick" manipulation to get what she wants. Likewise, Coraline's extraordinary capacity for empathy is matched only by other mother's "evil" callousness. Finally, other mother's deceitfulness provides a "weird" foil to Coraline's own use of trickery.

In becoming a hero, Coraline rejects the beldam's enticing supernatural agency, thereby reaffirming that her agency—as well as that of the reader—resides in one's ordinary capacities for creativity, empathy, and cunning put to extraordinary uses. Throughout the narrative, Coraline sacrifices much of her safety, her sanity, and even herself to help others. She battles a menacing supernatural foe in a world created only to trap her. She must learn to fail and succeed in equal measure and with equal grace. When Coraline returns home after defeating the beldam for the last time, she is no longer the neglected, anxious child that sought adventure and escape: "Normally, the night before the first day of term, Coraline was apprehensive and nervous. But, she realized, there was nothing left about school that could scare her anymore" (161). Coraline's reward is not fame, status, or acclaim—her parents do not even remember being adult-knapped—but the quiet contentment of feeling safe, accepted, and loved in a world that now seems less scary. Coraline's successful navigation of the other world and its trappings has reinforced the core tenants of her identity—wisdom, bravery, trickery—and given her the kind of security that comes with self-fulfillment. This self-actualized Coraline serves as an exemplar to young readers about the power of personal acceptance and self-affirmation.

"What an extraordinary child": *Coraline* and the Canon

At the end of the novel, Miss Spink marvels not once but twice at "what an extraordinary child" Gaiman's smart, sensitive, and savvy female hero has become. As a self-actualized hero, Coraline represents the triumph of normalcy and the power of finding the extraordinary in yourself and those around you. While Coraline certainly does not achieve these feats alone, Gaiman does position her as uniquely responsible for carrying the burden at the end of the narrative. In the final battle with other mother's hand, Coraline must face this last challenge alone, and she neither seeks nor asks for help from anyone in the text. When she finally defeats other mother, she does so as a self-actualized hero who feels confident and secure enough in herself to know what to do. In the book, readers are left with the powerful image of Coraline silently watching the hand of the other mother disappear down an abandoned well. In the movie adaptation, however, Coraline is not alone in this final scene. In Henry Selick's movie adaptation, the director introduces Wyborne "Wybie" Lovat, an awkward, insecure male sidekick, to the Coraline world. In a quasi-suspenseful action sequence, Wybie saves the day, an ending that incited a fervent backlash among *Coraline* reading audiences. Literary critic, Lindsay Myers, rightfully argues, "Far from challenging dominant stereotypes and conventions, as does Gaiman's literary masterpiece, Selick's *Coraline* presents a fundamentally unprogressive vision of childhood, trading off the novel's underlying theme of child empowerment for adult fears about child welfare" (247).

Selick defended his use of Wybie by suggesting that the character provides an important narrative device to the film. Throughout the text, Gaiman gives readers access to the full spectrum of Coraline's interiority, especially in her acceptance of and growth into an intellectual female hero; however, as many involved in the film have persuasively argued, the same strategy on the screen not only loses the intimacy of this narrative effect, but also threatens to produce a one-dimensional character whose sparse dialogue barely hints at her rich inner life. Selick describes how he and Gaiman agreed the first draft of the film was "not very good" because "The structure of the book wasn't working, it needed to be reshaped, I needed to add a character to give Coraline someone to talk to" ("Henry Selick," von Riedemann). Likewise, Gaiman himself has commented,

> Coraline has no conversations in the book, in the real world, with any adult who actually listens to her and answers anything that she has said. None of the adults actually pay enough attention to what she's saying to actually hear her. Mostly, they get her name wrong. That's great in a book because you are down there, at her point of view, and you're going along with her. In a film, you're kinda screwed because you're now in a world in which you just want her to be able to talk to somebody ["Interview"].

To combat this potentially alienating result, Selick created Wybie as a male sidekick for Coraline who basically serves as sounding board for the hero's interior monologue. While a more in-depth comparison of the narrative and film is needed, I would like to simply highlight the most problematic aspect of Wybie's inclusion in relation to Coraline's progressive heroism and the fantasy canon.

In order to fully integrate Wybie into the narrative, the filmmakers decided to change the ending of Gaiman's narrative and disrupt the culminating act of Coraline's heroic journey. Coraline's ultimate heroic endeavor rests with her cunning and her use of "protective coloration" at the doll's tea party. In the film adaptation, however, the doll's tea party is replaced with Coraline attempting to merely drop the black key into the abandoned well only to be attacked by other mother's right hand. Wybie literally rides into the scene to save the day, and after almost falling down the well himself, ends up saving Coraline. Instead of facing down the beldam's last trick alone, Coraline and Wybie bundle the shattered remains of the hand along with the key and drop it down the well together. Wybie's help in the last scene make Coraline appear weaker than the lone Coraline of Gaiman's novel, suggesting that Coraline's self-actualized heroism only works in the fantastical other world, but in the "real world," Wybie's pragmatism wins the day. While the designers went out of their way to deny Wybie the machismo of other male heroes by dressing him in oversized clothing and giving him a profound slouch, he still manages to smash other mother's hand with a rock in a show of brute force that is absent from the original narrative. Coraline does triumph over other mother, but this ending does not provide the catharsis of the original ending nor its unique perspective on achieving self-fulfillment.

While many readers were immediately disgruntled with the decision to include a sidekick, especially a male sidekick in an otherwise female-dominated cast, they were particularly outraged by this final scene. Indeed, the backlash against this character among *Coraline* readers was severe enough to warrant a response from Gaiman, who describes, "People got very upset. They were saying, 'Why did you let Henry put a boy in it? Does he come in and save her?' No, he really doesn't. Don't worry. He's the irritating kid next door, but he's there and she can talk to him, and it's great" (Gaiman, "Interview"). His use of the word "save" here, however, proves quite slippery, especially given the character's pivotal involvement in what is the climatic act of Coraline's heroism. In a more recent interview, Gaiman himself has backed away from his defense of this scene: "I was uncomfortable with feeling like Wybie had rescued [Coraline] at the end. She has to rescue herself" (qtd. in Rome, "Coraline"). Gaiman's grudging discomfort with this ending and his need to return to the issue four years after the film's release reflects the problematic tendency where, in many fantasy works, the female hero's agency is ultimately undermined—consciously or unconsciously—by the "helpful" interference of more male heroic figures. This interference is especially egregious in a story whose main argument revolves around the concept of personal acceptance and self-affirmation. Selick's introduction of Wybie into the Coraline universe has left many audience members to question "why born?" indeed.

What is most interesting about the backlash against the Wybie character in terms of this essay's discussion of Coraline's heroics is how this fervor translates into a desire for female-driven, intellectual fantasy stories. After all, the hallmark of Coraline's heroism is that she is decidedly a cerebral hero, and her heroic philosophy—"Be wise. Be brave. Be tricky."—emphasizes intellectual prowess over physical ability. In this way, Gaiman's Coraline is part of a continuing tradition of female fantasy heroes whose strength lies not with the power of their swords, but with the power of their minds. Lewis Carroll's inquisitive Alice, J. K. Rowling's scholarly Hermione Granger, Roald Dahl's precocious Matilda, and Philip Pullman's cunning Lyra Belacqua represent key figures within this tradition, and like Gaiman's Coraline, these characters have helped to establish a female fantasy hero who defeats interior and exterior obstacles through creativity, empathy, and cunning. Like these works, Gaiman's *Coraline* provides a strong female heroine who tests the boundaries of the fantasy genre and provides a useful, engaging, and strong model of the modern female fantasy hero. Ultimately, Coraline's success proves that while we may not live in a world inhabited by sadistic beldams, that even those who consider ourselves to be "normal" can become heroes by indulging normalcy and embracing what makes children—and perhaps some adults—extraordinary.

NOTES

1. The theorizations on Freud's uncanny here are drawn from various theoretical perspectives, and while discussing the merits of such readings are beyond the scope of this chapter, it is important to note that Gooding explores the concepts of double-readership and the "Ideal-I" using Lacanian analysis (398, 399); Rudd considers both Lacan and Kristeva through the concept of the abject and explores Coraline's ability to navigate between the Symbolic and Real (12, 13); and Muller draws largely on the work of Luce Irigaray to examine Gaiman's post-feminist politics ("Same Old").

2. Parsons, for instance, describes the final scene as Coraline's struggle with the patriarchy symbolized here by the key to the portal: "Coraline knows neither she nor her mother can have the phallus/the key, and the other mother's metonymic hand disappears forever in the well over which Coraline had laid her little girls domestic tea party" (382); and Gooding briefly mentions Coraline's "continued developmental struggles" as she comes back to the "real world" at the end of the novel (404). On the other hand, Rudd argues that the ending shows that Coraline is "no longer feeling oppressed by her status" and that "simply sees the world in different terms, and celebrates her own artifice" (14), and Russell views the doll-play scenes as a "subversive use of the patriarchal model of girlhood the other mother sought to impose" (173).

3. In his interview for Booksensewww, Gaiman describes the problem for writing for adults and children: "When I began it, I remember in 1990 showing the first couple of chapters to a very-respected, beloved English editor (now dead). He told me he thought it was absolutely brilliant and completely unpublishable. He said, 'There is no way that you can publish something that is a dark fantasy novel for children and adults—aimed at both markets for different reasons—that is essentially a dark and wonderful horror novel.'"

4. Danielle Russell describes this moment as a particularly feminist one by noting that it is Coraline's mother's voice, above all the others, that rallies her to shut the door: "Gaiman does not end the book with this victory, requiring Coraline to once again defeat the other mother in a continuation of the maturation begun in the other world. In order to succeed, Coraline must be meticulous in her planning and brave in the execution—traits her real mother models" (173).

WORKS CITED

David, Danya. "Extraordinary Navigators: An Examination of Three Heroines in Neil Gaiman and Dave McKean's *Coraline, The Wolves in the Walls*, and *MirrorMask*." *The Looking Glass: New Perspectives on Children's Literature* 12.1 (2008). Web. 1 April 2013.

Dresang, Eliza T. "Hermione Granger and the Heritage of Gender." *The Ivory Tower and Harry Potter: Perspectives on a Literary Phenomenon.* Lana A. Whited, ed. Columbia: University of Missouri Press, 2002. Print.

Gaiman, Neil. *Coraline.* New York: HarperCollins, 2002. Print.

_____. *Interview for* Booksense.com. May 2002. Web. 30 October 2013.

_____. *Interview with Neil Gaiman for Coraline by Mali Elfman.* Screen Crave. *Screen Crave,* 3 Feb. 2009. Web. 30 Mar. 2013.

_____. *Neil Gaiman on Coraline the Movie by Monica Valentinelli.* "Authors, Interviews, Movies, & TV." *Flames Rising,* 24 Jan. 2009. Web. 30 Mar. 2013.

Gooding, Richard. "'Something Very Old and Very Slow': Coraline, Uncaniness, and the Narrative Form." *Children's Literature Association Quarterly* 33.4 (Winter 2008): 390–407. *Project Muse.* 30 March 2013.

Keeling, Kara K., and Scott Pollard. "The Key Is in the Mouth: Food and Orality in Coraline." *Children's Literature* 40 (2012): 1–27. *Project Muse.* Web. 1 April 2013.

Knuth, Rebecca. *Children's Literature and British Identity: Imagining a People and a Nation.* Lanham, MD: Scarecrow Press, 2012. Print.

Lytle, Kandace. "Seeing Isn't Believing." *Neil Gaiman and Philosophy: Gods Gone Wild!* Tracy L. Bealer, Rachel Luria, and Wayne Yuen, eds. Chicago: Open Court, 2012. Print.

Muller, Vivienne. "Same old 'other' mother'? Neil Gaiman's *Coraline." Outskirts Online Journal* 26 Web. 3 April 2013.

Myers, Lindsay. "Whose Fear Is It Anyway? Moral Panics and 'Stranger Danger' in Henry Selick's *Coraline." The Lion and the Unicorn* 36.3 (September 2012): 245–257. *Project Muse.* 30 December 2013.

Parsons, Elizabeth, Naarah Sawers, and Kate McInally. "The Other Mother: Neil Gaiman's Postfeminist Fairytales." *Children's Literature Association Quarterly* 33.4 (Winter 2008): 371–389. *Project Muse.* 30 March 2013.

Rome, Emily. "'Coraline': Neil Gaiman and Travis Knight talk adaptation, scaring kids, and more at EW's CapeTown Film Festival." Inside Movies. *Entertainment Weekly,* 5 May 2013. Web. 1 July 2013.

Rudd, David. "An Eye for an I: Neil Gaiman's *Coraline* and Questions of Identity." *Children's Literature in Education* 39 (2008): 159–168. *Springer Link.* Web. 3 April 2013.

Russell, Danielle. "Unmasking M(other)hood: Third-Wave Mothering in Gaiman's *Coraline* and *MirrorMask.*" Tara Prescott and Aaron Drucker, eds. Jefferson, NC: McFarland, 2012. Print.

von Riedemann, Dominic. "Henry Selick on Neil Gaiman-Interview." *Suite101.* 11 Nov. 2009. Web. 22 Sept. 2013.

Wilkie-Stibbs, Christine. "Imaging Fear: Inside the Worlds of Neil Gaiman (An Anti-Oedipal Reading)." *The Lion and the Unicorn* 37.1 (January 2013): 37–53. *Project Muse.* 1 Nov. 2013.

Dancing with the Public:
Alethea Kontis's *Enchanted*,
Rachel Hartman's *Seraphina* and
Marissa Meyer's *Cinder*

Casey A. Cothran

In their seminal text, *The Female Hero in American and British Literature*, Carol Pearson and Katherine Pope respond to Joseph Campbell's *The Hero with a Thousand Faces* by reworking the stages of the archetypal hero's journey.[1] Pearson and Pope describe the stages of the hero's journey, when the hero is female. Her quest for personal and social transformation parallels the male hero's journey with its stages of "separation—initiation—return" (Campbell 30), but Pearson and Pope argue that the female hero's journey incorporates specific trials, such as the failed search for a male "savior" (Pearson and Pope 142–176) and a reconciliation with the mother (Pearson and Pope 177–222). In turn, Pearson and Pope argue that, although the female hero, like the male hero, is one who "departs from convention and thereby [...] challenges the myths that define the status quo" (16), the female hero faces unique challenges due to her sex. Specifically, the female hero, at the start of her journey, faces "the mirror and the cage" (16–62). Pearson and Pope write:

> Because a woman learns early that it is her destiny to gain the treasures of financial support, love, and social acceptance by pleasing others rather than by heroically acting and changing the world, she focuses not on what she sees, but on how she is seen. To the degree that she does so, her cage is a mirror [23].

Other scholars who address female archetypes agree that women are uniquely constrained by a culture that encourages them to act in a pleasing rather than in a heroic manner.[2] To achieve heroic status, women often must reject behaviors that would result in social validation.

Although female literary characters have struggled with the dragon of public censure in a myriad of historic and modern texts, it is notable that this particular aspect of the female hero's journey (facing public disgrace in order to embrace heroic behavior) is prominently featured in three popular American fictional works, all published in 2012, and all aimed at young adult females. Indeed, in each of the three texts discussed here, Alethea Kontis's *Enchanted*, Rachel Hartmann's *Seraphina*, and Marissa Meyer's *Cinder*, the female hero can save or transform her world only by revealing a truth that she believes will make her an object of public contempt. She must shatter the mirror, disregarding her desire to please others, and she must cultivate a self-confidence that is strong enough to withstand widespread public critique. This is a notable focus, one that pushes readers to ask if twenty-first century authors are responding to real-life anxieties of twenty-first century women.

Women and Identity Formation

In his groundbreaking *Ways of Seeing*, John Berger notes that women's identity-formation is tied to an awareness of themselves as beings that are constantly being observed (and appreciated). Within his analysis of the Western artistic tradition, he writes,

> Women watch themselves being looked at. This determines not only most relations between men and women but also the relation of women to themselves. The surveyor of woman in herself is male: the surveyed female. Thus she turns herself into an object—and most particularly an object of vision: a sight [47].

Berger argues that, within her own mind, a woman formulates a male voice that surveys and evaluates the beauty (and worth) of her person. In her frequently anthologized article, "Visual Pleasure and Narrative Cinema," Laura Mulvey builds on this theory, exploring how women are "simultaneously looked at and displayed" (442). In particular, Mulvey notes how film and life teach males and females that women "can be said to connote *to-be-looked-at-ness*" (442). This term, "to-be-looked-at-ness" continues to be a useful one, as living women still wrestle with their role as the object of the gaze. Females are taught that they are always on display and that, in consequence, their words, actions, appearance, and movement should reflect an awareness of their status as an observed object.

Indeed, it can be argued that women's "to-be-looked-at-ness" has been heightened in the twenty-first century by the function of the Internet within modern life. In "Self-Presentation 2.0: Narcissism and Self-Esteem on Facebook," Soraya Mehdizadeh notes that "any user with minimal knowledge of the Internet is able to relay information to a vast audience through personal blogging, videos, and photos" (357). In her study of "online identity constructions"

(357), she suggests that on Facebook women are more likely than men "to include revealing, flashy, and adorned photos of their physical appearance" (361). Indeed, a variety of online social networks (Facebook and Instagram, for example) encourage users to offer up their thoughts or their image for widespread public approval; often that approval is indicated by the number of "likes" on a picture or post. In turn, these sites provide opportunities for palpable public rejection of posts, pictures, or people; on many social networks, negative feedback is visible to all.[3]

In *Perfect Girls, Starving Daughters* (2007), Courtney E. Martin describes what she sees as an epidemic among American women aged 9–29, again related to Mulvey's notion of "to-be-looked-at-ness." Specifically, Martin sees a cultural sickness where women feel compelled to *appear* perfect. Martin describes this as the unintended consequence of feminism, where modern girls "are the daughters of feminists who said 'You can be anything'" and who heard instead "'You have to be everything'" (18). This trend is markedly visible when one observes the growing numbers of high-achieving young women in American culture _ perhaps the most highly educated generation of young women in history. Martin sees some of this generational success as the result of the modern young woman's drive to appear "perfect." Nevertheless, she goes on to argue that women's problematic obsession with self-image is most often played out privately, in fixations on food, exercise, and weight. These fixations reflect a hatred of the imperfect body. She writes:

> My generation is expending its energy on the wrong things [...]. We thought we would save the rain forest and find a cure for AIDS. Instead we are doing research on the most accurate scales and the latest diet trends. [...] We can't look up and out because we are too busy looking down, scrutinizing our bodies. (2–3)

The psychological, physical, and social problems Martin describes all stem from the stress of being perceived as the object of a disapproving public gaze. In modern life, as in fiction, the cage is a mirror (Pearson and Pope 23). Perhaps the most interesting thing about Martin's text is the way that she explores the psychology of women who actively embrace the pressure to be perfect. Unlike Naomi Wolf in *The Beauty Myth*, who describes a "social reflex" that posits images of female beauty "as a political weapon against women's advancement" (10), Martin explores how intelligent women (across the globe, and in a myriad of social classes) *choose* to bite the poisoned apple of self-destructive behavior. Like the heroines in the three novels described below, Martin recognizes the social pressures that various cultures place on women, but she sees self-acceptance as a potential, viable choice for women in modern society, one that they must make for themselves.

This message about the possibility of self-acceptance, even in the face of public disapproval, is repeated in the three 2012 YA novels I will explore here, each of which can be read as a full or partial reworking of the story of Cinderella: Alethea Kontis's *Enchanted*, Rachel Hartman's *Seraphina*, and Marissa Meyer's *Cinder*. It is my argument that Kontis, Hartman, and Meyer are providing young American women with tools that they can use to combat personal insecurities that blossom within the technology-filled world of the twenty-first century. The popularity of these three books indicates that real world readers are inspired by the science fiction/fantasy hero's struggle to disregard what she perceives to be her culture's view of "acceptable," or "good." As Jack Zipes argues, "fairy tales embody worlds of naive morality that can still resonate with us if their underlying dramas are re-created and re-designed to counter as well as collide with our complex social realities" (136).

In each twenty-first century text discussed here, the female hero successfully conquers her own self-destructive insecurities. Kontis, Hartman, and Meyer's literary presentations of the female hero's insecurities resemble Berger's twentieth-century description of woman's inner voice, the "surveyor of woman in herself" (47). Once she is able to overcome this imagined, critical, public voice, the modern-day female hero can allow herself to be viewed and judged by the public, as she truly is, and successfully endure painful, negative assessments of her person. In turn, as each fictional Cinderella allows her imperfections to be perceived publically, she battles systems that encourage exclusion or self-hatred, even as she suffers under them. As the female hero reveals her hidden self, she is able to defeat physical monsters. Perhaps more significantly, by publically acknowledging her forbidden powers, the female hero gains the authority to critique the prejudices which limit personal potential. The mirror, once a cage, becomes a tool she can use to shine a light into darkness.

Cinderella: The Underestimated Overachiever

Perhaps our culture's most famous underestimated overachiever is Cinderella: her tale has been repeatedly reworked in art, literature, film, and on television. Laurence Behrens and Leonard J. Rosen note that "more than 700 variants [of Cinderella] exist throughout the world—in Europe, Africa, Asia, and North and South America" (584), and Martin Hallett and Barbara Karasek refer to the story as "the core of the Western fairy-tale cannon" (94). Versions of the tale differ in detail.[4] Nevertheless, in almost all versions, Cinderella is portrayed as a sympathetic young girl who is all-but-orphaned and regularly abused. As Hallett and Karasek note, "the attraction of this tale has a lot to do with its theme of virtue revealed and rewarded" (94). It is not surprising that recent fairy tale rewrites, despite their divergence from earlier Perrault, Grimm, or Disney versions of this famous text, maintain the notion that the female hero seems, to those closest to her, an unlikely one; she perpetually starts out as the unwanted step-daughter or uncelebrated sister. Thus, these texts preserve the central charm of the tale: as Cinderella overcomes obstacles, she shows the reader that systems of authority *can* be reversed. Even the most disempowered can become empowered.

The version of Cinderella most familiar to modern Americans is the 1949 Disney film *Cinderella*, which generally follows the plot of Charles Perrault's "Cinderella, or The Little Glass Slipper," first published in 1697. This version features an uncomplaining protagonist, a fairy godmother, and a pumpkin that is transformed into a magnificent coach. Specifically, in Perrault's story, Cinderella is "a lovely and sweet-natured girl," who "bore everything patiently," cleaning her home and helping her family, despite the cruelty she regularly endures from her stepmother and stepsisters, who refer to her as "Cinderbritches" (97). On the day of the King's ball, she is left at home, in tears because she cannot attend. A fairy godmother suddenly appears, eager to help; the fairy uses magic to provide Cinderella with a beautiful dress and glass slippers, as well as a coach and horses. Cinderella is warned that, at midnight, the magic will disappear and "her coach would turn back into a pumpkin, her horses to mice, her footmen to lizards and her clothes back into overalls" (99). Cinderella notes the warning, thanks her fairy godmother, and rushes to the palace. Once she arrives, Cinderella impresses everyone at the ball (including her stepsisters) with her beauty and charm. Perrault writes, "Even the King himself, although he was an old man, could not help gazing at her" (100). During the ball, Cinderella inspires the court and wins the heart of the prince. Nevertheless, she races away before midnight, wary of her impending transformation. The same situation occurs the next night, at a second ball. This time, Cinderella leaves one of her glass slippers behind her (in her haste to escape). The King's son then publicly announces that he will marry the girl whose foot fits into the lost glass slipper. The only woman who can wear the slipper is Cinderella, and as she puts on the shoe (plus its mate which she has hidden in her pocket), her stepsisters realize the truth. Her fairy godmother appears and gives her a new, magical dress to wear. Cinderella then reconciles with her stepsisters, as she "forgave them with all her heart and wanted them only always to love her" (101), and she marries the prince.

What is sometimes noted (and critiqued) by scholars is the passive nature of Perrault's and Disney's Cinderella characters. Although Perrault's Cinderella preserves the secret of her true identity, avoiding discovery by quickness and secrecy, and although Disney's Cinderella dramatically escapes a locked room (with the help of her friends, the mice), neither are as heroic as other Ash Girls in different historic and international versions of the story. Notably, one of the morals presented at the end of Perrault's tale is "It is certainly a great advantage to be intelligent, brave, well-born, sensible and have other similar talents given only by heaven. But [...] they will never help you get on in the world unless you have either a godfather or a godmother to put them to work for you" (102). Terri Windling notes that, unlike the Perrault and Disney versions, other Cinderella stories feature "a stoic, clever girl in a cruel household" (1) who must use magical tools *to save herself*. Windling discusses the character Yeh-hsien from 9th Century China, the Italian "Cat Cinderella," the Grimm's Ash Girl, and an Iranian Cinderella, all clever, daring girls who work to bring about their own transformation (1–2). Windling concludes, "the oldest Ash Girl tales use simple language to tell stories that are not really simple at all" (2).

Kontis, Hartman, and Meyer revive Cinderella's latent heroic potential in their 2012 versions of the story. The Cinderellas they describe receive enchanted boons but must find the courage to use them in the face of potential danger and punishment. In turn, the three Cinderellas in these modern novels impact others. The Cinderella character's rejection of an insignificant social position proves transformative not only for herself but for her culture. In all three novels, Cinderella characters fall in love with princes who appreciate their unique charms, yet only one of the texts discussed here ends in marriage.[5] Romantic love, and the friendship and comfort that arise from it, are key parts of these texts, but they are not what determine the female hero's success. Indeed, Kontis, Hartman, and Meyer's protagonists become more than the wives of princes; they become female heroes who strive to save kingdoms from giants, dragons, and alien invaders.

While Kontis, Hartman, and Meyer recover Cinderella's historic agency, all three revise another traditional aspect of the fairy tale, the ballroom scene, in complex and significant ways. The new court scenes in these YA novels respond to morals imbedded in Perrault's influential version of the story and to Mulvey's idea of "to-be-looked-at-ness." Traditionally, Cinderella's unseen personal worth is validated by the public's response to her at the ball: she performs the role of the ideal female perfectly. In his version of the tale, Perrault writes, "All the women studied her hair and her ball-gown attentively so that they would be able to copy them" (100). Additionally, at the end of the piece, Perrault concludes: "*Moral*: Beauty is a fine thing in a woman [...]. But charm is beyond price and worth more [...] charm is the true gift of the fairies. Without it, one can achieve nothing; with it, everything" (102). In Perrault's and Disney's versions of Cinderella, the refined, aristocratic sensibility of the court intuits Cinderella's value by her appearance and her actions. In contrast, each of the 2012 novels discussed in this essay contains a dramatic, public ballroom incident, but it is not a successful one; in fact, it is disastrous for Cinderella's reputation. In Kontis's, Hartman's, and Meyer's novels, the Cinderella character does not leave the ball before her figurative rags are revealed. In consequence, she is rejected rather than adored by the public. This is a significant choice. It indicates that heroism requires a woman to reveal truths that displease her community. Cinderella can no longer charm.

Enchanted, Seraphina, and *Cinder*

Alethea Kontis's *Enchanted* centers on an insecure female hero who must learn to see herself as powerful before she can help to defeat a mad king and rule her country. Kontis's Sunday is the youngest of ten extraordinary siblings, a dreamer who often chooses to write about life instead of living it. Described by Kontis in an interview as "a slightly agoraphobic introvert writer" (qtd. in Scalzi), Sunday struggles with feelings of fear and inadequacy that arise from her youth and her family's poverty, and she must overcome the personal restrictions she puts on herself. In this text's notable ballroom scene, Sunday is physically attacked by the crowd, but she manages to save herself by using magic to put the crowd to sleep. As she does this, she symbolically puts to rest their criticism of her and her family.

Kontis's novel is an amalgamation of European fairy tales, Greek myths, and nursery rhymes, but one of its most compelling qualities is the way that both Sunday Woodcutter *and* her frog-prince lover, Rumbold, resemble Jacob and Wilhelm Grimm's Cinderella character, Aschenputtel. The female hero, Sunday, attends three balls at the royal palace, is aided by two white birds, and receives a marriage proposal as her prince returns her lost shoe. Rumbold, who at one point is called the "Cinder Prince" (121) for his tendency to sleep in the hearth ashes, is haunted and helped by the ghost of his dead mother. Both characters struggle to overcome complex family dynamics in their efforts to achieve self-actualization and to save the kingdom.

Sunday, the seventh daughter of a seventh daughter, is a "Creator," who is able to bring both living things and events into being by her will. She does not realize the extent of her powers when she first meets Rumbold, but she does tell him, "The things I write ... well ... they have a tendency to come true" (7). She and Rumbold (then living as a frog called Grumble) have only met three times when she impulsively chooses to write: "Sunday was nothing until she met Grumble—a beautiful man, with the soul of a poet. He was her best friend in the whole wide world, and she loved him with all her heart" (36). Sunday and Rumbold are moved by each other's conversation and drawn to one another, but it is only after Sunday proclaims her love in her journal that her kiss (the third one in three days) breaks the spell that has trapped Rumbold in the body of a fragile amphibian (42–46). In this moment, the female hero rescues the kind and helpless prince; she also sets events in motion that will destroy the evil that rules her land.

Kontis never clarifies whether or not Sunday and Rumbold's relationship is organic or shaped by Sunday's words, which magically bind them together in love. This important plot choice introduces one of the major questions of the novel: "is desire enough to make something true?" (79). In the book, the answer is yes; Sunday's great discovery is that she, like her mother before her, can bring events into being. As Kontis openly poses questions about dreams and their power, she pushes her readers to acknowledge their own desires. This novel's subtext is reminiscent of Courtney Martin's argument that women can *choose* to behave in self-destructive or in self-empowering ways, and that the modern woman only has to believe that "maybe things can be different" to discover that "power was not outside [my]self but inside" (Martin 12, 321).

Indeed, to be heroic in Kontis's novel is to *create*, to transform ideas into tangible reality. This power can be a frightening one to wield; Sunday's mother has it (everything she says comes true), but Seven speaks tersely and rarely, as a careless comment led to her daughter Tuesday's death years before. Sunday is frustrated by the way her mother refuses to use her power. Kontis's narrator notes, "Because Mama had eschewed her power, her daughter had no concept of the breadth and depth of her own" (99). Still, as she begins to manage her creative energies, Sunday realizes the complexity of the creative act, and she experiences the desire to eschew it, herself. To her surprise, a piece of paper on which she has angrily written "I AM NORMAL" comes to life (99). Afterwards she doesn't know what "purpose" to give the newly-made bird: "A few hours ago, it had been a piece of paper with a futile dream written inside it. Now it was flesh and blood and feathers and bone. Sunday hadn't the faintest clue what to do with it" (108). In *Enchanted*, women have the power to use narrative to influence reality. To become a female hero is to learn not to fear but to use that narrative power in constructive and meaningful ways, to consider purpose, to seek not a "happy ending" but an "interesting life," one that embraces continual growth and change (Kontis 293).

Sunday must overcome personal obstacles before she embraces her ability to change things in the physical world. It is troubling that she writes, "Sunday was *nothing* until she met Grumble" (36, my emphasis). She certainly is not "nothing," but she is the youngest in an extraordinary family, the eldest being the male "wunderkind" Jack, of whom Sunday writes *"all of Arilland's children grew up in Jack's shadow, his younger siblings more than most. I have never known a time when I wasn't surrounded by the overdramatic songs and stories of Jack Junior's exploits"* (1, emphasis in original). Inhibited by the beauty and talents of her nine siblings, Sunday attempts to escape her own life by writing in her journal. Indeed, in the novel's first line, Kontis shows Sunday writing, lamenting her belief that she is "doomed to a happy life" (1). Sunday and her six sisters are all named after the days of the week, and their personalities all match the children's rhyme[6] about these days; thus, Sunday feels underestimated, cursed to be "blithe and bonny and good and gay," rather than *"interesting,"* which she would rather be (21, emphasis in original). This desire reflects a common frustration of the archetypal female hero; Pearson and Pope note how female heroes must recognize the deeply limiting nature of "the goal of total purity and selfless innocence" (27) that is frequently placed upon women by a patriarchal culture.

In truth, it's only after Sunday becomes unhappy that she learns to see and harness the power inside her. She also learns to focus on herself instead of comparing herself to her siblings. This is an important step in her magical and personal development. Sunday, the youngest child in the family, is beautiful and powerful, but she has a tendency to put herself down. She regularly describes herself as "ungrateful," and indeed she is ungrateful—often focusing on her six sisters' talents or looks instead of valuing or celebrating her own. Over the course of the novel, she has to train herself to see other women (her mother, her sisters, her fairy godmother) as complex, imperfect individuals like herself. Each good woman is beautiful yet flawed in her own way, and Sunday learns that "normal is all relative" (100). The reward for Sunday's personal growth is the charming scene at the end of the novel where her older sisters lovingly and jokingly try on (and fail to fit into) the silver and gold dancing slipper that fits only Sunday. Putting on her own missing shoe symbolizes Sunday's newfound ability to walk her own path and focus on her own unique ability, rather than only writing about the adventures of others. The last chapter, "The Barefoot Princess," continues this theme. Now married to Rumbold, Sunday no longer wears shoes. Her dirty feet are referenced multiple times in this chapter, and they seem to signify her freedom to walk where and how she wishes, disregarding social expectations, her stained toes providing regular, visible evidence of her joy in her own imperfection.

Despite her evolving ability to see herself as worthy, over the course of the plot Sunday must face a dangerous public. Kontis's vision of a ball to which "every eligible woman in the land" (137) was invited is teeming with people and smells and colors. The line to get into the ballroom "wound through the lush hallways and out of doors, circling around itself on the cobblestones, colorful as a poisonous snake" (138). During the ball, Prince Rumbold finds Sunday amidst the "stifling sea of bodies" (139), and, as they dance, "[e]very eye in the room turned to them, and every other mouth whispered her name" (160). In consequence, Sunday suffers, "instantly reminded of her place in the world" (160). She is the child of a woodcutter, and despite the famed heroics of her brother Jack, she has grown up in a house that looks like an old shoe. Nevertheless, she battles her social anxiety and converses with the prince. "Enchanted" (154), they dance together. Afterwards, Sunday wishes to focus on her enjoyment of the dance, rather than on the public's response to her; still, as she steps away, she "did not want to look into the crowd and discover how many enemies she had just made. Sunday experienced a dreadful moment of inadequacy" (164). There is no reason why Sunday should not dance with the prince; she is a Creator, as well as a kind person. In this novel, it becomes apparent that the female hero's internalization of a negative public opinion limits her ability to see herself as someone's love-interest, much less a giant-killer or a future Queen of the realm.

Before she can embrace a heroic role, Sunday must disregard her concern with the public, no matter how tangible or violent their critique of her may become. Echoing many early versions of the Cinderella story, Kontis's book features three balls. At the second, the crowd turns against Sunday. As she and her sisters try to make their way through the sea of guests to the ballroom, Sunday is separated from her family, and soon

> [h]ands tore at her ribbons and ripped her dress to shreds; she heard shrieks like wild animals above the rending of fabric. One particularly strong blow sent her to her hands and knees, and someone's—or several someones'—pointed slipper connected with her ribs. If she did not stand, she would surely be killed. Pain blinded her briefly, and when her vision swam back to her, she saw blood on her fingers [196].

It is in this moment that Sunday pulls forth her magic, saving herself by putting everyone in the courtyard to sleep. It is significant that she is able to make up her own spell, in spite of the active malice of the crowd, later referenced as "the hellion horde" (252). As she puts the bodies to sleep, she also symbolically puts their critical voices to rest. From this moment on, Sunday is able to focus on her own plight, and on the plight of her family, rather than on what the "throng of strangers" (164) thinks. This is also the moment where Sunday truly begins to see her sisters, not as competitors, but as women worthy of love and respect. Sunday will no longer repeat the cycles of female competition that is so violently enacted by the other women at the ball.

The public plays a very small role in the rest of the book, as Rumbold works with Sunday's family to destroy his father the king (who has transformed into a cannibalistic giant). It's only in the final pages of the novel that Sunday writes of the people of Arilland, wondering what they think of her. In this moment, Kontis explores a more realistic vision of a woman's power to shape public narratives. Sunday has gathered the palace bards to her and told them "the complete truth" (304) of her adventures, requesting that they spread the tale, in part because she hopes that her lost brother, Jack Junior, will hear her story and know that his family is well. She considers the myths and stories she has heard about Jack over the years and thinks, "All those school chants and drinking songs about this man who slew dragons and saved worlds—now that I have slain and saved as well, I see an even better picture of what might be truth ... and what might be a lie" (304). The final moments of the book celebrate the power of public storytelling. Although Sunday has learned that the public may not ever truly know, understand, or accept her truth, there is magic in promoting new ways of seeing and knowing. Sunday, who is a Creator, capable of spinning tales, spinning wool into gold, and spinning the imagined into being, desires to participate in this public magic-making. Thus, she gives her story to the world. This is an appropriate final theme, as Kontis's book itself is a riotous rewriting of old myths and tales, a model of how a reader might rethink a traditional narrative and write herself a new one. As Sunday's fairy godmother demands, "Quit dwelling on other people's stories and make up some of your own" (101).

The theme of self-acceptance in the face of public prejudice also underscores Rachel Hartman's novel, *Seraphina*, the tale of a half-dragon and half-human who must come to terms with her identity as a central test of her hero quest. As Pearson and Pope explain, "The modern female hero comes to realize that even previously forbidden qualities must be assimilated into the self in order to achieve the ultimate boon of wholeness" (14). This is especially the case with Seraphina, whose most closely guarded secret is her half-dragon identity. At the end of the ball scene in this novel, Seraphina, along with the Prince and Princess of the realm, find themselves facing a belligerent dragon, and Seraphina saves their lives by revealing her racial identity, to the shock and horror of both the humans and the dragon who stand before her (320–331). Nevertheless, her revelation, despite the consequent outpouring of public prejudice, saves the day. At the end of the novel, she realizes her honesty will allow her new opportunities to seek great adventures.

Seraphina lives in a world where religious fanatics wander the streets, celebrating St. Ogdo the Dragonslayer and shouting, "Cursed be thine eyes, worm! [...]. All Saints curse thee, Eye of Heaven curse thee, thy every serpentine thought turn back upon thee as a curse!" (14). Although dragons can take human form and live among the people in the city, they must wear a visible item (a bell) that designates them as non-human, and they are regularly abused while in their human bodies. In Hartman's novel, the relationships between humans and dragons echo historic and modern epidemics of racial discrimination and religious persecution.

Seraphina sees herself as a frightening abnormality, her half-dragon status a burdensome secret that must never be revealed. Her dragon-ness is concealable; she hides the scales on her waist and arm with clothing and downplays her extraordinary musical talents. Seraphina's father warns her, "do not imagine for one moment that the citizenry wouldn't know what to do with you if they found out. They need only to turn to scripture for that!" (35). Even though she must maintain secrecy for her safety, Seraphina also has learned to enjoy being "comfortably anonymous" (21). She embraces her feelings of self-loathing, often reminding herself, "I was a monster; that could never change" (139) or "I was monstrous. There were things in this world I could not have" (180). Ignored and feared by her step-mother and step-siblings, she looks forward to going to the palace to work as the assistant music mistress.

Despite her need and preference for anonymity, her musical abilities, as well as her intellect, soon bring Seraphina to the attention of many important people. Her mentor (whose role in her life is reminiscent of a fairy godfather) encourages her to take a more active role, noting, "You will get nowhere at court by isolating yourself, Seraphina," to which she replies, "I am exactly where I wish to be" (49–50). She privately decides, "My own survival required me to counterbalance interesting with invisible" (56). This becomes an impossibility, however, as she gains the trust of the princess and the heart of the prince. The novel describes her suffering as she attends a series of small court gatherings, experiencing social anxiety at each. Ultimately, however, at the novel's crucially important political ball, Seraphina not only wears a transformative new dress and dances with the prince, she conducts the entire royal orchestra, and afterwards she performs a musical solo which leaves the audience in stunned, moved silence (303–305).

By the time of the ball, Seraphina has overcome her self-loathing and her fear of being the center of attention. Indeed, in this scene, she is able to both perform her music publically *and* uncover an insidious plot to destroy the Kingdom. Seraphina thus releases her creativity and bravely risks her physical safety, saving the two heirs of the realm from a dragon. Critic Lee R. Edwards argues, "Heroic labor is not a job, narrowly defined, but rather a means of restructuring society and its representations" (146). Seraphina, like Sunday and Cinder, restructures her world by multiple means. She performs heroic feats, and she also inspires through the creation of art. In turn, by publically revealing the racial duality of her own person, she pushes her community to rethink their notions of identity and value. Most people and dragons consider her mere existence an impossibility (320); by announcing it, she pushes both groups to begin to reformulate their understanding of what it means to be human and what it means to be dragon.

Before she reveals her dragon-ness, Seraphina must learn to accept herself. Her journey to self-acceptance is marked by her growing comfort in social situations and specifically by her new knowledge that she cannot please everyone. Midway through the novel, she thinks: "I scrupulously hid every legitimate reason for people to hate me, and then it turns out they don't need legitimate reasons. Heaven has fashioned a knife of irony to stab me with" (98). She realizes she must judge herself, rather than basing her sense of self-worth on others' opinions of her. She comes to understand her dead mother's words: "*I cannot perch among those who think I am broken*" (163, emphasis in original). Seraphina's mother, Linn, was a dragon who managed to "pass" as human, until the day of Seraphina's birth (and her own death), when her silver dragon blood gave her away. As the novel progresses, Seraphina is able to access more and more of the memories Linn transferred to Seraphina's mind while she was a child in the womb; in doing so, Seraphina learns that Linn faced challenges similar to her own. Her mother acted heroically by articulating and defending her beliefs about the value of humanity to other dragons. Linn worked to transform her world, even in the face of her father's emotional wrath and physical violence.

Despite being excluded from all of dragon society because of her views, which labeled her a "dangerous deviant" (234), Linn made choices she felt were ethical.

Of course, her mother's brand of heroism, standing up for right in the face of public scorn, is not easy for Seraphina to emulate. Interestingly, Seraphina finds herself repeating her mother's efforts, but in reverse; she must explain and defend dragons to humans. This effort becomes especially challenging when the man she loves misreads her actions and decides she is a traitor to the state. At first, she is unable to handle the internal effects of outside condemnation. After losing Prince Kiggs' trust, Seraphina resorts to despair and even self-mutilation. She thinks, "I could not live, hating myself this hard" (221). She locks herself in a filthy public latrine and uses a knife to pry off one of her scales, causing herself immense physical pain. She thinks, "Hatred tore at my insides. I was desperate to stop feeling it; like a fox in a snare, I'd have gnawed off my own leg to escape it" (220). In this scene, Hartman has Seraphina parallel her feelings not with her brave mother but with her ancient dragon ancestors:

> Orma had once told me that when dragons first learned to take human form, centuries ago, some had been prone to harming themselves, rending their own flesh with their teeth because the intensity of human emotions had taken them unprepared. They had rather endure physical pain than mental anguish [221].

Over the centuries, dragons have trained themselves to suppress the emotion that assaults them when they take human form, flooding and confusing their normally calculating, rational minds. Like them, Seraphina must learn to control her feelings. She must see beyond her emotions in order to become a female hero, able to conduct both orchestras and groups of people.

In Hartman's novel, Seraphina achieves self-acceptance by learning to see herself as part of a world that teems with wondrous difference. In a time of personal stress, she finds herself in an underground bar where dragons, humans, and even quigs (lesser dragons who live in the piles of garbage outside the city) gather together. She thinks, "I had never seen both my ... my peoples together like this. I found myself a little overcome" (147). As the evening continues, she comes to revel in "this peculiar, smelly slice of interspecies coexistence, the treaty's mad dream come to raucous life" (152). This is only the beginning of her new vision of her body, her mixed race, and her "peoples." At the end of the novel, as she looks out over the city, Seraphina concludes, "We were all monsters and bastards, and we were all beautiful" (358). She realizes that she exists in a world where *all* life deviates from an imagined "normal" standard, and that to believe in or to strive for this imagined standard is to harm not just herself but all human and dragonkind.

What Seraphina has formerly defined as deformity has been transmuted into a thing of beauty. This is not the result of a fairy godmother's magic spell, but a transformation that is achieved through thoughtful consideration and personal choice. In consequence, Seraphina is empowered. She thinks, "Tomorrow I'd give some back, restore and replenish the world. I'd play at Princess Dione's funeral; I'd put myself on the program this time [...]. I might as well stand up and give what I had to give" (358). Seraphina realizes that she has something of value to share with the world, and she embraces the opportunity to see and be seen. No longer haunted by the belief that her difference makes her hideous and hateful, she accepts her responsibility to perform. Thus, her heroism continues. She plans to use her art to move the people of the realm, and she decides to travel, seeking out more dragon-humans to fight against the war between species that is brewing. Perhaps most powerfully, the female hero, by making herself visible, has and will influence public perception. In this final textual moment, the reader concludes that Hartman's "unlikely" female hero has the potential to change the world's vision of who is or isn't a "likely" candidate to wield power, show heroism, or deserve love.

Like Kontis's Sunday and Hartman's Seraphina, Marissa Meyer's Cinder struggles to discover the self-acceptance she needs to embrace heroic action. *Cinder* takes place in the post-apocalyptic city of New Beijing and follows the adventures of the young cyborg mechanic, Linh Cinder. In Cinder's world, Kai, the prince, struggles to maintain peace as humanity struggles with the eruption of a new, deadly plague and the inhabitants of a former lunar colony make preparations to conquer the earth. Over the course of the novel, Cinder discovers that she is not simply a second-class citizen and hated ward, but the lost niece of the Lunar Queen and the rightful heir to the Lunar throne: she is Princess Selene (377–380). While at the ball, Cinder uses her cyborg and Lunar abilities to save the life of the prince, but her actions result in public humiliation and imprisonment. Afterwards, she must silence the inner, critical voice that insists that she is less than human, escape her prison cell, and start on her next heroic quest. Like Sunday and Serephina, and also like the female hero discussed by Pearson and Pope, Cinder must overcome her "society's restrictive myths" (Pearson and Pope 17).

In particular, Cinder must overcome the emotional consequences of being raised by a woman who openly abuses her, in a culture where her kind is considered repulsive and expendable. The novel opens as a mother pulls her child away from Cinder's work booth, frightened that her child will be damaged simply by playing too close to a cyborg. Although Cinder mutters, "It's not like wires are contagious" (3) at the woman's retreating back, it soon becomes evident that the novel's protagonist has internalized her culture's critique of her different body. Early in the novel, Cinder's body is scanned by scientists, and she is horrified to discover that she is 36.28 percent machine (80). Her only visible, non-human parts are her mechanical leg and hand, but she also has a steel reinforced skeleton, wires that run down her spine, and a chip in her brain that allows her to mentally access the internet and to mechanically read the facial expressions of others, perceiving when they are lying (114–118). As Cinder views the doctor's holograph of the amazing mechanical and biological symbiosis of her body, all she can think is, "A girl. A machine. A freak" (123).

Cinder is proud of the fact that she is the best mechanic in New Beijing; nevertheless, both her money and her person belong to her stepmother. Meyer's narrator notes, "Legally, Cinder belonged to Adri as much as the household android" (21). Consequently, Adri is able to "volunteer" Cinder for the plague's cyborg draft, despite her protestations. Meyer writes:

> Every morning, a new ID number was drawn from the pool of so many thousand cyborgs who resided in the Eastern Commonwealth. Subjects had been carted in from provinces as far-reaching as Mumbai and Singapore to act as guinea pigs for the antidote testing. It was made out to be some sort of honor, giving your life for the good of humanity, but it was really just a reminder that cyborgs were not like everyone else [26].

In addition to the daily draft, cyborgs can be "volunteered" for the program. The obvious consequence of living in this world is that Cinder's stepmother chooses to donate her ward to medical science, basically condemning Cinder to die (62–66). Although Cinder acts in brave, self-sacrificing ways throughout the text, she has no wish to become a martyr. In Meyer's novel, the female hero must recognize and assert the value of her life. This theme is reminiscent of Pearson and Pope's discussion of the female hero who "does not give up her life for others," thus "violat[ing] female sex-role conditioning" (14–15). This is the first step in Cinder's heroic journey; she must reject her stepmother's vision of her as worthy of no role but that of test subject.

Despite her desire to live, it is apparent that public attitudes towards cyborgs have influenced Cinder's psyche. She refers to her hand and foot as "metal monstrosities" (30), and in spite of her attraction to Prince Kai, who has come to her for help with a broken android, Cinder fears his friendship. As she looks at her face in the mirror, she reminds herself, "She was not looking at a girl in the mirror. She was looking at a machine" (75). In turn, in addition to attitudes toward cyborgs (which she has faced all of her life), midway through the novel, Cinder must face her new knowledge that she is Lunar. Following her discovery about her own bloodline, Cinder thinks, "To be cyborg *and* Lunar. One was enough to make her a mutant, an outcast, but to be *both*? She shuddered. Lunars were a cruel, savage people. They murdered their shell children. [...] She was not one of them" (emphasis in original 176). Cinder must confront the fact that multiple facets of her identity render her susceptible to public ostracism. Indeed, she realizes that her Lunar heritage is something that she herself has previously defined as "savage" and "mutant" (176).

Over the course of the novel, widespread public attitudes about cyborgs and Lunars do not change. At the end of the book, Cinder has no reassurance that

Kai, who has finally learned that she is cyborg and Lunar, is not repulsed by her. Nevertheless, Cinder must begin to value herself before she can undertake the quest to save the prince. Notably, echoing the heroic journeys of Sunday and Seraphina, Cinder's quest to save a prince in danger will result in saving a world from danger. In each text, the female protagonist's initial romantic heroic action and consequent public heroic action (against a powerful, wicked enemy) designate her a hero in the mind of the reader, if not in the eyes of her community.

Cinder's will and confidence are tested most thoroughly at the ball, where she faces a series of public humiliations in order to warn Kai about Queen Levana's plans to invade Earth. To attend the event, Cinder must wear her dead stepsister's crushed and abandoned gown, and she must don a child's mechanical foot that is too small and that hurts her. She drives to the palace in a dilapidated (pumpkin-orange) automobile she has rehabilitated from the junkyard, so her dress and gloves are stained with oil and mildew. It soon begins to rain, and she must enter the palace late and dripping wet, her dress spattered with mud. Because of her bedraggled appearance, the guards question her right to be there; in doing so, they realize she is Kai's special guest, and they introduce her to the crowd below with a fanfare of trumpets. She has no choice but to descend the staircase on her "mismatched feet" (333). After her dance with Kai, Cinder determines she must humiliate herself further in order to save his life. Even though she has always dreaded being the object of the public gaze, Cinder publically kisses Kai, besmirching his reputation in an effort to disuade Queen Levana from lobbying for a political marriage. Cinder is humiliated by this series of events, and she knows she may be killed for what she has done, but she takes the risk, hoping to save the planet from the Lunar Queen, who plans to usurp Kai's lands and use them as a base for her invasion of Earth (322–348).

The consequence of kissing Kai is that Cinder must face Queen Levana, who recognizes Cinder as Lunar and suspects that she is the lost heir to the throne. During this public confrontation, Levana uses her mental powers to force Cinder to steal a gun from a nearby guard, but Cinder manages to evade Levana's mind control, shooting into the chandelier instead of into her own head (349–355). This is both an important plot moment and a crucial symbolic moment. Cinder fights for and wins control of the machine in her hand, as well as the machine that *is* her hand. Soon after, Cinder is able to see behind Queen Levana's glamour to the "ugly" face underneath her bioelectric spell. It is possible to read this moment as one where Cinder gains the ability to disregard false images of beauty and power. Cinder is able to see that the Queen's culturally lauded presentation of feminine beauty is, ultimately, fake. More importantly, Cinder decides that she will not allow the lying voice that emanates from this false icon of female beauty to force her to harm or destroy herself. Cinder will take control of her own body, no matter how flawed others may believe it to be, and she will use her person to bring about good. This action is presented by Meyers as a heroic one. The female character must fight villains, but she also must fight lies. She must ignore voices (even within her own mind) that tell her that she has no agency or power.

Interestingly, Levana is the master of manipulating crowds, while Cinder is degraded in every possible way. Unlike Disney's Cinderella, who ran off into the night without a shoe, Cinder's poorly-fitting mechanical foot falls off as she races to the garden, the wires in her leg sparking visibly, announcing her cyborg identity to all in attendance. She is rendered immobile, captured, and jailed. After this moment, Cinder suffers, imagining how the people must hate her. Yet, as Dr. Erland sneaks into Cinder's cell with a new foot he has made for her, he tells her that her concerns are "silly" (373). Although Cinder is shocked at his casual description of her public humiliation, she comes to realize that he is right, and that there are more important things for her to think about, like her own escape. As the novel ends, Cinder cuts into her wrist and removes her ID chip. As she does so, she thinks, "Soon the whole world would be searching for her—Linh Cinder. A deformed cyborg with a missing foot. A Lunar with a stolen identity. A mechanic with no one to run to, nowhere to go. But they would be looking for a ghost" (385–86).

By facing Queen Levana, by doing what she thinks is right despite the social consequences, Cinder takes her first step toward being Earth's hero. At one point in the novel, Dr. Earland tells Cinder, "It is easier to trick others into perceiving you as beautiful if you can convince yourself you *are* beautiful" (170). He is telling Cinder how Lunars use bioelectricity to control the minds of Earthlings; nevertheless, this message echoes the theme of the novel, which pushes the reader to reconsider how she sees herself. Cinder must realize that her culture's notion of beauty is a constructed phenomenon, as is her culture's notion of "human." Although she has Lunar blood and cyborg parts, Cinder repeatedly exhibits her humanity: her ability to feel, her desire to help random people (specifically children) around her, her identification with the endangered population of Earth. She must embrace her intrinsic humanity, her intrinsic beauty, rather than using cultural standards as tools to determine self-worth. The novel ends as she prepares to escape from the literal and symbolic jail cells that have kept her from reaching her heroic potential.

Conclusions: Breaking the Mirror

All three of these 2012 YA novels focus on the underestimated female hero's struggle to disregard what she perceives to be her culture's view of "acceptable," "normal," or "good" in favor of an intrinsic, organic personal sense of identity. After she embraces this identity, the female hero allows herself to be viewed and judged by the public, as she is, without fear of their assessments of her person. By privately accepting her underestimated, imperfect persona as heroic, the female hero exposes the falseness of the imagined female ideal, thus destabilizing systems of power and oppression. In turn, by allowing herself to become a visible object, she forces her community to reconceptualize their idea of who can wield power. Meyer's Cinder disregards popular prejudices against cyborgs and Lunars as she considers her potential to do good, and as she allows her cyborg body to become visible to those attending the ball, she actively transgresses her culture's rules about different body types and their ability to interact (romantically or otherwise) with other bodies. In consequence, her character shows her world (and the book's readers) that physical difference does not limit a woman's potential. Similarly, Hartman's Seraphina, forced to reveal her half-dragon identity as she speaks with dragons to save the Prince and Princess, assaults the religious and social ideologies that assert that her person (half-dragon, half-human) cannot even exist. She forces others to reassess the complexity, variety, and beauty of human life. Readers can interpret Seraphina's dragon-difference as a metaphorical discussion of race and ethnicity. In Hartman's text, powerful social forces actively resist the natural merging and blending of different groups. As the female hero's body is the literal embodiment of such merging, the vocal, visual presence of her person uproots the dualistic thinking that characterizes her world, and, perhaps, the world of the reader. Kontis's Sunday promotes the idea that the insecure daughter of a simple woodcutter has the power to change reality, as "everything in the world was about creativity: belief and creation" (112). Sunday can turn herself into a rose tree, but, more importantly, she can write her own destiny, if she can find the courage and imagination to believe she can. Notably, Sunday's story is based on traditional fairy tales, rhymes, and myths: literary forms that are frequently read as misogynistic. Kontis's novel subverts the reader's expectations about men, women, and traditional stories. As Sunday's child chooses to be more than "blithe and bonny and good and gay" (frontispiece), she rebels against cultural forces that limit women's roles and attitudes. Ultimately, Kontis as author encourages readers to rewrite both their own stories *and* the ones told to them by their culture. All three heroines illustrate how imperfect women can affect their worlds in extraordinary ways; in turn, the books inspire readers to do the same.

Ultimately, the female heroes in these novels accept that they are different, but they transform their perception of difference. They determine that difference will not hinder their heroism. *This decision is a heroic act in itself.* It takes more effort (and courage) for Sunday, Seraphina, and Cinder to love themselves than it does for them to face giants, dragons, or alien queens. This may be because each character must ignore the public's expectations of her, as well as the voice within her own mind that recognizes those expectations: Berger's "surveyor of woman in herself" (47). As critic Valerie Frankel notes, "Fairytales show silent, virtuous maids like Cinderella and the little mermaid, who never complain of their vicious treatment [...]. While silence teaches discipline and patience, the heroine must absorb her adversary's voice in order to ascend" (22). Sunday must not, like her mother, fear or deny her magical ability to change the world around her; Seraphina must stop hating herself because she is biracial; Cinder must overcome her aversion to both her cyborg body and her Lunar heritage. The female hero must recognize and exhibit the strength within herself that she initially condemns. In turn, Kontis, Hartman, and Meyer seem to argue that the twenty-first century female hero must endure widespread visibility—or even hatred. In this way, she becomes a public symbol. She may be a symbol of disgrace, but her visibility is, in itself, a recognition of her world's flaws. Cinderella can no longer run away from the ball when her beautiful gown turns to rags. She must show the world her sparking wires, her dragon scales, her dirty feet. This is because to embrace visibility and truth, to stand up and be seen, is potentially to perform a transformative magic.

Notes

1. Over the course of the text, Pearson and Pope also address Dorothy Norman's *The Hero: Myth/Image/Symbol* and Lord Ragland's *The Hero: A Study in Tradition, Myth and Drama*, in addition to Campbell's work.

2. See Annis Pratt's *Dancing With Goddesses: Archetypes, Poetry, and Empowerment* (Indiana UP, 1994) and Maureen Murdock's *The Heroine's Journey: Woman's Quest for Wholeness* (Shambhala, 1990), for example.

3. Typical girls and women feel the pressure of the public gaze, but American women in visible positions of power face higher levels of public observation and judgment. Pippa Norris's *Women, Media, and Politics* and Mary Douglas Vavrus's *Postfeminist News: Political Women in Media Culture* examine the impact of the media on feminism and politics in America, concluding that "Electoral politics is [...] a cultural arena, a site on which struggles for meaning about the appropriateness of women's relationships to socioeconomic power take place" (Vavrus 2). Print, television, and internet media loudly scrutinize the choices (and the bodies) of women who rise to positions of social power or political leadership.

4. For example, in Jacob and Wilhelm Grimm's 1812 version, "Aschenputtel," emphasis is placed on the hazel tree that grows up out of the dead mother's grave and the magical birds that perch within it.

5. In *Cinder* and *Seraphina*, Prince Kai and Prince Kiggs face arranged marriages and must do their duty to their people, in spite of their feelings of love for the female hero. In turn, Cinder and Seraphina have their own responsibilities, and, at the end of each novel (each the first in a trilogy), they stand poised to fight for justice or to seek out the unknown. Marriage is not an option, though it is possible that it may become feasible in later books. *Enchanted*, while it does end with a marriage of the Cinderella character to her prince, rebels against the traditional romance formula as it pushes readers to ask if the couple's love is organic or simply fabricated by Sunday's creative magic. Sunday's companionate romance with Prince Rumbold also is contrasted with the unhealthy marriage of her sister Wednesday to the King. Wednesday's marriage, which arises from the King's sinister desire to use a beautiful young woman, rather than to love her, is an example of the dark ways one can read traditional tales of whirlwind royal courtships.

6. The rhyme goes, "Monday's child is fair of face, Tuesday's child is full of grace, Wednesday's child is full of woe, Thursday's child has far to go, Friday's child is loving and giving, Saturday's child has to work for a living, but the child that is born on the Sabbath Day is blithe and bonny and good and gay."

WORKS CITED

Behrens, Laurence, and Leonard J. Rosen. "Fairy Tales: A Closer Look at Cinderella." *Writing and Reading Across the Curriculum: Tenth Edition*. New York: Pearson, Longman, 2008. 584–653. Print.

Berger, John. *Ways of Seeing*. London: Penguin, 2009. Print.

Disney, Walt. *Cinderella*. Burbank: Walt Disney Home Entertainment, 2005.

Edwards, Lee R. *Psyche as Hero: Female Heroism and Fictional Form*. Middletown CT: Wesleyan University Press, 1984. Print.

Frankel, Valerie. *From Girl to Goddess: The Heroine's Journey through Myth and Legend*. Jefferson, NC: McFarland, 2010. Print.

Grimm, Jacob, and Wilhelm. "Aschenputtel," *Kinder- und Hausmärchen* [Children's and Household Tales—Grimms' Fairy Tales], 7th ed. Trans. D.H. Ashliman. Göttingen: Verlag der Dieterichschen Buchhandlung, 1857, no. 21, 119–26. Web.

Hallett, Martin, and Barbara Karasek. *Folk and Fairy Tales*, 4th Ed. Buffalo: Broadview Press, 2009. Print.

Hartman, Rachel. *Seraphina*. New York: Random House, 2012. Print.

Kontis, Alethea. *Enchanted*. New York: HMH Books for Young Readers, 2012. Print.

Martin, Courtney E. *Perfect Girls, Starving Daughters: The Frightening New Normalcy of Hating Your Body*. New York: Atria Books, 2007. Print.

Mehdizadeh, Soraya. "Self-Presentation 2.0: Narcissism and Self-Esteem on Facebook." *CyberPsychology, Behavior and Social Networking* 13.4 (August 2010): 357–364. Print.

Meyer, Marissa. *Cinder*. New York: Fiewel and Friends, 2012. Print.

Mulvey, Laura. "Visual Pleasure and Narrative Cinema." *Feminisms: An Anthology of Literary Theory and Criticism*. eds. Robyn R. Warhol and Diane Price Herndl. New Brunswick NJ: Rutgers University Press, 1997. 438–448. Print.

Murdock, Maureen. *The Heroine's Journey: Woman's Quest for Wholeness*. Boston: Shambhala, 1990. Print.

Norris, Pippa. *Women, Media, and Politics*. Oxford: Oxford University Press, 1996. Print.

Perrault, Charles. "Cinderella." *Folk and Fairy Tales*, 3d ed. Eds. Martin Hallett and Barbara Karasek. Toronto: Broadview Press, 2002. 39–44. Print.

Pratt, Annis. *Dancing with Goddesses: Archetypes, Poetry, and Empowerment*. Bloomington: Indiana University Press, 1994. Print.

Scalzi, John. "The Big Idea: Alethea Kontis." *Whatever: The Heart Opens Wide Like It's Never Seen Love*. 2 October 2013. Web.

Vavrus, Mary Douglas. *Postfeminist News: Political Women in Media Culture*. Albany: State University of New York Press, 2002. Print.

Windling, Terri. "Cinderella: Ashes, Blood, and the Slipper of Glass." *Endicott Studios*. Spring 2006. Web.

Wolf, Naomi. *The Beauty Myth: How Images of Beauty Are Used Against Women*. New York: HarperCollins, 2002. Print.

Zipes, Jack. *The Irresistible Fairy Tale: The Cultural and Social History of a Genre*. Princeton: Princeton University Press, 2012. Print.

"This huntress who delights in arrows": The Female Archer in Children's Fiction

Zoe Jaques

Nor does laughter-loving Aphrodite ever tame in love Artemis, the huntress with shafts of gold; for she loves archery and the slaying of wild beasts in the mountains, the lyre also and dancing and thrilling cries and shady woods and the cities of upright men
> —Homer, "Hymn to Aphrodite" 407

"I brought you this." Gale holds up a single, ordinary arrow.
"It's supposed to be symbolic. You firing the last shot of war."
> —Collins, *Mockingjay* 427–8

"Susan, Eve's Daughter," said Father Christmas. "These are for you," and he handed her a bow and a quiver full of arrows and a little ivory horn. "You must use the arrow only in great need," he said, [...] "battles are ugly when women fight."
> —Lewis, *The Lion, the Witch and the Wardrobe* 271

One of Katniss Everdeen's earliest acts of rebellion in Suzanne Collins's *The Hunger Games* series is to sneak beyond the bounds of District 12 in order to take up her bow and arrows. This hidden weapon, nestled in a hollowed log, facilitates her resistance to political and economic oppression—it allows her to provide food for her family while experiencing freedom in the liminal space of the forbidden woodlands. As the series develops, imagery of Katniss's prodigious skill with a bow continues to operate in increasingly complex ways. From the arrow fired at the roasted pig on the Gamemakers' table through to the final shot that brings a permanent end to the Hunger Games, Katniss's coterminous role as archer, girl, and child shapes the ensuing narrative and complicates the construction of a female hero "on fire" (Collins, *Catching Fire*, 316).

The popularity of the series, and its subsequent filmic transformation, has, according to the *New York Times*, "helped to make archery hip" (Rubin)—an outcome perhaps somewhat misaligned with *The Hunger Games'* overt critique of violence. Collins's series is hardly unique, even among young adult fiction, in repositioning the young female hero as a warrior figure. Yet this transformation has potentially negative implications. Speaking about recent film and television transformations of fairy tales, Jack Zipes argues that "the message films such as *Mirror Mirror* and *Snow White and the Huntsman* deliver is that women must compromise their femininity to succeed," contending that such representations suggest that "[t]o become a true woman, you first must become a man" (qtd. in Benthuysen). Zipes goes on to add that in the recent animated film *Brave*, Princess Merida "uses a bow and arrow and wants to become a man, subliminally" (qtd. in Benthuysen). Such a critique highlights the anxieties inherent in the figure of the fighting female hero. Indeed, concerns about the ambiguous gender roles of female warriors date back to classical antiquity; in the *Iliad*, for example, Homer terms the Amazons, "antianeirai" or "those who fight like men" (*II*.6.186). For J. H. Blok, this comparative language, whereby female warriors are termed "like men," is fundamentally paradoxical, as its "very equivalence underscored the fact that they were not men but women" (434).

The female warrior-hero in children's literature has thorny antecedents, and the archer in particular deploys a weapon with a complexly gendered past. From volatile Amazonian warriors through to classical imagery of the huntress Artemis, mythologies of female archers are continually alluded to and revised in modern transformations and retellings. Despite their violent nature and penetrative purpose, the bow and arrow also have real histories of being deployed as "female" weapons. Writing in his 1840 *Book of Archery*, George Agar Hansard expresses a debt of gratitude to the "good sense and discrimination of 'the Woodmen of the Ancient Forest of Arden'" for their introduction of archery "as a perfectly unexceptionable recreation for ladies" (151). This cultural positioning might relate to the fact that bows are wielded at a distance as opposed to sword fighting's mandatory close combat. It is perhaps because of this detached nature that C. S. Lewis felt able to give Susan Pevensie a bow in *The Lion, the Witch and the Wardrobe*, while still retaining a belief that "battles are ugly when women fight" (271). Such tensions between femininity and fighting also occur in more recent children's literature, such as Rick Riordan's *Percy Jackson* series, where the all-female followers of Artemis are bow-wielding warrior-hunters, yet must also swear eternal chastity and, interestingly, never grow up. Riordan's initial depiction of these huntresses as comically man-hating offers a hardly more sophisticated gendered model than the supine damsel of the fairy-tale tradition might be said to afford, and seems to be in keeping with Zipes's critique of contemporary female warriors. With these concerns in mind, this essay examines the extensive and often conflicting ways in which the female archer is depicted in modern children's fantasy, to explicate how these texts navigate tensions concerning female identity, violence, childhood and survival.

It seems fitting, given that her archer-girl is "such a big shot" (Rubin), to begin by exploring how Collins positions the figure of Katniss Everden as a female-archer hero. While this dystopian series is set in a futuristic America—a space plagued by famine, inequality, and the sacrificial Hunger Games themselves—it is apparent from the opening moments that "certain tacit norms of gender" (Butler 53) remain in this post-apocalyptic space, albeit on a reductive and stereotyped level. Ostensibly, this ravaged and dying society is one of male and female equivalence: both "[m]en and women with hunched shoulders" and "swollen knuckles" (Collins, *Hunger* 4) make up the District 12 coal-mining populace; the Hunger Games require a tribute of "one girl and one boy" (22) from each district, pitted in the arena against each other regardless of differences of age, physicality or sex; and the cruelties of the Capitol regime—its annual reaping and daily starvation—reach both men and women alike. Yet while Collins characterizes the populous at large as biologically equal in sufferance, she repeatedly offsets and opposes male and female capabilities, with the latter seeming ineffectual, fragile, or self-absorbed when compared to the former. The first book of the series opens with a picture of domestic peace, as Katniss reflects on the recumbent forms of her mother and sister:

> There's enough light in the bedroom to see them. My little sister, Prim, curled up on her side, cocooned in my mother's body, their cheeks pressed together. In sleep, my mother looks younger, still worn but not so beaten-down. Prim's face is as fresh as a raindrop, as lovely as the primrose for which she was named. My mother was very beautiful once too [3].

We here encounter women prone, beautiful (or once-beautiful), and objectified. That Katniss's sister is named after a primrose immediately highlights her delicateness for, as Michael Ferber notes, "[f]lowers, first of all, are girls. Their beauty, their beauty's brevity, their vulnerability to males who wish to pluck them—these features and others have made flowers, in many cultures, symbolic of maidens, at least to males who have set those cultures' terms" (74). The opening image of the narrative is thus one of domesticity, feminine repose, and inherent fragility.

The depiction of Katniss, however, offsets what is essentially a maternal idyll in a more broadly dystopian universe. Dressed in her hunting garb, "[s]upple leather that has moulded to my feet [...], trousers, a shirt" (4), Katniss leaves her sleeping mother and sister to enter the ruins of District 12, manoeuvring her way beyond the electrified fence and into the woods where she stores her illegal bow. This spatial shift takes Katniss not only into the liminal space of the forest, but also into the realm of her father, who both crafted her bow and taught her the ways of the wood. His spectral voice continually echoes in the background, while her companion, Gale, becomes a physical substitute for him, offering up what Katniss describes as "a sense of security I'd lacked since my father's death" (135). The forest itself is replete with the bestial threats of "wild dogs, lone cougars, [and] bears" (5), plus the "added concerns of venomous snakes, rabid animals, and no real paths to follow" (6), yet the woodland assumes none of the folkloric associations for Katniss that it might for Red Riding Hood. As Roger Sale observes, "[a]lmost no one in fairy tale literature goes into the forest to play" for "it is a space in which one can get lost, or encounter known, suspected or unknown dangers" (29). While Katniss's experience of the woods might not offer the freedom of childhood play as such, the space nonetheless permits her a moderate sense of liberty dislocated from District 12: "Gale says I never smile except in the woods" (7).

Katniss and Gale join forces to support their households. Forced into the role of the head of the family, responsible for a surrogate child and a helpless mother-wife figure, Katniss assumes an identity akin to her absent father in order to survive:

> They're not our kids, of course. But they might as well be. Gale's two little brothers and a sister. Prim. And you may as well throw in our mothers, too, because how would they live without us? Who would fill those mouths who are always asking for more? [11].

Writing on the trope of the sacrificial child in the *Hunger Games* series, Susan Tan identifies Katniss as part of a "system constructed to turn children into agents of their family's survival: adults cannot provide but children can" (56). This role as provider is also one that is traditionally, if archaically, assumed by a man; as Betty Freidan observes "[t]he work that a man had to do to eat, to stay alive, to meet the physical necessities of his environment, dictated his identity" (458), while the feminine mystique determines that for a woman there could be "no other way she can even dream about herself, except as her children's mother, her husband's wife" (Friedan 115). Both the tragicomic imagery of Gale holding up "a loaf of bread with an arrow stuck in it" (Collins, *Hunger* 8) and Peeta's later alias as "the boy with the bread" (Collins, *Hunger* 113), hints at a mythologized relationship between "breadwinning" and male enterprise, while Katniss's immediate female influences assume the role of passive recipients— the docile bodies of Freidan's oppressed wives and their children. The other female characters who are directly associated with District 12 can be read as equally, if differently, deficient. A visit to the mayor's house exposes "a girl with a gold pin and no tesserae" (Collins, *Hunger* 16) who is foolishly flippant and tactless; the baker's wife, who leaves Katniss starving in the rain and beats her young son, aligns with a fairy-tale tradition of step-mothers and witches, as she shouts ugly, abusive words from a house of "mesmeriz[ing]" heat and "luscious scent" (Collins, *Hunger Games* 35); and the "[b]right and bubbly" (Collins,

Hunger Games 23) Effie Trinket, who enters the district once a year, is not only an embodiment of the affectation and "trinketry" of the Capitol, but also a surrogate for the self-absorbed vanity of womanhood. Even Prim, almost entirely raised by Katniss, seems to be trapped in this cycle, as exposed by her inability to learn to hunt: "The woods terrified her, and whenever I shot something, she'd get teary and talk about how we might be able to heal it is we got it home soon enough" (Collins, *Hunger* 42). Women in District 12 can thus be sad, stupid, selfish or sweet but they appear as poor counterparts to the more active, and often kinder, men who live alongside them.

This new dystopian world order, it would seem, revives the numerous "ideological expressions of sexual asymmetry" that equate maleness "with being strong, durable, and aggressive, while femininity is associated with being silly, passive, and transient" (O'Laughlin 315n). Katniss, unlike her sister, embodies the austerity and impassivity of a hunter—part of the fairy-tale tradition, certainly, but far more masculine in origin. The anecdote of how "Catnip" became Katniss's official nickname epitomizes this rejection of a feminized, fairy-tale mythology; when a "crazy lynx" (Collins, *Hunger Games* 8) starts to follow her, as if a pet looking for treats, Katniss dispatches him, for he scares away the game. Such a moment is "almost" (Collins, *Hunger Games* 8) regretted, for the creature offers good company, but the price for his pelt quickly offsets a more nostalgic relationship with the animal. A similar rejection occurs in her sighting of a beautiful "young buck" beside a stream:

> Less beautiful perhaps when the two arrows caught him one in the neck, the other in the chest. [...] Momentarily, I'd felt a pang at killing something so fresh and innocent. And then my stomach rumbled at the thoughts of all that fresh and innocent meat [Collins, *Hunger Games* 326].

In Katniss's role as family provider there is no space for the sentimental befriending of woodland creatures in the tradition of Snow White, nor can the forest be permitted its dangerous heritage when it offers up sustenance for those who "know how to find it" (Collins, *Hunger Games* 6). If the "fairy-tale forest embodies isolation and non-community" and is demonstrably "more dangerous for females than for males" (Wilson 90), perhaps it is little wonder that Katniss seeks to dominate this space for the purposes of familial advance, pairing up with a character who represents a "masculine ideal" (Henthorne 58) and assuming for herself a mantle of male identity. By this reading, the survival techniques demanded by District 12, a region physically and culturally distanced from the Capitol, offer a post-apocalyptic vision of humanity that emphasizes an andocentric "Man-the-Hunter" model of (d)evolution that makes the parts women play "relatively invisible" (Wiber 26).

Yet this focus on providing for the family from nature is not, of course, inherently a masculine enterprise. The importance of amassing organic matter to the history of human development is demonstrable in the reworking of the long-standing paleoanthropological Man-the-Hunter hypothesis, which "largely ignored the behaviour and social activity of one of the two sexes" (Haraway 40), to offer an alternate model of evolution based upon the role of Woman-the-Gatherer. In the opening to her acerbic and witty essay on the andocentric role of the hero, Ursula Le Guin recounts a parable of human development that relies less upon the loosing of arrows and rather more upon gathering pursuits:

> In the temperate and tropical regions where it appears that hominids evolved into human beings, the principal food of the species was vegetable. [...] The mammoth hunters spectacularly occupy the cave wall and the mind, but what we actually did to stay alive and fat was gather seeds, roots, sprouts, shoots, leaves, nuts, berries, fruits, and grains, adding bugs and mollusks and netting or snaring birds, fish, rats, rabbits, and other tuskless small fry to up the protein [149].

Le Guin goes on, however, to contend that this reality of gathering as a mainstay for human existence, with its emphasis upon localized, monotonous and repeated tasks, lacks the glamor of "the sticks and spears and swords, the things to bash and poke and hit with, the long, hard things" (Le Guin 151) that embody the familiar story of the ascent of man:

> It is hard to tell a really gripping tale of how I wrested a wild-oat seed from its husk, and then another, and then another, and then another, and then another, and then I scratched my gnat bites, and Ool said something funny, and we went to the creek and got a drink and watched newts for a while, and then I found another patch of oats.... No, it does not compare, it cannot compete with how I thrust my spear deep into the titanic hairy flank while Oob, impaled on one huge sweeping tusk, writhed screaming, and blood spouted everywhere in crimson torrents, and Boob was crushed to jelly when the mammoth fell on him as I shot my unerring arrow straight through eye to brain [Le Guin 149–150].

Here the hero is not fed by the seed plucked from its husk, or even by the meat he kills with arrow or spear. His hu*man*ity is assured by the power of the story that accompanies his triumph over beasts and by its self-serving phallic overtones. This emphasis upon the gallant struggle of the male hero creates a cyclical and autonomous connectivity between epic narratives or fairy tales and the "mature writing about serious subjects" (Lewin 36) that comprise scientific accounts of evolutionary history. As Misia Landau first noticed, and several other paleoanthropologists have subsequently explored, accounts of the history of human development "conform in many details of their structure to the classical hero myth" (Lewin 36) and its andocentric bias. The power of story, it would seem, might account for why "this image of man the hunter has proven surprisingly resilient" (Wiber 23).

What the story of Katniss suggests, however, is that the role of the gatherer is just as important to the wellbeing of humanity as the role of the hunter. For

Le Guin, the male hero emerges from a culture of "bashing, sticking, thrusting, [... and] killing" (151), and Katniss seems to embody exactly this mode of masculine violence: dressing as a hunter, carrying a bow, drowning kittens, killing lynxes, and fearlessly dominating a landscape frequented by snakes, cougars and bears. Surely this is the story of Ool and Boob and the anonymous central male "I" who thrusts his spear and shoots his "unerring arrow straight through eye to brain?" Indeed, it is Katniss's ability to kill in this "eyeballing" manner that marks her as especially gifted, albeit against prey demonstrably less imposing than the "titanic" mammoth: "She's excellent," says Peeta. "My father buys her squirrels. He always comments on how the arrows never pierce the body. She hits every one in the eye" (Collins, *Hunger Games* 109). Yet even before we learn of her prodigious skill with arrows, we are aware of her role as gatherer: "I pull on trousers, a shirt, tuck my long dark braid up into a cap, and grab my forage bag" (Collins, *Hunger Games* 4). We are thus first exposed to Katniss in possession of a bag, not a bow—an object used not to bring *down* magnificent beasts in the manner of the hero story, but to bring *back* food for communal benefit. The primacy of this bag, as a means to familial survival, is also central to Le Guin's conception of the fraught relationship between feminized gathering and masculine hunting; drawing upon what Elizabeth Fisher terms the "Carrier Bag Theory" of human evolution, Le Guin comically, but categorically, underscores the value of this "recipient" device over its more celebrated pointed counterpart:

> If you haven't got something to put it in, food will escape you—even something as uncombative and unresourceful as an oat. You put as many as you can into your stomach while they are handy, that being the primary container; but what about tomorrow morning when you wake up and it's cold and raining and wouldn't it be good to have just a few handfuls of oats to chew on and give little Oom to make her shut up, but how do you get more than one stomachful and one handful home? [...] [F]or what's the rise of digging up a lot of potatoes if you have nothing to lug the ones you can't eat home in—with or before the tool that forces energy outward, we made the tool that brings energy home [150–151].

The need to maintain a supply of food and, more importantly, to find a way to share it, requires the possession of "a gourd a shell a net a bag a sling a sack a bottle a pot a box" (Le Guin 150); if women are established as society's primary gatherers, it is perhaps not so substantive a leap to suspect that "the female hominid probably invented such containers" (McGrew 62).

We know that for Katniss survival depends upon just this process of gathering—a repetitive, quiet and unremitting exercise that proves far more reliable than the one-off chance involved in slaying game. Despite the persistent imagery of Katniss as a bow-wielding huntress, accounts of successful large kills, in terms of animal prey at least, are relatively few. Outside of the slaying of the pet-like Lynx, the occasional kill of a wild dog, and the slaughter of three deer—one of which, Katniss recalls, was "a doe that had injured her leg somehow" and thus "almost didn't count" (Collins, *Hunger Games* 326)—the majority of the animals Katniss hunts are smaller creatures, like rabbits and squirrels, secured as often as not by snares as opposed to at the point of an arrow. Katniss ensures familial sustenance primarily through the skills she develops as a gatherer and forager. At first this takes the form of filling a bucket, another kind of container, with "dandelion greens, stems and flowers" (Collins, *Hunger Games* 60) found in the meadow, before the fecund woodlands offer up more bountiful harvests:

> The woods became our savior, and each day I went a bit further into its arms. It was slow going at first, but I was determined to feed us. I stole eggs from nests, caught fish in nets, sometimes managed to shoot a squirrel or rabbit for stew, and gathered the various plants that sprung up beneath my feet [Collins, *Hunger Games* 62].

Set against the backdrop of the "squat grey houses" and "black cinder streets" (Collins, *Hunger* 5) of the Twelfth District, the valley beyond offers a vision of natural abundance, "teeming with summer life, greens to gather, roots to dig, fish iridescent in the sunlight" (Collins, *Hunger Games* 10). Even at the semantic level, Katniss's survival is encoded in her innate ability to live with the land:

> In late summer, I was washing up in a pond when I noticed the plants growing around me. Tall with leaves like arrowheads. Blossoms with three white petals. I knelt down in the water, my fingers digging into the soft mud, and I pulled up handfuls of roots. [...] "Katniss," I say aloud. It's the plant I was named for. And I heard my father's voice joking, "As long as you can find yourself, you'll never starve" [Collins, *Hunger Games* 63].

Katniss roots here combine both the vegetable nourishment associated with the gatherer and an "arrowhead" shape reminiscent of the hunter. Through this emphasis, breadwinning does become a process of wresting "a wild-oat seed from its husk, and then another, and then another" (Le Guin 149), and although the voice of Katniss's father still echoes here, the ethos of gathering permits feminine engagement. Prim might recoil from the slaughter of animals, but she readily engages in gathering greens and delights in milking her goat, while their mother becomes reanimated by a fertile harvest and uses her apothecary skills to turn plants into saleable medicinal remedies. Via different methods and drawing upon diverse skills, Katniss's whole family becomes part of this "'humble hero(ine)'" (Wiber 19) process of filling the communal foraging bag. It is perhaps telling that Katniss's first moments in the arena, poised before the ultimate symbol of nourishment and plenty that comprises the cornucopia, are characterized by an internal struggle between a hunter's desire to do battle for a sheath of arrows or a gatherer's need to escape with some useful "pickings" in the form of a "backpack that could hold anything" (Collins, *Hunger Games*

182). That the bag turns out to be the "right choice" (Collins, *Hunger Games* 189), laden with further containers in the form of a sleeping bag and water bottle with which Katniss can warm the cold body of Rue and douse the fevered brow of Peeta, is in keeping with a narrative that values community over individuated defense.

At the same time, however, the inclusion of a bow at the mouth of the cornucopia reminds us that the tool is crucial to Katniss's survival, although here it is more than a hunting weapon. The arena exposes complexities inherent in the figure of the bow-wielding female hero, as Katniss the hunter is transformed into an archer-warrior. Le Guin's narrative of female gathering, of course, eschews mention of the mythological stories of female hunters upon which Collins clearly in part bases Katniss's identity. Allusions to the Goddess Artemis in the series are fairly obvious: Katniss is a huntress "who delights in arrows" (Homer *Hy*.9.1) and finds solace in the freedom of the woodland grove, in keeping with her divine counterpart. Just as Katniss reconciles contradictory ontological modes through the conflation of masculine hunting devices with feminine gathering ones, so too is Artemis a goddess comprised of merged symbols of ferocity and compassion. As Lewis Farnell writes in *The Cults of the Greek States* (1896): "[...] while Greek poetry and art more usually describe her as the huntress and destroyer, the older religion was more familiar with the conception of her as the protector and patroness of wild animals, and especially of those that were young" (434). Katniss's protective capacity over young human-animals, shown most demonstrably in the form of Prim the "little duck" (Collins, *Hunger Games* 18) and Rue the "baby animal" (Collins, *Hunger Games* 285), thus aligns with a tradition of the huntress as both a pursuant of game and a patron of the defenseless. The combative role that the arena demands of Katniss, however, is disassociated both from the mythologies of Artemis and from her own history. Her place in the Games transforms the communal huntress into a hunted individual; her bow becomes a weapon by which she must defend herself from an army of human foes. Yet, as Jean Pierre Vernant argues, Artemis herself was ill suited to the theatre of war: "She does indeed carry a bow, arrows and a quiver [...]. Yet neither epic poetry, nor Homeric hymns, nor lyric, nor tragedy portrays her in the guise of a warrior engaged in battle" (244). Vernant adds, "there is only one instance in the *Iliad* where [Artemis] partakes in combat" and here she "shows herself to be a weakling" (245), as Hera chastises her attempt "to fight amain with those mightier than thou" (Homer, *Il*.21.487). Katniss's own skepticism at her chances in battle is couched in similar terms, as she reflects upon tributes possessing skill, training and physicality "far beyond my abilities" (Collins, *Hunger Games* 44). Gale's advice to "get your hands on a bow" as a "best chance" (Collins, *Hunger Games* 47) of survival offers a somewhat reductive perspective on the process of transforming a huntress into an archer:

"Katniss, it's just hunting. You're the best hunter I know," says Gale.

"It's not just hunting. They're armed. They think," I say.

"So do you. And you've had more practice. Real practice," he says. "You know how to kill."

"Not people," I say.

"How different can it be, really?" says Gale grimly.

The awful thing is that if I can forget they're people, it will be no difference at all [Collins, *Hunger Games* 48].

War requires the combatant to disconnect both from her own humanity and from that of her enemy; in order to "overcome those moral inhibitions" against killing another person, "it is necessary to resort to the kind of distancing which blinds killers to the humanity of the killed" (Norman 183). As Katniss later reflects, shifting from the human-focused huntress to human-blind archer is not as simple as either she or Gale might have first conceived: "Amazingly similar in execution. A bow pulled, an arrow shot. Entirely different in the aftermath. I killed a boy whose name I don't even know. Somewhere his family would be weeping for him" (Collins, *Hunger Games* 294).

Katniss's effective ability to "play war' in the Games does not, however, rely upon her ability to kill or disconnect from humanity by hardening to slaughter. Localized success in Katniss's first Games is instead encoded in placing the players on an "equal footing" (Frankel 56) by destroying the miniature Capitol represented in the artificial plenty of the cornucopia; a process which is, of course, reflected on a larger scale in the subsequent rebellion and overthrowing of a corrupt governmental regime. Katniss's first offensive plan, which involves destroying the ill-gotten provisions of her enemies by shooting a hole into a burlap sack so as to release its apples and trigger the surrounding mines, echoes her "game-changing" tactics in training, in which she skewers the apple in the pig's mouth upon the Gamemakers' table and secures herself the highest tribute score. It is the most significant arrow fired in the arena, but it is not one that directly ends the life of another tribute—instead it resonates with the power of a unified hunter's bow and gatherer's bag. Yet while this annihilation of resources begins the Games afresh for Katniss, playing to her natural survival skills and knowledge of "how to be hungry" (Collins, *Hunger Games* 252), the greater significance of this act rests in its cementing of communal bonds. In teaming up with Rue, Katniss relishes the "comforting presence of another human being" (Collins, *Hunger Games* 252) and thus reaffirms the humanness the Games seek to destroy. The co-operation of Katniss and Rue to obliterate the Career tributes' supplies represents an instance of effective teamwork and mutual dependence that transcends an individualized attack. Supporting this idea, after Rue's death, Collins shows Katniss being gifted sponsorship bread from the people of District 11, a unique instance of "[a] district gift to a tribute who's not your own" (*Hunger Games* 289). The mysterious "effect" (Collins,

Hunger Games 111) that Katniss is said to have upon people is here literalized—she is able to act as a bridge between communities just as she acted as a bridge between her own blighted District 12 and the fecund woods beyond. Katniss here resembles an Artemis who is "situated on the margins, on the frontier between the wild and the civilized, she is the patron of the young on the borders" (Vernant, 209).

Although ostensibly ill-fitted for battle, Katniss draws together communities in conditions designed not only to keep them apart but to pit them against each other. Yet at the same time this ultimate manifestation of communal bonding sits somewhat ill-at-ease alongside Katniss's role as a revisioned Artemis, whereby engagement in fictions of heteronormative love are part of the game of survival. Although Katniss eschews romance from the opening of the series, very much in the manner of the Goddess of chastity, her subjugation to the Capitol regime and role as tribute force her to quickly accept an objectifying sexualized gaze that Artemis infamously and violently forbids. Katniss's body is subjected to numerous beautifications designed to ensure her erotic appeal to the eager viewers of the Hunger Games, and, as her "story" unfolds, she actively builds upon this initially visual and passive performance by kissing Peeta in order to generate enough donations to keep him alive. The fiction of their romance is an essential component to their overall success, and critics have been vocal as to the implications of Katniss's subjugation to, and ultimate manipulation of, a sexualized identity. As Rodney M. DeaVault points out, "Katniss's survival over the course of the series is often predicated on her ability to perform femininity, the practice of which she initially scorns" (191)—a point which Jennifer Mitchell seconds when she argues that Katniss can be read as "actively playing with her gender presentation" (133). This eroticization of the bow-wielding hero, and her reluctant acceptance and subsequent manipulation of this role, shows how Collins's adaptation of Artemis tropes forces the virgin huntress into the uncomfortable territory of the sex symbol. Although the final reproductive drive of this particular communal engagement is made clear, the narrative is never comfortable with Katniss's and Peeta's somewhat forced union.

Writing as to why the goddess of chastity who is poorly adapted to war might intervene on the battlefield, Vernant explains that the "links between Artemis and warfare appear less in normal conflicts than in [...] wars of total annihilation, where the prize is no longer the victory of one city over another but the survival of an entire human community" (246). He argues that Artemis "goes into action when one of the combatants violates the limits set either on the use of violence during battle" or "when war goes beyond the civilized boundaries within which rules of military engagement are maintained and veers abruptly into savagery" (246). There are no such rules of engagement in the Hunger Games; they are savage and violent at their core. But, more terrifyingly, the Games embody exactly this threat of "total annihilation," destroying not just the hopes of individual districts but also the essence of a humanity that allows children to slaughter each other in the name of punishment and entertainment. The victors of these "war games" also become properties to be bought and sold—sexualized commodities that quite literally annihilate the sanctity of the self. Modeled on Artemis and similarly mythologized by becoming a Mockingjay of rebellion, Katniss comes to represent a huntress who unifies communities through a bridging spirit first shown in her unification of the hunter's bow with the gatherer's bag, and in the narrative's concluding reproductive positioning of a marriage to Peeta that is at least somewhat an act of choice. The final shot of war, which sends a just arrow into President Coin and terminates the deviance of the Capitol regime, resonates with the same power as the gathered poisoned berries that Katniss looses from their pouch to end the first Games. With bag or with arrow, with berries or blood, Katniss's rebel agency operates in the spirit of unification, first for her family, then her community, and finally for the good of all humanity.

While Collins's female hero is here fashioned to draw upon a spirit of Artemis that can unify "chaos and savagery" (Vernant 256) for communal good, other children's fiction situates the fashionable archer-hero in a more ostensibly egocentric context. Princess Merida, the lead in Disney-Pixar's 2012 animated film *Brave*, shares many of Katniss's symbolic associations with Artemis. Merida is a fiery huntress who finds her greatest pleasure in traversing woodlands with bow in hand, and who furthers the connection by scaling mountains, in accordance with Artemis's request to her father that "all the mountains be mine" (Callimachus *Hy*.III). Yet while Katniss's use of the bow is intricately connected to communal survival, Merida's devotion to the arrow amounts to a defense of a reproductive self that Katniss is forced to sacrifice, with the mirrored "Hunger" and "Highland" Games marking two distinctive depictions of female archery. In keeping with her royal lineage, Merida is not often required to use her arrows as a means of securing sustenance; the closest her bow gets to food at first is in the repeated refrain that a Princess should "not put her weapon on the table" (Andrews & Chapman, *Brave*). Yet this comedy underpins a different kind of obligation, focused around Merida's feminine duties, which are endorsed by patriarchal tradition and voiced through the queen's continual training in princess "perfection" (Andrews & Chapman, *Brave*). Merida is thus trapped in a cycle of female oppression that is ironically endorsed by her mother; a point made clear by Merida's initial outburst on the inevitability of feminine responsibility: "I'm the princess. I'm the example. I've got duties, responsibilities, expectations. My whole life is planned out, for the day I become, well, my mother! She's in charge of every single day of my life" (Andrews & Chapman, *Brave*). The narrative works to oppose duty and obligation against days free from "lessons" or "expectations," where Merida can instead "ride through the glen, firing arrows into the sunset" (Andrews & Chapman, *Brave*). However, the arrangement of a betrothal event, in which suitors from the neighboring clans will vie to secure her engagement, recasts the symbolism of her weapon. Her bow becomes the mechanism by which she defends her right to bodily freedom—archery is the contest in which the heirs of the Macintosh, MacGuffin, and Dingwall clans must compete to be her husband, but Merida herself remains secretly intent upon shooting for her "own hand" (Andrews & Chapman, *Brave*).

Such fierce resistance to marriage, of course, provides one of the most direct associations between Merida and the huntress Artemis. In Lucian's *Dialogue of the Gods*, Eros explains to his mother that Artemis cannot be trapped in love, for she is already devoted to other pursuits:

> APHRODITE: And why do you never take a shot at Artemis?
> EROS: Why, the great thing is that I cannot catch her; she is always over the hills and far away. But besides that, her heart is engaged already.
> APHRODITE: Where, child?
> EROS: In hunting stags and fawns; she is so fleet, she catches them up, or else shoots them; she can think of nothing else [Lucian, *Dial*.XIX].

Merida's response to her impending betrothal is encoded in this mythology of a resistant heart engaged elsewhere that "might never be ready" (Andrews & Chapman, *Brave*) for marriage—an allusion that is also in keeping with Katniss's inherent hostility to the trappings of romantic love. Yet this emphasis upon chastity is somewhat eschewed in *The Hunger Games*, where Katniss learns that desirability is yet another tool of survival—much like a bag, bow or berry—which she both manipulates and is in turn manipulated by. Katniss is thus largely compliant as she is maneuvered into various outfits and wedding dresses designed to appeal and dazzle a world of onlookers, aware of the broader implications for her loved ones if she doesn't play this part in the Games. Conversely, Merida angrily resists such material containment, protesting that her dress is "too tight" and that she "can't move" (Andrews & Chapman, *Brave*), while repeatedly freeing a strand of her fiery red hair from her wimple. This resistance to the aesthetics of patriarchy clearly "places […] free will at the center of a strong female character's plot line" (Waston), yet her angry protestations that "[i]t's not fair" (Andrews & Chapman, *Brave*) equally ring with a certain infantilism that values the personal above the communal. Merida's rebellion finally culminates in a display of her archery prowess that locates the arrow as a symbol of individualized female defense. As is also the case with Katniss, Merida's bow is gifted to her by her a father—a process that initiates her into a male order and offers a means to avoid an ostensibly feminine fate. Although aware that a rejection of the sons of the three clans might lead to "declarations of war in the morning" (Andrews & Chapman, *Brave*), Merida nonetheless steps forward to demonstrate that her skills exceed those of the emasculated first-borns who shoot alongside her. This moment is accompanied by some rather bald symbolism of rebellion against male oppression, characterized most acutely by her freeing her hair, breaking the binds of her dress and splitting the arrow of the most successful suitor (a post–Freudian moment that is accompanied by several jump cuts that slow down the action as her arrow repeatedly penetrates the target).

The film insists that Merida's gendered radicalism comes entirely at the point of an arrow. At the same time, however, the visualizations of directors Andrews and Chapman here directly counter George Agar Hansard's depiction of archery as a gentile pursuit suited to the temperament and the attire of aristocratic women:

> Requiring no excessive corporal exertion, a combination of the most graceful positions of all the bodily exercises, and invariably associated with refined and polished society, the bow appears especially adapted for relieving the sedentary occupations to which women are still far too much devoted [151].

Hansard goes on to recall a real history of women who, "long rebels in heart," delight in the "occasion for emancipating themselves from the ancient tyranny of harpsichord, spinet, backboard and embroidery frame" (151), but there is no mention here of either cursing or bursting one's dress. Perhaps *Brave's* quasi–Medieval context predates such emancipation, for the narrative stresses not the adaptability and appropriateness of women to the pursuit of archery, but instead encodes Merida's shooting as an act of rebellion against her corporal form and the material that binds it. Such revolt against one's human form is reminiscent of what Kathryn Schwarz terms "the much mythologized amazonian body" (148) in which the restrictions of womanhood result in fables of mutilation to remove the right breast and thus improve archery skill. Merida's competitive shooting equally recalls the somewhat less brutal, but equally legendary, tales of Robin Hood, and in particular Disney's own 1973 anthropomorphized version, in which Robin competes for a kiss from Maid Marion in the "Tournament of the Golden Arrow." Clearly working to rewrite a tradition in which "women cannot chart their own lives without male manipulation and intervention" (Zipes, 36), Andrews and Chapman here allude to and recreate this scene of masculine triumph and feminine compliancy from the Disney archives, but reverse and problematize the gendered terms.

Merida thus emerges as a fierce defendant of the capabilities of women and their rights to personal freedom, but her fury and resistance is not aimed directly at patriarchy. While her relationship with her likable but buffoonish father is largely comfortable and undemanding, Merida directs her anger towards what Janet Alderman terms, in another context, the "suffocating maternal matrix" (3) represented by Queen Elinor. The demands of betrothal, the limitations upon Merida's body, and the cultural conditioning of her daughter to the traditions of the princess, are all initiated by Elinor, while at the same time she is depicted, at least from her daughter's perspective, as having the power and potential to break such tradition: "You're the queen, you can just tell the lords, the princess is not ready for this. In fact, she might not be ever ready for this" (Andrews & Chapman, *Brave*). This emphasis upon maternal influence and patriarchal authority both occupies and subverts the traditions of the Disney canon, which, as Susan O'Brien has observed, demonstrably occludes appropriate "mothering":

> Disney's films' affirmation of patriarchal values [...] is strongly evident in the persistent absence of matriarchal support in animated fairy tales. Disney's princess and princes do not have mothers or grandmothers and the princesses do not have sympathetic sisters. Thus the only system in which Disney characters can potentially find happiness is a patriarchal one because that is the only option [180].

Although offering a rare instance of a biological mother-daughter relationship, the film's rendering of Queen Elinor as the sole impediment to Merida's freedom is in keeping with a tradition that makes mothers absent at best and wicked surrogates at worse.

Taken in isolation, Merida's act of loosing an arrow against the express command of her mother could thus be read as a moment of empowered female rebellion against a corrupted maternal order that unflinchingly parrots and perpetuates patriarchal regimes. Conversely, the shot can offer a different, but equally clichéd, depiction of women vying against women—the scene's final image of mother and daughter stubbornly staring each other down embodying the "divide and conquer" tactics that work to "sow disunity and undermine solidarity" (Hammer 60). Yet while Merida's fiery visage and ready bow might be the most pervasive and widespread symbol of the film, just as the majority of stills from the filmic version of *The Hunger Games* focus upon Katniss with bow in hand, *Brave*'s narrative arc focuses less upon this individuated act of personal rebellion and attends instead to the importance of learning from others and negotiating a desire for freedom with societal responsibility. While Elinor does reproduce the patriarchal order, she does not do so unquestioningly, alluding to her own experience of having "reservations when I faced betrothal" but recognizing the larger implications of individualized defiance: "are you willing to pay the price your freedom will cost?" (Andrews & Chapman, *Brave*). The film's overall narrative rewrites a fairy-tale ethos that makes mothers either mere memories or treacherous villains by including tender bookends to the more infamous archery scene, in which Elinor endorses her daughter's inherent bravery and spirit as a young child and Merida as an adolescent learns to understand the queen's conflicted courtly and maternal role.

The principal mechanism by which the women become unified is more magical than maternal, demonstrated through a somewhat ironic animal metamorphosis. Many myths of Artemis symbolically connect her with bears, and in particular her angry transformation of her nymph Callisto into a great She-bear. Here *Brave's* transformation of Elinor reverses its Greek symbolism; while at the festival of *Arkteia* Anthenian girls would appear "disguised as she-bears [as] part of a *rite de passage* into womanhood" (Ballesteros-Pastor 334), Merida directs an animalizing transformation onto her mother in order to both defend her own chastity and resist a metamorphic transition into maturity. By becoming animal, and thus reevaluating what it means to be human and to ascribe to human ideologies, Elinor learns that her daughter possesses useful skills outside of her own relentless schooling in feminine arts. In a moment surprisingly reminiscent of the hunter-gatherer motifs depicted in *The Hunger Games*, Merida teaches her mother "real" survival skills, such as how to catch fish from the river or avoid eating poisonous berries, while she in turn learns to accept and appreciate the care her mother bestows upon her. The narrative resolution thus rests upon the two women finding ways to unify tropes of the masculine and the feminine, by both learning to understand each other and working together for their common good. Drawing upon the skills in oratory that she learns from her mother, Merida is able to calm the rising tempers of the clan leaders, and negotiate a freedom from tradition, not just for herself, but also for the pawn-like first-born males who unquestioningly follow the laws laid down by their own fathers. Merida has to learn that while the system bestowed upon her might not be entirely "fair," neither is an act of individual, localized defiance. The story's final reversion of Elinor into a human, which relies upon Merida sewing up the hole she rent in her mother's family tapestry, undoubtedly recalls the "ancient tyranny of harpsichord, spinet, backboard and embroidery frame" (151) from which Hansard suggests archery offers an escape. Yet while this return to the feminine arts is on the one hand rather disappointingly patriarchal, it also avoids the pitfalls associated with a young woman simply assuming the equally problematic tropes associated with the "unerring arrow" (Le Guin 150) of the male hunter-hero. Importantly, Merida's weaving places her in a demonstrably active role in which she works to save her mother; while Hansard aligns such embroidery with "the sedentary occupations" (151) of women, Merida's love of archery is in fact emblematic of her initial desires to be somewhat sedentary in freedom, in that it divorces her from the responsibilities associated with an active role in society. While learning to do one's duty might be a fairly traditional message, the narrative overall works to redeploy misdirected anger and to endorse female agency, albeit on limited terms. Despite its somewhat reductive geography of Scotland as a "bare rugged land, inhabited by men in kilts" and slightly "mixed up [...] periods" (Ornam), *Brave* offers a surprisingly "real" account of reconciling passions and politics through compromise instead of demand, "negotiation" itself being "a necessary modality in feminism because feminism itself is contradictorily situated" (Orr 8).

Merida's movement from avoiding marriage via Artemis's arrow to negotiating a stay of execution with Penelope's warp recasts an individuated act of staged and showy rebellion into something rather more conciliatory and communal, utilizing the skills embodied by her mother to create a coalition that unifies difference in order to prompt mutually beneficial change. This focus upon communal engagement, so central to the journeys of both Katniss and Merida, is also crucial to the depiction of female archers in Rick Riordan's *Percy Jackson & the Olympians* series, although here the huntresses play secondary roles to the series' titular character. While *The Hunger Games* and *Brave* allude to classical tradition in the creation of their female leads, Riordan's narrative directly deploys Artemis and her community of maidens as characters in his series, in keeping with the series' overall focus on modernizing and adapting Greek myth. As a single-sex grouping, the hunters of Artemis immediately emphasize sisterhood over other forms of communal bonds, particularly those of family or marriage. Thus the negotiations of gendered identity are different from those learned by Katniss (who unites a community through the expected heterosexual relationship) and Merida (who unites by maternal bonding). But while Katniss and Merida are able eventually to negotiate a mode of relative gendered freedom, albeit within confines that might still be identified as patriarchal, the hunting group of Riordan's narrative seek to achieve an absolute rejection of patriarchy and in so doing face the dangers of an ironic communal isolation.

Drawing upon the centrality of chastity to mythology of Artemis, Riordan's hunters are at first subsumed in an overwhelming ideology of virginity. They pledge to evade any fraternization with men, and in doing so develop a fierce hostility towards them that is in keeping with Amazonian traditions. Such hostility is made manifest in Percy's first encounter with them in *Percy Jackson and the Titan's Curse*:

> "You must forgive my Hunters if they do not welcome you," Artemis said. "It is very rare that we would have boys in this camp. Boys are usually forbidden to have any contact with the Hunters. The last one to see this camp...." She looked at Zoë. "Which one was it?"
> "That boy in Colorado," Zoë said. "You turned him into a jackalope."
> "Ah, yes." Artemis nodded, satisfied. "I enjoy making jackalopes" [38].

Zoë Nightshade, an established hunter, joined Artemis because Hercules betrayed her, and her initial banter has an obviously misanthropic tone. Although the allusion to Artemis and Actaeon is comical, it includes a direct threat to boys who transgress. Riordan's focus upon man-hating here overlooks the contradictory nature of Artemis: she is both the Goddess of chastity and of childbirth; a champion of the hunt but a protector of young animals; her arrows can kill, but she is not a warrior. The mythological complexity of Artemis is here instead reduced to a group of cool and aloof Vestal virgins, who react fiercely to even the implication of sexualized contact:

> Zoë ordered the Hunters to start loading. She picked up her camping pack, and Apollo said, "Here, sweetheart. Let me get that."
> Zoë recoiled. Her eyes flashed murderously.
> "Brother," Artemis chided. "You do not help my Hunters. You do not look at, talk to, or flirt with my Hunters. And you do *not* call them sweetheart" [*Titan* 49].

Although ostensibly part of a wider heroic community, the hunters of Artemis are thus highly individuated in their fierce separation from and dislike of mankind. Riordan takes pains to position the hunters as sexually off-limits, but such distancing makes them almost cult-like and inhuman, working to lure other young girls into their fold with promises of "A BOY-FREE TOMORROW" (*Titan* 77). Artemis suggests that girls who "go astray" are those who: "Grow up. Become smitten with boys. Become silly, preoccupied, insecure. Forget themselves" (*Titan* 33). The emphasis upon staying young here recalls the misogyny implicit in C. S. Lewis's denial of Susan Pevensie's reentry to Narnia in *The Last Battle* because she has become interested in "nylons and lipstick and invitations" (165). Such a model offers a reductive stance upon femininity, which encodes a female body with value only while it remains childlike, and a woman's body valuable only when it commits to sanctioned marriage matches.

Against such unisex isolationism, Riordan's narrative, or at least his male characters, are at pains to highlight the limitations of a life with Artemis. Percy, for instance, explains to Bianca:

> "Camp is cool! It's got a pegasus stable and a sword-fighting arena and... I mean, what do you get by joining the Hunters?"
> "To begin with," Zoë said, "immortality."
> I stared at her, then at Artemis. "She's kidding, right?"
> "Zoë rarely kids about anything," Artemis said. "My Hunters follow me on my adventures. They are my maidservants, my companions, my sisters-in-arms. Once they swear loyalty to me, they are indeed immortal... unless they fall in battle, which is unlikely. Or break their oath."
> "What oath?" I said.
> "To foreswear romantic love forever," Artemis said. "To never grow up, never get married. To be a maiden eternally."
> "Like you?"
> "I tried to imagine what she was saying. Being immortal. Hanging out with only middle-school girls forever. I couldn't get my mind around it" [*Titan* 41].

Jokes about boys and girls of middle-school age not getting along aside, the narrative foregrounds the rejection of hetero-normative love as a stereotypical aspect of the female warrior, one that conforms neatly to Disney-Pixar's initial representation of Merida. Riordan's first-person positioning of the "I" voice as

Percy's provides a narrative trajectory that tends to silence the case for a homosocial life. Yet in keeping with the new narrative traditions I have outlined for female warriors in *The Hunger Games* and *Brave*, Percy Jackson's female archers are shown as able to embrace a broader range of identities as the story progresses. Artemis and her followers undergo a sea-change that makes the earlier Amazonian stereotyping redundant, or at least suggests that the complexities of community render this particular version of feminism unwieldy. Instead of being a man-hater, Artemis becomes the goddess most ardently in support of Percy's campaigns. Her hunters endure the greatest sacrifice when Zoë Nightshade is killed by her father, Atlas, while trying to save Percy's life. Her death at the hands of the father of course represents the potentially inescapable oppressions of patriarchy, yet Zoë's communal sacrifice, like Katniss's, turns her into an even greater hero than her ability to kill with a bow might initially seem to warrant. In her death, she is "passed into the stars" (*Titan* 291) alongside the Greek male heroes, as a new constellation in the southern sky, the Huntress. The heroism of the female warrior here, as with Katniss and Merida, comes as much from self-sacrifice as from direct acts of violence. Even if the Hunters do not engage in romantic love, there can be little doubt of Zoë's final affection for Percy. In keeping with the narratives of *The Hunger Games* and *Brave*, Zoë at first manifests a resistance to heterosexual love or marriage that is strongly figured upon her tendencies towards violence, and especially violence with a bow. In the end, however, the very strength given by her archery skill enables her to exceed simple trajectories from girl to wife in order to have a more substantive engagement with community, politics, and humanity.

In tracing the contemporary representations of three very different female archers, I have aimed to show that female heroic violence can be more sophisticated than mere replications of male aggression. Offsetting the somewhat singular skills of the violent male hero, these female heroes deploy a wide skill-set, including archery, gathering, and strategy, to enable themselves and their clans to survive. All of the heroes have skills beyond the bow—Katniss and Merida in particular are also shown to be knowledgeable about plant life, partaking of Ursula Le Guin's trope of heroic gathering. The authors and directors of these texts and films build upon popular traditions associating chastity with Artemis, but each also grants the characters further wisdom in their deployments of violence and rebellion. The huntresses make very different sexual choices, and the narratives paint these choices as equally valid, eschewing stereotypes that place women as either virgins or wives, or see them solely as potential sexual conquests. Importantly, these narratives work against traditions that separate virgins from their communities, keeping them in isolated bowers away from male predators. Instead, these female archers use their hunting and survival skills to benefit their communities, participating at least equally among men while doing so. Both their marriage choices and violent rebellions are shown in varying degrees to have communal consequences, but these consequences are not at the expense of their relative autonomies. As such, female archers are more than just violent men in skirts; they offer complex negotiations of contemporary gendered identities against their mythological forebears.

WORKS CITED

Adelman, J. *Suffocating Mothers: Fantasies of Maternal Origin in Shakespeare's Plays, Hamlet to The Tempest.* New York: Routledge, 1992.

Ballesteros-Pastor, L. "Bears and Bees in Themiscyra: A Sanctuary for Artemis in the Land of the Amazons?" *From Artemis to Diana. The Goddess of Man and Beast.* Eds. T. Fisher-Hansen and B. Poulsen. Copenhagen: Museum Tusculanum Press, 2009. 333–344.

Benthuysen, G. V. "Are new raft of fairy tale films and TV shows fair to their female characters?" Foxnewswww. 13 Aug. 2012. Web. 6 June 2013. http://www.foxnews.com/entertainment/2012/08/13/are-new-raft-fairy-tale-films-and-tv-shows-fair-to-their-female-characters/#ixzz2SijKuqru.

Blok, J. H. *The Early Amazons: Modern and Ancient Perspectives on a Persistent Myth.* Leiden: Brill, 1994.

Brave. Dirs. M. Andrews and B. Chapman. Walt Disney Studios and Pixar Animation Studios, 2012. Film.

Butler, B. *Undoing Gender.* London: Routledge, 2004.

Callimachus. "Hymn III: To Artemis." *Hymns and Epigrams.* Trans. A. W. Mair. Cambridge: Harvard University Press, 1960.

Collins, Suzanne. *Catching Fire.* New York: Scholastic Press, 2010.

_____. *The Hunger Games.* New York: Scholastic Press, 2008.

_____. *Mockingjay.* New York: Scholastic Press, 2010.

DeaVault, R.M. "The Masks of Femininity: Perceptions of the Feminine in *The Hunger Games* and *Podkayne of Mars. Of Bread, Blood and* The Hunger Games. Eds. M.F. Pharr and L.A. Clark. Jefferson, NC: McFarland, 2012. 190–198.

Farnell, L.R. *The Cults of the Greek States.* Vol. 2. Oxford: Clarendon Press, 1896.

Ferber, M. *Dictionary of Literary Symbols.* Cambridge: Cambridge University Press, 1999.

Frankel, V.E. "Reflection in a Plastic Mirror." *Of Bread, Blood and* The Hunger Games. Eds. M.F. Pharr and L.A. Clark. Jefferson, NC: McFarland, 2012. 49–58.

Freidan, B. *The Feminine Mystique.* 1963. London: Norton, 2010.

Hammer, R. *Antifeminism and Family Terrorism: A Critical Perspective.* Lanham, MD: Rowman & Littlefield, 2002.

Haraway, D. "The Past Is the Contested Zone: Human Nature and Theories of Production and Reproduction in Primate Behaviour Studies." 1978. *Simians, Cyborgs and Women.* New York: Free Association Books, 1991. 21–42.

Henthorne, T. *Approaching the Hunger Games Trilogy: A Literary and Cultural Analysis.* Jefferson, NC: McFarland, 2012.

Homer. *The Iliad.* Vol. 1. Trans. A.T. Murray. Cambridge: Harvard University Press, 1924.

_____. "V: To Aphrodite." *The Homeric Hymns and Homerica.* Trans. H.G.E. White. London: Heinemann, 1964. 407–427.

_____. "IX: "To Artemis." *The Homeric Hymns and Homerica.* Trans. H.G.E. White. London: Heinemann, 1964. 435

Le Guin, U. "The Carrier Bag Theory of Fiction." 1986. *The Ecocriticism Reader: Landmarks in Literary Ecology*. Eds. C. Glotfelty and H. Fromm. Athens: University of Georgia Press, 1996. 149–154

Lewin, R. *Bones of Contention: Controversies in the Search for Human Origins*. 1987. Chicago: University of Chicago Press, 1997.

Lewis, C.S. *The Last Battle*. 1956. New York: HarperCollins, 1998.

_____. *The Lion, the Witch and the Wardrobe*. 1950. New York: HarperCollins, 1994.

Lucian. "Aphrodite and Eros." *Dialogues of the Gods. The Works of Lucian of Samosata*. Trans. H. W. Fowler and and F. G. Fowler. Oxford: Clarendon Press, 1905.

McGrew, W.C. "The Female Chimpanzee as Human Evolutionary Prototype." *Woman the Gatherer*. Ed. F. Dahlberg. New Haven: Yale University Press, 1981. 35–74.

Mitchell, J. "Of Queer Necessity: Panem's Hunger Games as Gender Games." *Of Bread, Blood and The Hunger Games*. Eds. M.F. Pharr and L.A. Clark. Jefferson, NC: McFarland, 2012. 128–137.

Murry, R. "'Brave' Princess Merida Gets a Sexy Makeover, But Fans Aren't Pleased." *New York Daily News*. 13 May 2013. Web. 19 June 2013. http://www.nydailynews.com/lifestyle/fury-brave-princess-merida-makeover-article-1.1342482.

Norman, R. *Ethics, Killing and War*. Cambridge: Cambridge University Press, 1995.

O'Brien, P.C. "The Happiest Films on Earth: A Textual and Contextual Analysis of Walt Disney's Cinderella and The Little Mermaid." *Women's Studies in Communication* 19 (Summer 1996): 155–181.

O'Laughlin, B. "Mediation of Contradiction: Why Mbum Women Do Not Eat Chicken." *Women, Culture and Society*. Eds. M.Z. Rosaldo and L. Lamphere. Palo Alto: Stanford University Press, 1974. 301–320.

Ornam, R. "A Scottish historian on Brave." *The Guardian*. Interview by L. Barnett. 29 Aug. 2012. Web. 9 June 2013. http://www.guardian.co.uk/film/2012/aug/29/scottish-historian-view-brave.

Orr, E. N. *Subject to Negotiation: Reading Feminist Criticism and American Women's Fictions*. Charlottesville: University of Virginia Press, 1997.

Riordan, Rick. *Percy Jackson and the Titan's Curse*. New York: Hyperion, 2007.

Robin Hood. Dir. W. Reitherman. Buena Vista Distribution, 1973. Film.

Rose, S.R. *Margaret Atwood's Fairy-Tale Sexual Politics*. Jackson: University Press of Mississippi, 1993.

Rubin, C. "The Odds Are Ever in Their Favour." *The New York Times*. 28 Nov. 2012. Web. 5 June 2012. http://www.nytimes.com/2012/11/29/fashion/hunger-games-heroine-helps-make-archery-hip.html?_r=0.

Sale, R. *Fairy Tales and After: From Snow White to E.B. White*. Cambridge: Harvard University Press, 1978.

Schwarz, K. "Missing the Breast: Desire, Disease, and the Singular Effect of Amazons." *The Body in Parts: Fantasies of Corporeality in Early Modern Europe*. Eds. D. Hillman and C. Mazzio. New York: Routledge, 1997. 147–169.

Tan, S. "Burn with Us: Sacrificing Childhood in The Hunger Games." *The Lion and the Unicorn* 37.1 (January 2013): 54–73.

Vernant, J.P. *Mortals and Immortals: Collected Essays*. Princeton: Princeton University Press, 1991.

Watson, T. "'Brave' Is Actually Quite Brave: Pixar's Fantastic Feminist Document." Forbeswww. 7 June 2012. Web. 17 June 2013. http://www.forbes.com/sites/tomwatson/2012/07/06/brave-is-actually-quite-brave-pixars-fantastic-feminist-document/.

Wiber, M. *Erect Men, Undulating Women: The Visual Imagery of Gender, Race and Progress in Reconstructive Illustrations of Human Evolution*. Waterloo, ON: Wilfrid Laurier University Press, 1997.

Zipes, Jack. "Breaking the Disney Spell." *From Mouse to Mermaid: The Politics of Film, Gender and Culture*. Eds. E. Bell, L. Hass and L. Sells. Bloomington: Indiana University Press, 1995. 21–42.

III. SHOW-STEALERS: HEROIC FEMALE SIDEKICKS AND HELPERS

Sublime Shape-Shifters and Uncanny Other-Selves: Identity and Multiplicity in Diana Wynne Jones's Female Heroes

Apolline Lucyk

Heroes. These are mythical beings, often selected at birth, who perform amazing deeds of courage, strength, and magical mayhem, usually against huge odds. The Rule is that the Hero is always Out There. If you get to meet a so-called Hero, she/he always turns out to be just another human, with human failings, who has happened to be in the right place at the right time (or the wrong place at the wrong time, more likely). Tourists, too, may perform amazing deeds and quite normally end up SAVING THE WORLD, but cannot qualify as Heroes because they are not Out There.
—Diana Wynne Jones, *The Tough Guide to Fantasyland*, 88

Among the most influential and inventive fantasy writers of the twentieth century, Diana Wynne Jones stands out for her constant subversion of traditional fantasy conventions, and the distinctly postmodern feel of her work. As David Rudd notes, "Diana Wynne Jones is particularly adept at demonstrating how what we think of as solid ground is always prone to dissolution" (258). This sense of metaphysical uncertainty is created primarily through Jones's sustained use of parallel worlds, and in many texts, alternate identities. However, as Farah Mendlesohn observes in *Rhetorics of Fantasy*, Jones is also a master of "the casualization of the fantastic," artfully constructing worlds "from pieced-together hints and gradual explanations," and creating characters who are clearly indigenous to and comfortable in their magical worlds (75–76). Her characters are consistently complex, eluding classification into the traditional character-types, such as the (male) hero or passive heroine.

As Mendlesohn argues in *Diana Wynne Jones: Children's Literature and the Fantastic Tradition*, "Jones is both a fiction writer and a critic and ... her fiction can be viewed as a sustained metafictional critical response to the fantastic" (XIII). One of the many conventions that Jones revises and critiques in her texts is the hero character-type. In her critical essay, "The Heroic Ideal," Jones explains how important it was for her to write a truly heroic female character. She describes the characteristics of the hero type, and her endeavor to write a female hero within her novel, *Fire and Hemlock*—one who behaved "like a woman and not like a pseudo-man" (Jones, "Heroic" 135). She sought a narrative structure for *Fire and Hemlock* "which did not simply put a female in a male's place" (Jones, "Heroic" 135). *Fire and Hemlock*'s Polly is not Jones's only resourceful female hero, however; Jones is a master at crafting heroic female characters. These characters do not usually perceive themselves as heroes initially, though. At the outset of her novels, they position themselves in supportive roles, usually to a man they respect, and it is only after gradually realizing their own potential that they become truly heroic, and accomplish heroic deeds that have monumental consequences in their respective worlds. Through this structural scheme, Jones creates narratives that appear to abide by the conventional female-male dynamic, but ultimately turn this dynamic upside down when the female turns out to be the world-saver after discovering her own power and potential.

Jones's female heroes are unique because each of them has another "self," an alternate identity, in some sense. Polly from *Fire and Hemlock* has a parallel set of memories that reveal a mysterious plot from her past that had been wiped from her memory; Vierran from *Hexwood* has a false identity (Ann Stavely) imposed on her that the reader initially believes to be an autonomous character, and a number of voices in her head who help her to understand her surroundings; and Roddy from *The Merlin Conspiracy* has a compendium of knowledge from an ancient sorceress transferred into her mind, which adds a similar duality to her character as well. Each protagonist has to find herself amid her multiple psyches, and this process of self-discovery ultimately leads her to discover her heroic powers and become a pivotal world-saver within the narrative: a hero in her own right. Through an analysis of Jones's female helpers-turned-heroes in *Fire and Hemlock, Hexwood,* and *The Merlin Conspiracy*, I will explore how Jones's use of multiple character identities enables her to create complex, resourceful female heroes who are not simply shadows of male heroes, nor passive female heroines such as Sleeping Beauty or Rapunzel.

Heroes, Heroism and the Call for a Female Hero

The hero character-type has existed since the beginning of storytelling, and has been defined and redefined countless times over the centuries. Jones defines the traditional hero primarily as "the one you identify with in the story" (Jones, "Heroic" 129). Further, she observes, "heroes are brave, physically strong, never mean or vicious, and possessed [*sic*] a code of honor that requires them to come to the aid of the weak or incompetent and the oppressed when nobody else will" (Jones, "Heroic" 130). She also notes that heroes are always somehow connected with higher powers such as supernatural beings or the gods, and that having the supernatural connection serves two purposes: it forces the hero to uphold a code of honor, but it also "suppl[ies] a huge extra set of dimensions that put the hero in touch with the rest of the universe and render his actions significant for the whole of humanity" (Jones, "Heroic" 130). Finally, she attests that "above all, heroes go into action when the odds are against them. They do this ... often knowing they are going to get killed, and for this reason they impinge on a hostile world in a way others don't" (Jones, "Heroic" 130). So, for Jones, the tradition of the heroic character-type is very important, and heroism is linked intrinsically with courage and selflessness.

Jones does not simply replicate the traditional hero figure in her own writing. Rather, as Mendelsohn observes, Jones's heroes "are heroes because the gods and the fates *and we* take notice of them. ... Heroes get to do what we *want* do to [*sic*], without subtlety, without symbolism" (*Diana Wynne Jones* xxi–xxii, emphasis in original). Mendelsohn maintains that Jones's concept of the hero builds on Joseph Campbell's monomyth, but "[w]hereas Campbell's ideas about heroes are about following the rules of a moral narrative, Jones argues 'No.' The thing about heroes is that they will not follow the rules" (*Diana Wynne Jones,* xxii). In Mendelsohn's view, Jones's heroes "are not something you emulate but a scapegoat, to be blamed for doing exactly what you would do yourself" (Jones qtd. in Mendelsohn, *Diana Wynne Jones* xxii), which is an innovative modulation of the traditional hero type.

Traditionally, the hero role has, unfortunately, not been available to women in fantastic fiction. As Rene Fleischbein comments in "New Hero: Metafictive Female Heroism in *Fire and Hemlock*,"

> There are far too few true female heroes—girls who are active, adventurous, intelligent, just, and independent—in literature. Other female heroes are not really female; they are boys and men who have had a feminine name given to them, like Pippi Longstocking, a young girl who lives by herself with her pet monkey and who beats up pirates by herself [235].

This is not to say that there is anything wrong with female heroes who assert themselves in battles and take on masculine roles; however, it is important for there to be female heroes of all sorts, ones that are complex and unique, and not simply repetitions of previous models, or of male versions. In "The Heroic Ideal," Jones comments, "it seemed to me women [characters] were a mess. All over the world they were either goaded into taking vengeance, ... or they were passive" (131). She remarks that a medievalist she consulted "opined that Christianity had substantially affected the heroic ideal, especially where women were concerned, by introducing ideas of patience and endurance and solitary personal struggle against one's own fleshy instincts" (Jones, "Heroic," 131–132). Ruth B. Bottigheimer claims that female roles in fiction have had fluctuating levels of agency over the centuries, but that in twentieth-century literature, they moved back into subjective roles: "girls had become frightened damsels, their mothers had retreated into the shadows, and maids and sisters who had formerly lent their mistresses a helping hand had disappeared" (Jones, "Heroic" 37). Similarly, Fleischbein observes, "[t]here are yet other females such as Cinderella [figures] ... who are heroines by virtue of their socially approved womanly beauty, complaisance, silence, and passivity, all of which result in a lack of what we would normally consider heroic action" (Fleischbein 235). The disenfranchised position females have often occupied is very disheartening for female readers and writers, but perhaps that is partly why recent fantasy has been gradually revising the traditional place of women in new and exciting ways. Jones, as author and critic, is perhaps the most influential innovator in developing the female hero as a character-type in her own right.

Polly Whittacker, *Fire and Hemlock*

Fire and Hemlock (1984) is an early example of how Jones uses multiple character identities to create truly heroic female characters. As Martha Hixon notes, *Fire and Hemlock* is "a complex story constructed of interconnecting narrative layers that questions the nature of time, reality, and the linearity of narrative itself" ("Tam Lin," 86). Polly Whittacker, an ordinary-seeming girl, discovers a hidden set of memories that reveal an old friend, Thomas Lynn, who had been erased from her memories completely and is in grave danger due to something she did. Rather than embarking on a quest into an unknown land, Polly journeys into the depths of her memory and relives a past she has since forgotten. She revisits her hidden memories from her forgotten adolescence, which begin with the funeral she gatecrashed when she was ten where she meets Tom (Jones, *Hemlock,* 16–47), and end with the Hudson House gathering where she agrees to forget Tom at Laurel's behest (Jones, *Hemlock,* 345–352). As Hixon observes, the nineteen-year-old Polly we see in "Part Four" is "now armed with the truth and a deeper understanding of the meaning of those past events" ("Nowhere," 98). Through revisiting her past from the perspective of an outsider, Polly is able to realize that Tom is in great need of her help, and that she must find a way to save him from his ex-wife, Laurel. As Alice Mills maintains, "[a]t the end of *Fire and Hemlock* it is Polly who is the least lost; she functions as the most powerful, wise and healing character" (10). Polly realizes, through the exploration of her hidden memories, that it was when she tried to "hang on" to Tom that the worst things happened to them. For example, at the Middleton Fair, Tom avoids Polly, but she clings to him, and when they go through the House of Horrors together, he is almost killed by a suit of armour and a falling portcullis (Jones, *Hemlock,* 288). Similarly, when Polly spies on Tom and Laurel with the Fire and Hemlock photograph, it leads Laurel to erase all Polly's memories of Tom. Thus, to save Tom, Polly must become wholly independent and let go of him.

Polly's process of discovery, prompted by the discovery of her alternate set of memories, gives her the strength to become a fully independent individual, and to see herself as her own hero, rather than someone else's assistant. In the beginning of Polly's narrative, she continually places herself in a supplementary role to her outgoing friend, Nina, "a big, fat girl with short, frizzy hair, glasses and a loud giggle" (Jones, *Hemlock,* 16), who is continually threatening never to play with Polly anymore if she does not come up with a fun game idea, or if she cannot figure out what "High Priestesses *do*" (Jones, *Hemlock,* emphasis in original 18). When Polly meets Tom, she immediately positions herself as his assistant, explaining to him, "Really you're secretly a hero, a very strong one who's immortal— ... Your name is really—um—Tan Coul and I'm your assistant" (Jones, *Hemlock,* 28). Polly's constant scripting of herself as an assistant suggests that this is how she perceives herself; however, as Polly gradually redis-covers her past and realizes that Tom has been erased from the memory of almost everyone she knows, it finally becomes clear to her that she must act on her own—independently and selflessly—if she is to have any chance of saving Tom from Laurel. Once Polly realizes this, she is finally able to embark on her heroic journey and save him from Laurel, a feat that has been seldom accom-plished in the past. Therefore, for Polly, the process of discovering heroic poten-tial and unleashing female agency is intrinsically connected to her gradual discovery of her full identity, and her ability to ultimately withstand loss.

It is significant that Polly's ability to save Thomas ultimately requires that she let go of him, at least outwardly; in this move, Jones creates a heroic task unlike the sort of tasks a typical male hero would need to perform in order to save someone. As Fleischbein notes, "[Polly] understands that full agency occurs when she is independent and when Tom does not depend on her either" (243). While a masculine hero would usually physically fight someone or something to save someone, Polly's ultimate conflict is internal: it is a fight with her own will that she wins, which enables her to let go of Tom and ultimately save him, which is not a characteristically masculine struggle. Polly realizes that "[w]hat saves Tom is her not helping him but rather recognizing his independence, learned through the story they created and—ironically—from the books Tom sent her" (Fleischbein 243). Yet, it is also not a passive letting go, as one might expect from a traditional heroine. Polly is not a hero who lacks a voice, like the female heroes that Fleischbein observes, who allow "men to speak and act for her ... such as Briar Rose ... or Cinderella" (235). Polly actively abandons Tom in order to save him. Instead of holding on to him, as Janet holds on to Tam in the "Tam Lin" ballad, Polly rejects Tom, yelling at him in front of Laurel's whole court: "You took me over as a child to save your own skin.... You're not doing that again, ... I never want to see you again!" (Jones, *Hemlock* 386–387). With this act, Polly successfully frees Tom from Laurel through a heroic act that is neither a typical male hero's task, nor passive.

Polly's multifaceted identity also helps her evade placement into a certain static character-type. In *Fire and Hemlock*, Polly evolves from a young child to a young woman, both naïve and ordinary, but also savvy and learned, with an acute knowledge and awareness of the supernatural plots unfolding around her as well as a keen mind for logic, strong resolve, and all the qualities of the traditional male hero that Jones describes in "The Heroic Ideal." Further, as Fleischbein notes,

> [i]n modeling Polly on heroes of both sexes, Jones has created a multifaceted character who is not bound to traditional female roles. Thus, Polly provides the young reader with a more fluid and open example of gender construction than is often found in previous writing for children [234].

This dynamic identity construction enables Polly to play an active role in the plot, yet still remain feminine.

Vierran Guaranty/Ann Stavely, *Hexwood*

Nearly a decade after the publication of *Fire and Hemlock*, in *Hexwood* (1993) Jones presents another female hero, Vierran Guaranty/Ann Stavely who exhibits multiple identities. In *Hexwood*, however, the multiple identities function slightly differently than in *Fire and Hemlock*. Rather than introducing the female hero as a girl with dual memories at the outset of the narrative, the female hero of *Hexwood*, whose real name is Vierran Guaranty, is first introduced as a character with a completely different persona and backstory, Ann Stavely. As Deborah Kaplan explains,

> like several other Jones characters, Ann does not know that she is in disguise. Her disguise not only conceals her name, family history, and planet of origin, but also makes her appear substantially younger than her actual age. Ann is actually Vierran, a powerful twenty-one-year-old noblewoman from another planet, with a job of her own as well as a role in an anti-government rebellion [198].

Vierran as herself is not introduced until Part Four of the novel, and it is not until chapter two of part six that her role in the novel finally becomes significant—over two hundred pages into the novel. Also, not only does Vierran have an alternate identity in the beginning of the novel, but there are also four voices with which she communicates in her head throughout the novel, both when she is Ann, and later when she is Vierran, adding further multiplicity to her character. Vierran's ability to think independently and resist deception, which she achieves in part through contact with these voices and the realization that she has had a disguise imposed on her, enables her to play her part in conquering the previous Reigners and prompts her to make the choices that mark her as truly heroic.

Vierran is not an independent hero figure like Polly; rather, she is a part of a team of heroic individuals who have to conquer the evil force—the previous Reigners—*together*. She is an important part of this team, though, and instrumental in defeating the previous Reigners and solving the puzzle of the bannus—the fantastical device that distorts characters' realities throughout the novel, and ultimately chooses the new set of rulers for their Universe (the Reigners). Even towards the beginning of the novel, Mordion and Hume—the characters with whom she works to conquer the previous Reigners—value her opinions greatly; as [Vier]Ann reflects, "[b]oth of them seemed to think of her as a sort of consultant" (Jones, *Hexwood,* 106), and seek out her opinions and advice when she visits them at Hexwood Farm as Ann Stavely. Throughout the novel Vierran continues to be an important member of the Mordion-Hume-Yam team, operating as their connection with the outside world, and giving them an objective perspective when their minds are under the influence of the bannus.

In addition to being a part of the Mordion-Hume-Yam group, Vierran is also one of the future Reigners, a group of people who communicate with each other telepathically. However, this group, which is introduced simply as Ann's "four imaginary people" (Jones, *Hexwood,* 27), works in the narrative as a dimension of Vierr[Ann]'s psyche, rather than as a group of living people. These people can be seen as aspects of Vierran's psyche, and it is partially through communicating with them that Vierran realizes how magically adept she is. In communicating with the voices in her head, Vierran becomes the first person in the bannus's field to understand what is happening in Banners Wood: who is caught in the role-playing game, and how strong and large the bannus field really is. Gaining this knowledge leads Vierran to realize her unique power, and it enables her and her companions to take control of the bannus field and subsequently become the new leaders, "Reigners," of the surrounding worlds.

In Part Seven, once Vierran has been on Earth for some time, she finds a strange message she left herself on the tape recorder her father gave her before she left for earth. Upon hearing it, and realizing the bannus is playing tricks on her, she consults the voices in her head to figure out how long she has been on Earth and to confirm that she is in fact Vierran, that Ann Stavely is merely an alternate version of herself. Her voices tell her that the termination of the controller (the last event before she arrived on Earth) had been "*Quite a while ago. Ten days at least*" (Jones, *Hexwood,* emphasis in original, 261), which informs Vierran that she has been on Earth for over a week. When Vierran asks them who they think she is: "*[I am] Not Ann Stavely?*" (258), the King answers, "*I was puzzled by that name*" (Jones, *Hexwood* 259), and they all tell her they think of her as the "*Girl Child*" (Jones, *Hexwood,* emphasis in original, 258). In this way the voices in her head also enable her to confirm that she is really Vierran, and that Ann Stavely is only a disguise the bannus made for her, as well as enabling her to piece together how long she has been on earth.

These discoveries, prompted by the multifaceted nature of her identity, are what lead her to make the first decision that marks her as heroic: the decision to return to the Banners Wood in order to do *what is right*, even though she does not want to return. After discovering that she has been living disguised as Ann for over a week, and especially after remembering flashing her legs to Mordion from up in the tree, Vierran is so embarrassed that she never wants to see Mordion again. Yet, she realizes immediately that she must return to the wood to help her friends out of danger: "no sooner had Vierran decided [not to see Mordion again] than she found she would have to. She had to warn Mordion" (Jones, *Hexwood,* 263). She realizes that although she does not wish to re-enter the bannus, she must return because she has information that Mordion needs: "Mordion would think he was going to the castle to face Reigners Two and Four. She did not think even he knew that Five had also came to Earth. He certainly had no idea that Three and One were here too" (Jones, *Hexwood,* 263). It is arguably at this moment that Vierran becomes truly heroic, because as Tom tells Polly in *Fire and Hemlock,* "being a hero means ignoring how silly you feel" (Jones, *Fire and Hemlock* 349).

It is this sense of selfless integrity, rather than outright heroic action that makes Vierran heroic. Vierran, like Polly, does not engage in the type of action that characterizes traditional male heroes: for example, she does not "[set] out to do a deed which no one else dares to do and/or at which others have horribly failed" as Jones claims most male heroes do (Jones, "Heroic," 131); and she does not save a person's life singlehandedly, as Polly does, either. However, Vierran is still equally heroic. Vierran's heroism comes from the sum of many smaller heroic acts that combine to make her a truly heroic sidekick character, or team player, rather than an independent hero herself. Most significantly, she decides to return to the bannus to help Mordion and Hume defeat the corrupt Reigners. As Deborah Kaplan observes, once Vierran has come to Banners Wood and "realizes she has been Ann all along due to the reality-warping powers of the wood ... [her] story, at least, moves forward linearly in time, even if the context around her warps and flows" (199). She plays her part in this battle by keeping a level head—helping to unravel the bannus's illusions, and to work out the true identities of those around them. At the crux of the novel, she is instrumental in revealing people's true identities to all those deceived by the bannus. The physically heroic acts of the novel's climax, however—the killing of the previous Reigners—are performed by Mordion, making him the primary hero character of the narrative, whose sidekick she seems to be.

Although Vierran plays a largely supportive role to Mordion, her supportive heroism does not evoke female-heroine passivity. As previously noted, Vierran is very perceptive of her surroundings, and returns to Banners Wood in Part Seven to warn Mordion that *all* of the Reigners are now in Banners Wood, so he has a much more difficult task ahead of him than he anticipated. Similarly, in Part Nine, when Mordion has transformed into a Dragon, Vierran and Hume come to warn him that Morgan la Trey—Reigner Three—knows he is still alive, and is coming to kill him. Endearingly, Mordion assumes Vierran is just worried for him, and tells her, "You needn't be afraid" (Jones, *Hexwood,* 334) to which she answers, "We're *not* afraid.... But we came to warn you, Mordion" (emphasis in original Jones, *Hexwood,* 334). Additionally, Vierran and Hume also have some advice for Mordion on how their group should manage their battle against the corrupt Reigners: "And I thought you ought to take Vierran and Martin back to their parents.... If you fly away with them over the lake, you'd be safe too" (Jones, *Hexwood,* 334). This exchange is illustrative of exchanges between Mordion, Vierran and Hume. Mordion is more powerful than Vierran and Hume, and is therefore the leader and authority figure; however, Vierran and Hume advise him, and keep him updated on the happenings in the bannus. Moreover, Vierran, Hume and Mordion all work together as a team to fight the original Reigners. While Mordion ultimately terminates Reigners One and Three, they all work together to defeat the original Reigners, and once their adversaries are overcome, they each earn a place as the new Reigners in the House of Balance. Thus, Vierran does not play a passive heroine role in *Hexwood*, but is a genuine heroic sidekick with a strong character and agency.

Arianrhod (Roddy) Hyde, *The Merlin Conspiracy*

Alongside Polly and Vierran stands another young female hero with a unique twofold identity that pushes her to grow and eventually become a hero. Rather than having a disguise or false identity imposed upon her, and having to figure out who she really is in order to discover her power, Roddy obtains the complete knowledge of the ancient Flower Witch. Roddy explains, "the law is that you have to pass your knowledge on to someone" (Jones, *The Merlin Conspiracy,* 130). However, because the Flower Witch had been ritually injured by the people in her village for being a powerful witch, she looked elsewhere: "she had searched the centuries and the millennia for the right person to pass her magic to. And she had found me" (Jones, *The Merlin Conspiracy,* 130).

Roddy inherits this wisdom after meeting the witch "in a time slip" (Campbell 195) that enables her to travel to a "ruined village where people lived before History began" (Jones, *The Merlin Conspiracy,* 195). After this brief encounter, the Flower Witch's wisdom is Roddy's own; she possesses all of the witch's expertise in her own mind, and can access it whenever the need arises: "I had the knowledge all at once in a bundle—all she knew, all she could do, and her entire life with it" (Jones, *The Merlin Conspiracy,* 195). It is this possession of the Flower Witch's knowledge, the "flower files," that functions as Roddy's other-identity in *The Merlin Conspiracy,* leads her to discover her immense power, and enables her to save the world once she has "learn[t] to control and implement it" (Campbell 196).

Like Polly and Vierran, Roddy has to gradually realize her own magical potential before she is able to save her world from "the process of corruption that has begun in the magic of Blest" (Hixon, "Power Plays," 176). Throughout the novel, Roddy progresses from a young girl who exerts most of her energy caring and looking out for her younger friend, Grundo (who has a terrible mother and sister, but who is actually a very strong magic-user himself), to an immensely powerful witch who "raise[s] the land" of Blest (Jones, *The Merlin Conspiracy,* 149). The magical act of raising the land is "a process [that] involves setting all the magic of Blest free from the authoritative structures that keep it in place" (Hixon, "Power Plays," 176); thus Roddy essentially "pull[s] up the very foundations" of the land and magic of her entire world in order to save it from corruption (Jones, *The Merlin Conspiracy,* 302).

When Roddy inherits the Flower Witch's files, she begins the process of self-realization and growth that will culminate in her eventually raising the land and saving her world. Before saving the world, however, she has to learn how to use the flower files to find and implement the spells she needs. When Grundo asks Roddy, "Can you out-magic the Merlin now?" she muses, "There was certainly stuff in my head that would do that, but you had to learn what it was and how to work it first" (Jones, *The Merlin Conspiracy* 133–134). As Roddy gradually discovers the depths of the flower files, she realizes that not everything she and Grundo were taught in court was correct: "I realized that all the magic we had learnt at Court was small and one-sided and incomplete. The reality was huge—and all the things our teachers said were complicated were really quite simple. And the other way round" (Jones, *The Merlin Conspiracy,* 134). As she sifts through the flower files in her head, she realizes she is an enormously powerful witch. Thus, Roddy's inheritance of the Flower Witch's memory motivates her to grow as a magic user, which helps her become knowledgeable and powerful enough to save Nick from being made a sacrifice, and Blest from becoming overrun with black magic.

It is not only magical ability that Roddy needs in order to raise the land and save Blest; it is not until she realizes the full danger her world is in that she is able to raise the land and save Blest. The Little People had originally advised her to raise the land, declaring "Blest thing, booming big thing, you raise the land" (Jones, *The Merlin Conspiracy,* 149), but Mrs. Candace had cautioned her against it. When Roddy tells Mrs. Candace the Little People had told her to raise the land, the very powerful witch exclaims, "On no account! ... I'm surprised he even mentioned it. The Little People are usually so wise" (Jones, *The Merlin Conspiracy,* 301). Mrs. Candace does not want Roddy to raise the land because she is worried that "pulling up the very foundations" of the magic of Blest could "make it all come loose or perhaps even blow apart" (Jones, *The Merlin Conspiracy,* 302). She explains, "we can't have that, because Blest magic keeps the magics of several hundred surrounding worlds in their right place" (Jones, *The Merlin Conspiracy,* 302). When Grundo tells Romanov that the Little People told Roddy to raise the land, however, he responds otherwise: "When one of the Little People gives advice like that, you take it!" (Jones, *The Merlin Conspiracy,* 405). Romanov believes Roddy must raise the land because the Little People would only advise someone to do such a monumental task if it were truly important. However, even after Roddy decides to raise the land and Romanov instructs her on how to do it, she is still scared of the task before her: "I just kept hoping that we would arrive in time and that I could manage to raise the land in the way I had discussed with Romanov. And wondering what awful thing might happen if I did" (Jones, *The Merlin Conspiracy,* 434).

It is only when Roddy understands the significance of the damage the conspirators are about to do to Blest that she finds the power and the will to raise the land. As the false Merlin tells the King and Prince Edmund that he is taking over their throne, Roddy suddenly understands what he is really doing:

> As soon as he said "raise the land," I realised that this was exactly what he was doing. And he couldn't be allowed to, not like this! Doing it by a blood sacrifice would bring Blest and all the worlds surrounding it into the realm of purest black magic. The balance would be tipped entirely the wrong way [Jones, *The Merlin Conspiracy,* 457].

She had been attempting to sort through the flower files for a while at this point, but it is only at this moment that she is finally able to use them to raise the land:

> [The hurt woman's files] rushed into my head, file after file ... in a wild waterfall of spells.... At first they seemed to be no use at all. But that phrase raise the land had given me such a jolt that before long it seemed to steady the rush down. I saw that they did not come into my head in any old order[,] ... [a]nd I knew that I had known how to raise the land, long before Romanov tried to explain it to me [Jones, *The Merlin Conspiracy,* 451–452].

Thus, Roddy does not flippantly decide to raise the land; it is a considered decision. She realizes how difficult a task it is, and how severe the consequences can be. She raises the land because she knows she must in order to save Blest from total corruption. The fact that she takes on this task fully aware of the possible consequences and of the necessity of her action makes Roddy's decision to raise the land even more heroic.

Roddy fits perfectly into Jones's definition of a hero. Jones says that a hero is "the one you identify with in the story" (Jones, "Heroic" 129), and although the reader may identify with Nick as well, he or she will certainly identify with Roddy, as she is a co-narrator, and her narration opens the book. As Jones puts it, "heroes are brave, physically strong, never mean or vicious, and possessed [sic] a code of honor that requires them to come to the aid of the weak or incompetent and the oppressed when nobody else will" (Jones, "Heroic," 130). Although Roddy is not physically stronger than the other characters of the novel, she is very strong mentally and emotionally, and she comes to Nick's defense when no one else will, saving him from the evil Merlin who has chosen him for his blood sacrifice. Jones also states that heroes are often connected with the gods, or other supernatural characters who "supply a huge extra set of dimensions that put the hero in touch with the rest of the universe and render his actions significant for the whole of humanity" ("Heroic," 130). Roddy is connected with the Flower Witch, who is certainly supernatural, and the Flower Witch's ability to transcend space and time in order to pass on her wisdom to Roddy does make Roddy's actions universally relevant and significant. Finally, Jones identifies that a hero "go[es] into action when the odds are against him" ("Heroic," 130), and Roddy does just that. She realizes that raising the land could have grievous consequences for Blest and the surrounding worlds, but she also realizes that raising the land is the only thing she can do to save Blest, and this is why she does it. Thus, Roddy is truly heroic in Jones's terms, and since Jones's notion of the hero greatly contributes to our overall understanding of heroism in fantasy, particularly modern fantasy, Roddy's embodiment of Jonesian heroic qualities situates her as a significant female hero in the greater fantasy tradition as well.

Roddy's unique double identity as both herself and the vessel for the Flower Witch is also important because it enables her character to evade female stereotypes often used in fantasy writing. Polly, Vierran, and Roddy are all very dynamic female heroes, and the multiplicity of their identities makes them all more dynamic. By giving their personalities different layers, Jones allows them the chance to act "out of character." Jones's rejection of female stereotypes is especially interesting in *The Merlin Conspiracy*, because she enables Roddy to evade classification into a certain female stereotype by situating her in two diverse female roles simultaneously. Roddy's original self is somewhat naïve, yet smart and driven: all typical traits of a young female protagonist. The inheritance of the Flower Witch's memory thus complicates Roddy's character by adding to it the boundless wisdom of an old woman. Roddy becomes more knowledgeable about the technical aspects of magic use in her world than any other character, including her Grandad Hyde and Romanov; however, she retains a youthful naiveté towards the full extent of her new knowledge, which prevents her from fully taking on the position of the wise old woman. Therefore, she is not a simple heroine character, ignorant or passive, but neither is she a wise old woman, as she retains her youthful perspective. Thus, in Roddy Jones creates a character with exceptional depth for a young female protagonist, revising the options for heroic young women in fantasy with her mixture of both old and young woman in one.

It is also significant that Roddy rescues Nick from the false Merlin, reversing the traditional gender roles of the male hero and female damsel in need of rescuing. The false Merlin takes Nick as a blood sacrifice in order to raise the land, and tortures him:

> [Nick's] body became covered at once in hurrying silver ripples.... He was in obvious agony from it. He rolled about, trying to scream—or not being able to scream—and every time the ripples formed into a leaf-shape this seemed to hurt him even more. He curled up, he uncurled, he flung his legs and arms about, much as the salamanders were doing in the false Merlin's fist [Jones, *The Merlin Conspiracy*, 449].

Nick is unable to save himself or lessen his pain, but Roddy wants to save him: "I am entirely in a muddle as to whether this was what I would have done for anyone or whether it was because it was Nick," Roddy reflects (Jones, *The Merlin Conspiracy*, 448). Shortly after this, Roddy is able to raise the land, foiling the conspirators' plans, and saving Nick in the process. So, as in *Fire and Hemlock*, the female hero of *The Merlin Conspiracy* ultimately comes to the rescue of her male protagonist counterpart.

Conclusion: Reflecting on Jones's Female Heroes

Through an examination of a handful of novels from Jones's vast opus, it is clear that her work in re-imagining and revitalising female roles has greatly contributed to the construction of the female hero in modern fantasy fiction. Her narratives boast numerous heroic female characters that break away from the roles traditionally reserved for women in fantasy. Her use of multiplicity in her heroic female characters—for example, characters with uncanny other-selves, characters with mysterious disguises that have been imposed on them, and characters with a wealth of knowledge inherited from ancient witches—works to set Jones's female heroes apart from the demure heroines of earlier fantasy, who wait to be saved by their male counterparts. This multiplicity also sets her heroes apart from assertive female heroes who essentially play the part of a male hero in the body of a female, such as Arya Stark from George R.R.

Martin's *A Song of Ice and Fire*. Jones's heroes must complete unique, unconventional tasks to save their worlds from destruction. They must discover the extent of their powers and become comfortable with their complex identities before they can complete their heroic tasks.

Therefore, for Jones's characters, becoming heroic is intrinsically connected with coming to terms with one's identity, and processes of maturation. Only after Jones's female protagonists have matured throughout the narrative, and grown comfortable in their multifaceted identities, are they able to accomplish their heroic feats. But once they discover their power, they complete their tasks with extreme ease; so Jones's female heroes always possess the skills to accomplish these feats from the outset of her novels, but must come to terms with themselves and their identities in order to use their powers effectively. For Polly, her process of maturation is fundamentally connected with her journey to independence. She has to become emotionally self-sufficient in order to save Tom, and also discover both sides of her memory. Once she has done this, she is able to let go of Tom, the act which saves him. For Vierran, her need to come to terms with her identity is very literal: she must discover who she is amid the confusion of the bannus in order to help Mordion and Hume defeat the Reigners. Additionally, she must be mature enough to go back into Banners Wood to help Mordion and Hume even though she dreads seeing Mordion again, but once she figures out her identity and begins to make choices for the right reasons, she becomes a hero and a key force for good. For Roddy, she must figure out how to infuse the Flower Witch's wisdom into her very self, and trust her instinct in using the files, but once she has become really motivated to use them against the powers of evil, she is able to raise the land with tremendous, almost uncanny ease. Thus, the potential for heroism is inherent in all of these characters, but that they must mature and accept their identities for what they are before they can actually be heroic, and use their power to its potential. This suggests that Jones's female heroes are inherently underdogs and must work at constructing their own sense of identity before they can take on the hero mantle and see themselves as heroes, because they're not immediately viewed as having hero potential due to their sex.

Mendlesohn asserts that the "equation that creates much of the tension in Jones's work [is that] adulthood is a combination of agency, power, and the ability to withstand loss" (Mendlesohn, *Diana Wynne Jones,* 29), and these four components are crucial to the development of Jones's female heroes—not just Polly, Vierran, and Roddy, but Sophie, Millie, Charmain, Helen, Hayley, and the heroic female characters of all her novels. Further, in "The Importance of Being Nowhere," Hixon opines that "[f]or Jones, the fantasy element, or the magic of her stories, often works as a metaphor for human imagination and creativity, the 'right-brain' approach to grappling with the problems of everyday life" (Hixon, "Nowhere," 99). Not only does Jones's use of multiple identities in her female hero characters enable her to create complex, dynamic female heroes who escape the roles in which most female characters are trapped in conventional fantasy fiction, but perhaps the journeys these identities create for her female protagonists are meant to suggest to the reader that she, too, can be a hero, if she can only become comfortable in her complex, perhaps confusing, identity.

WORKS CITED

Bottigheimer, Ruth B. "Fertility Control and the Birth of the Modern European Fairy-Tale Heroine." *Fairy Tales and Feminism: New Approaches.* Ed. Donald Haase. Detroit: Wayne State University Press, 2004. 37–52. Print.

Campbell, Lori M. *Portals of Power: Magical Agency and Transformation in Literary Fantasy.* Jefferson: McFarland, 2010. Print.

Fleischbein, René. "New hero: Metafictive female heroism in *Fire and Hemlock.*" *Journal of the Fantastic Arts* 21.2 (2010): 233–245. Print.

Herbert, Frank. *Dune.* New York: Ace, 1987. Print.

Hixon, Martha P. "The Importance of Being Nowhere." *Diana Wynne Jones: An Exciting and Exacting Wisdom.* Ed. Rosenberg, Teya, et al. New York: Peter Lang, 2002. 96–107. Print.

_____. "Power Plays and Paradigms of Power in The Pinhoe Egg and The Merlin Conspiracy." *Journal of the Fantastic in the Arts.* 22. 2 (Spring 2011): 169–186. Print.

_____. "Tam Lin, Fair Janet, and the Sexual Revolution: Traditional Ballads, Fairy Tales, and Twentieth Century Children's Literature." *Marvels & Tales: Journal of Fairy-Tale Studies* 18.1 (2004): 67–92. Print.

Jones, Diana Wynne. *Fire and Hemlock.* London: Methuen Children's, 1985. Print.

_____. "The Heroic Ideal—A Personal Odyssey." *The Lion and the Unicorn: A Critical Journal of Children's Literature* 13.1 (June 1989): 129–140. Print.

_____. *Hexwood.* London: Collins, 2000. Print.

_____. *Howl's Moving Castle.* London: Collins, 2000. Print.

_____. *The Merlin Conspiracy.* London: Collins, 2004. Print.

_____. *The Tough Guide to Fantasyland: The Essential Guide to Fantasy Travel.* New York: Firebird, 1996. Print.

Kaplan, Deborah."Disrupted Expectations: Young/Old Protagonists in Diana Wynne Jones's Novels." *Journal of the Fantastic Arts* 22.2 (Spring 2011): 197–209. Print.

Mendlesohn, Farah. *Diana Wynne Jones: Children's Literature and the Fantastic Tradition.* New York: Routledge, 2005. Print.

_____. *Rhetorics of Fantasy.* Middletown, CT: Wesleyan University Press, 2008. Print.

Mills, Alice. "Archetypes and the Unconscious in Harry Potter and Diana Wynne Jones's Fire and Hemlock and Dogsbody." *Reading Harry Potter: Critical Essays.* Ed. Giselle Liza Anatol. Westport, CT: Praeger, 2003. 3–13. Print

Rudd, David. "Building Castles in the Air: (De)construction in Howl's Moving Castle." *Journal of the Fantastic Arts* 22.2 (Spring 2011): 257–270. Print.

A New Kind of Hero:
A Song of Ice and Fire's Brienne of Tarth

John H. Cameron

Like many writers in the fantasy genre, George R. R. Martin is interested in knights and heroes. Not only is he interested in knights, but, more importantly, he is also interested in the problems associated with knighthood. An example of the ideal of knighthood is laid out in an oath from one of Martin's novellas set in the earlier world of Westeros, *The Hedge Knight*:

> ... touching the blade to the squire's right shoulder, "in the name of the Warrior I charge you to be brave." The sword moves from right shoulder to left. "In the name of the Father I charge you to be just." Back to the right. "In the name of the Mother I charge you to defend the young and innocent." The left. "In the name of the Maid I charge you to protect all women..." [518].

Throughout his writings, and particularly in *A Song of Ice and Fire*,[1] Martin shows many knights that try to live up to these ideals of bravery, justness, and charity. These are ideals that Martin, a keen reader of medieval history and romance, would have borrowed freely from Arthurian romances with an equal awareness of how these ideals have been used and abused throughout history (Archibald 151–52).[2] Equally problematic, the issue was not merely that knights found living up to such ideals difficult for, as Meera Reed reminds Bran Stark in *Storm of Swords*, "sometimes the knights are the monsters" (*SS* 339). As Martin is well aware, the ideals expressed by Chrétien de Troyes and Thomas Malory rarely reflected the knights of history as described by Frances Gies, who "had little in common with the courtly heroes of the Round Table. Ignorant and unlettered, rough in speech and manners, he earned his living largely by violence, uncontrolled by a public justice that had virtually disappeared" (17).

It is important to note that Martin does more than simply condemn such injustices; instead, he tries to show the genuine difficulties of being a knight and of trying to maintain one's vows in a world where such vows are constantly being forsaken. Interestingly, and in a way entirely in keeping with all of the other genre rules that he breaks, Martin's main testing ground for true knighthood is a character few may expect: Brienne of Tarth. The sole surviving child of Selwyn Tarth, Brienne finds herself trying to negotiate the trials of knighthood in increasingly perilous circumstances. During the course of *A Song of Ice and Fire* she serves under a succession of leaders, from Renly Baratheon to Catelyn Stark to Jaime Lannister, and each of these stints of service teaches her something new and unexpected about what it means to be a knight and a hero. In this sense through Brienne Martin presents a true negotiation of knighthood, a negotiation that is threefold, for it involves the reader of *A Song of Ice and Fire*, as well as Brienne's antagonist and eventual ally Jaime, and Brienne of Tarth herself. Readers unaccustomed to Martin's representation of knighthood are asked to come along with Brienne and experience her tests and trials through her eyes, and this experience has led both readers of the series and viewers of the HBO series to see her as a "fan favorite" (Collins). Jaime begins his encounters with Brienne in an entirely negative vein, mocking and criticizing her whenever and wherever he can; however, as the story progresses he comes to truly respect Brienne and regard her as a true knight and hero. At the same time, Brienne herself must negotiate her own way through the difficult world of knighthood, and it is during this negotiation that she learns just how difficult ideals like honor and chivalry are to maintain. Brienne's struggles show that living up to the ideals of knighthood may not only be difficult, but it may not be possible, for while "words [are] easy," "deeds [are] hard" (*FC* 81). It is through her negotiation of knighthood in *A Song of Ice and Fire* and, secondly, in HBO's *Game of Thrones*, that Brienne of Tarth truly emerges as a new kind of hero, and one that helps to redefine the parameters, challenge old stereotypes, and expand the development of the female hero in modern fantasy in innovative ways.

Martin, Fantasy Fiction, and Feminism

As Martin shows, such redefining, challenging, and expanding will not be easy. The world of *A Song of Ice and Fire* is one in which "the weak" seem to exist only "for the strong to play with," one in which "all the stories" that have been told of good people and "true knights" seem little more than "lies" (*CK* 757). Perhaps it is because of his strong awareness of such injustices that Martin is always more engaged with exploring the more powerless and marginalized voices of Westeros. Such engagement extends to his female characters, and Martin gives them a voice that is often denied them. Perhaps thinking less of *A Song of Ice and Fire* than of the genre as she imagines it, Ginia Bellafante nevertheless dismisses the entire series as "boys' fiction," and even argues that the television series' more adult content reflects not just adult concerns but a trick "tossed in as a little something for the ladies, out of a justifiable fear, perhaps, that no woman alive would watch otherwise" ("A Fantasy World"). To Bellafante, Martin's female characters, with all of their struggles, defeats, and triumphs, are little more than a "patronizingly" unsuccessful attempt by Martin "to reach the population's other half" ("A Fantasy World"). Embedded within Bellafante's critique, of course, is a far more patronizing view of female readers and viewers than the one she charges Martin with having. Another reviewer, equally dismissive of the series and of what he perceives as Martin's take on gender, argues that both the books and the show are "so screamingly aimed at the adolescent male mind that [he felt] slightly embarrassed about once being a male teenager" and that "women viewers" must "feel differently about *Game of Thrones*" than male ones (Doyle). In keeping with such perceived differences, *The Guardian* even recently had an online poll to ask readers the old clichéd question about whether the fantasy genre could even be enjoyed by women, only to have 90% strongly respond that it could ("Is fantasy fiction a guy thing?").

To anyone who has actually read *A Song of Ice and Fire* or fully watched *Game of Thrones*, such charges are ludicrously unfair, for the fact remains that most "of the major players ... in the game of thrones are women" (Meslow) and that these female characters all play tremendously important roles in the series, an importance perhaps best expressed by Martin's somewhat sarcastic response to an interviewer's comment that his female characters are, actually, rather well written: "you know, I've always considered women to be people" ("George R. R. Martin."). Martin's female heroes offer a direct challenge to his critics, for they are not only as interesting and as complex as his male characters, but they are often more so. In fact, Martin says that the large number of female fans his series has been able to attract is "one of the things that pleases [him] most" (Salter). He is also pleased when fans criticize one of his female characters because of "things that they've done [as characters], not because the character is underdeveloped" or overlooked (Salter). While reticent about being called a feminist, Martin nevertheless feels that, for him, "being a feminist is about treating men and women the same," and that he "regard[s] men and women as all human—yes there are differences, but many of those differences are created by the culture that we live in, whether it's the medieval culture of Westeros, or 21st century western culture" (Salter).

The world that Martin creates is certainly misogynistic, but to show is not to approve, and the lens through which we see that world is always more complex, with female characters having to navigate their way through this world as best as they can. Much to Martin's credit, such navigation reveals not only female strength, but the wide varieties in which such strength manifests itself as, Charli Carpenter summarizes:

Catelyn draws on her maternal power to guide her son's army. Daenerys, buoyed by the soft-power tactics she learned from her handmaid, seizes power in the wake of her husband's death, using it to, among other things, advance a feminist liberation policy in the lands across the Narrow Sea. Cersei uses her beauty and family connections ruthlessly, but constantly risks ensnarement by the very gender scripts she has so cleverly manipulated. Osha the wildling toys with Westerosi class and gender norms in conversations with Theon, then playfully throws them away in favor of a blunt eco-libertarianism. Arya refuses the roles society has set for her as a girl; warriors Brienne and Asha (whose name has been changed for the TV series) follow different paths to power on masculine terms ["Game of Thrones as Theory"].

While apt in many ways, this is unfair to Sansa, in Carpenter's assessment a clichéd character "who appears to buy into notions of chivalry" and is "pitiably naïve"; however, this assessment overlooks Sansa's own quiet strength, for she is forced to try to survive in King's Landing following her father's execution, a world in which she is entirely on her own with no friends or allies to help her. Martin's interest in such ambivalent and ambiguous characters is heightened by his use of POV chapters that place readers alongside the Starks one minute and the Lannisters the next, so much so that they often "end up rooting, tragically, for both sides" (Hodgman). Even distinguishing sides can be daunting. For the POV chapters Martin has taken to using titles for characters in recent books—such as Sansa Stark and Theon Greyjoy—other than their own names to suggest the shifting nature of their allegiances and even identities. Such chapter divisions also suggest the degree to which identity and gender distinctions are constructed rather than fixed, and they force readers to ask important questions about our oft-thwarted desire for easy categorization. Not only is such categorization wrong from a moral standpoint, but it is also simply inaccurate, for such labels can never account for the unaccountable.

Brienne of Tarth as Ideal Knight?

Such unaccountability is in evidence as readers first experience Brienne of Tarth, for she does not receive a POV chapter until *A Feast of Crows* despite appearing in two previous entries of the series, *A Clash of Kings* and *A Storm of Swords*. When we first encounter her it is through the eyes of Catelyn Stark, who has come to Bitterbridge to negotiate terms with Renly Baratheon. Renly has staged a tourney, in which Brienne manages to defeat numerous other nights, including Renly's champion and lover Ser Loras Tyrell, and remains the sole knight standing. However, the fact that Brienne has done the defeating is not initially clear, as she is dressed in blue armor that masks her gender, so much so that Catelyn believes her to be a man and is shocked and even "horrified" to discover otherwise (*CK* 343).[3] Even in her victory Brienne is mocked by her fellow nights—"though not to her face" (*CK* 344)—but Renly is sufficiently impressed to allow Brienne to serve as one of his seven most elite knights, the Rainbow Guard. Although a strong female hero herself, Catelyn is less impressed by Brienne's skill on the battlefield than she is moved to pity by her appearance: *"Is there any creature on earth as unfortunate as an ugly woman?"* (*CK* 344, emphasis in original).[4] This mix of admiration for her skill as a fighter and disapproval over her gender typifies the response of many in Westeros; even when Brienne is formally inducted into the Rainbow Guard, "her smile lit up her face, and her voice was strong and proud," but it "was painful to see" the "way she looked at the king—looked *down* at him" (*CK* 344, emphasis in original). Seated at a point of honor at the high table, Brienne is nevertheless shunned by her fellow knights, suffering in silence and constantly looking down at her food instead of engaging with the others (*CK* 347–48). Perhaps the strongest example of the complex nature of Brienne's reception at Renly's court is the fact that Renly gives her the cloak that he has reserved for Ser Barriston when he had hoped that he, the greatest in Westeros, might join his cause (*CK* 351). She is a woman in a man's world, and though Renly will later call on her to "carry his banner," she will do so wearing "plate armor that [gives] no hint of her sex" (*CK* 475). In any case, it is not the last time that Brienne will be given a gift initially meant for another famous knight, and these gifts will come to reflect the degree to which she is trying, above all else, to be a knight and a hero on her terms. Brienne's attempt to be an ideal knight help to make her a new kind of hero.

Martin lets readers see Brienne through Catelyn's eyes so that they, like Catelyn, can begin to gain a better understanding of this, and this allows Martin's readers the chance to better negotiate their own conceptions of knighthood and heroism. This negotiation is affected by Brienne's own motivations for joining Renly's Rainbow Guard, for as much as she wants to prove herself, she also wants to be close to the man she loves. Catelyn sees this, and she feels pity for a love that can never be requited: *"She loves him, poor thing, she thought sadly. She'd play his squire just to touch him, and never care how great a fool they think her"* (*CK* 483, emphasis in original). From Lancelot and Guinevere to countless others, the theme of unrequited love is common to knightly tales and romances of courtly love; however, Martin's twist on the convention is quite unique, for his knight is not a man in love with an unapproachable maiden but a female knight in love with a king, one who is both married to another and engaged in an affair with his wife's brother. Oblivious to this, Brienne sees Renly—in the best courtly love tradition—as a wholly perfect king and man, and so the enormity of her grief when Renly is later murdered is almost palpable (*CK* 502). One may not feel that Renly is quite as perfect as Brienne does, but one does feel, as Catelyn does, that Brienne is to be pitied when she loses her love at the moment that it is closest: "I never held him but as he died" (*CK* 504). It is at this moment of grief and pain that Brienne swears a new vow to kill Renly's brother Stannis; she may not have been able to protect Renly, but she can avenge his death. Catelyn can see Brienne's worth and can—whatever her initial misgivings—begin to appreciate it. Thus Catelyn manages to direct Brienne's grief to a new purpose, forswearing her vow of revenge and instead swearing a new vow of fealty to Catelyn herself to be her "liege man, or ... whatever [she] would have [her] to be" (*CK* 562). In yet another twist on tradition, Brienne swears fealty not to a king but to a lord's wife, a twist that Catelyn notes with some amusement. Just as Brienne had sworn "by the old gods and the new" to protect Renly (*CK* 344), so too does she now swear to "shield" Catelyn's "back and keep [her] counsel and give [her] life for [hers], if need be" (*CK* 562).

The only problem for Brienne is that this service does not involve, at least initially, much fighting or protecting of honor or any of the other things typically associated with knighthood. In fact, Catelyn is at first chagrined to find that Brienne will not act in accordance with what everyone else feels that she ought to be doing as a woman (*CK* 649–50).[5] Again Martin presents an underhanded compliment to Brienne's abilities as a knight, for while she has been asked to stay back and defend Riverrun, it is only because all "the able-bodied men" have been "taken for the fords" and there is no one left "to protect a castle crammed full of women and children" (*CK* 650). Catelyn respects Brienne, but she seems to forget that Brienne was the last knight left standing in a tourney involving 116 knights-at-arms. Although she is a strong woman herself, Catelyn's views often reflect the chauvinistic attitudes prevalent in her world. Catelyn has been raised to believe that she should be protected by "the men of [her] House," but "while they are away from" her, she "suppose[s] that [Brienne] must fill their place" (*CK* 652). Much to Catelyn's surprise, Brienne is more than capable of doing so, advising on military strategy (*CK* 656) and providing support when Catelyn is questioning a foe (*CK* 659). However, when the subject of her singing abilities come up, particularly when they are linked to her service of Renly (*CK* 660), Brienne's complexities can truly be seen, for although she may have a strong arm, she also has a heart. It is perhaps for this reason that Catelyn begins to see Brienne as a truly worthy knight, for she has compassion as well as skill at combat, and she can be trusted in a way that few of the other knights in *A Song of Ice and Fire* can.

Here lies the interesting irony of Martin's challenge to the idea of female heroism. Is compassion a mark of female heroism in a way that it is not for a male hero? Is Brienne's compassion a way of bowing to stereotypical gender expectations, or is it because Catelyn is female that she perceives this compassion is a positive quality? Whatever the case may be, here Brienne manages to elevate herself in Catelyn's eyes. This elevation shows the degree to which Brienne has to navigate knighthood in her own way. As many critics have noted, medieval romances—the key source for many of Martin's conceptions of knighthood ("My Hero")—often deal with the problems of heroism: "as they celebrate male prowess, many romances reveal the burden of masculinity, the shame of dishonor, the difficulty of sacrificing one's sentimental life for the greater cause ... or a knight's failure to adhere to a code" (Krueger 143). All of the factors that plagued the more traditional hero are complicated by the fact that Brienne is a woman who tries to live up to more masculine ideals of knighthood while also following her own moral code of heroism, one that challenges the prejudices of those around her. This will become particularly clear in her dealing with Jaime Lannister, whose attitudes are reflective of the very stereotypes concerning heroism that Brienne combats; and their relationship serves to show just how much Brienne can be seen as a new kind of hero.

Brienne of Tarth: A New Kind of Hero

Martin has shown the way that Brienne is a new kind of hero by allowing Catelyn to see her with respect, but he now explores this heroism by means of contrast with another knight: Jaime Lannister. Through the contrast with Jamie Lannister, many of Brienne's heroic traits emerge. The fact that he is a man points up the fact that Martin means for us to compare them in gendered terms. Jaime Lannister does not share Catelyn's high estimation of Brienne, and so he is clearly surprised when he finds that Catelyn tasks Brienne with the responsibility of taking him and Cleos Frey to King's Landing to exchange Lannister for Catelyn's daughters Sansa and Arya. Jaime is amused at this arrangement, and he refuses at first to give Brienne any kind of respect, either as a woman or as a knight. To Jaime, Brienne appears as "*a big strong peasant wench to look at her, yet she speaks like one highborn and wears longsword and dagger. Ah, but can she use them*? Jaime meant to find out..." (*SS* 18–19, emphasis in original). "Wench" is the name Jaime will continually use for Brienne, but she serves him one better and refuses to call him anything other than "Kingslayer," a reference to his killing of Aerys II. If Brienne saw Renly as perfect, as being someone who "would have been the *best* king," for "he was so good" that he cannot be equaled (*CK* 561, emphasis in original), she sees Jaime as a monster, for "a man who would violate his own sister, murder his king, and fling an innocent child to his death deserves no other name" (*SS* 21). Unperturbed by her disapproval, Jaime does his best to perturb Brienne, mocking her unattractiveness and her unrequited love of Renly, all in an attempt to make her drop her guard and allow him a chance to escape. While his attempts are largely unsuccessful, Brienne *is* perturbed by the "knightly" behavior she sees on display throughout

Riverrun, with dead bodies strewn about and "a live oak full of dead women" (*SS* 25). In one of her earliest lessons in the realities of knighthood, Jaime sarcastically counters Brienne's charge that "this was not chivalrously done" and that "no true knight would condone such wanton butchery" with the reflection that "true knights see worse every time they ride to war.... And *do* worse, yes" (*SS* 25, emphasis in original). His sarcasm is underscored further by the revelation that this brutality was committed by the Starks, the very family Brienne is serving (*SS* 26). Just because one is serving a cause faithfully does not mean that a cause is faithful. Nevertheless, Brienne "swore an oath to bring [Jaime] safe to King's Landing," and she, much to Jaime's annoyance and "wonder[,] ... mean[s] to keep it" (*SS* 32).

Words are easy, but deeds are difficult. Jaime Lannister, the knight infamous throughout Westeros for killing the king he had sworn to protect, knows this better than anyone. He mocks Brienne insistently, particularly over her intense devotion to her word, but his own difficult negotiation with knighthood begins to make him more empathetic to her situation. However, such empathy does not keep Jaime from taking delight in Brienne's discomfort, such as in the many moments when—as Jaime puts it—"*the wench* ... [is] *reminded that she's a wench*" (*SS* 148, emphasis in original). Whatever Jaime or others may call her, Brienne acts as courteously as she believes a knight should, paying for provisions and horses when most in arms would have simply just taken for themselves. Despite such courteousness, Brienne is not naïve, and she earns Jaime's respect when she takes a road different from the one that they were recommended, as the recommended road likely has outlaws waiting at the other end of it: "Well, she may be ugly but she's not entirely stupid. Jaime gave her a grudging smile" (*SS* 154). It may be "grudging," but it is a smile nonetheless, for Jaime begins to respect this knight in spite of himself. He may mock her, call her a "wench," and take delight in her describing herself as her father's only son, but Jaime will nevertheless ask her forgiveness for his behavior. Brienne rejects such apologies and takes Jaime to task for having "harmed others," particularly those he was "sworn to protect" such as "the weak" and "the innocent," but Jaime gives Brienne another lesson in the realities of knighthood when he tells her not to "presume to judge" what she can "not understand" (*SS* 155). Brienne is right when she says that Jaime has broken his vows, but she will come to realize that while words may be easy, deeds truly are difficult. Like Jaime, like everyone, Brienne has her own sins to bear, and he almost manages to take her off her guard and away from her sword when he calls her out—in reference to her being accused of Renly's murder in *A Clash of Kings*—as a fellow kingslayer, only one who was able to lie better than he could: "your wits are quicker than mine, I confess it. When they found me standing over my dead king, I never thought to say, 'No, no, it wasn't me, it was a shadow, a terrible cold shadow'.... Tell me true, one kingslayer to another..." (*SS* 157). Nevertheless,

Brienne, unlike Jaime, will not break her vow to Catelyn no matter how much she is tested.

Jaime is annoyed by this loyalty, but he also learns from it as well, and this stands as the strongest example of his ability to see Brienne as a true hero and respect her for her qualities. This can be seen when Brienne and Jaime both take on the outlaws who have killed Cleos, a scrape that is immediately followed by a swordfight between them, for Jaime manages to take Cleos' sword. Jaime has frequently been called the one of the best swordfighters in Westeros, and yet Brienne, much to Jaime's surprise, is able to hold her own: "he stepped back and let the point of the sword fall to the ground, giving her a moment of respite. 'Not half bad,' he acknowledged. 'For a wench'" (*SS* 289–90). As the fight proceeds Jaime upgrades his assessment of Brienne's talents, as she goes from "wench" to "a squire," perhaps "a green one," in his identification of her, but as the fight proceeds further he comes to realize to his horror that "*she is stronger than*" he is (*SS* 290–91).[6] For a knight such as Jaime, a man who has defeated so many other knights, this is too much to bear: "with speed and skill, Jaime could beat them all. But this was a *woman*" (*SS* 291, emphasis in original). His pride does not allow Jaime to yield, but it is clear that he has lost this match against Brienne, to be saved—if that is the right word—from his humiliation by the arrival of The Brave Companions, who promptly take them both captive (*SS* 291–97). Jaime may not be willing to admit it, but Brienne shows him that she is a true knight and hero and that she deserves his respect as such.

Unfortunately, The Brave Companions are not knights, true or otherwise, and they honor none of the rules of war, particularly those involving the treatment of prisoners. Sellswords who were initially in the pay of Jaime's own father Tywin Lannister, they have chosen to disregard each and every rule associated with the conduct of war. As much as the knights of Westeros might fail to live up to their codes of honor, they at least swear a very strict oath to try to do so (*The Hedge Knight* 518). The Brave Companions care for none of these oaths of protection, and their behavior reflects that as described by the Hound above. When they say that they have "trade[d] [their] lion pelts for wolfskins" because the Starks seemed to be winning the war against the Lannister, Jaime mockingly retorts: "and men say I have shit for honor?" (*SS* 293). Despite such quips, Jaime realizes how dangerous these men are, and he instructs Brienne not to resist when they attempt to rape her, for if she "fight[s] them, [she]'ll lose more than a few teeth" (*SS* 294). Brienne will not heed his advice, and so Jaime tries to save Brienne not by appealing to the mercy of The Brave Companions but by appealing to their greed. Although "Tarth is called the Sapphire Isle for the blue of its waters," Jaime convinces The Brave Companions that the name actually means that Brienne's "father is rich in gemstones" (*SS* 295). The lie manages to save Brienne, but it does not save Jaime, for he loses his hand to The Brave Companions, who—in addition to being simply sadistic—worry about a

Bolton-Lannister alliance and feel that such a mutilation may help to prevent it.[7] Brienne tries to save Jaime, but she is severely beaten by her captors for her efforts. Brienne cites her oath to keep Jaime safe, but such words, as she is beginning to find out, mean little in a world of oathbreakers. In a phrase that will be repeated again and again through *A Feast for Crows*, "words are wind" (*FC* 363).

As Brienne and the mutilated Jaime make their way to Harrenhal and Roose Bolton, they are mocked by one of their captors in a jest that reflects, on the one hand, the misogyny of Westeros and, on the other, the degree to which Martin has upended our understanding of such attitudes, both in Westeros and in our own world: "The lovers ... and what a lovely sight they are. 'Twould be cruel to separate the good knight and his lady.... Ah, but which one is the knight and which one is the lady?" (*SS* 413–14). Again the text is suggestive of the courtly love tradition, but we are also reminded of the degree to which Martin is working to redefine that tradition. This becomes even clearer as Brienne begins to discover a new side to knighthood, one that involves more than just swords and armor. Seeing that Jaime has given up on life in despair, she encourages him to "live ... live, and fight, and take revenge" (*SS* 415). Jaime appreciates her encouragement, and perhaps this is why he begins to see her as both "protector" (*SS* 424) and confidante, for she has "protected [him] as well as any man could have, and better than most" (*SS* 505). And so Jaime tells Brienne the full story of his role in Aerys II's murder, a story he has never told anyone (*SS* 505–08). It is not a tale for the naïve or the innocent, or for those trying to stick to a vow, for it reveals one of the central issues at the heart of Martin's world, an issue earlier described by Jaime to Catelyn:

> "So many vows ... they make you swear and swear. Defend the king. Obey the king. Keep his secrets. Do his bidding. Your life for his. But obey your father. Love your sister. Protect the innocent. Defend the weak. Respect the gods. Obey the laws. It's too much. No matter what you do, you're forsaking one vow or the other" [*CK* 796].

Brienne is troubled by Jaime's revelations, but in many ways she still remains— as Jaime calls her—"*an innocent*" (*SS* 516, emphasis in original), unable to fully grasp just how it is that good people can be capable of evil. At the same time, she begins to learn that the reverse may be true, that bad people can sometimes be capable of good, for Jaime, despite having all of his instincts demand that he do otherwise, risks[8] his life to save Brienne from being raped and murdered by The Brave Companions. The man who is most infamous for having broken his word decides to keep his word to Brienne, for he has learned from her something valuable about what it means to be a true knight. In one of the more famous scenes in *A Storm of Swords*, Jaime races back to Harrenhal to find Brienne in a bear-pit, with a wooden tourney sword and "no shield, no breastplate, no chainmail, not even boiled leather, [but] only pink satin and Myrish lace"

(*SS* 616). Like a true knight, Jaime saves Brienne, but, in a true twist on convention, he has learned how to be a knight and a hero from Brienne herself. Perhaps this is why Jaime, who has so often called Brienne a "wench," corrects someone else who uses that term with "her name is Brienne" (*SS* 618).

Jaime's adventures with Brienne represent a real negotiation of knighthood, one that involves a true reevaluation of his own and of Brienne's actual worth. In a real sense, Jaime not only learns to respect Brienne, but he learns about just what it means to be a knight as a result of his encounters with her. This becomes all the more clear when they both arrive at King's Landing, the very place that Brienne has vowed to bring him, only to find out that Catelyn Stark has been killed along with her son Robb and most of the Stark forces at the Red Wedding.[9] Brienne has kept her vow to bring Jaime back to King's Landing, but "that was only half," for she had also promised to bring back Sansa and Arya Stark (*SS* 844). Left without a lady to serve, Brienne balks at the idea of serving "oathbreakers and murderers," but Jaime reflects that such are those who most knights have to serve: "*Then why did you ever bother putting on a sword?*" (*SS* 845, emphasis in original). Jaime is also an oathbreaker and a murderer, but, seeing that Brienne "does have honor" (*SS* 847) and is "loyal past the sense of sense" (*SS* 924), he manages to keep her from being punished for Renly's murder by Loras Tyrell, not on the basis of his influence, but on that of her merits. Loras comes to see Brienne's worth as a knight, for while he remarks that Renly had initially thought Brienne absurd for being "a woman dressed in man's mail, pretending to be a knight," he soon sees that all the other knights "wanted things of him," but "all that Brienne wanted was to die for" Renly (*SS* 925). The fact that two of the greatest knights in the realm come to such conclusions suggests just how much Martin has upended conventions, for Brienne finally becomes a true knight, one far greater than the other knights who may mock her. Seeing this, Jaime decides to maintain his own vow to Catelyn Stark, a vow spoken "with a sword at [his] throat" (*SS* 1007), but one that he nevertheless decides to honor by sending Brienne to find the missing Sansa Stark and protect from his sister Cersei. He also gives her the very sword that his father Tywin had given him, a sword of Valryian steel that has been made from Eddard Stark's own sword Ice. The gift of this sword signifies just how Jaime— however much he may try to avoid fully admitting it—has come to respect Brienne, and he asks her to name the sword "Oathkeeper" so that Brienne can "make good [their] stupid vows to … precious dead Lady Catelyn" (*SS* 1008–09).

The New Knight's Quest

Martin chooses to relay the quest to find Sansa from Brienne's own perspective, and so readers of *A Feast for Crows* finally get to see things through her eyes. Brienne faces many trials, but her sole focus is her "promise [to] Lady Catelyn that she would bring back her daughters," for "no promise was as solemn as one sworn to the dead" (*FC* 83). Things do not begin especially well for Brienne, for she soon comes upon a pair of older knights, who mockingly remark that they "took her for a knight as well" (*FC* 84). Such a qualification of praise has been with Brienne throughout her life, and in *A Feast for Crows* Martin provides a much fuller picture of her upbringing, including her father's frustrated attempts to find a suitor for her, a daughter who wanted to be a knight and not a wife. One suitor, Ser Humfrey Wagstaff, learned the hard way, as Brienne defeated him on the battlefield in order to avoid becoming his wife: "He was her third prospective husband, and her last. Her father did not insist again" (*FC* 202). Brienne's complicated love life will continue to be explored throughout the series. Martin also provides a fuller picture of Brienne's early love for Renly, a love that inspires her to try to join his Rainbow Guard (*FC* 87). Brienne still has to face the taunts of her fellow knights and companions—who try to protect her like "some great lady ... though this lady dwarfed both of her protectors and was better armed and armored in the nonce" (FC 89)—but she still has faith. And so, Brienne prays to the Crone for guidance she decides to hold firm to her knightly quest: "*Lead me,* she prayed, *light the way before me, show me the path that leads to Sansa.* She had failed Renly, had failed Lady Catelyn. She must not fail Jaime" (emphasis in original *FC* 99).

Her task to bring back Catelyn's daughters is difficult, if not impossible, for Sansa is hiding under an assumed name and Brienne has little to no leads on her whereabouts (*FC* 192–93). Further complicating things are the constant insults Brienne receives at the hands of everyone she meets, from knights on the road to the daughters of farmers, whose taunts "were just as cruel as" those of "men" (*FC* 286). Such incessant criticisms take their toll, and even Brienne sometimes wonders whether she is a real knight (*FC* 285), but she refuses to lose hope: "*I will never stop looking. I will give up my life if need be, give up my honor, give up all my dreams, but I will find her*" (*FC* 200, emphasis in original). Her task is lightened somewhat when Brienne, like any real knight, finds herself a squire, Podrick Payne, a young boy who had once squired for Tyrion Lannister (*FC* 204–05). Their adventures continue as they navigate the ruins of Riverrun, with numerous examples of the atrocities being committed by all sides of the conflict (*FC* 186, 779) and the lack of honor among men. However, even as "men will always underestimate" her (*FC* 203), Brienne manages to stay one step ahead of her foes, including former members of The Brave Companions whom she manages to defeat when they believe that they have led her into a trap (*FC* 414–23). Such victories are satisfying, but they are often not enough, for Brienne's life as a knight is one filled with compliments on the one hand and chastisements on the other, particularly from those such as Lord Randyll Tarly, who angrily declares that she should have never "donned mail, nor buckled a sword," and that when she is raped she should not look to him for justice, for she "will have earned it with [her] folly" (*FC* 295–96). Tarly was the one who had ended the mock courting Brienne had received from other knights while serving Renly at Highgarden (*FC* 299–301), but to Tarly the blame for the knights' behavior laid at her door alone: "The blame is yours .... The gods made men to fight, and women to bear children .... A woman's war is in the birthing bed" (*FC* 301). It is interesting that Brienne should recall such troubling comments while she is on a quest as a knight, for they indicate that, however much she may disagree with such accusations, she can sometimes feel as uncomfortable with herself as others do: "the only child the gods let [her father] keep. The freakish one, not fit to be a son *or* daughter" (emphasis in original *FC* 672). Brienne's achievements as a knight will always be discounted and ignored by many in Westeros, and she despairs at the idea that Sansa may have left for Essos, for she would be seen as "*even more* [of] *a freak there,*" and that "*they will laugh at* [her], *as they laughed at Highgarden*" (*FC* 299, emphasis in original). A truly complex character, Brienne is never wholly confident in her abilities, but this lack of confidence ultimately inspires her to go further. This persistence shows that she truly is, regardless of the chastisement of Tarly and others, whose "*words are* [only] *wind*" (*FC* 520, emphasis in original), a real knight and hero. As she later says to Tarly, after he has yet again tried to dissuade her from being a knight, "all I can do is try" (*FC* 519).

Arguably, it is because she continues to try, that readers and audiences have responded so strongly to Brienne of Tarth. She is truly trying her best to be a knight, and Martin's representation of her struggle confirms just how much he is to be applauded for showing us a new kind of female hero, one that truly challenges the status quo as maintained by those who mocked her and tried to stop her. Her path to knighthood may be "a crooked one," but she is navigating it as best she can (*FC* 657). It is a path that has many tests, all of which are difficult, but this is the path that Brienne has chosen. Believing that "*a true knight is sworn to protect those who are weaker than himself, or die in the attempt*" (*FC* 665, emphasis in original), Brienne follows a series of false leads in her quest to Sansa, including one that has her following the Hound, a man who is already dead (*FC* 669–70).[10] She often wishes that she could just return home, or go back to Jaime at King's Landing (*FC* 788), but she always decides to keep going and following the leads as they come. One of those leads results, in a series full of ironic reversals, with one of the most ironic reversals of all, as Brienne is ultimately captured during her quest by members of The Brotherhood Without Banners as she tries to fight off the remaining members of The Brave Companions who try to attack and rape her (*FC* 794–99). The Brotherhood Without Banners has been hanging members of the Frey family throughout Riverrun in retaliation for their role in the Red Wedding, and they are led by none other than Catelyn Stark, who has been resurrected from the dead by Beric Dondarrion and who has taken on the name of Lady Stoneheart to symbolize her cold resolve to enact her vengeance. Brienne and Podrick are brought to a cave to be hanged by The Brotherhood Without Banners, men who, like Brienne, have come to realize how difficult it is to serve and keep true to a sacred vow: "We were king's men when we began, ... but king's men must have a king, and we have none. We were brothers too, but now our brotherhood is broken. I do not know who we are, if truth be told, nor where we might be going" (*FC* 907). This seems an appropriate passage to support the point, not only because it reflects Brienne's predicament as well, but also because it reflects my own predicament as a critic, for I am writing about a character whose story is not yet finished. In the most recent entry in the series, *A Dance with Dragons*, Brienne finds herself in the hands of her former master, but her master has changed not only in appearance but in every way. Even though her service to him is ultimately in Catelyn's name, Brienne's connection to Jaime is enough to seal her fate with The Brotherhood, and they accuse her of being a Lannister and a traitor.

In yet another ironic twist, Brienne's sword, Oathkeeper, signifies not her loyalty but her betrayal, for she has received it from none other than the Kingslayer himself: "Deny it all you want. That swords says you're a liar" (*FC* 912). Although her voice has been affected by her wounds, Catelyn whispers to her companion that the sword should be called not "Oathkeeper" but "Oath-breaker," for "it was made for treachery and murder" and that the sword should be called "*False Friend*" to symbolize Brienne's betrayal (*FC* 913, emphasis in original). The dramatic irony comes from the fact that Brienne has spent so much of the story proving that she is not a false friend, and so many readers may be shocked by such accusations. If so, they are all the more shocked when Catelyn orders that Brienne should be executed if she does not agree to kill Jaime for The Brotherhood. Brienne insists that they are wrong about Jaime and that he has changed, but her words fall on deaf ears: "you do not understand, Jaime ... he saved me from being raped when the Bloody Mummers took us, and later he came back for me, he leapt into the bear pit empty-handed.... I swear to you he is not the man he was" (*FC* 915). Forced to make a choice between "the sword [and] the noose," Brienne refuses to "make that choice" (*FC* 915). As difficult and fraught with complications as it may have been, Brienne's negotiation of knighthood has always involved her staying true to her word. She may reprimand herself for failing in her services (*FC* 406), but she has never gone back on her oath to remain true.

A Quest Unfinished...

Or has she? As mentioned above, this is a story that is not yet finished, and Brienne's narrative in *A Feast for Crows* ends with her being struck up to a tree, forced to watch her page Podrick die alongside her and forced likewise to feel the pain of the rope as it strangles her. Ending her story in *A Feast for Crows* with a tremendous cliffhanger, Martin writes: "She screamed a word" (*FC* 916). As Brienne hangs from a tree about to die, she screams a word that we have yet to learn. However, this is not merely a cliffhanger involving danger or suspense, for it also involves our understanding of Brienne as the character that Martin has created. Does Brienne agree to break her oath? Does she yell out "sword" and, in doing so, agree to use Oathkeeper to do so? At present, we do not know for sure. All we do know is that Brienne is later found in *A Dance with Dragons* to be alive, for she manages to find Jaime at Pennytree, where he is spending the night after securing the surrender of Raventree Hall of House Blackwood. Instead of calling her "wench," Jaime calls Brienne his "lady," even though he thinks *"she looks ten years older than when* [he] *saw her last"* (*DD* 645–46, emphasis in original). Brienne's face is bandaged from her attack, but such a things as appearance is of no concern, for she has come, with Oathkeeper by her side, to remind Jaime of her "quest" (*DD* 646). Claiming to have found Sansa, Brienne says that she is being held by the Hound "a day's ride" away (*DD* 646). What are we to make of this, particularly since, as Brienne is well aware (*FC* 669–70), the Hound seems to be dead? Did Brienne choose to betray Jaime over keeping her word? Has her negotiation with knighthood ended with the conclusion that, as the Hound had once said, "there are no true knights" (*CK* 757)?

At this time we cannot say for certain either way. One certainly hopes that Brienne will keep her oath, but *A Song of Ice and Fire* abounds with oathbreakers. Brienne herself has made several vows over the course of the series, to Renly, to Catelyn, and even to Jaime, but, like Jaime, Brienne may come to realize one of the central issues at the heart of Martin's world, that, as Jaime says, "no matter what you do, you're forsaking one vow or the other" (*CK* 796). Martin has left Brienne in a real cliffhanger before we see her again in *A Dance with Dragons*, but Martin insists that despite the more physical and dramatic cliffhangers, he is most interested in such moments as "a character moment" and as "a moment of revelation," "something that makes you want to read more about this character" (qtd. in Poniewozik). What does this moment reveal about Brienne of Tarth? As Lev Grossman notes, "Martin is fond of sudden reversals," such as "the tasty but poisoned dish, the false god who abruptly proves all too real," and "the unsalvageable rogue who strikes a hidden vein of decency when we— and he—least expect it" (Grossman). In regards to that last reversal, might the reverse also be true? If a reversal can reveal goodness, can it also reveal its opposite? Has Brienne become a villain, or are such titles, just like gender titles, the very notions and codes that Martin seeks to question and undermine? As Andrew Serwer notes in his comparison between Martin and J. R. R. Tolkien, who is commonly viewed as the architect of modern fantasy:

Tolkien's monsters are literally monsters—his orcs, uruk-hai, and ringwraiths lack genuine free will, let alone the potential for individual moral redemption. Most of Martin's monsters are people—and just when you've decided to hate them, he writes a chapter from their perspective, forcing you to consider their point of view [Serwer].

Martin's monsters are more complex, and his works suggest that monstrousness is always, like righteousness, a very complicated affair. In Martin's world, "we're never quite so righteous as we think we are" (Serwer), and that many of "Tolkien's imitators" have created "terrible clichés" that have hurt the genre, with one of the worst of these being the treatment of the problem of good and evil:

I think the battle between good versus evil is within the individual human heart. We all have the capacity for good in us, we all have the capacity for evil, and I've always been attracted to grey characters rather than black and white characters. You read about these people who perform a heroic act and then the next day or the next year, ten years from now, perform a horrible act. And it's the same person ["Martin talks"].

In Brienne of Tarth Martin has created not simply a wonderfully nuanced and complex female hero, but a human being, with all the good and bad that that entails. It may be that Brienne has forsaken her vows, or it may be that she will still find a way to keep them. However, she is a hero nonetheless, regardless of what happens later, and her negotiation of knighthood has shown that she is as good "as any man could have, and better than most" (*SS* 505).

NOTES

1. The following abbreviations will be used to designate the works from *A Song of Ice and Fire*: *A Game of Thrones* (*GT*), *A Clash of Kings* (*CK*), *A Storm of Swords* (*SS*), *A Feast for Crows* (*FC*), and *A Dance with Dragons* (*DD*).

2. For more on this interplay between the ideal and the real, see Archibald's "Questioning Arthurian Ideals."

3. It should be noted that Brienne is not the only mystery night in *A Song of Fire and Ice*, nor may she be the only female mystery knight. Speculation is rife among fans of the series that the Knight of the Laughing Tree, who defeated three nights during the Tourney at Harrenhal that is described by Meera Reed in *A Storm of Swords*, may have been Lyanna Stark, although this has yet to be confirmed.

4. Interestingly, some fans of the books have responded negatively to the casting of Gwendoline Christie as Brienne, precisely because she is believed by some to be too attractive for the role. According to James Hibberd, who interviewed Christie after she had been cast, Christie said that "she was rather startled—and pleased—by the response" ("Christie on being 'too pretty'").

5. In an odd case of life imitating art, and of people reflecting the very narrow and biased views that Martin is attacking, tabloids such as *The Daily Mail* often make much of Gwendoline Christie when she is spotted wearing a dress (Strang), and have devoted whole headlines to this single topic ("Forget the armour"). One wonders whether they are actually reading the series or watching the show.

6. During the filming of the fight scene for television, Christie noted with satisfaction the moment when Nikolaj Coster-Waldau, who plays Jaime, asked her to "hit [him] 10 percent less hard" (Hibberd, "stars talk Jaime and Brienne's big fight").

7. In the television episode depicting this scene, the men who take Jaime and Brienne are not The Brave Companions but members of Roose Bolton's army, and Locke, the man who cuts off Jaime's hand, does it as much to show Jaime that he is not as strong as he thinks. As Locke tells Jaime, all the while pressing a blade to Jaime's face, "you are nothing without your daddy, and your daddy ain't here. Never forget that" ("Walk of Punishment").

8. As Christie refers to the scene in the third season episode "Kissed by Fire," Brienne recognizes [Jaime's] humanity, and his own struggle with what it is to be honorable. She's also seeing something of him in her—she's seeing his striving for the good of all, to an extent. It's a revelatory moment. It really expands Brienne's mind, shows her not to regard everything as being quite so black and white. We start to see the complexity of a person's mind developing" (Collins).

9. Of course, as readers of the series are aware, Catelyn is not dead, at least not quite, for she has been resurrected by Lord Beric Dondarrion and has taken on the name of Lady Stoneheart, leader of the Brotherhood without Banners and revenger upon anyone who has had any hand in the Red Wedding.

10. However, it should be noted that this, like so many other things in *A Song of Ice and Fire*, is a matter for debate, as some readers believe that he may have lived on to become anything from a gravedigger to a novice in a monastery.

Works Cited

Archibald, Elizabeth. "Questioning Arthurian Ideals." *The Cambridge Companion to the Arthurian Legend*. Ed. Elizabeth Archibald and Ad Putter. Cambridge: Cambridge University Press, 2009. 139–53. Print.

Barber, John. "George R.R. Martin: At the top of his Game (of Thrones)." *The Globe and Mail*. 11 Jul. 2011. Web. 15 Jul. 2013.

Bellafante, Ginia. "A Fantasy World of Strange Feuding Kingdoms." *The New York Times*. 14 Apr. 2011. Web. 15 Jul. 2013.

Carpenter, Charli. "Game of Thrones as Theory." *Foreign Affairs*. 29 Mar. 2012. Web. 15 Jul. 2013.

Collins, Sean T. "*Game of Thrones*' Q&A: Gwendoline Christie on the Education of Brienne of Tarth." *Rolling Stone*. 22 May 2013. Web. 15 Jul. 2013.

"Forget the Armour! *Game of Thrones* Star Gwendoline Christie Opts for a Thigh Skimming Dress at UK Series 3 Launch." The Daily Mail. 27 Mar. 2013. Web. 15 Jul. 2013.

"George R. R. Martin." *George Stroumboulopoulos Tonight*. George Stroumboulopoulos. CBC. 21 Aug. 2012. Television.

Gies, Frances. *The Knight in History*. New York: Harper Perennial, 1987. Print.

Grossman, Lev. "The American Tolkien." *Time*. 13 Nov. 2005. Web. 15 Jul. 2013.

Hibberd, James. "*Game of Thrones*': Christie on being 'too pretty' to play Brienne." *Entertainment Weekly*. 11 Mar. 2013. Web. 15 Jul. 2013.

_____. "*Game of Thrones*' Stars Talk Jaime and Brienne's Big Fight." *Entertainment Weekly*. 7 Apr. 2013. Web. 15 Jul. 2013.

Hodgman, John. "George R.R. Martin: Storyteller." *Time*. 21 Apr. 2011. Web. 15 Jul. 2013.

"Is Fantasy Fiction a Guy Thing?" *The Guardian*. 20 Apr. 2011. Web. 15 Jul. 2013.

Keen, Maurice. *Chivalry*. New Haven: Yale University Press, 2005. Print.

Krueger, Roberta. "Questions of Gender." *The Cambridge Companion to Medieval Romance*. Ed. Roberta Krueger. Cambridge: Cambridge University Press, 2000. 132–49. Print.

Martin, George R. R. *A Clash of Kings*. New York: Bantam, 1999. Print.

_____. *A Dance with Dragons*. New York: Bantam, 2011. Print.

_____. *A Game of Thrones*. New York: Bantam, 1996. Print.

_____. *A Feast for Crows*. New York: Bantam, 2005. Print.

_____. *The Hedge Knight*. *Legends: Short Novels by the Masters of Modern Fantasy*. Ed. Robert Silverberg. New York: Tor, 2005. 451–534. Print.

_____. *A Storm of Swords*. New York: Bantam, 2000. Print.

"Martin Talks About New Series *Game of Thrones*." *Digital Guardian*. 2012. Web. 15 Jul. 2013.

Meslow, Scott. "'*Game of Thrones*' Finale: The Powerful Women of Westeros." *The Atlantic*. 20 Jun. 2011. Web. 15 Jul. 2013.

Poniewozik, James. "George R. R. Martin Interview." *Time*. 15 Apr. 2011. Web. 15 Jul. 2013.

Salter, Jessica. "*Game of Thrones*'s George RR Martin: 'I'm a Feminist at Heart.'" *The Telegraph*. 1 Apr. 2013. Web. 15 Jul. 2013.

Serwer, Andrew. "A Liberal's Guide to Middle Earth." *The American Prospect*. 4 Apr. 2011. Web. 15 Jul. 2013.

Strang, Fay. "She's the Very Essence of Leggy! *Game of Thrones* Star Gwendoline Christie Sheds the Armour." *The Daily Mail*. 12 Jun. 2013. Web. 15 Jul. 2013.

"Walk of Punishment." *Game of Thrones*. Season 3. Dir. David Benioff. Writers: David Benioff and D. B. Weiss. HBO. 13 Apr. 2013. Television.

And *Her* Will Be Done:
The Girls Trump the Boys in
The Keys to the Kingdom and
Abhorsen Series by Garth Nix

Lori M. Campbell

"A mortal who wields the Key will become its tool as much as it is his. It will change you, in blood and bone, remaking you in the image of its maker."

—The Old One [Nix, *MM* 248][1]

The surface meaning of this quotation from *Mister Monday*, the first book of Garth Nix's *The Keys to the Kingdom* series is straightforward: by using the keys, the "mortal" alluded to here, Arthur Penhaligon, will be magically transformed over time from his skinny, asthmatic, human self into a being of supreme power. With closer scrutiny, however, and the knowledge that the maker of the keys is the *female* Architect of the entire universe, a more complex idea emerges. Does the Old One mean that Arthur will be transformed from he to she? Or, will Arthur be transformed into a Creator as she is a Creator, but only as an "image," a facsimile rather than a true being of power? In the first scenario, the sexual identification seems to be unimportant, while in the second such identification is emphasized. The female maintains supreme authority; Arthur can only be a lesser copy, not her equal. Either way, the passage offers a prime example of Nix's treatment of gender, not only in this series but across his work. It is not that gender does not matter in Nix's fantasy worlds, but that it typically does not define or inhibit the abilities and choices of his characters—at least not for girls.

Among the writers of literary fantasy working in the past twenty years,

Nix is one of the most prolific and progressive in his use of female heroes. In both *The Keys to the Kingdom* (2003–11) and *Abhorsen* (1995–2003), Nix overturns or simply ignores stereotypical sex-based expectations. In the terms delineated by Carol Pearson and Katherine Pope, then, Nix must be applauded for showing that he "understands at some level that women are primary beings, and that they are not ultimately defined according to patriarchal assumptions, in relation to fathers, husbands, or male gods" (12 emphasis in original). Yet, while he creates empowered, wise female characters, most often Nix pairs his female heroes with weak, indecisive, and insecure male protagonists, demonstrating what Maria Nikolajeva terms the "new male" increasingly populating YA fiction who is "encumbered by the social pressures and uncomfortable in his conventional gender role" (Nikolajeva 106). Such a character offers a more realistic, less stereotypical approach to gender, but how does his, by comparison, weaker status help to shape the identities of the girls with whom he interacts, and vice versa? By exploring Nix's empowerment of girl heroes in relation to his portrayal of boys who would be heroes but typically fall short, this essay teases out the nuances of the author's contribution to the female hero's development—and its inherent influence on masculine identity—as demonstrated in his two most popular series to date, *The Keys to the Kingdom* and *Abhorsen*.

Empowered Maternity: The Architect and the Doctor[2]

Before analyzing how Arthur Penhaligon's companions Suzy and Leaf overshadow him in *Keys to the Kingdom*, it is necessary to first consider the influences of two less visible yet pivotal adult female characters, The Architect and Arthur's adoptive mother, Emily. The Architect is arguably the most significant and certainly the most powerful character of the series, even though she is present only through the descriptions of other characters until the final book, *Lord Sunday*, when she embodies the fused parts of the Will (*LS* 305). Imparting her history to Arthur, she tells of how she emerged "from Nothing ... made the stars and waited while the planets were born" (*LS* 305). Refraining from intervention, which to her is the highest sin and the main tenet of her "Will," she decided "to create an entity who would oversee [the] work" of making the rest, and fashioned the Old One out of herself (*LS* 305). Reversing the Christian Creation story, the Architect, as supreme Creator, appears from "Nothing," and commits an act of maternity, bringing forth a male from her own being. When she and the Old One disagree, she punishes him, but after ten thousand years, she tires of the feud and of her position as overseer of the House and its environs. Unable to release the Old One without destroying all that she has made, she fashions the Will as a way to insure her wishes are carried out while she "go[es] beyond" (*LS* 306). Her whereabouts are never entirely explained, which further elevates her position; she is too great and powerful to remain material and chooses to become an elusive, non-interfering presence; integrated into the cosmos.

As representatives of the Architect, seven Trustees, collectively known as the Morrow Days, are charged with carrying out and protecting Her Will, but in her absence they have gone astray, pursuing self-interests. To save Creation, including his own world, Arthur must recover each piece of the Will, defeat each Trustee, and claim his or her Key. As the first part of the Will that Arthur meets and the eventual personification of its fused parts, Dame Primus manifests after he defeats Mister Monday. She becomes physically larger and more formidable each time Arthur claims another key and each newfound part of the Will fuses with her person. Her expanding shape is a continual reminder of the Architect's supreme power, and while Primus is not nurturing, she is Arthur's primary guide. Her advice is usually self-serving—as the personification of the Will she remains most concerned with saving the House (and herself) from destruction. At the same time, these goals tie into the greater good since destruction of the House means destruction of Arthur's world as well, and her advice is born from the Architect's vast knowledge. Primus' insistence that Arthur remain or return to the House whenever he tries to leave or to stay away longer amount to a maternal tough love that signifies Arthur being pushed forward in the maturation process he is subconsciously trying to avoid.

More than mere adventure, I submit that the series metaphorically renders Arthur's appropriate response to the loss of his biological parents, doctors who had worked with his adoptive mother Emily, and who died in "the last really big influenza epidemic" (*MM* 33). Near the end of the series, Dame Primus morphs into the Architect, who has a human double in Emily. While Arthur loves his adoptive father, a famous rock musician, Bob seems rather immature—more like a cool older brother than a parent. Arthur clearly elevates Emily over Bob in his affections and in his estimation of their characters and abilities. Even though he laments that Emily's work "[takes] her away from her own family," Arthur takes pride in the fact that her research "benefit[s] the whole human race" (*MM* 33). In contrast, his father, known as Plague Rat in his earlier days, tours the country with his band, The Ratz. Thus Nix cleverly lowers our estimation of Arthur's father, whose work brings to mind the spreading of pestilence, and in the process elevates his mother, the curer of diseases.

Emily embodies heroism for Arthur, and the series aligns the Architect with the adoptive mother whose presence "transform[s]" their large house "from a quiet retreat into a family home" (*MM* 52). Together, Dame Primus/the Architect and Emily may be viewed as two sides of "the great mother" that Flo Keyes pinpoints as a "principle archetyp[e]" of fantasy, from medieval to modern. As a crucial influence in the hero's journey, the great mother "provides the support necessary to break away from one's own limitations and strike out on the adventure that will help form the self and, simultaneously, [she is] the deadly enemy against whom the hero must battle for that selfhood" (Keyes 141). Being the admirable yet largely absent adoptive mother, Emily inspires Arthur to adventure because if the House is destroyed, his world—including and in some ways synonymous with Emily—will be destroyed. She is bound up with the Architect, who, while not an enemy, torments Arthur in her persona as Dame Primus and in the end presents him with an impossible choice that is both a natural result of his quest and a symbol of his maturation. That he is ultimately tasked with rescuing Emily after she is kidnapped by Lord Sunday, and that Arthur fails that task, demonstrate the veneration and formidability of female power—specifically of maternal power—that drives the series.

When Helpers Become Heroes: Suzy, Leaf, and Arthur

Nix blurs the connection between Emily and the Architect until near the end of the series by making both of Arthur's maternal figures just as inaccessible to him as his deceased biological mother. In their place, Nix supplies two girls of about Arthur's own age who trump him in pretty much every way. Their continual support of Arthur, often to their own peril, makes them present in ways that his mothers are not. Again borrowing from Keyes' model, Suzy and Leaf equate "the maiden" in the ancient concept of the "tripartite goddess of which the mother is an integral part" (Keyes 151). Representing "innocence ... intuition and innovation ... [the maiden] is the spark of a new idea when old ways do not suffice" (Keyes 151). Read this way, Suzy and Leaf stand in for the women who are such powerful yet elusive influences upon Arthur as he works toward becoming mature enough to reconcile their loss. In that final test, he is left alone but with the benefit of his past interactions with Suzy and Leaf to help him figure out how to defeat Lord Sunday; to be finally worthy of meeting the Architect—and accepting her loss.

Arthur's main helper throughout the series is Suzy Turquoise Blue, who first appears in *Mister Monday* as he faces an onslaught of Nithlings. Establishing the inequality that will define their relationship, Suzy says, "Hey! Idiot! Up here!" and he turns to see her "small grimy face look[ing] down on him ... [from] several stories up" (*MM* 142). Positioning Suzy physically above Arthur, Nix clearly establishes her leadership position. Her words reinforce her superiority as she calls him "stupid" or "idiot" three times within the space of a few pages. Once the initial danger of the Nithling attack is past, he realizes she is "a girl about his own age, perhaps younger, though she is dressed as a boy" (*MM* 144). When he hesitates about following her, the voice of the Will speaks through her: "The Will has found a way and you are part of the way .... Follow Suzy Turquoise Blue" (*MM* 144). That Suzy is the vessel through which the

Will first operates confirms her value and, especially in the first few books, she completely outshines Arthur. Admittedly, he finds himself a stranger in an alternate world where he does not know the rules, but in the brief glimpses we have of him in his own world, he demonstrates nothing like Suzy's strength, cleverness, and courage.

Suzy's heroism is perhaps best illustrated in her uncanny ability to come to Arthur's rescue in the nick of time, and usually when he is feeling most hopeless. Rare occasions find Arthur in control, such as when he spends a lot of time "dragging" Suzy around in the latter chapters of *MM*, because being the Rightful Heir enables him to use the Improbable Stair while she cannot. Still this is a temporary condition and she quickly regains her superiority as they face the conclusive battle with the slothful Mister Monday. Meaning to "bolster [Arthur's] confidence" as he prepares to retrieve the first Key, Suzy ends up implying his weakness: "I reckon you can take on Mister Monday.... He'll probably be flat out snoring anyway" (*MM* 293). Arthur finds courage to take action, but when the battle goes awry, Suzy throws herself at the knife-wielding Denizen to "gai[n] Arthur precious time" (*MM* 313). Left on his own, he immediately lands in trouble again: Mister Monday transforms into a giant snake and calls for the Key, which is lodged inside Arthur, making its way toward his heart. Never fear, Suzy re-emerges, "bloody but triumphant," and stabs Mister Monday. Arthur calls for ink, and being that her position in the House is "Ink-Filler Sixth Class" (*MM* 151), Suzy has the technology to write on Monday's snake tail, inciting the bibliophages to attack the Trustee (*MM* 325–6). The idea to use the ink comes from Arthur, yet it is Suzy who has the courage to put the plan into action, immediately understanding what he wants her to do without him having to explain.

Admittedly, Arthur does show courage sometimes—not only in taking action, but more often in overcoming his own feelings of despair and inadequacy. Still, Nix undercuts Arthur's heroism by usually having him find his strength because help arrives just when his impulse to give up is the strongest. Most often at these times, Arthur's hopelessness is bound up with his inability to view himself as a hero. In *Grim Tuesday*, Arthur resists Suzy's effort to encourage him, which she does by reminding him that he is the "Master of the Lower House." The narrator describes Arthur thinking: "He wasn't Monday .... He was just a boy caught up in great events and as soon as possible he would try to go back to his normal uneventful life" (*GT* 121). Likewise, in book three, when he learns that Dame Primus (the incarnation of the Will part one) has had a propaganda book written that embellishes his physicality and describes him as "Hero of the House," Arthur has no idea why Primus would portray him in this way (*DW* 125). His confusion is understandable given that the image the book puts forth bears no resemblance to Arthur. As complications mount in his effort to rescue part three of the will, Arthur thinks, "*Why is nothing straightforward?*

... I bet heroes who had only to beat up dragons or monsters never had to worry about whole populations and their friends, not to mention what might be happening to their family back home" (*WW* 330, emphasis in original). Here Arthur misses the point, since most heroes *exist* to serve the greater good, as Joseph Campbell tells us: "A hero is someone who has given his or her life to something bigger than oneself" (123).

Further, the hero's tasks and tests are rarely if ever "straightforward." What Arthur means is "why can't things be easy," which does nothing to improve his hero status, though it makes him more relatable to the reader who feels similarly helpless. In "The Deconsecration of the Hero" Gary Gumpert points out, "during childhood and adolescence ... a cadre of heroes is required, perhaps to satisfy inner frustrations, perhaps to provide secret visions and dreams in contrast to the external pressures imposed by growing up in an adult world" (134). Arthur's misunderstanding of heroism reflects his resistance to his own maturation and his confusion about what it means to be an adult. These emotions are comprehensible to any reader, male or female. As such, Arthur helps to overturn some of the qualities normally associated with what Elizabeth Heilman calls "hegemonic masculinity" in her look at gender stereotyping in J.K. Rowling's *Harry Potter* series. This "straight, strong, and domineering" masculinity "oppresses not only women but the many men excluded from it" (Heilman 231). Arthur's distance from and inability to achieve the hegemonic male ideal operates in tandem with Nix's empowerment of the girls who so often outshine him. In this way, Nix' weakening of Arthur can be read as much less problematic for its potential to ease some of the trauma of maturation for the reader who sees himself in Arthur, as well as for the one who sees herself in Suzy, or Leaf, who will be discussed later in this essay.

In particular, Arthur's hesitations make Suzy's bold eagerness for adventure make her that much more heroic, especially given that he benefits from the magical aid and protection of the Keys and the Atlas. She relies on Arthur's magic to help her as well, but more often it is her own resourcefulness that enables her to help him and protect herself (usually in that order.) Unlike Arthur, Suzy *never* shows despair—she only *acts* - repeatedly, and without thought for her own safety. She is motivated as much by her love of adventure as by self-interest stemming from her pact with Arthur that if he can succeed in defeating the Morrow Days, he will help her and all of the other children who had "followed the Piper all those years ago" to return to their own times and places (*MM* 155). Her heroic self-sacrifice becomes particularly noticeable in book four when Arthur is drafted into the Glorious Army of the Architect, presided over by Sir Thursday, and Suzy volunteers to go with him. Arthur's first response is "I'm not going" (*ST* 69), but as he realizes he has no choice, Suzy says, "I reckon if Arthur wants me to go along, then it is my job" (*ST* 71). Feeling "tremendous relief," Arthur says, "I do want you to come. You always cheer me up, not to mention helping me" (*ST* 72). Here Arthur severely under-states Suzy's contribution, but his private thoughts reiterate the contrast between Suzy's courage and his own weakness.

As Arthur worries about what is happening at home, the narrator describes, "After all, he was only a boy. He shouldn't be a recruit in the army, let along one full of immortal Denizens who were much tougher and stronger than he was" (*ST* 73). Arthur is "only a boy," but while Suzy has been in the House for centuries, she is frozen at about his age, and *never once* in the series does she think or utter the words, "I'm only a girl." Even if we are to understand Suzy as more capable than Arthur due to her experience of being in the House, she has had her memory erased numerous times. Also, despite her job as Monday's Tierce, and later as Arthur's self-appointed General, we must keep in mind that his quest is not her quest. Regardless, she attacks it with a sense of honor and duty that are nothing short of heroic, as well as being qualities that would not have been taught or innate to her as an impoverished child of the seventeenth century, her situation prior to following the Piper and finding herself in the House.

Some might detect a problem in Nix's portrayal of female empowerment since Suzy often looks like a boy and demonstrates few feminine qualities. Rather than undercutting her girl power, though, I would argue that Suzy's appearance re-confirms the gender bending that elevates her while, yet again, diminishing Arthur. For example, when Suzy shows up in book three looking most unlike herself, he wonders if "[t]his beautifully dressed ramrod straight girl ... might be an imposter" and doubts her ability to "be much help" (*DW* 257). His thoughts can be read ironically since Arthur, who never looks like anything but male has already benefitted numerous times from Suzy's help. As it turns out, despite the "frock" Suzy is still the same "bold adventurer" Arthur has come to know, and she definitely helps; she's only wearing the clothes because she "swore to be all ladylike and proper" so that Dame Primus would send her to the Border Sea to help Arthur (*DW* 264). Suzy's sudden feminine appearance should not and does not matter. Rather than undercutting her hero-ism, doubting her abilities based on her feminine appearance casts a shadow on Arthur by emphasizing his limited view of what girls are capable of achieving, a view that Suzy's behavior throughout the series regularly contradicts.

One useful way to look at Arthur and Suzy's gender role confusion is in the context of the common notion that all humans inherently possesses both masculine and feminine qualities. For the male, this "anima ... must be accepted and incorporated into himself in order to reach self-awareness" (Keyes 142). From this perspective, Suzy's male attire signals her invaluable contribution to Arthur's development as a hero and to his maturation journey. At first glance this might define her as a combination guide/sidekick, but her repeated demon-strations of courage and strength, as well as Arthur's relief in seeing her whenever he is in trouble, reinforce her position as a hero in her own right. More importantly, by reminding us that she is female, rather than portraying her as wholly tomboyish, Nix defines her as a female hero, allowing such a character type to exist without having to fit herself into the long-established male model. Valerie Smith helps to clarify in her assessment of the qualities of a hero that override sexual identification:

> The female hero demonstrates that characteristics of equality, support, and interdependence, are inherently human, not specifically female. While illustrating that inherently human qualities of heroes may threaten the current power structure, it allows a reconceptualization of hero to include qualities typically associated with females and not just those characteristics usually identified with masculinity [201–02].

In the world of the House, Suzy epitomizes this "reconceptualization." Her wearing of girly clothes forced upon her by Dame Primus *reminds* us that she is female, then her negative response to wearing them articulates her *rejection* of the most obvious traps of femininity.

Dame Primus herself provides another important example of this idea by wearing ultra-feminine garb that is completely at odds with her increasingly masculinesque body. With each book she gains in height, her size being commensurate with the additions of successive parts of the Will. Even though it is Arthur—with a lot of help from Suzy and Leaf—who recovers these parts, Dame Primus—whose name says it all—is the one who embodies the awesome power of the Architect. Her beauty matches her power and is often described in the same breath; for instance in book four when she points out that Arthur's "attachment to [his] original world and mortality is a serious weakness" (62), he feels "an almost overpowering urge to bow before her because she was so beautiful and so powerful" (*ST* 62). Dame Primus overturns any possible weakness associated with femininity by being both beautiful and powerful, just as Suzy not only maintains her heroism but emphasizes it as a female trait by donning "female" clothes and continuing to behave as she always does—heroically. Ultimately, then, the matter of Suzy's clothes not only makes Arthur appear less heroic by comparison, but further complicates the notion of heroism as Nix imagines it so that the sex of the hero is less precisely significant.

Nix adds another girl to the mix to ensure that Suzy's example cannot be too easily explained away by her knowledge of and longevity in the House. Arthur's friend Leaf is from his own world and much less interested in adventure than Suzy, but her lack of knowledge and experience do not prevent her from stepping up when she becomes part of Arthur's quest by stopping to help him after he collapses from an asthma attack on the running track in book one (*MM* 18–21). Leaf and her brother Ed both stop to help, but it is Leaf who becomes involved in the adventure while her brother ends up hospitalized with the sleeping sickness, suggesting that Nix purposely chooses a second girl rather than a boy helper for Arthur. Leaf's heroism largely occurs when she is apart from Arthur, making her that much more heroic for having to act alone, relying on her own instincts while he enjoys the benefit of Suzy's help and magical aid.

Leaf enters the adventure proper in book three when she is swept out of his hospital room and onto the high seas. Paralleling Suzy's gender bending, she is taken aboard a pirate ship in Arthur's place and "forcibly enlisted" as a "ship's boy" (*DW* 22–3, 25–7, 200). While Arthur can look into a special mirror given to him by Scamandros to see how Leaf is faring, he can do little to help her and finds his own courage by replaying in his mind her suggestion "that he should do something first instead of waiting for the Trustees to do something to him" (*DW* 136). Meanwhile Leaf figures out how to negotiate with the Rats, and after escape, her first thought is to try to "get in touch with Suzy Blue" (*DW* 148). Both being Arthur's helpers but with vastly different backgrounds, Leaf and Suzy share an uneasy relationship, yet Leaf immediately thinks of Suzy as the person to help both her and Arthur. Further, when Arthur learns that Leaf signed unbreakable "articles" of indenture, even though he "wishe[s] ... he could have helped Leaf get off the ship" (*DW* 201), he quickly determines his best option is to leave her there, rationalizing, "she was probably better off than he was" (*DW* 201). He turns out to be correct as Leaf finds her own way out and ends up helping Suzy save the day near the end of the book with a "true soccer striker-style" kick of the pirate Feverfew's head that turns a dire situation in Arthur's favor (*DW* 347).

Leaf's first solo adventure, and arguably her most important for enabling Arthur's success, occurs when she volunteers to return to their world to retrieve a pocket believed to be the source of a Spirit-eater's impersonation of Arthur as it tries to infect the population with grey-mold (*ST* 47–51). Perhaps thinking of himself, Arthur points out, "You don't have to try .... I know people who wouldn't do anything unless it directly affected them," but Leaf responds, "Yeah, well, I don't want to be one of those people" (*ST* 47). Despite her fear and her own desire to be "normal" again, Leaf accepts the quest and uses no magic to retrieve the pocket, falling to mold contamination in the process (*ST* 108, 114). As Suzy does when she places herself in the service of Grim Tuesday in book two, and echoing her own indenture to the Rats in book three, Leaf faces enslavement as she knows that the grey-mold will slowly allow the Spirit-eater to control her mind. Leaf begins to feel the mold's effects while she struggles to return the pocket to the House so it can be destroyed. Beyond the saving of her own life, she focuses on the idea that "Not just Arthur but everyone else too" are "depending on her" (*ST* 157).

In the later volumes of *Keys*, Arthur, Suzy, and Leaf fight separate battles in service of the greater goal to prevent the Nothing from destroying the House and the Secondary Realms. Invariably Suzy and Leaf embody the "rare exception" Jennifer Stuller allows for in her description that traditionally "girl sidekicks were generally less capable than their male counterparts, of whom they were character spinoffs" (Stuller 25). Stuller admits that "sometimes ... supergirls often attempted to handle situations above and beyond their capabilities which ultimately necessitated their rescue by the hero" (25). To her point, in dire circumstances, Suzy and Leaf separately hope that Arthur will fix everything, yet both are more often the leaders of their own quests and end up getting themselves (and him) out of trouble. Arthur remains the hero, as the closing chapters prove, but Nix orchestrates the contributions of Suzy and Leaf to define their heroism in two primary ways. First neither Suzy nor Leaf seems to need Arthur; each girl is more than capable of saving herself. Second, Arthur is nothing like so capable—without them he would almost certainly be defeated by one of the first Trustees.

More than the challenges involved in his claiming of the keys, Arthur's interactions with and reliance upon Suzy and Leaf prepare him for the final task of his quest: meeting the Architect. Following his battle of wits with Lord Sunday near the end of the last book, the Architect names Arthur as her successor, and he realizes that his final acts have resulted in the loss of his adoptive mother Emily (*LS* 309). Arthur splits into two selves: the "New Architect ... known to his friends as 'Art'" (*LS* 317), who looks like Arthur at about age twenty-one, confronts the twelve-year-old who cries at the knowledge of Emily's loss to the Nothing that destroyed almost everything. The relation between his birth and adoptive mothers is reinforced in Art's offer: "I could make her again, solely from our memory, but she would not be exactly right" (*LS* 313). The boy Arthur says "No!" and in his clearest act of heroism he decides he will return to Earth with Leaf to help his adoptive family cope with Emily's loss. Like the toy elephant that appears at key moments in his development and which is finally sacrificed in Arthur's effort to defeat Lord Sunday, Emily becomes a casualty as the boy must reconcile his feelings of grief for his birth mother— and indeed for his childhood—if he hopes to mature into a man. The interaction between his pre-teen and adult selves brings the coming-of-age journey full circle. Even with a lot of help from Suzy and Leaf, the younger doubles for adoptive and biological mothers, Arthur is unable to rescue Emily the way that she rescued him through adoption. In the end Arthur achieves heroism *and* maturation. His efforts still pale in comparison to those of the two girls who move well beyond "sidekick" roles to become true heroes, but that is just the point. His less-than-heroic moments throughout his journey are necessary growing pains, and the undeniable heroism of the girls (and women) who guide and lead him through these challenges—rather than retreating into the background in the end—appear all the more heroic for their part in his very tumultuous transformation. Ultimately, by giving Arthur such formidable and admirable "sidekicks" Nix reimagines the notion of heroism itself, freeing it from its gendered boundaries and suggesting that true change—whether of the world, a society, or an individual—is only possible through cooperation, friendship, and acceptance.

"Dirt and flower petals": Female Heroism in *Lirael* and *Abhorsen*

> "Remember that while the Clayr can See the future, others make it. I feel that you will be a maker, not a seer."
> —Filris [Nix, *Lirael* 128]

Coping with orphan status and identity confusion around absent parents also drives much of Lirael's hero journey from its beginning in the second book of Nix's *Abhorsen* series. In *Lirael* and its sequel *Abhorsen*, however, Nix does not paint parental absence as such an overwhelming condition that it prevents Lirael from action or solely motivates that action in the way that it does for Arthur in *Keys to the Kingdom*. In fact, the opposite is true since Lirael finds her way despite her feelings of inadequacy. Like Arthur, Lirael begins as an unlikely hero: besides being female (a traditional mark of unlikelihood), she is insecure and isolated from her fellow Clayr. On her fourteenth birthday, she still lacks "the Sight" that most Clayr manifest around age eleven, a condition she associates with being an orphan: "No mother, no father, no Sight" (*Lirael* 16). Lirael would be a quite likely hero if her noble paternity and status as Abhorsen-in-Waiting were immediately revealed, but Nix guards these secrets until almost the end of *Lirael*. Her eventual companion, Prince Sameth, enters the story as the expected hero, but repeatedly falls short while Lirael gains strength and confidence, particularly after they meet about halfway into *Lirael*. The son of the Abhorsen Sabriel and her husband King Touchstone, Sam is repulsed at the idea of being the next Abhorsen, mirroring Lirael's dejection at her lack of the Sight. That her hero traits reveal themselves against Sam's less impressive qualities intensifies Lirael's heroism so that she outshines even Suzy and Leaf from *Keys*.

Like Sam's parentage, being a Clayr should be a tool of great empowerment for Lirael. The Seers' ability to access the future makes them a repository of knowledge and an invaluable asset for upholding the side of good in the tension between the Charter and Free Magic in the Old Kingdom. Lacking the Sight, however, Lirael does not participate in this process, at least not initially; and her sense of isolation and difference weigh so heavily that she more than once contemplates suicide in the early chapters of *Lirael*. Each time, though, her curiosity and survival instincts intervene (*Lirael* 49, 107), leading her to an unexpected though perhaps predestined way forward. As famously delineated by Vladmir Propp, and reiterated by W.H. Auden and Joseph Campbell, among others, one key way that the hero is identified as such is when he (or she) "obtains some agent (usually magical) which permits eventual liquidation of misfortune" (Propp 39). As Lirael's path unfolds, Nix provides her with a few such agents who offer aid just when she feels at her lowest point. In her first move toward suicide, she is discovered by some of "the most important Clayr in the Glacier" (*Lirael* 55), who sympathize with her for not yet having the Sight and offer her a chance to work in the library. The position provides Lirael not only with purpose and identity, but also with access to the vast secrets of the Clayr.

As the Third Assistant Librarian, Lirael is not supposed to be able to work any but the most basic spells required for her job, but she finds she can unlock most of the other spells on the bracelet that marks her position. Her innate magical ability and curiosity lead to her first hero test "thousands of feet underground" (*Lirael* 98) in Nix's version of the descent into "the belly of the whale" (Campbell 146), a central feature of the traditional hero's journey. Calling upon the biblical story of Jonah, Campbell defines this necessary test as one where the hero faces his own subconscious, "learn[s] ... to come to terms with this power of the dark and emerge[s] ... to a new way of life" (Campbell 146). Nix puts a female twist on this test without undercutting any of its danger or compromising the extent of Lirael's heroism, as she navigates a cavern full of red flowers and awakens a monster in the shape of a "sleeping, naked woman" (*Lirael* 105). Struggling to escape, Lirael recalls the librarians' credo of "self-sacrifice," and counter to her earlier suicidal impulses, she determines that she very much "want[s] to stay alive" (*Lirael* 107). Knowing that she must save herself, Lirael calls upon the Charter, creating a "single master mark ... of great power that she had never before dared to use" (*Lirael* 108). As the narrator describes, "With the spell ready, pent up inside her by will alone, Lirael did the bravest thing she had ever done. She touched the door with one hand, the creature's hook with the other, and spoke the master Charter mark to cast the spell" (*Lirael* 108). She gets away, but knows the creature remains a threat to the Clayr. Lirael's first hero test compels her second, and in this she has the encouragement of an extremely powerful and revered female, her previously unknown great-great grandmother, who tends Lirael in the infirmary after she succumbs to her injuries in the first fight with the Stilken. Saying, "Remember that while the Clayr can See the future, others make it. I feel that you will be a maker, not a seer," Filris also confirms what Lirael already knows: "You must learn about the creature and you must defeat it!" (*Lirael* 128). In true guide fashion, Filris dies soon after this encounter (according to her own prediction), but Lirael is not entirely alone.

In the underground chamber Lirael found a dog statuette that kindled her desire for a "true friend" (*Lirael* 115), and in another illustration of her latent power, Lirael's "dog-sending" turns out much better than she hoped, producing an "entirely real" dog, a female one at that (*Lirael* 144–5). The Disreputable

Dog, as she identifies herself, gives Lirael the idea and helps her to "borrow" the Chief Librarian's sword, the only object with the power to bind the Stilken (*Lirael* 153–8). Near the end of *Abhorsen*, Dog is revealed to be an ancient power, but all along Lirael accepts that the mongrel is not what she appears. Again in the traditional mode, Dog's loyalty to Lirael helps to mark her as a hero; and as Max Luthi notes, when a "helping" character is an animal, it "can embody unconscious forces within us" (Luthi 80). Lirael's finding of the dog statue and transfiguration of it into the living form of the bell Kibeth which "gives freedom of movement to the dead, or forces the dead to walk at the piper's will" (*Lirael* 537), hints at the ancient power that lives within Lirael, connecting her to all previous Abhorsens and even to the making of the Charter itself.

For her second test Nix further reveals Lirael's heroism by putting a legendary weapon in her grip. Like the mythical Arthur who becomes king by being the one to remove the sword from the stone, Lirael, without any aid (other than Dog's advice), liberates an incredibly powerful Clayr artifact, one that as the narrator describes would choose for itself "who would—or would not—wield it" (*Lirael* 165). Lirael recognizes "this was probably the first time [the sword] was being wielded by a girl who didn't really know what she was doing"; but at the same time she engages the "latent strength of the sword's magic" (169) and makes it do her bidding. Her ability to do so despite her inexperience, combined with her determination to defeat the Stilken and protect the Clayr, are marks of true heroism.

If the chamber of flowers were not enough to feminize Lirael's hero task to defeat the Stilken, Nix describes the site of the vanquishing with obvious Edenic imagery: "The tree was the most likely place for the creature to be, Lirael thought, imagining it twined around a branch like a snake" (*Lirael* 172). As she feels "her completely untrained muscles [take] over" (*Lirael* 174), Binder (the sword) communicates the proper order of the Charter marks to her mind (*Lirael* 176). Immediately after defeating the Stilken, Lirael unearths a book of power from a hole she had "tripped over" during the battle (*Lirael* 179). The image of Lirael "caked in dirt and flower petals" as she takes stock of the fact that "[s]he had bound the Stilken. All by herself" presents an interesting juxtaposition of stereotypically masculine and feminine associations, "dirt" and "flower petals." To bind a monster makes her a hero in the traditional sense of dragon-slaying, but Nix complicates things since both slayer and monster are female, and the Stilken dwells in a dark cavern around a tree evoking the transgression of the biblical Eve.

On the one hand, Lirael's act may be read as a challenge to her own femininity, to the part of her that longs to be like all of the other Clayr, to be a Seer. She could be trying to annihilate her femininity in taking up the phallic sword as her weapon, which would limit her hero status by suggesting such may only be achieved by a woman if she appropriates masculinity. However, such a reading would contradict Nix's characterization of Lirael, and also of the many strong female characters that populate his work, including the Clayr, who, while all female, are not overtly feminine. Rather, I read Lirael's defeat of the Stilken as her effort *not to defeat but to usurp*: by binding the Stilken as monstrous Eve, Lirael claims power for herself. Her own transgression of the Clayr's rules—releasing power in the bracelet to which she is not yet entitled and unlocking doors she is not authorized to pass through, not to mention stealing the ancient sword—*aligns* her with the Stilken's ancient and terrible power. Lirael binds the female monster with the heroic instrument that is the sword, symbolically accepting power as a condition for herself who feels most powerless while rejecting the evil the Stilken represents. Her discrete separation of good and evil, also symbolized by the sword's cutting, illustrates Nix's sophisticated approach to female heroism. Lirael's transgression of the Clayr's rules propels her forward by demonstrating her ability to rise above needing to be a part of their society, even though she has yet to consciously recognize this.

While Lirael epitomizes Miriam F. Polster's view of "heroes [as] agents of change ... [who] move other people—sometimes whole societies—forward with them" (49), she also overrides Polster's limitation that "[t]he woman hero usually relies less on muscular strength than her male counterpart and invents other ways to achieve a desired end" (31). To Polster's point that "[w]omen rely more on persuasion and argument" (31), Lirael often logically thinks things through, but in the Stilken battle it is the combination of her magical ability and sword-wielding that enables success. The sword-wielding obviously aligns her with the masculine heroic ideal, but the image of her "caked in dirt and flower petals" leaves her femininity not only intact but intensified. Before she is ever Seen by the Clayr as a chosen one, Lirael has already proven herself to be a very satisfying kind of female hero: she claims the sword in the name of heroism itself, not in imitation of male heroism but as a woman and an "individua[l] of great physical and mental courage" (Polster 22).

As with her first hero test, Lirael's heroism in the Stilken battle carries larger social implications regarding female empowerment. As Roberta Seelinger Trites points out,

> The feminist character's recognition of her agency and her voice invariably leads to some sort of transcendence, usually taking the form of a triumph over whatever system or stricture was repressing her. The character defeats some force of evil ... or she succeeds at a typically male task, or she comes to believe in herself despite the doubts of those around her [7].

Supporting Trites' idea, after her first run-in with the Stilken, Lirael loses her voice for a time as a result of speaking the powerful Charter mark in her effort to escape (*Lirael* 123). Lirael's silence becomes a "long established habit," a defense against the pain of still having not gained the Sight when her story resumes at age nineteen (*Lirael* 280). At that time, venturing into a previously unexplored part of the glacier leads her to "Lirael's Path" and a destiny seemingly carved out thousands of years before (*Lirael* 300). By finding this path and the three magical objects, Lirael makes a giant step toward "triumph over whatever system ... [is] repressing her" (Trites 7); in her case, the Clayr. Upon finding her, Sanar reveals that Lirael, who "alone amongst the Clayr [had] never been Seen" (*Lirael* 423) up until this time, has finally been envisioned as destined to "face great tests" and with "the potential for great power" (*Lirael* 424). Lirael's lack of the Sight makes her an "outsider" (*Lirael* 430) to the Clayr, and it takes her some time to recognize that this status places her *above* them. Their identification of her "potential for great power" (*Lirael* 424) is more than enough to support Lirael's transcendence over gendered expectations altogether.

Even though Lirael's obstacles at least initially have female origins (the Stilken and the Clayr), ultimately she achieves her birthright as the Abhorsen-in-Waiting, as a matter of heredity. She soon finds her voice, making noise in taking up the Abhorsen's bells, and in speaking words of power from the Charter. Further, Nix sees to it that the position of Abhorsen is not limited by sex: Sabriel inherits from her father, and mistakenly believes her son Sam will inherit from her. Rather than being limited to the female exclusivity of Clayr society, and sheltered by the glacier to See and report without experiencing, Lirael will go into the dangerous world where she can *define herself* in ways that would be impossible if she had become a "proper Clayr" (*Lirael* 450). At first she sees this quest as "the opposite of her heart's desire" (*Lirael* 452), as the Clayr "throwing [her] out" (*Lirael* 426); but when she prepares to depart, Lirael sees leaving as "escape, from a life that she couldn't admit was stifling her" (*Lirael* 526). She also equates the journey with "doing something important" (*Lirael* 527), in heroic terms signifying that she understands her role as a chosen one whose decisions and sacrifices will resonate far beyond herself.

Her eventual partner, Sam also leaves home with the goal to do something important, but both his introduction into the story and his true motivation for leaving differ in ways that place him in Lirael's shadow and keep him there. Unlike Lirael, Sam starts out with obvious hero potential. He triumphs with a "personal best" on the cricket field (*Lirael* 193–4), then recognizes danger as his school team bus heads toward the Wall (*Lirael* 203), and takes charge against an onslaught of Dead Hands (*Lirael* 207–15). Sam's courage wanes, however, when he finds that he must go into Death if he has any hope of defeating the necromancer controlling the Hands. While Lirael claims the sword and uses it to bind the Stilken, Sam "wish[es] desperately" for his mother, since in his only previous passage into Death he felt somewhat secure being led by her (*Lirael* 218). Fear is certainly reasonable in such situations; Lirael feels it as she goes to face the Stilken, as does Arthur upon first entering The House in *Keys*. Sam's desire for his mother is not itself a weakness; at sixteen, he has had only the most rudimentary training and experience. Yet, his lack of knowledge mainly derives from his own avoidance—despite believing himself to be "Abhorsen-in-Waiting" Sam is physically and emotionally repulsed by *The Book of the Dead* (*Lirael* 269). What's more, he lacks the courage to confide these feelings to anyone, least of all his mother, who upon learning about his effort against the Dead Hands confuses it as evidence of his being "ready to formally begin training" (*Lirael* 272–3).

Sam survives his solo journey into Death and just misses being possessed by Hedge, who mistakenly uses Sam's friend Nick as his vessel (*Lirael* 242–3). Thus an innocent boy with no working knowledge or even belief in the magic of the Old Kingdom takes the place of the prince and supposed Abhorsen-in-Waiting. Sam's heroism is curtailed and postponed, signifying that he is not ready to challenge the Necromancer, which Nix confirms as Sam lies in hospital. When his father arrives alone, all Sam can think of is that "he could have died and apparently that still wasn't enough for his mother to come and see him" (*Lirael* 252), though he half-heartedly admits Sabriel has a good reason "being the Abhorsen and everything" (*Lirael* 253). He feels comforted by the presence of his father, King Touchstone (*Lirael* 248), but he only reinforces Sam's weakness by explaining, "as a result of your going unprepared and unprotected, some small fragment of your spirit has been leached away ... enough to make you weaker, or slower .... But it will come back in time" (*Lirael* 251). Similar to Lirael's loss of her voice after calling up the powerful Charter mark against the Stilken, Sam is temporarily injured but permanently scarred by his first major hero test. Unlike Lirael, however, Sam has no intention of trying again.

Not only does she lack the nurturing family and royal privilege that Sam enjoys, but Lirael follows her first meeting with the Stilken by returning to defeat it. In contrast, after meeting the necromancer in Death, Sam goes home to be berated by his older sister, Ellimere, who by birth order is "named 'co-regent'" (*Lirael* 261) while their parents are away and who believes "one of her duties ... [is] to address the shortcomings of her younger brother" (*Lirael* 262, 264). When he discovers that his friend Nicholas may be in grave peril, Sam uses the situation as an excuse to avoid his royal duties, deciding that "he must go to save [Nicholas]" while acknowledging "that what he [is] really doing [is] running away" (*Lirael* 388). This moment marks one of many in which Sam, like Arthur in *Keys*, consciously feels his own cowardice. These moments also find Sam comparing himself to his mother or wishing for her presence, which for him connotes aid and protection. Again this is reasonable given her position as Abhorsen, but since his father is king, Sam's reliance upon female aid remains significant. His decision to head "off to adventure—and of course, to rescue Nicholas" (*Lirael* 404) emphasizes his reliance upon his mother and his desire not to disappoint her since, by his own admission, it is Sam's inability to own up to his repulsion for Death that motivates his leaving.

Their first meeting defines their hero/sidekick relationship as Lirael, traveling in a magical boat called *Finder* that can guide itself, reaches Sam, unconscious and sprawled in a metal bathtub (*Lirael* 567). Lirael takes charge, rescuing Sam from the bathtub and using the Charter to heal his leg (*Lirael* 580). While "surprised by how easy it is to talk to him" (*Lirael* 581), she initially views him as "a nuisance" (*Lirael* 587) as they set a course for the Abhorsen's house to regroup. By this point, Sam has overcome (albeit sloppily) several dangers. To his credit, he usually tries to rise above his weaknesses and like Lirael, he possesses innate but as yet unrealized magical power. Paralleling the ancient power of Lirael's Dog, Sam has a spirit helper in animal form, Mogget, who notes more than once that the prince is "skilled—surprisingly so" in magic (*Lirael* 497). Even so, like Arthur with Suzy and Leaf in *Keys*, Sam never surpasses or even equals the heroism of Lirael, who counterbalances her insecurities by *seeking* danger. This is best illustrated when they reach the Abhorsen's house and it becomes revealed that it is Lirael, not Sam, who is Abhorsen-in-Waiting, much to his very great relief (*Lirael* 685–6). Instead of re-committing to help Nicholas, his abiding thought is of safety: "Lirael could go on alone" (*Lirael* 594), and "if I'm not the Abhorsen-in-Waiting I'm not going to be able to do much" (*Lirael* 692). Still, his "conscience" troubles him as he privately recognizes, "It's *your* job to deal with necromancers. And it's *your* parents who would expect you to face the enemy" (*Lirael* 594, emphasis in original).

In a telling exchange that sums up Sam's character and echoes his own thoughts, Lirael reminds him, "[Y]ou are still a Prince of the Kingdom. You cannot just sit here and do nothing" (*Lirael* 693). In response to Sam's sobbing as he confides his fear of death, Lirael challenges, "I'm afraid, too…. But I'd rather be afraid and do something than just sit and wait for terrible things to happen" (*Lirael* 693–4). With such scenes Nix dilutes Sam's display of courage in the battle against the Dead he and Lirael fought in order to reach the Abhorsen's house, and intensifies Lirael's heroism by showing that she has the strength to move forward herself as well as to push Sam to do the same. Her challenge to him is all the more heroic since she has only just discovered that "the gift she had longed for her entire life [is] finally and absolutely denied to her" (*Lirael* 687), while he has been given a massive reprieve to avoid the supposed birthright he has been dreading.

As their quest moves toward its conclusion in *Abhorsen*, Lirael increasingly emerges as the hero while Sam matures but never becomes more than a sidekick for her. The most revealing examples occur as the Destroyer nears success and Lirael realizes she must go into Death and use the Dark Mirror to learn how Orannis was bound the first time so the process might be repeated (*Abhorsen* 383). Deciding she "must do what must be done, regardless of the risk" (Abhorsen 446), Lirael relies on Sam to protect her body in life while she faces Hedge in Death. Sam stumbles a few times, but remembering her words, he determines, "It's always better to be doing" (*Abhorsen* 462). Rather than reinforce his heroism, though, his efforts to keep the Dead Hands from reaching her body become undercut by his longing for her to return to fix everything as she is "the last hope for the entire world against the Destroyer" (*Abhorsen* 465–6).

Sam "trie[s] desperately to think of some stratagem or cunning ploy" against the Dead, but he is no more effective than the non-magical Major Green and Lieutenant Tindall. It is Sabriel who rings the bell to disperse the Dead (*Abhorsen* 467–8, 474), and Sam's spirit guide Mogget who rescues Nicholas (*Abhorsen* 474). After Nicholas dies, Sam despairs, believing he has "failed" (*Abhorsen* 480), and it is Lirael who must remind him that he is a "Wallmaker" with the power to forge "blood and metal" to create a sword to re-bind the Destroyer (*Abhorsen* 481–2). Without this special sword, Lirael knows the binding will not succeed, so in the end Nix creates important work for Sam and enables him to finally overcome his fears by doing what he loves the most in aid of the greater good. Sam achieves a degree of heroism, yet even here Nix qualifies it by having Lirael explain to Sabriel, Touchstone, and the others, "Sam is making the sword that I will use to break the Destroyer once It is bound" (*Abhorsen* 492), to which the narrator adds, "At least she *hoped* he was" (*Abhorsen* 492, my emphasis). While doubting Sam's ability to perform under pressure, Lirael remains the true hero for organizing and leading the Seven in the binding with the knowledge that "Everything depended upon her" (*Abhorsen* 489). This is true despite the presence of Sabriel, the king, and two ancient powers (Mogget and the Disreputable Dog), all of whom follow Lirael's orders.

Going far beyond Filris' prediction that she would be a "maker, not a seer" (*Lirael* 128), Lirael does both. Her last journey into Death gives her a view of the ancient past that she correctly interprets to know "what she would have to do" (*Abhorsen* 496) in the present in order to enable a future. More importantly, as the narrator describes, "Lirael had known and accepted the certainty of her own death in this venture, and thought it a fair price for the defeat of Orannis and the saving of all she loved and knew" (*Abhorsen* 506). One might expect Lirael to be thwarted by the kind of insecurity that Sam endures since for much of her life she has focused on gaining the Sight, but unlike Sam she accepts her role as Abhorsen-in-Waiting and in the end she willingly offers herself as a sacrifice to save a world in which she has yet to fully participate. As a Remembrancer, she becomes a Seer not only of the past but of the entire panorama of what is at stake, rather than seeing in bits and pieces as the Clayr do. Sam acts heroically in small ways throughout the last two books of the series, but he nearly always does so from a place of self-centeredness. In contrast, Lirael often internally voices fear and insecurity but these feelings never make her hesitate, and in fact, spur her forward in the true spirit of self-sacrifice that defines the hero archetype. As a result, Sam's heroic moments do nothing to diminish Lirael as the true hero of the series. Instead he enhances her heroism, which is not dependent upon Sam's contrasting weakness nor threatened by his developing strength, as is the case with Arthur and his female sidekicks-turned-heroes in *Keys to the Kingdom*. From beginning to end, Lirael is just as the Disreputable Dog describes on the final page: "Lirael Goldenhand... Remembrancer and Abhorsen, and much else besides" (*Abhorsen* 516).

Notes

1. For brevity purposes, the novels of *The Keys to the Kingdom* series will be abbreviated: *Mister Monday* (*MM*), *Grim Tuesday* (*GT*), *Drowned Wednesday* (*DW*), *Sir Thursday* (*ST*), *Lady Friday* (*LF*), *Superior Saturday* (*SS*), *Lord Sunday* (*LS*).

2. Despite the earlier publication of the *Abhorsen* series, I want to begin with the *Keys to the Kingdom*, which utilizes female sidekicks who become heroes, as opposed to *Abhorsen*, where Nix complicates things by having the main male character rather unexpectedly becoming the helpful but clearly less capable sidekick to the female hero.

Works Cited

Campbell, Joseph, with Bill Moyers. *The Power of Myth*. New York: Doubleday, 1988.

Gumpert, Gary. "The Deconsecration of the Hero." *Heroes in a Global World*. Susan J. Drucker and Gary Gumpert, eds. Cresskill, NJ: Hampton Press, 2008. 129–47.

Heilman, Elizabeth E. "Blue Wizards and Pink Witches: Representations of Gender and Identity and Power." *Harry Potter's World: Multidisciplinary Critical Perspectives*. Elizabeth Heilman, ed. New York: RoutledgeFalmer, 2003. 221–39.

Nikolajeva, Maria. *Power, Voice and Subjectivity in Literature for Young Readers*. New York: Routledge, 2010.

Nix, Garth. *Abhorsen*. New York: HarperCollins, 2003.

_____. *Drowned Wednesday*. New York: Scholastic, 2005.

_____. *Grim Tuesday*. New York: Scholastic, 2004.

_____. *Lady Friday*. New York: Scholastic, 2007.

_____. *Lirael*. New York: HarperCollins, 2001.

_____. *Lord Sunday*. New York: Scholastic, 2010.

_____. *Mister Monday*. New York: Scholastic, 2003.

_____. *Sir Thursday*. New York: Scholastic, 2007.

_____. *Superior Saturday*. New York: Scholastic, 2010.

Pearson, Carol, and Katherine Pope. *The Female Hero in American and British Literature*. New York: R.R. Bowker, 1981.

Smith, Valerie. "Female 'Heroes' at Ground Zero: Verbal and Visual Accounts Reconceptulize the 'Heroic.'" *Heroes in a Global World*. Susan J. Drucker and Gary Gumpert, eds. Cresskill, NJ: Hampton Press, 2008. 185–204.

Stuller, Jennifer K. *Ink-Stained Amazons and Cinematic Warriors: Superwomen in Modern Mythology*. New York: I.B. Tauris, 2010.

Trites, Roberta Seelinger. *Waking Sleeping Beauty: Feminist Voices in Children's Novels*. Iowa City: University of Iowa Press, 1997.

IV. Unwilling Do-Gooders: Villains and Villain-Heroes

The Problem of Mrs. Coulter: Vetting the Female Villain-Hero in Philip Pullman's *His Dark Materials*

Amanda M. Greenwell

Critics who discuss Mrs. Coulter of Philip Pullman's *His Dark Materials* tend to treat her as a power-hungry female whose late realization of her own motherhood triggers a self-sacrificial act to save her daughter and the universe (see, for example, Hatlen, Lenz, and Rutledge). While this description is generally sound, a central irony in her final self-sacrifice suggests there is more to her story than the neatness this reading implies: her maternal instincts play a crucial role in her act to save Lyra, but her manipulative seduction of Metatron is made possible by her *femme fatale* attributes as well as her hideously corrupt past. Further complicating her move from the villainous to the heroic is that Mrs. Coulter does not switch from "Evil" to "Good," nor does her villainy become heroic in a new light; rather, her transition involves an energizing of subject-hood that breaks free from a villainous pattern and resists external moral absolutes. Thus, the trilogy swerves past the conventional villain-with-a-heart-of/turned-gold and villain-whose-villainy-is-heroic story arcs. Instead, *His Dark Materials* posits a key act in the salvation of the universe on a morally corrupt human being who commits a good, heroic act through violent means. We are left, then, with a question: what do we, as readers, do with this paradox of evil-and-good, with this vicious mother and villainous lover?

In exploring the mechanisms by which Mrs. Coulter's transformation occurs and its attendant implications, it is helpful to turn to rhetorical narrative theory. According to James Phelan and Peter J. Rabinowitz, fictional characters have mimetic, synthetic, and thematic properties, in that they "do resemble possible people, they are artificial constructs that perform various functions in the progression [of the story], and they can function to convey the political, philosophical, or ethical issues being taken up by the narrative" (Herman et al. 111). Throughout most of the trilogy, Mrs. Coulter's mimetic character is systematically obscured by a narrative progression that emphasizes her synthetic and thematic functions as archetypal villain. In the third volume of the trilogy, however, the narrative progression resituates its emphasis so that Mrs. Coulter's mimetic properties make possible a shift in her synthetic and thematic importance to the story, aligning her not with forces of Good, but with the force of an individual's capacity to achieve liberty and act according to one's own sense of purpose.

Central to the case of Mrs. Coulter as villain-hero is that in its presentation of Mrs. Coulter, *His Dark Materials* impugns the reader's impulse to vilify. Examining the cognitive approaches readers take to fictional villains, Enrique Cámara Arenas claims that readers often make a "fundamental attribution error":

> Although we tend to justify our own failures and wrong doings by alluding to our circumstances—"I had had a very bad day," etc.—the conflicting behaviors of others are invariably linked to their inner dispositions. In the case of villains, they behave badly just because they are bad [18–19].

The narrative progression of *His Dark Materials* mires the reader in this practice that oppresses the growth of others, and then explodes it by forcing an acknowledgement of Mrs. Coulter's heroic potential.

As part of this process, *His Dark Materials* relies upon the impressionability and resilience of what Phelan and Rabinowitz refer to as the "authorial audience," a "hypothetical group" that "readers typically join (or try to join)" that "shares the knowledge, values, prejudices, fears, and experiences that the author expected in his or her readers and that ground his or her rhetorical choices" (Herman et al. 6). First isolating Mrs. Coulter's mimetic character by way of examining her back-story as a woman through the lens of Simone de Beauvoir's *The Second Sex*, then analyzing the way the narrative progression initially encourages the reader to dismiss Mrs. Coulter's mimetic qualities and label her as an archetypal villain, this essay ultimately argues for her late emerging heroics as key to the trilogy's attempt to reshape the authorial audience's— and therefore actual audience's—conceptions of the villainous and the heroic.

Contextualizing the Woman (in a Man's World)

Mrs. Coulter grew up in a world where, according to Sarah Gamble, "feminism has not happened" (190). Critics have characterized the Church-governed society in Pullman's trilogy as a "hierarchy of mad patriarchs" (Rutledge 120) with "sexist and misogynistic attitudes" (Allen 121) adopted even by the young girl protagonist, Lyra (Allen 121; Rutledge 127). Affected by many of the same situational influences endured by the women Simone de Beauvoir discusses in *The Second Sex*, Mrs. Coulter negotiates a delicate relationship between her quest for power and the strict expectations of the patriarchy. Tellingly, much of the biographical information *His Dark Materials* offers about Mrs. Coulter is by way of male characters, which makes the process of examining Mrs. Coulter's back-story more based on guess-work than it might be if she were described more directly by the narrator. This limitation, rather than making such a process worthless, actually emphasizes the extent of the oppression of Mrs. Coulter. Such oppression manifests doubly: on Mrs. Coulter's mimetic character, a woman whose personal agency is limited by a ruthless patriarchy, but also, as later sections of this essay will demonstrate, on Mrs. Coulter as textual construction whose potential heroics are problematized by narratorial dynamics that, for the first two volumes, position her as villain. Examining the complexities of Mrs. Coulter's mimetic character, then, is crucial to understanding her eventual steps toward subject-hood and agency.

The furthest back the story goes into Mrs. Coulter's past is her age of marriageability, the time when she became interesting to the male world. Lord Asriel reports that her first attempt to secure power, for which she has "always been ambitious," was "the normal way," via marriage (Pullman, *Golden* 374). De Beauvoir agrees: "A more advantageous career than many others" (*Second* 431), "marriage is the only means of integration into the community" (*Second* 427). However, a wife "is allowed no direct influence upon the future nor upon the world" (de Beauvoir, *Second* 430), and when Mrs. Coulter's husband dies, she continues her quest for power outside of a marriage contract. According to Lord Asriel, "she had to set up her own order, her own channels of influence," a practice he calls "unorthodox" (Pullman, *Golden* 374). The phrase "had to" emphasizes the limits that would have thwarted Mrs. Coulter's attempt to rise within an already established arm of the patriarchal Church, and Asriel's repetition of the word "own" highlights his perception of her ownership of her rise to power. Testament to this power is that it is recognized by herself and others, notably witch Queen Serafina Pekkala, who calls her a "powerful agent of the Magisterium" (Pullman, *Golden* 318). If "only independent work of her own can assure woman's genuine independence" (de Beauvoir, *Second* 475), then Mrs. Coulter strives beyond the immanence to which so many women are relegated because they "*do* nothing" (de Beauvoir, *Second*, emphasis in original 258). Never guilty of inaction, she seeks to carve a path to power by aligning her work with a major concern of the Church: Dust. Leveraging the fearful curiosity the leaders of the Church feel about this substance they maintain is the mark of original sin, Mrs. Coulter sets out to investigate and eradicate it (Pullman, *Golden* 374), thus ruthlessly creating for herself a niche she believes she can control.

In securing power within a patriarchy, however, Mrs. Coulter must acquiesce to some of its expectations, and her seemingly subversive power is inherently problematized since she capitalizes on gender expectations to secure it. Since both an extra-marital affair—unpalatable to a strict patriarchy—and a traditionally enacted motherhood—unprofitable within a strict patriarchy—would keep her from her goals, she has "turned her back" (Pullman, *Golden* 123) on her infant daughter, Lyra, the child born of her passionate affair with Lord Asriel. Other aspects of what Allen refers to as "traditional femininity" in her world (114) she finds useful, for appearance and sexuality work well in a setting where "man wants woman to be object" (de Beauvoir, *Second* 615). The beautiful Mrs. Coulter is a master of manipulation—in de Beauvoir's terms, the ultimate "exploiter" of the parasitical role forced upon women in a male-dominated society (*Second* 614). Her flat is a manifestation of her "mannered femininity" (Cox 136), its appearance and contents described as "pretty," "delicate," "charming," "frilled," "flowery," and "soft" (Pullman, *Golden* 75). Both luring and lulling men by its embodiment of domestication, the flat allows the performance of feminine bustling and poise at gatherings that are "at once a party and a ceremony" (de Beauvoir, *Second* 539). Mrs. Coulter wears the clothing that "offer[s] her as prey to male desires" (de Beauvoir, *Second* 539), and she indulges those desires when they suit her political ends. Her seductive manipulation of Lord Boreal/Sir Charles in *The Subtle Knife* is testament to her gendered stratagems; using wine, coy conversation, and physical intimacy, she employs her feminine wiles to gain information from a conniving yet smitten colleague whom she eventually murders (Pullman, *Subtle* 198–202, 310–312).

For all the independence these tactics afford, the result is, ironically, not subversion of the patriarchal status quo, but submission to it. Wielding the "tyranny [woman] accepts through self-interest" (de Beauvoir, *Second* 615), the patriarchy treats as vassal women like Mrs. Coulter. She must step with extreme care, conforming to its rules and expectations, or risk losing everything she has gained, for "a woman who has no wish to shock or to devaluate herself socially should live out her feminine situation in a feminine manner; and very often ... her professional success demands it ... the woman who also is subject, activity [must] insinuate herself into a world that has doomed her to passivity" (de Beauvoir, *Second* 683). If Mrs. Coulter has stepped out of the domestic sphere and entered the male world of political action, then she has done so without disrupting the meta-structure of gender binaries she believes she has either been exploiting or has left behind: that is, she's really just taken as (metaphorical) husband the entire patriarchy of the governing Church. Though her position of influence makes her synonymous with a powerful branch of the government—"she *is* the Oblation Board" (Pullman, *Golden*, emphasis in original 89), says one man at her party—it has also isolated her in that branch as her new sphere, which is only indirectly sponsored by a cautious Magisterium that can determine it "renegade" at any given moment (Pullman, *Golden* 373). The first interaction the trilogy presents between Mrs. Coulter and one of her superiors makes clear her status: the Cardinal speaks about her in the third person while in her presence, and when the other men in the room quail at her passionate fury, he "[does] not flinch" as he continues to deny her information about the prophecy concerning Lyra (Pullman, *Subtle* 36–37). Mrs. Coulter is valuable only insofar as she serves the aims of the patriarchy, and should she even appear to inhibit those aims (the Cardinal here suspects her of withholding information herself), she loses her political footing. Engaged in a race for power within the paradigm and confines of the male-dominated power structure, she must not only acquiesce to the superficial gender expectations of the patriarchal status quo, but also, like a wife, she must accept without question its values, its goals, and its moral vision (de Beauvoir, *Second* 463–465). She commits crimes against humanity—particularly by separating children from their daemons— that coincide directly with the desires of the patriarchal Magisterium.

Her "utilitarian alliance" (Fox 129) with the Church that requires her to "attach ready-made values to her ego" (de Beauvoir, *Second* 636) has thwarted Mrs. Coulter's opportunity to develop her own. When a woman continues to submit to the customs and ideals of the oppressive patriarchy, "she takes herself simultaneously as self and as other, a contradiction that entails baffling consequences ... she seeks salvation spontaneously in the way that has been imposed on her, that of passivity, at the same time when she is actively demanding her sovereignty" (de Beauvoir, *Second* 718). The namelessness of Mrs. Coulter's daemon in a trilogy wherein even very minor characters' daemons are named, as well as her disregard for the personal integrity of the children she separates, speaks to the crippling identity crisis that such a position can cause. One of the major characters in the trilogy, Mrs. Coulter, as desperate, oppressed woman, is lacking in actual "character."

Given the extensive power of the Church in Mrs. Coulter's world, that she has neglected to free herself from its confines is not surprising. According to de Beauvoir, "the real reason why [woman] does not believe in liberation is that she has never put the powers of liberty to a test; the world seems to her to be ruled by an obscure destiny against which it is presumptuous to rise in protest" (*Second* 602). Hence, when Lord Asriel invites Mrs. Coulter to come with him into the new world, she can only stutter out a series of answers that betray her fear as well as her perception of her life as "immanent enterprise" (de Beauvoir, *Second* 702): "They'll [the Church] never allow it... No—no— they're coming... I daren't... No, Asriel—my place is in this world..." (Pullman, *Golden* 395). Her references to Lyra, tangled in the midst of these protests, betray the latent and troubled mothering instincts she purposefully thwarted years ago as well as her attraction to Lord Asriel, her former lover and daughter's father. Mrs. Coulter rejects the validity of the feelings that feed her internal conflict when she chooses the sovereignty of the Church over these potential interpersonal relationships; she perceives the Church as her only means to personal agency.

Configuring the Villain (We Love to Hate)

Commonly, a woman attempting to assert power in a man's world can be seen as heroic; likewise, her subjugation by an oppressive patriarchy can be construed as tragic. However, most readers of *His Dark Materials*, especially as they work their way through the trilogy for the first time, see Mrs. Coulter as neither heroic nor tragic, which has as much to do with the narrative progression of the trilogy as with her villainous crimes. Studying the series of rhetorical moves that make up a narrative and their effects on the reader involves examining the interplay between *textual dynamics* and *readerly dynamics*: "textual dynamics are the internal processes by which narratives move from beginning through middle to ending, and readerly dynamics are the corresponding cognitive, affective, ethical, and aesthetic responses of the audience to those textual dynamics" (Herman et al. 6). The first two volumes of *His Dark Materials* capitalize on the preconceptions of their implied reader—or authorial audience, that ideal audience the text anticipates—who is aware of the basic good vs. evil conventions of heroes and villains. In the case of Mrs. Coulter, examining the process of "configuration"—"the reader's experience of an unfolding text during the act of reading" (Rabinowitz 110–111)—helps us understand how narrative constructs of the first and second books work to "other" her as a female archetypal villain capable only of immanence, not heroic transcendence.

The audience first meets Mrs. Coulter in the guise of a beneficent, angelic woman: "a beautiful young lady whose dark hair falls, shining delicately, under the shadow of her fur-lined hood ... standing in the doorway of the oratory" with "light com[ing] from the doorway behind her" (Pullman, *Golden* 41). Her appearance is complimented by her daemon, "no ordinary monkey" whose "fur is long and silky and of the most deep and lustrous gold" (Pullman, *Golden* 41). However, her sweet offer of "chocolatl" to a young boy is followed by a jarring narrative intrusion: "He's lost already" (Pullman, *Golden* 42). The authorial audience of *His Dark Materials*, schooled in western fables and fairy tales, immediately recognizes the evil stepmother figure—complete with chocolatl-as-poison-apple—and its attendant connotations: ruthlessness, manipulation, danger, malevolence. From this point forward, Mrs. Coulter's seeming benevolence serves only to confirm her villainous role.

When she proceeds to toss into a furnace the letters the boy and others have written to their parents (Pullman, *Golden* 44), the reader who has joined the authorial audience, appalled by her treatment of the children, seeks to "other" the evil stepmother, a reaction Bruno Bettelheim claims is a common attempt by a child to maintain safety from a domineering parental figure (68–69). Whether or not Bettelheim's psychological interpretation of the evil stepmother is accurate, his theory, according to Maria Warner, has caused "the bad mother [to] become an inevitable, even required ingredient in fantasy, and hatred of her a legitimate, applauded stratagem of psychic survival" (212). The implied reader of *His Dark Materials*, whether through psychological instincts or by way of learned "stratagem," finds quick comfort in dealing with Mrs. Coulter by categorizing her as object of hate, thus distancing her from sympathy and rejecting the potential integrity of her subject-hood.

Deepening the collusion of readerly and textual dynamics to position Mrs. Coulter as "other" is her initial appearance in a hypothetical sidebar. The section in which she is introduced begins "It [children disappearing from Oxford] would happen like this" (Pullman, *Golden* 40), so making her a mere suggestion, Mrs. Coulters' narratorial "initiation" (Herman et al. 61) suspends her in a fairy tale style story. The reader, then, never quite reaches the point of "entrance" (Herman et al. 60) into her tale because it exists outside of the story proper. Outsider by way of narrative structure and by way of archetype, Mrs. Coulter is also villainous according to a key "rule of signification" that "Space Invaders are to be distrusted" (Rabinowitz 91). Her sudden invasion of the main plot provokes a horrifying moment of shock and recognition when a guest at Lyra's college is described as "beautiful and young. Her sleek black hair framed her cheeks, and her daemon was a golden monkey" (Pullman, *Golden* 65). These words, which constitute a chapter end, mirror the description of the evil stepmother figure from the hypothetical sidebar and pull that figure into the realm of the protagonist hero, her daughter, Lyra. Furthermore, the use of Mrs. Coulter's name—unmentioned in the fairy tale sequence—by the Master of Jordan College to introduce her to Lyra, serves less to humanize than to villainize her, for a villain interacting with the hero is crucial to the plot development of most works of fantasy (Edwards and Klosa 37).

Lyra's initial interactions with Mrs. Coulter invite the reader to judge her villainy on multiple levels. Mimetically, she is the flesh-and-blood woman to whom Lyra is dangerously attracted, and thematically and synthetically, she is the archetypal evil woman whom the hero must fight. When, after spending her first full day with Mrs. Coulter, Lyra feels "too enchanted to question anything" (Pullman, *Golden* 78), the audience can read that enchantment in the psychological sense and in the magical sense—Lyra is overwhelmed by the "feminine mysteries" (Pullman, *Golden* 77) and glamorous lifestyle filled with shopping, clothes and luncheons to which Mrs. Coulter has exposed her, and also Mrs. Coulter bewitches Lyra into a subdued state through her "warm drink with milk and herbs" (Pullman, *Golden* 77) that recalls the chocolatl from the hypothetical sidebar. Encouraging the reader to other Mrs. Coulter over and over, the text rewards compliance by confirming suspicions about Mrs. Coulter's character: her daemon physically attacks Lyra's daemon Pan with a "cold, curious force" (Pullman, *Golden* 86), earning his "hatred" (Pullman, *Golden* 87) and Lyra's uneasiness, and spurring their escape from Mrs. Coulter's ultra-feminized lair.

In colluding to relegate Mrs. Coulter to this villainous role, the textual and readerly dynamics have positioned the authorial audience as oppressor: this woman must be beyond redemption of any kind. Despite the few sympathetic mimetic qualities she acquires in her back-story as told by John Faa (Pullman, *Golden* 121–122), the narrative works to cement rather than mitigate the vision of her as evil. Leaving Mrs. Coulter unnamed at the beginning of his story, John Faa does attribute positive, human qualities to her: she is "passionate," "clever," and capable of romantic "love" (Pullman, *Golden* 121). She also feels "fear" when she finds herself pregnant by her lover rather than her husband (Pullman, *Golden* 122). The tale, however, soon divorces her from these recognizable feelings: after the death of her husband and her lover's punishment, she "wanted nothing to do with" the child (Pullman, *Golden* 123), and the last we hear about her past from John Faa is that the gyptian woman who cared for the baby "told [him] she'd often been afeared" of the way she would have treated the baby "because she was a proud and scornful woman" (Pullman, *Golden* 123). The interpretation of Mrs. Coulter's mimetic character I present above is rendered almost impossible at this point in the reader's configuring experience because John Faa's dismissive "so much for her" (Pullman, *Golden* 123) undermines the interest the audience might have had in the mimetic character he first describes. Subsequently revealing that the woman in his story is not only Mrs. Coulter, but also Lyra's biological mother (Pullman, *Golden* 124), the narrative encourages the reader to move immediately to an ethical and affective judgment of righteous horror: Mrs. Coulter is not an evil *step*mother—she is an evil *mother*.

Her mimetic role obscured by the interplay of textual and readerly dynamics, Mrs. Coutler is locked into the immanence of her archetypal role. One main way that readers make sense of texts is by their "understanding of causation": they "move from cause to effect" or "from effect to cause" in order to determine what will happen or why things have happened (Rabinowitz 104–105). In *The Golden Compass* the narrator withholds any causal information about Mrs. Coulter until it has pressed upon the reader prejudices against her, and even then, the information it offers is scant. If, mimetically, Mrs. Coulter has little in the way of personal "character," then, synthetically, the readerly and the textual dynamics have worked together to supply a villainous one.

Yet even after this seeming solidification of her villainy, there is a turn. If rules of configuration are "basically predictive" in that they guide the reader to expect what will come next (Rabinowitz 111), then the expectations of Mrs. Coulter set up by the narrative progression so far are both satisfied and confounded by the scenes at Bolvanger. Edwards and Klosa characterize classic villains as "selfish, hav[ing] no concern for others, and [willing to] use any means necessary to achieve their goals" (Edwards and Klosa 35), and the reportedly "ghoulish" (Pullman, *Golden* 274) enjoyment Mrs. Coulter experiences when she witnesses the dreadful process of intercision (by which humans are severed from their daemons and lose conscious selfhood) is the most convincing testament to that selfish lack of concern. Yet during the Bolvanger episode—where this villain, as expected, creates a "cold drench of terror" (Pullman, *Golden* 245) in her own daughter and "suppressed hysterical fear" among other children (Pullman, *Golden* 267)—Mrs. Coulter, "haggard and horror-struck" (Pullman, *Golden* 278), rescues Lyra from the silver guillotine that is about to sever her from Pan, "la[ys] her gently on the bed," and "stroke[s] her head" with a "tender hand" (Pullman, *Golden* 279).

The authorial audience reels at this chapter end: what has happened to the evil mother? What of our "metonymical rules of enchainment" that encourage us to "assume that one moral failure naturally accompanies another" (Rabinowitz 91)? The audience reads on only to experience readerly and textual dynamics that again collude to distance Mrs. Coulter from their sympathy. The golden monkey "prowl[s] about restlessly" in his search for Lyra's alethiometer (Pullman, *Golden* 284) while Mrs. Coulter attempts to explain intercision in a positive light, and Mrs. Coulter's un-motherly reaction of stepping back when her daughter dry heaves (Pullman, *Golden* 283) prompts the reader to agree, quite naturally, with the free indirect discourse focalized through Lyra: "Oh, the wicked liar, the shameful untruths she was telling!" (Pullman, *Golden* 284). The narrative progression very neatly undoes most of the confusion the reader might have felt about Mrs. Coulter in the previous scene. Even if Mrs. Coulter's rescue of Lyra and Pan from a horrible fate remains a disquieting exception to her evil classification, the reader is invited to find comfort in the text's subsequent suggestion that she is still, indeed, the villain of the story whose daemon attacks Pan while she "drag[s] Lyra to the back of a motorized sledge" and "shriek[s] a high command" (Pullman, *Golden* 297).

Thus, when readers learn the rest of Mrs. Coulter's back-story from her former lover and father of her child, they are already positioned to continue with the vilification the text overtly encourages. If the authorial audience is used to villainous characters "manifest[ing]" often in "political discourse" and "popular culture" (Edwards and Klosa 35), then the political bent of Lord Asriel's first description of her as power hungry (Pullman, *Golden* 374) provokes the audience to understand Mrs. Coulter not as the desperate oppressed woman described in Beauvoir's terms above, but as an evil authority figure whom it last saw commanding an army of child-stealers. Since such evil figures are painted by the media as "one-dimensional" with "no depth to their experience" (Edwards and Klosa 65), we cling more to Asriel's comment that intercision was her own, original idea (Pullman, *Golden* 376) than we do to any insight into her mimetic situation.

The final scene of *The Golden Compass*, however, most overtly confronts the reader's impulse to view Mrs. Coulter as one-dimensional, hearkening back to John Faa's earlier revelation that Mrs. Coulter has been in love (Pullman, *Golden* 394) and Lord Asriel's comments about her as a woman within a patriarchy, and also prefiguring her eventual heroics. Alternately kissing Lord Asriel passionately and protesting against his invitation to accompany him into a new world, she seems legitimately torn about the choice offered her. The golden monkey, whom the reader has become used to seeing as a prowling, calculating creature, is instead "relaxed, blissful, swooning" (Pullman, *Golden* 395) in Lord Asriel's daemon's embrace as she wrestles with her decision. Even Lyra notices that her tears "were real" (Pullman, *Golden* 397). At the end of a novel wherein Mrs. Coulter's formal name has been used and withheld strategically and her daemon has no name at all, Lord Asriel's use of her first name "Marisa" (Pullman, *Golden* 395) is a shocking reminder of Mrs. Coulter's humanity. If "eyes are among the more reliable visual guides to characters in fiction" (Rabinowitz 88), then Mrs. Coulter's being filled "with an infinite beautiful sadness" (Pullman, *Golden* 396) as she turns down Lord Asriel's invitation certainly suggests depth to her mimetic character. Here the reader must also make sense of the revelation that Mrs. Coulter fears the controlling Church—a fear articulated in her own voice: "They'll forbid it! They'll seal it off and excommunicate anyone who tries! ... They are stronger than anyone, Asriel! You don't know—" (Pullman, *Golden* 394).

Hearing this "evil woman" struggle to communicate her terror challenges the reader to reconfigure Mrs. Coulter on the mimetic, thematic, and synthetic levels. Mimetically, her protests might even cause the audience to remember and possibly re-read the information John Faa and Lord Asriel have offered about her past, persuading them to acknowledge Mrs. Coulter's experience as a woman in a man's world. Synthetically and thematically, the shock of Mrs. Coulter's humanity forces a reevaluation of her role: if she is not a one-dimensional evil mother, what is she? What purpose will she serve in Lyra's story? What is the significance of her internal struggle?

If we remain in the archetypal mode the text has encouraged so far but shift our focus therein, one way to understand Mrs. Coulter here is as refusing the hero's "call to adventure." According to Joseph Campbell, when a potential hero refuses the call, "the refusal is essentially a refusal to give up what one takes to be one's own interest. The future is regarded not in terms of an unremitting series of deaths and births, but as though one's present system of ideals, virtues, goals, and advantages were to be fixed and made secure" (60). Mrs.

Coulter's protests about the consequences of rebelling against the Church make explicit her fear of repercussion and imply her internal struggle: she is both attracted to Asriel's invitation and committed to (perceived) self-interest via her espousal of the Church's values. At this point in the story, allegiance to the Church wins—in light of possible excommunication, Asriel's invitation seems far too risky and promises little reward—because allegiance is the only route she can see that maintains her own power. Therefore, examining Mrs. Coulter synthetically and mimetically suggests that thematically, fear of the patriarchy can perpetuate villainy not *in spite of*, but *due to* the complexity of those it oppresses.

At the point of refusal, "the subject loses the power of significant affirmative action" (Campbell 59) and continues on "walled in boredom, hard work, or 'culture'" (Campbell 59). As agent of the Magisterium, Mrs. Coulter enters *The Subtle Knife* wielding the Church's culture like a battering ram against the protagonist, the protagonist's helpers, and her own possibilities for transcendence. Her warning to the witch she physically tortures aligns her firmly with the villainous purposes of the Magisterium: "We have a thousand years of experience in this Church of ours. We can draw out your suffering endlessly" (Pullman, *Subtle* 38). Thematically and synthetically, Mrs. Coulter is a villain on a mission to thwart whatever "destiny" the child hero Lyra possesses (Pullman, *Subtle* 38).

The Subtle Knife abstains from developing the complexities *The Golden Compass* raises about Mrs. Coulter; instead it confirms and indulges the reader's original configuration of Mrs. Coulter as evil woman, which the scenes with Lord Boreal/Sir Charles evidence. In the first she is pumping Boreal for information about the multiple worlds he's visited while her daemon "crouch[es] ... turning its head this way and that, searching for something" (Pullman, *Subtle* 202), and she refers caustically to her daughter as "the child" (Pullman, *Subtle* 199). Will, as a young man, must fight his attraction to her "brilliant dark eyes wide with enchantment, her slender shape light and graceful" (Pullman, *Subtle* 204), and he does so by understanding that the "evil monkey" is part of her "being" (Pullman, *Subtle* 204). Her witch-like character grows to epic proportions in her final scene, where her graphic seduction and poisoning of Boreal emphasizes her cold, calculating nature. After asking "would you like me to please you even more?" (Pullman, *Subtle* 310), the monkey massages his serpent daemon, "squeezing just a little, lifting, stroking as Sir Charles sighed with pleasure" (Pullman, *Subtle* 312). Once she learns from him the information she needs, she poisons him; as he is dying, "the monkey shook her [the serpent daemon] off with contempt" (Pullman, *Subtle* 312), and in these actions the authorial audience recognizes what Sarah Appleton Aguilar refers to as the "castrating bitch" stereotype. A "marvel of integration," the castrating bitch "incorporate[s] all of the bitch stereotypes: domineering shrew, witch, femme fatale, and devouring mother. Demanding, devious, sexually predaceous, egocentrically possessed, she chews men up and leaves them bereft of their manhood" (Aguilar 50).

The narrative progression even attributes to Mrs. Coulter superhuman powers: she controls the Specters who feed on conscious life (Pullman, *Subtle* 310), and the second witch she tortures perceives that "Mrs. Coulter ha[s] more force in her soul than anyone she had ever seen" (Pullman, *Subtle* 313). The finale of Mrs. Coulter's villainous performance in this volume is her vow upon learning that her daughter is the next Eve: "Why, I shall have to destroy her" (Pullman, *Subtle* 314). Upholding the Church's campaign against human consciousness as a devouring mother, femme fatale, and superhuman witch on the loose, Mrs. Coulter manifests to the reader as a force of Evil, and the reader is encouraged to view her that way. *The Subtle Knife*'s insistence on Mrs. Coulter's archetypal character mires its authorial audience in prejudice that is difficult and even dangerous to avoid, tied as it is to the basic psychological impulse to other the evil (step)mother. And yet the final volume of the trilogy seeks to undermine this foundation laid by the narrative progression of the first two volumes, thereby casting those psychological impulses as oppressive of the possibilities engendered by growth and change.

Acknowledging the Heroic (in Spite of Ourselves)

Though *The Subtle Knife* works against readerly acknowledgment of Mrs. Coulter's complexities, the majority of *The Amber Spyglass* capitalizes on them. This shift serves a major synthetic purpose: Mrs. Coulter is key to the plot, since her vanquishing of Metatron makes possible Lyra's ability to "fall" in freedom and safety. However, since "one typical consequence of an author's foregrounding the synthetic component of character is the heightening of our interest in the thematic" (Herman et al. 113), the reader wants to make sense of her actions beyond the level of plot. Mrs. Coulter's character arc in *The Amber Spyglass* engages the reader in a strenuous process of *coherence*, in which he strives to make sense of the part-to-whole relations in a text, especially when it seems to resist unity (Rabinowitz 147). Her synthetic shift—from the "principal villain" (Hatlen 79) she plays throughout the majority of the trilogy to unexpected helper of the protagonist and hero in her own right—has thematic effects that stem from the relationship between her synthetic and mimetic qualities and reach beyond the page to urge a shift in the audience itself. Dogging the reader with its insistence on possibilities beyond an exclusive good/evil dichotomy, the narrative progression provokes the audience to examine its oppressive preconceptions about villainy and heroic potential.

The Amber Spyglass makes inroads towards Mrs. Coulter's eventual heroics by engaging with her point of view. The first chapter, in which she keeps Lyra in a drugged sleep in a remote cave, includes the first instances in the trilogy of free indirect discourse focalized through Mrs. Coulter, and they do not convey a clear malevolent purpose: "she wondered what in the world she thought she was doing, and whether she had gone mad, and, over and over again, what would happen when the Church found out" (Pullman, *Amber* 7). The foregrounding of Mrs. Coulter's confusion in these early cave scenes sets the stage for her mimetic struggle with her heroic impulse as well as the reader's struggle to overturn judgments about her villainy.

For the reader this struggle is of epic proportions after witnessing her superhuman badness throughout *The Subtle Knife*. The large narrative gap regarding Mrs. Coulter's psychological shift between the second and third volumes is difficult to surmount even with the "license to fill" that readers invoke when confronted with insufficiencies or discrepancies (Rabinowitz 148); applying understanding of causation is troublesome when the effect in question is curiously unclear. First appearing domestically "over a naphtha stove" (Pullman, *Amber* 2) and laughing at the notion that she can "tell the truth" (Pullman, *Amber* 3), she forces Lyra to choke down a sleeping potion. Her daemon seems nasty as ever, "ready to seize Pantalaimon" (Pullman, *Amber* 5) and displaying obvious "contempt," but Mrs. Coulter sponge-bathes Lyra and tidies her hair (Pullman, *Amber* 7). Furthermore, the reader has been discouraged from understanding Mrs. Coulter as a person, so the possible mimetic causes of her behavior in the cave sequences are doubly obscured.

The narrative progression probes this uncertainty. Balancing the narrative gap between books two and three, the cave sequences extend throughout the entire first third of *The Amber Spyglass*, and the drawing out of the audience's "temporal experience" (Herman et al. 58) of Mrs. Coulter's fugitive activities forces the reader to examine their significance. Arenas calls "the average reader … a cognitive miser, who construes character as fast and loosely as he or she can" (17), and, as demonstrated above, the first two volumes of the trilogy encourage such a stance in relation to Mrs. Coulter. However, as Arenas explains,

> sometimes fictional villains surprise us by behaving in ways which break … expectations. It is in such cases that readers get perplexed and may leave their position of cognitive misers to become motivated tacticians; now automatic processes of perception may be substituted by controlled processes through which we weigh up all possible mitigating factors [19].

Therefore, when the newly tactical audience sees Mrs. Coulter slap a waking Lyra "hard across the face" (Pullman, *Amber* 51) before "crooning baby songs, smoothing the hair off the girl's brow" and kissing a lock of her hair before enclosing it in a locket (Pullman, *Amber* 52), the reader is being encouraged to feel "distrust" for her (Russell 216), but is more likely to be interested in the direction the confused woman will take rather than write her off as mad. When the golden monkey tears apart a bat for the entertainment of it while "the woman lay moodily on her sleeping bag by the fire and slowly ate a bar of chocolate" (Pullman, *Amber* 52), a tactical reader notes the discrepancy between a woman and daemon heretofore joined in malevolent calculation and perceives their internal division manifesting in depressed stasis.

Mimetically, Mrs. Coulter is lost in "a hopelessly confused protectiveness—or possessiveness" (Rutledge 123), and archetypally, she is on the verge of a breakthrough. Of potential heroes who refuse the call to adventure, Campbell writes "not all who hesitate are lost. The psyche has many secrets in reserve ... sometimes the predicament following an obstinate refusal of the call proves to be the occasion of a providential revelation of some unsuspected principle of release" (64). This "predicament" is rooted in her choice to hide Lyra away even as she fears "what would happen when the Church found out" (Pullman, *Amber* 7) that she has done so. Though hiding does risk patriarchal retribution, it is actually necessary for her to gain any perspective on her own subject-hood: "one must first emerge from [society permeated by gender-specific expectations] into a sovereign solitude if one wants to try to regain a grasp upon [subjecthood]: what woman needs first of all is to undertake in anguish and pride, her apprenticeship in abandonment and transcendence: that is, in liberty" (de Beauvoir, *Second* 711). Indeed, Rutledge points out that most of the surrogate parents in *His Dark Materials* exist outside of the governmental hierarchies that populate Lyra's world, an exile that makes possible their ability to nurture (121). Mrs. Coulter's time in the cave is a time of incubation for her own existential and heroic impulses: she needs isolation from all society, even that of her own daughter, to make sense of the inner conflict she is experiencing. This isolation is necessary for the implied reader, too, who is mired in configurations prompted by the narratorial dynamics of the previous volumes which exploit conventional expectations of the evil female. If "the traditional stereotype of [the bitch] maintains its tenacious hold upon the imagination" (Aguilar 9), then by isolating Mrs. Coulter in the cave for the reader's examination, the narrative obliges the reader to see her as more than the sum of a group of interrelated archetypal manifestations. She has potential beyond that of "villain," and the cave sequences make her future heroics not only possible, but palatable.

In their work to slowly dismantle the box in which the textual and readerly dynamics have kept her, however, the narrative progression of *The Amber Spyglass* does not forge ahead with the expectation that the reader is fully ready to see Mrs. Coulter "on our side." Once she is captured from the cave, counterpointing her rather convincing outbursts about her love for her daughter (Pullman, *Amber* 204–206) are the moments of free indirect discourse focalized through Lord Asriel (who sees her tears as a "shameless" ploy) and Lord Roke's sense of her "scorpion" nature (Pullman, *Amber* 206). The authorial audience is tempted to agree, for the sake of ease, with Lord Asriel's perception of the "glitter of sly triumph in the depths of her beautiful eyes" when she convinces his council she should stay on as informer. Yet the narrative ties any indictment of Mrs. Coulter to another character's point of view, not to its limited omniscient perspective. Furthermore, when the narrative voice indulges Mrs. Coulter's perspective, it remains neutral regarding her intentions. For example, though "an idea [comes] to Mrs. Coulter's mind," we are not privy to the idea itself. We do know, however, that it must be important, for "she and the monkey daemon exchanged a glance that felt like a powerful anbaric spark" (Pullman, *Amber* 207). That she and the monkey are again aligned provokes the reader to wonder whose side they've chosen: Mrs. Coulter's germinating instinct to nurture, or the monkey's need to "torment" (Pullman, *Amber* 148).

Either way, the textual and readerly dynamics accept as given that Mrs. Coulter is not one to remain inactive; if "no existent can be satisfied with an inessential role" (de Beauvoir, *Second* 604), then a woman "full of joy and life and energy" even in the danger of battle (Pullman, *Amber* 156) needs the exhilaration of activity to thrive. Her escape from Lord Asriel's fortress is a step towards a true exercise of liberty, which occurs just after she is "genuinely shocked" (Pullman, *Amber* 210) by the information that the Authority is not the creator. As the top of the patriarchy crumbles in her mind, she and her daemon exhibit the effects of their potential freedom from its tyranny: "another idea struck even more forcibly, and she hugged the golden monkey with glee" (Pullman, *Amber* 218). The connotations of the word "glee" are intensely positive, and though the reader may still be distrustful of Mrs. Coulter's agenda (that she believes she must trick Asriel in order to leave for her spying mission sets off warning bells about her deceptive *modus operandi*), he or she cannot avoid acknowledging the narrative's emphasis on Mrs. Coulter's ability to feel non-anger-based passion.

As it details her steps towards liberty from patriarchal oppression and works to soften the reader's judgment, the narrative voice even aligns itself with Mrs. Coulter's in one of the most overt instances of gender discourse in the trilogy. She argues with Fr. MacPhail:

> If you thought for one moment that I would release my daughter into the care— the *care*!—of a body of men with a feverish obsession with sexuality, men with dirty fingernails, reeking of ancient sweat, men whose furtive imaginations would crawl over her body like cockroaches—if you thought I would expose my child to *that*, my Lord President, you are more stupid than you take *me* for [Pullman, *Amber*, emphasis in original 326].

Already convinced of the Church's obsession with sexuality, the authorial audience appreciates Mrs. Coulter's vitriol as insight into her own experience as a sexualized woman in the patriarchy, an experience that has, heretofore, likely stifled her impulse to speak out to a high-ranking Church official. Later in the same conversation, she questions the power base of the Church itself: "Well, where is God ... if he's alive? And why doesn't he speak anymore? ... Is he still alive, at some inconceivable age, decrepit and demented, unable to think or act or speak and unable to die, a rotten hulk?" (Pullman, *Amber* 328). Finding it "intoxicating, to speak like that to this *man*" (Pullman, *Amber*, my emphasis, 328), she delights in the liberating effect of breaking away from subaltern status.

Having positioned her as more sympathetic to the reader, the narrative progression now makes Mrs. Coulter's new direction quite certain, not so late as Coulter's "departure to seduce Metatron" as Rutledge argues (123), but during the bomb scene at Saint-Jean-les-Eaux. The textual dynamics shift again to privilege Mrs. Coulter's perspective, revealing her focus on Lyra rather than herself: "The problem for Mrs. Coulter was not how to get out of this situation alive: that was a secondary matter. The problem was how to get Lyra's hair out of the bomb before they set it off" (Pullman, *Amber* 344). Most profound in terms of readerly dynamics here is that when Mrs. Coulter engages in the physical fight that means the difference of life or death for her daughter, the narrative *demands* that the reader be on Mrs. Coulter's side, the side of Lyra's hope to live. Though in the cave Mrs. Coulter is torn between her varying impulses and allegiances, here she is unified of purpose: "the golden monkey leapt for Father MacPhail, but not to attack: he scrambled up and over the man's shoulders to reach ... the resonating chamber" (349). Not distracted by his relish for violence, even Mrs. Coulter's daemon passes over an attempt to attack his captor, and Mrs. Coulter herself "hurl[s] her whole weight against the machine" (Pullman, *Amber* 350), symbolic of her full investment in saving Lyra's life. In this enormous physical ordeal focalized through Mrs. Coulter, the narrative forces the audience to acknowledge her authenticity as Lyra's defender, thus eroding her status as villain.

According to Rabinowitz, "authors frequently create their effects by tricking readers" into believing, for example, that a character is bad when he or she is actually good (90). The case of Mrs. Coulter is much more complex than this trick: Mrs. Coulter *does* commit a series of villainous acts that *cannot* be re-cast as heroic and that *do* deserve the reader's repulsion, and she certainly does *not* engage in a cut-and-dry shift from Evil to Good. In fact, *His Dark Materials* works explicitly against such categorization when protagonist and female hero Lyra agrees with helper figure Mary Malone that "good and evil are names for what people do, not for what they are. All we can say is that this is a good deed, because it helps someone, or that's an evil one, because it hurts them. People are too complicated to have simple labels" (Pullman, *Amber* 447).[1] The trilogy makes clear that Mrs. Coulter has both performed villainous deeds and also has the capacity (and even impulse) to perform heroic ones; when she makes the decision to infiltrate the Clouded Mountain to destroy Metatron and enable Lyra's life, the narrative does not emphasize stark reversal from one "side" to another, but rather personal evolution: Mrs. Coulter "found the eyes of her daemon. The golden monkey's expression was as subtle and complex as it had ever been in all their thirty-five years of life" (Pullman, *Amber* 382). The attention to eyes, age, and the golden monkey (who has heretofore represented her villainous impulses) all serve to highlight not repression of or divorce from a villainous past, but growth towards a heroic future.

In terms of archetype, growth marks the traditional hero's readiness to answer a call: "the familiar life horizon has been outgrown; the old concepts, ideals, and emotional patterns no longer fit; the time for the passing of a threshold is at hand" (Campbell 51). But growth does not erase one's past, and *His Dark Materials* is emphatic that Marisa Coulter's villainous choices are key to her character's fruition. The main trial she must overcome on her way to her heroic finale is her deception of Metatron, which she accomplishes by way of "the most searching examination [she] had ever undergone ... she stood naked, body and ghost and daemon together, under the ferocity of Metatron's gaze" (Pullman, *Amber* 398). This examination of what Mrs. Coulter thinks is "her nature" (Pullman, *Amber* 398) yields the only result that could allow her to come to her heroic end. Metatron sees

> corruption and envy and lust for power. Cruelty and coldness. A vicious, probing curiosity. Pure, poisonous, toxic malice. You have never from your earliest years shown a shred of compassion or sympathy or kindness without calculating how it would return to your advantage. You have tortured and killed without regret or hesitation; you have betrayed and intrigued and gloried in your treachery. You are a cesspit of moral filth [Pullman, *Amber* 398].

Metatron's indictment powerfully coincides with the authorial audience's assessment of Mrs. Coulter throughout the first two volumes of the trilogy and functions as a grotesque moment of absolution. Scoured for her worth, Mrs. Coulter emerges as morally reprehensible and therefore valuable to archangel Metatron's goal of defeating Lord Asriel—which is to say that the notion of actual absolution does not apply to Mrs. Coulter. Mrs. Coulter, for instance, never expresses remorse for her child-torturing past (which can be troubling to readers), and therefore the text emphasizes that her past actions do not need to be and *cannot* be eradicated or boxed away in order for her to be able to perform a good deed. Mrs. Coulter, perpetrator of so many harmful acts, is *also* capable of making a choice that will result in help, and Metatron's labeling her a "cesspit of moral filth" confronts the audience with this notion unequivocally.

Mrs. Coulter's and Metatron's mistaken belief that he is assessing her entire "nature" speaks to the same exclusive good/evil dichotomy that has its grip on the authorial audience. According to the narrator, Mrs. Coulter is "lying with her whole life" (Pullman, *Amber* 398), the sum of which *has been* "treachery" and the "glor[y]" therein, but Metatron can only see Mrs. Coulter's past, as his verb tenses demonstrate, and from that he makes his present tense judgment about her entire being (using the verb "are"). Mimetically, however, as a human with free will and a growing sense of her liberty to use it, Mrs. Coulter's future is for her to enact on no one's prediction.

In emphasis of the continuity among past, present, and future, Mrs. Coulter draws on her well-nuanced understanding of patriarchal desire for female submission to defeat Metatron, for she is aware that her success is predicated upon his need to dominate a woman. Putting herself in the precarious position of subservience—"is it not time you had a consort?" (Pullman, *Amber* 399)—works specifically because Metatron's desire, piqued by reminders of his past as a human male (Pullman, *Amber* 399), outweighs his intelligence: "The Regent was a being whose profound intellect had had thousands of years to deepen and strengthen itself, and whose knowledge extended over a million universes. Nevertheless, at that moment he was blinded by his twin obsessions: to destroy Lyra and to possess her mother" (Pullman, *Amber* 404). Here, Mrs. Coulter is enacting the role of hero who "brings knowledge of the secret of the tyrant's doom" (Campbell 337). Furthermore, if Metatron is "the dragon to be slain by [the hero] ... the monster of the status quo" (Campbell 337), then in her use of her past to enable the world's future, Mrs. Coulter both embodies and makes possible movement beyond stasis.

The stasis out of which Mrs. Coulter breaks includes her enslavement to the patriarchy and, to use de Beauvoir's term, their "ready-made values" (de Beauvoir, *Second* 636) which fostered her villainous choices and repression of love. Her refusal of the call at the end of *The Golden Compass* binds her in the immanent roles of woman in a man's world and villain in the hero's journey, but the parallel scene with Lord Asriel over the abyss in *The Amber Spyglass* has her moving beyond these restraints towards transcendence. Instead of protesting to Lord Asriel about her fear of the patriarchy, she questions him to ensure Lyra's safety. Instead of wrestling with her conflicting desires, "she felt as soft and light in [Asriel's] arms as she had when Lyra was conceived thirteen years before" (Pullman, *Amber* 405). As Mrs. Coulter attempts to articulate the love she feels for her daughter, the narrator infuses metaphors of growth into her story as she compares the love to a "mustard seed" that "had taken root and was growing, and the little green shoot was splitting [her] heart wide open" (Pullman, *Amber* 405).

Traditionally, the hero is "the champion not of things become but of things becoming" (Campbell 337), and Mrs. Coulter herself is still in the process of "becoming." As she expresses this love for Lyra she also expresses her confusion about Metatron's gaze: "I wanted him to find no good in me, and he didn't. There is none. But I love Lyra" (Pullman, *Amber* 405). The juxtaposition of "there is none" and "but I love Lyra" aligns Mrs. Coulter with the authorial audience; like them, she is schooled in the exclusive good/bad binary. Thus, this speech demonstrates her engaging in the process of individuation, which psychoanalyst Ann Ulanov claims "by no means ceases at adulthood but recurs throughout life whenever nonrational unconscious contents excluded by a conscious ego adaptation press for integration" (70–71). Newly integrating her love for her daughter into her understanding of herself, Mrs. Coulter is "recovering an inner value" more than "establishing outer adaptation" (Ulanov 71). Mrs. Coulter, like the reader, is called to move past, or transcend, those external cues that have forced her to separate rather than integrate. Now that "her own consciousness, as her 'hero,' [is freeing] her from eternal dedication to the paternal masculine, as given through some authority external to her" (Ulanov 276), she is able to engage in the meaningful "human relationships" that, according to de Beauvoir, are "the only way for each individual to find the foundation and accomplishment of his being" (de Beauvoir, "Existentialism" 213). Mrs. Coulter's earlier search for power forced her into vassalage to the Church, but her later movement towards liberty has made possible her ability to transcend the roles of oppressed female and evil villain.

His Dark Materials dissolves the "the popular angel/whore division that has plagued female characters for centuries" (Aguilar 9) by way of emphasizing that Mrs. Coulter is both. In the end she performs, as betraying seductress *and* loving mother, her heroic act of throwing out the tyrannical patriarch who has been aiming to squash the selfhood of all conscious life. Russell claims that the final narrative appellation for Mrs. Coulter is "descriptive of her mothering function that now dominates all she does: she is only and essentially 'Lyra's mother'" (Russell 216–217), but the qualifiers "only" and "essentially" need some tempering. According to Terri Frongia, "'the mother as hero' conveys a truth basic to female experience ... [but also] imprisons women in an all-too-familiar conceptual and representational 'box' ... it is yet another manifestation ... of woman's old nemesis, biological determinism" (15). The love Mrs. Coulter expresses for Lyra spurs her heroic act, but it neither reduces nor encompasses the extent of her heroism. For she is the woman brave and clever enough to fool a powerful, uber-intelligent angel, and she is also Asriel's "love" (Pullman, *Amber* 406). She has the audacity to presume that she and Asriel can "wrestle with [Metatron] and bring him to the edge of the gulf" and the determination to "go down with him" (Pullman, *Amber* 406). And in the detailed violence that has her "[digging] her fingers deep into [Metatron's] eyes" and "bar[ing] his throat for [Lord Asriel's daemon's] teeth" (Pullman, *Amber* 408), she ends her life on the note of the power of her physical existence. While motherhood is key to her final act, defining her by one particular role is not in keeping with the textual and readerly dynamics that have exposed the many levels—one of which is hero—on which Mrs. Coulter rightfully exists.

Conclusion

If *His Dark Materials* confirms, complicates, and ultimately undermines early expectations about Mrs. Coulter's synthetic role, then the trilogy is exploiting the preconceived notions of its authorial audience in order to subvert them. This exploitation is not simple, for "we make aesthetic judgments both as we read and again once we have finished the narrative and can look back on it as a whole ... aesthetic judgments are made by actual audiences about the quality of our participation in the authorial audience" (Herman et al. 160). In capitalizing on and subsequently calling into question the authorial audience's expectations of a villainous woman, the trilogy asks its readers to participate in an authorial audience that is *in the process of being constructed*, and therefore risks their possibly negative aesthetic judgment. The narrative's continual obscuring and refocusing of Mrs. Coulter's mimetic characteristics in many cases serve to suspend such judgment by creating the confusion and suspense that turn "cognitive misers" into "tacticians" (Arenas 19). In this process of becoming a new type of audience, members must be goaded into an acceptance of Mrs. Coulter that is, for many, grudging. Anticipating the implied reader's unease, the narration emphasizes the significance of such acceptance through the character of Serafina Pekkala, who functions as a surrogate mother figure for Lyra. Serafina Pekkala remarks, "I saw that woman torturing a witch, and I swore to myself that I would send that arrow into her throat. Now I shall never do that. She sacrificed herself with Lord Asriel to fight the angel and make the world safe for Lyra. They could not have done it alone, but together they did it" (Pullman, *Amber* 479). Just as Serafina Pekkala's speech emphasizes the importance of human relationships to Mrs. Coulter's heroics, so does it highlight the importance of reconsidering earlier valuations and acknowledging their shortcomings. Narratively, Mrs. Coulter has ceased to be villain and has become an embodiment of the freedom to choose—even if that choice is difficult or terrifying—in all human circumstances.

His Dark Materials' insistence on the acceptance of Mrs. Coulter's evolution as a person as well as a villain-hero speaks to philosopher Phillip Cole's claim that people must move beyond "the discourse of evil":

> We are not excusing [the perpetrators of villainous crimes] of being evil at all; we are rejecting evil as a category that can meaningfully be applied to human beings.... The deeply *unethical* aspect of the discourse of evil is that it closes any space for future redemption ... the rejection of the discourse of evil does not rule out moral condemnation and legal punishment of the most extreme kind, but it does rule out the notion that such people are irredeemable [173].

Mrs. Coulter's death can be construed as just punishment for her crimes in the terms Coles suggests and can satisfy a reader's need for justice. However, following Cole's argument, it is important to acknowledge that she ends her life by choosing to perform deeds that help others (namely, Lyra). Rather than allying herself with an external force of "Good," Mrs. Coulter takes steps towards "redemption" not as a result of a perfect paradigm shift (as evident in the lack of remorse, mentioned above) but in answer to a grassroots-style morality germinating from (but not restricted to) her latent motherly instincts. Such steps send an intensely positive and hopeful message about the generative power of human beings.

According to Edwards and Klosa, many "mythic fantasy narratives serve to simplify the world around us and demonstrate who is undoubtedly good and clearly evil" (33), but *His Dark Materials* works against this notion of simplification not just as champion of ambiguity and complexity, but as ethical crusader: in regards to Mrs. Coulter, the human impulse to vilify can manifest as a limiting, oppressive act. On the mimetic, thematic, and synthetic levels, Mrs. Coulter forces us to allow for her subject-hood as villain and as woman, reminding us that by right of humanity, all of us are capable of originating our own actions, of transcending boundaries imposed on us by others, of participating in the villainous as well as the heroic by means of our own individual agency. Jack Zipes explains, "a reader ... will always be impelled by the dynamics of the fantastic to reflect seriously and imaginatively about the customary ways she or he engages with the world" (83). In tearing our eyes from the past, from what is comfortable, to look ahead to what might be, Mrs. Coulter's character calls the reader to a new heroic cycle, which he or she can complete with a "return" to the real world to champion the recognition of subject-hood and possibility not only in himself or herself (such introspection is often prompted by stories of heroism) but also in others: even those we might label villains.

NOTE

1. In contrast to Mrs. Coulter, Lyra, at the start of the trilogy, is marked as heroic: she is the protagonist, she embarks upon a journey, and she crusades for what she believes is right, in the end saving the world from loss of consciousness itself. It is important to note, however, that similar to her mother, even Lyra must work out a concept of "right" that is not always tied to cultural preconceptions. In *The Golden Compass*, Lyra swallows her own culturally-induced repulsion at the sight of a daemon-less child and, with the help of armored-bear Iorek, carries the boy back to the company of humans who quail at the sight but whom she convinces to care for him in his last hours (Pullman, *Golden* 216–217). Lyra's feeling obligated to flout the status quo in the name of what she feels to be personally important is emphasized throughout the trilogy, and set against her example, Mrs. Coulter appears to be capable of a similar trajectory, albeit from a different past.

WORKS CITED

Aguilar, Sarah Appleton. *The Bitch Is Back: Wicked Women in Literature.* Carbondale: Southern Illinois University Press, 2001. Print.

Allen, Nicola. "Exploring and Challenging the Lapsarian World of Young Adult Literature: Femininity, Shame, the Gyptians, and Social Class." Cox and Barfield 111–125. Print.

Arenas, Enrique Camara. "Villains in Our Mind: A Psychological approach to Literary and Filmic Villainy." *Villains and Villainy: Embodiments of Evil in Literature, Popular Culture, and Media.* Eds. Anna Fahreaus and Dikmen Yakali Camoglu. Amsterdam: Editions Rodopi B. V., 2011. 3–29. Print.

Bettelheim, Bruno. *The Uses of Enchantment: The Meaning and Importance of Fairy Tales.* 1976. New York: Vintage, 1989. Print.

Campbell, Joseph. *The Hero with a Thousand Faces*, 2d ed. Princeton: Princeton University Press, 1973. Print.

Cole, Phillip. *The Myth of Evil: Demonizing the Enemy.* Westport, CT: Praeger, 2006. Print.

Cox, Katharine. "'Imagine Dust with a Capital Letter': Interpreting the Social and Cultural Contexts for Philip Pullman's Transformation of Dust." Cox and Barfield 126–142.

Cox, Katharine, and Steven Barfield, eds. *Critical Perspectives on Philip Pullman's* His Dark Materials: *Essays on the Novels, the Film, and the Stage Productions.* Jefferson, NC: McFarland, 2011. Print.

de Beauvoir, Simone. "Existentialism and Popular Wisdom." Trans. Marybeth Timmermann. *Simone de Beauvoir: Philosophical Writings.* Ed. Margaret A. Simons. Chicago: University of Illinois Press, 2004. Print.

_____. *The Second Sex.* Trans. and ed. H. M. Parshley. New York: Knopf, 1983. Print.

Edwards, Jason, and Brian Klosa. "The Complexity of Evil in Modern Mythology: The Evolution of the Wicked Witch of the West." *Millenial Mythmaking: Essays on the Power of Science Fiction and Fantasy Literature, Films, and Games.* Ed. John Perlich. Jefferson, NC: McFarland, 2010. 32–50. Print.

Fox, Quinn E. "Paradise Inverted: Philip Pullman's Use of High Fantasy and Epic Poetry to Portray Evil in *His Dark Materials.*" *Vader, Voldemort, and other Villains: Essays on Evil in Popular Media.* Ed. Jamey Heit. Jefferson, NC: McFarland, 2011. 125–144. Print.

Frongia, Terri. "Archetypes, Stereotypes, and the Female Hero: Transformations in Contemporary Perspectives." *Mythlore* 18.1 (1991): 15–18. Print.

Gamble, Sarah. "Becoming Human: Desire and the Gendered Subject." Cox and Barfield 187–201.

Hatlen, Burton. "Pullman's *His Dark Materials*, a Challenge to the Fantasies of J.R.R. Tolkien and C.S. Lewis, with an Epilogue on Pullman's Neo-Romantic Reading of *Paradise Lost.*" Lenz and Scott 75–94.

Herman, David, James Phelan, Peter J. Rabinowitz, Brian Richardson, and Robyn Warhol. *Narrative Theory: Core Concepts and Critical Debates.* Columbus: Ohio State University Press, 2012. Print.

Hopkins, Lisa. "Dyads or Triads? *His Dark Materials* and the Structure of the Human." Lenz and Scott 48–56.

Lenz, Millicent. "Awakening to the Twenty-first Century: The Evolution of Human Consciousness in Pullman's *His Dark Materials.*" Lenz and Scott 1–21.

Lenz, Millicent, and Carole Scott, eds. His Dark Materials *Illuminated: Critical Essays on Philip Pullman's Trilogy.* Detroit: Wayne State University Press, 2005. Print.

Pullman, Philip. *The Amber Spyglass.* New York: Knopf, 2000. Print.

_____. *The Golden Compass.* New York: Knopf, 1995. Print.

_____. *The Subtle Knife.* New York: Knopf, 1997. Print.

Rabinowitz, Peter J. *Before Reading: Narrative Conventions and the Politics of Interpretation.* Ithaca: Cornell University Press, 1987. Print.

Russell, Mary Harris. "'Eve, Again! Mother Eve!' Pullman's Eve Variations." Lenz and Scott 212–222.

Rutledge, Amelia A. "Reconfiguring Nurture in Philip Pullman's *His Dark Materials.*" *Children's Literature Association Quarterly* 33.2 (Summer 2008): 119–134. *Project Muse.*

Ulanov, Ann Belford. *The Feminine in Jungian Psychology and in Christian Theology.* Evanston: Northwest University Press, 1971. Print.

Warner, Maria. *From the Beast to the Blonde: On Fairy Tales and Their Tellers.* New York: Farrar, Straus and Giroux, 1994. Print.

Zipes, Jack. "Why Fantasy Matters Too Much." *Journal of Aesthetic Education* 43.2 (Summer 2009): 77–91. *JSTOR.*

"All little girls are terrible": Maud as Anti-Villain in Catherynne M. Valente's *The Girl Who Circumnavigated Fairyland in a Ship of Her Own Making*

Jill Marie Treftz

"Now," said the Green Wind, ... "there are important rules in Fairyland.... I am afraid that if you trample upon the rules, I cannot help you. You may be ticketed or executed, depending on the will of the Marquess."

"Is she very terrible?"

The Green Wind frowned into his brambly beard. "All little girls are terrible," he admitted finally, "but the Marquess, at least, has a very fine hat."

—Valente, *The Girl Who Circumnavigated Fairyland in a Ship of Her Own Making*, 2–3

When September, the hero of Catherynne M. Valente's *The Girl Who Circumnavigated Fairyland in a Ship of Her Own Making*[1] (2011), asks the Green Wind if Fairyland's ruling Marquess is "very terrible," the Green Wind's response serves two key narrative functions. First, his statement establishes the Marquess as the novel's antagonist, and, second, it reinforces the ways Valente has already begun to subvert the models of little girlhood set forth in children's fantasy literature of the late nineteenth and early twentieth centuries. Valente's choice of the word "terrible" echoes the confrontation between Oz the Great and Terrible and Dorothy "the Small and Meek" in L. Frank Baum's *The Wonderful Wizard of Oz* (Baum 88), but reverses the power dynamics set forth in that novel. By asserting that it is little girls, not adult men, who are great and terrible—who wield the power to control their own and others' destinies—*GWCF* reimagines the roles of little girls in fantasy fiction.

In an interview appended to the 2012 paperback edition of the novel, Valente says that *GWCF* "was always meant to stand against a troubling aspect of the wonderful heroines of my youth, Dorothy and Alice and Wendy—all characters who, some sooner, some later, wanted to go home, and rejected the magical world in favor of our own. I wanted to create a book about saying yes to magic, about seeing a new world, a new way of living and embracing it instead of turning away" (252). In September and the child-tyrant Marquess (later known as Maud[2]), both of whom enthusiastically embrace the "new world" of magic that they find in Fairyland, Valente creates characters that serve as focal points for her critique of the home-centeredness of these earlier figures. More importantly, as she intertwines September's story with that of Maud in an increasingly grim exploration of children's fantasy tropes, Valente constructs a narrative that brings to light the troubling assumptions about gender and maturity that lie at the heart of the genre. In all of the novels to which Valente refers (and in many others), the transitions between the magical world and the human world and the various adventures of the girl hero within Fairyland function as metaphors for or harbingers of her incipient adolescence. For Valente, who describes seeing C. S. Lewis's *The Lion, the Witch, and the Wardrobe* as "a horror novel" (252) for its treatment of its child heroes, the girl hero's eventual escape or expulsion from her Fairyland marks not a turn to adult independence, but a traumatic loss of freedom and autonomy brought about by the betrayal of Fairyland itself.

Thus, in *GWCF*, Valente critiques the literary tradition that limits fantastic adventure to the province of children in general, and specifically deconstructs the ways in which children's fantasy has traditionally privileged little girlhood far above adult womanhood. In *The Rhetoric of Character in Children's Literature*, Maria Nikolajeva maps out the ways in which the protagonists of children's literature mimic the monomythic hero delineated by Joseph Campbell in *The Hero with a Thousand Faces*. She concludes this analysis by observing that for both the mythic and the child hero, upon the conclusion of their adventure "there is also a promise of further adventure; that is, *as long as children remain children*, they can cross the boundaries between the ordinary and the magical world" (30, my emphasis). Nikolajeva does not examine the gendered dynamics of this convention, but children's fantasists from Lewis Carroll to J. M. Barrie to C. S. Lewis have specifically adopted as their protagonists little girls—not little boys—who are (whether figuratively, as with Carroll, or literally, as with Barrie and Lewis) cast out of the realms of magic when they grow up.

Of course, as Valente herself notes in an address she delivered at the feminist science fiction/fantasy convention WisCon in 2005, the expulsion of girls from magical lands and their subsequent confinement to domestic roles merely mirrors the relatively limited options available to women in the late nineteenth and early twentieth centuries. However, Valente goes on to ask, "in the post-modern world, where the experience of women is no longer limited to hearth and childbed, where can they look for their own exempla, for heroines that perform the heroic cycle in their own right?" ("Follow the Yellow-Brick Road," par. 2). Valente provides her own answer and allows September and especially Maud to embrace both traditionally masculine quest-heroism and the more traditionally feminine domestic heroism, imagining a children's literature that defies those gendered binaries. In short, Valente reinvents the girls of fantasy. September is invited to Fairyland because she is "ill-tempered and irascible" (Valente 2), a far cry from meek Dorothy, one of the little girl heroes David Emerson argues uses "innocence" as a super-power (132). Similarly, though Maud, as the Marquess, initially appears to be yet another seductive female villain who seeks to manipulate the hero for her own selfish ends, she proves to be a complex triune character whose interactions with September position her as an anti-villain foil to September's heroic quester. By creating Maud as this anti-villain—a complicated figure that is at once antagonist, mentor, and double—Valente establishes a critical counternarrative to September's fantastic adventures, so that *GWCF* both celebrates the quest adventure and calls attention to the toll that adventure has, traditionally, demanded of its female questers.

After a brief discussion of the anti-villain figure, this essay examines how Maud tries to use her familiarity with fantastic narratives to shape September's heroic development. Admittedly, a full reading of the complexity of September and Maud's characters and relationship may be beyond the scope of this essay. Yet, by focusing primarily upon the externalities of Maud's personae and particularly upon the ways in which her character(s) adopts various modes of villainous and heroic femininity, I will show how Maud's function as anti-villain is central to September's development as a hero and to Valente's (de-)construction and revision of the roles of little girls in children's fantasy literature.

Shaping the Hero: The Anti-Villain

Though there are hints throughout the book that the Marquess is not entirely who she claims to be, it is only at the end of *GWCF* that September discovers her antagonist's real identity—she is a teenage girl named Maud Elizabeth Smythe, who once "Stumbled" into Fairyland by way of an old armoire and became its now-lost Queen Mallow:

> I had a sword and I'd faced down King Goldmouth and his army of clouds, and I was queen. I ruled long and well and wisely. Anyone will tell you. I married my sorcerer.... I discovered, by and by, that I was with child.... With one awful ticking, I was swept out of Fairyland as though I had never been there. I woke

up in my father's house, curled up inside the armoire, as though no time at all had passed.... I was twelve again and hungry, and my father was just getting home from his day's work [Valente 224–5].

In Valente's Fairyland, the adventures of children who accidentally find their way into Fairyland—who "Stumble" into a magical world—are controlled by a magical clock, and when the clock strikes midnight, the child returns to the human world (Valente 221–2). Though the clock is original to Valente, the trope of the child who must leave Fairyland behind when he or she becomes an adult is a familiar one in coming-of-age and portal fantasies—it is used repeatedly and in varying ways in C. S. Lewis's *The Chronicles of Narnia*, of course, and also appears in J. M. Barrie's *Peter Pan*, to give just two examples. Yet Valente invokes this familiar trope as a shattering revocation of independence and personal agency. It is not adulthood and maturity that await Maud when she is returned to her father's home, but the catastrophic loss thereof. This narrative of traumatic loss initially repositions the Marquess as a sympathetic villain whose defeat is as tragic as it is necessary, but a careful reading of the ways Maud has influenced September up to this point in the novel shows that Maud does not easily fit into the standard villain categories available. Neither fully villain nor authentically heroic, Maud is truly an anti-villain, a troubled character whose idealistic ends can be reached only through horrific means.

The anti-villain, which can be nearly indistinguishable from the sympathetic villain, the anti-hero, and the villain hero, has its roots in the long literary tradition that created brilliant, appealing, and misguided characters such as Milton's Satan, *The X-Men*'s Magneto, or Gregory Maguire's Elphaba, each of whom commits villainous acts out of a kind of perverse idealism. Though the term "anti-villain" has been used occasionally in both academic and popular discussions of villainy in fiction, to date, its meaning has never been adequately delineated. One working definition, found on the website *TV Tropes*,[3] defines "the Anti-Villain [as] a villain with heroic goals, personality traits, and/or virtues. Their desired ends are mostly good, but their means of getting there are evil" ("Anti-Villain"). I would qualify this definition further by suggesting that a key hallmark of the anti-villain would be his or her engagement with the hero's development; positioning the anti-villain as a potential mentor figure to the hero allows for a clearer distinction between this figure and the various roles to which it is related. Unlike the anti-hero, for instance, the anti-villain is narratively positioned in such a way as to draw the reader's and the protagonist's ire, rather than their sympathy. Whereas the anti-hero is usually a dark protagonist, a character who is at once the focus of the reader's attention and whose borderline villainy yet discourages the reader from entering into full sympathy with him or her, and the villain—even the sympathetic villain—consistently works against the hero, Maud inhabits a middle ground from which she can influence September's development, in order to achieve her own (arguably) laudable goal of making Fairyland safe for human children like herself (Valente 228).

Leroy G. Dorsey uses a similar definition of anti-villainy in his discussion of *The X-Files'* Cigarette Smoking Man as a trickster figure, suggesting that an anti-villain is "someone ... more amoral than truly wicked, perhaps even more tragic than diabolical" (454). This assessment rings hauntingly true of Maud, and like the Smoking Man in Dorsey's analysis, Maud, too, is a trickster figure—alternately tempting, threatening, and protecting September along her journey. Dorsey suggests that in this role the trickster ultimately functions as "society's conscience: his or her behavior may stretch the bounds of what is considered normal, yet, in taking such action, the trickster reveals important information for that culture's development" (454). As anti-villain, Maud reveals to September the real cost of heroism and justifiably critiques Fairyland for its treatment of human children. Maud, like the Cigarette Smoking Man and other contemporary anti-villain figures, chooses and helps to mold a hero who is compassionate, who will see and be outraged by the injustices that have created the anti-villain's position.[4] In theory, when the anti-villain unmasks herself in the final act, the fully developed hero, shaped by the perverse guidance of the anti-hero, will be drawn to support the anti-villain's cause. Of course, in reality, the anti-villain's role is always self-defeating. The very same compassion and sense of justice that helps to define the hero will ultimately prevent her siding with an antagonist—in *GWCF*, September weeps for Maud as she tries to send her back to the human world, but she does it all the same.

Maud presents September with a series of increasingly difficult choices, each of which pit September's own desires against the needs of those around her; and with each decision she makes, September furthers her heroic development. Throughout the novel, September wrestles with her understanding of heroism, unable to reconcile her definition, which she has learned from stories, with the helplessness, terror, and frustration she herself feels. Yet Valente makes it clear that this definition of heroism, in which a Chosen One goes forth to defeat evil, is the wrong one. When September asks the Green Wind if she is a "chosen one," he proposes a different model of heroism, saying, "No one is chosen .... you chose yourself. You could have had a lovely holiday in Fairyland and never met the Marquess, never worried yourself with local politics.... But you didn't. You chose" (Valente 205–6). Though September's reading of fairy tales has probably taught her that a hero is "brave, physically strong, never mean or vicious, and possessed of a code of honor that requires them to come to the aid of the weak or incompetent or oppressed" (Jones 130),[5] the Green Wind instead suggests that September is heroic precisely because she is not *required* to do any of the things she has done. She chooses not to abandon her friends to the Marquess even when she is repeatedly offered the opportunity to leave Fairyland and return home,[6] and she chooses, repeatedly, to sacrifice her own desires in exchange for the safety and happiness of those around her. However, September's ability to make those choices are, in many ways, shaped by Maud's interventions—Maud manipulates the situations in which September finds herself in order to ensure that September will be able to make the hardest choice of all when they meet at the Lonely Gaol.

Maud shapes September's heroic development by setting her on the path of heroism that Maud herself once walked—in the form of Mallow. Though the Marquess orders September to journey to the Autumn Provinces, retrieve a magical sword, and bring it back to the Marquess's palace, the Briary, this is a false quest (Valente 98). It is not the sword itself that the Marquess needs, but the sword *September* will draw from the casket. The magical, shapeshifting sword takes on a form that represents its bearer's mother, and for September, whose mother is an airplane mechanic, the sword becomes a magical wrench (Valente 154). Maud needs September to use that wrench-shaped sword to decouple Fairyland from the human world via the massive gears that connect the two worlds—thus preventing any future children from Stumbling into a magical existence and making it impossible for Fairyland to send anyone back (Valente 218). To ensure September's compliance, the Marquess kidnaps September's friends and imprisons them at the Lonely Gaol—a prison-fortress built atop the very gears that connect Fairyland to the human world. The journey to that prison, which forms the heart of the novel (and gives it its title), literally strips September bare, paring her down to a core self capable of sacrifice.

Though her actions in the novel are not, Maud's motivations are, again, at least partially benevolent. She does seem to believe that she is making Fairyland safe for human children. Even in her repeated manipulations of September, Maud claims to be acting in September's best interest. For instance, when September points out that Maud set the Tsukumogami (a race of sentient household objects) on her, Maud replies that she had to do it in order for September to believe that her quest was "real" and thus believable (Valente 216); for September to reach her innermost heroic self—to make the small sacrifices necessary to harden her to the larger sacrifice Maud hopes she will make—she has to believe that her life, along with those of her friends, is in real danger of ending. As Emerson notes, "successful completion of the Hero's Journey" requires "acceptance of the quest and determination to complete it" (147)—that is, active choice and the will to carry it through. It is in large part because of Maud, who forces her to make those choices, that September is able to complete her hero's journey.

"A very fine hat": The Marquess

The Marquess's rule over Fairyland is a reign cemented by magic, might, and manipulation, but behind each lies the power of the "very fine hat" mentioned by the Green Wind (Valente 3). Indeed, the hat is so fundamental to the Marquess's persona that nearly every time she is mentioned, the hat is mentioned in the next breath. In Chapter IV ("The Wyverary"[7]), A-Through-L (Ell) explains to September that, though he is bigger than the Marquess, he cannot contest her will, because "she's *the Marquess*. She has *a hat*. And muscular magic, besides" (Valente 44, emphasis in original). Ell places even the Marquess's "muscular magic" below the power of the hat, suggesting that it is the Marquess's appearance of power, even more than the magic itself that cements her authority. Though she has magical ability and several dangerous big cats, and further secures her reign by harnessing and abusing the gifts of the wish-granting Marids (Valente 106), the Marquess's interactions with September suggest that the Marquess relies most strongly upon her reputation—that is, upon appearance and story—to bend others to her will.

It is quite telling that the Marquess's first physical appearance in the story is literally onscreen—on a movie screen, as part of a pre-film newsreel that September watches. That neither the reader nor September sees the Marquess first in person, and that nearly the entirety of this description focuses on her clothing slyly hints at the ultimate revelation of the Marquess's identity. Even once she actually appears in the novel, hers is a mediated presence—first literally mediated by appearing through film, and then mediated through her disguises. The multiple and changing layers of magic and millinery that the Marquess adopts are a visual signifier of her carefully-guarded secret—no one can look too closely at her, because, after all, the Marquess does not truly exist. She is only one of the several faces of Maud.

Though the filmed scene shows the Marquess shaking hands with a bear as she seals a treaty, Valente's narrator focuses almost entirely upon detailed description of the Marquess—a tall girl "not a day older than September herself" (Valente 88)—and on her clothing. Particular attention is given to the hat, which "looked a bit like a cake that had fallen over to one side under the weight of peacock and pheasant feathers and chains of jewels that cascaded down from a silk rosette on its flat top. Ribbons, bows, and satin ropes made delicate tiers like icing on its body, and the brim was so crisp and perfect it seemed deathly sharp" (Valente 88). Maud constructs her villainous identity in such a way that neither Maud nor Mallow is easily visible in the Marquess, but the Marquess's clothing and demeanor, read closely, reveal nearly as much as they conceal. The hat, of course, is particularly revealing; both stereotypically "girlish," with its "ribbons, bows, and satin ropes," and sharply masculine, with its "crisp and perfect" brim, the hat combines a child's images of beauty of power—the elaborate decorations combined with the "crisp" brim suggest a game of dress-up, as though a little girl has draped her father's business hat in ribbons. At once whimsical and sternly sensible, this hat thus reflects both the damaged sweetness of the child who became Mallow and the hard-edged sorrow and hatred of the girl who becomes the Marquess, and symbolizes the internal conflict that shapes Maud's complex role in September's journey. In its mix of appealing softness (the decorations) and dangerous authority (the shape), the hat, like a number of other sartorial signs that September cannot yet read, is a visual marker of the ways Maud will function as both antagonist and as mentor/friend.

Chief among these other signs are the way the Marquess herself, whenever September encounters her in person, enacts the bizarre pairing of frivolity and danger suggested by the hat. The Marquess, like her hat, is dramatically playful and threatening, and at least part of her terrible power is rooted in the disconcerting innocuousness of her exaggeratedly childlike dress:

> In the center of the heart-shaped staircase sat a little girl, holding her chin in her hands. She had thick cherry-purple hair that hung in old-fashioned sausage curls to her shoulders and that magnificent, terrible hat poised on her head like a cake tipping to one side. The hat was black.... The feathers shone blue and green and red and cream-colored. The jewels glittered dark and violet [Valente 92].

Everything about the Marquess is "dark"—her hair; her hat; the jewels and feathers on the hat; even her dress and stockings are "blackberry colored" and "violet"—but also childishly feminine, with her "old-fashioned sausage curls" and her hat "like a cake tipping to one side," her dress short and "all lace and stiff magenta petticoats" (Valente 97). In this scene, the Marquess is a surreal blend of Edwardian child and fairy tale villain, theatrically upholding the Green Wind's claim that "all little girls are terrible" by exaggerating the trappings of idealized little girlhood. Adopting this girlish persona empowers the Marquess because it plays upon her opponents' (and the readers') presumed belief in the harmlessness, even inferiority, of little girls.[8]

In this first meeting, the Marquess constructs her appearance in response to September's expectations of villainy; though she presents herself as a child, she drapes that childishness in darkness in order to play the part of the wicked queen. In their second meeting, however, the Marquess adopts the dress and mannerisms of an Edwardian angel-child, as though to neutralize the threat she has to this point presented

> a little girl in a frilly white dress ran full tilt across the many-colored rug, her golden curls bouncing. She embraced September like a long-lost sister, still laughing and exclaiming with joy.
> "Oh, September, you're safe! I'm so happy you've come, finally, and not a scratch on you! ... What fun we are going to have!" [Valente 215].

This exuberant greeting serves to throw the battered and exhausted September further off-balance, but it also signifies the final stage of Maud's agenda. Now that Maud has created the hero, she can reconstruct herself as a friend, in the hopes of finally winning the hero, September, over to her cause. The apparent inconsistencies of Maud's clothing and behavior resolve themselves into coherent meaning if we read enthusiastic welcome as sincere—that is, if we accept that she truly believes she is doing the right thing, and believes that September will agree to help her.

Though the Marquess uses the trappings of villainy (as well as actually villainous behavior) to force September into her service, when she does so she is using September's own knowledge of fantasy conventions against her. September expects to find a wicked queen in the Briary, and the Marquess fulfills these expectations by looking and acting the part. The Marquess's manipulations of her appearance and her reliance on disarming cuteness aligns her with villains like Lewis's White Witch, who tempts Edmund Pevensie as much with her icy beauty as with the infamous hot chocolate and Turkish Delight for which he agrees to betray his siblings (Lewis 36). Feminine beauty like that of the White Witch and the Marquess is in most fantasy fiction particularly untrustworthy. While male fantasy villains are frequently unattractive, even deformed[9] (Sauron, Darth Vader, and Lord Voldemort are the most obvious examples), their female counterparts are often disturbingly, deceptively beautiful and prone to luring in unwise heroes with the promise of domestic or (though rarely in children's fantasy) sexual comforts. Bryan Dove characterizes the White Witch (and thus similar villains) as "the classic honey pot, made all the more symbolically obvious by the fact that she is actually using sweets ... in order to entrap and coerce" (113). In another "classic honey pot" move, the Marquess initially tries to use both her appearance and the promise of comfort and play to sway September to her side. However, whereas Edmund Pevensie naively trusts the White Witch because she is beautiful and offers him treats, September, a child who is well-read in fairy tales and quest stories, recognizes that the Marquess is "a wicked Queen" in part because the Marquess offers her such temptations (Valente 92).

When they meet in the Briary, the Marquess offers September physical comforts that she has been, to this point, denied: first, new shoes, to replace the single shoe she is wearing, and then "a silver plate piled high with wet red cherries, a wedge of black cake crusted with sugar, swollen raspberries and strawberries, several lumps of dark, dusty chocolate, and a tall goblet of steaming hot cider" (Valente 93). Despite her cold, blistered foot, her hunger, and her thirst, September recognizes the potential danger of the Marquess's offered gifts, and resists: "taking gifts from wicked Queens, even if they are called Marquesses, even if they are very pretty children not big enough to hurt anyone, is a dangerous business, and September knew it" (Valente 92). Though September's resistance is largely symbolic—as the Marquess forces her to accept the shoes, and September has already eaten and triggered the "Persephone clause" (Valente 18) that will require her return to Fairyland for the rest of her life— her refusal of the Marquess's temptations still marks a crucial point in her early development as a hero. She has demonstrated her willingness to accept discomfort, even sacrifice, through her refusal, however symbolic, to trade her ethics for her physical comfort.

Yet, just as September's resistance is symbolic, these temptations function more as tests of the latter's heroic mettle than actual attempts at seduction. Just as September is fully cognizant of her adversary's duplicitous nature, the Marquess, too, recognizes September's store of knowledge, and her initial temptation of September is merely an exercise in practiced villainy—and, more importantly, a lesson in heroic behavior. The Marquess does not expect September to take her offer of food or clothing, and only "persuades" September to take a pair of proffered shoes when Ell's life depends upon September's ability to reach the Autumn Provinces in a week (Valente 101). These tests are part of September's heroic initiation, and will ultimately help September to understand what the Marquess means when she says that September needs to be "a bit more discerning" (Valente 95) to survive in Fairyland. If September can resist this first set of tests, then she may be better prepared to resist the next set when they come.

Until they actually meet in Chapter VIII ("An Audience with the Marquess"), for September the Marquess is a kind of bogeyman—a frightening but largely unreal figure. September encounters multiple examples of the Marquess's petty despotism on her journey towards Pandemonium (the capitol city of Fairyland): the Marquess has persecuted the witches for their failure to look into her future (Valente 35); she has declared flight an "Unfair Advantage" and all winged creatures' wings are chained (Valente 44); and at her command, the once-tea-filled Barleybroom River has been stripped of its tea leaves in order to fit the Marquess's expectations of a "real" river (Valente 66). Despite seeing the effects of the Marquess's decrees, the real impact of her cruelty does not register with September until the Marquess threatens Ell's life to ensure September's compliance with her demands. In other words, it is not until someone September holds dear is threatened that she can recognize what tyranny is and how the Marquess uses it to shape the world to her will. The deaths of the witches' brothers and Ell's chains are status quo for September when she reaches Fairyland; though she recognizes that the Marquess's actions are wrong, the true meaning of that "wrongness" is purely abstract. It is only the Marquess's cruel interventions in September's adventures that allow September to understand that heroism will require her to make painful choices, choices that will force her to give of herself and will further lead her down the road she chose in Chapter III—the road by which September will "Lose [Her] Heart" (Valente 26).

"Cherries for all": Queen Mallow

Mallow is by far the most shadowy of Maud's three personae; already long missing when September arrives in Fairyland, she exists only as an ideal myth-memory among her former subjects. Although Mallow has a profound impact upon September and, of course, upon Maud, her influence is almost entirely passive—mediated through stories and the memories of those who knew her. Yet despite this passivity, Mallow serves as a powerful mentor to September, offering her a model of kindness and strength that helps September to make wise choices along her journey. In this, as in all things, Mallow is a mirror of the Marquess, because the Marquess's entire identity is constructed around being that which Mallow was not. Though September does not learn Maud's true identity until the end of the novel, her initial encounters with the remnants of Mallow clearly parallel her initial encounters with the Marquess. Just as she first sees the Marquess on a film reel, the first and only time she sees Mallow "in person," it is through a mediated image. Moments before she meets the Marquess herself, September sees a "grandiosely framed painting" in which stands

> a tall, lovely woman with long golden hair tied back with a velvet bow. Her hand rested on a Leopard's head, and in her other, she held a simple wooden hunter's bow.... In the painting, she seemed to glow. *That is what a grown-up looks like*, thought September. *Not like the grown-ups in my world who look sad and disappointed and grimy with work and bored with everything. What do the storybooks say?*
> *In the fullness of her strength* [Valente 91–2].

September can identify this woman as Mallow because the painting visually echoes the ways Mallow has been presented to September throughout her journey—as a source of warmth and strength, embodied in the radiant presence of the goddess-queen. Just as she knows the Marquess by reputation long before she meets her, September knows Mallow by the stories that have preceded her.

The novel first mentions Queen Mallow when September meets Ell, but in no more than a passing reference to "the days of Good Queen Mallow" set up in nostalgic contrast to the present (Valente 44). It is only when September and Ell reach The House Without Warning (the last way station before Fairyland's capitol city, Pandemonium) in the next chapter that Mallow truly enters the story. Lye, the soap golem who tends the baths at The House Without Warning, welcomes Ell and September in the name of her mistress, the woman who created her and for whose return she waits—Mallow (Valente 55). Ell immediately connects Lye's Mallow to the lost Queen Mallow, and at September's bewildered questioning, describes Mallow's reign as a time when "every table groaned with milk and wheat and sugar and hot chocolate," while Mallow "governed with rhyming songs and cherries for all on Sundays" (Valente 56). That Ell can tell stories of the days of Mallow's reign testifies to the strength of her myth-memory, because his store of knowledge is largely limited to those subjects that fall under his alphabetical range (A-L). When September asks Ell how he knows so much about her reign, even though Mallow begins with an M, he replies, shocked, "*Everyone* knows about Good Queen Mallow" (Valente 56).

Though Ell's version of events is implausibly nostalgic, his central image of a queen who translated domestic comforts into benevolent power is validated by the physical markers she left behind her in Fairyland. Her former subjects have elevated Mallow into a goddess figure, in no small part because she literally created much of the world as they know it. Pandemonium, for instance, is a "city of cloth"—much of it woven by Mallow herself. Ell describes Mallow's creation of the city in the language of battle juxtaposed against the language of domesticity, "Fierce was her needle, and she wore it like a sword. Wielded it, too! Brandished, even! Woven things are so warm, she said, so kind and home-like" (Valente 83). Like the baths at The House Without Warning, the woven city of Pandemonium is a tangible artifact that testifies to the essential truth of the mythic history of Mallow's rule.

Though the physical remnants of her reign testify to the truth of her existence, for September, the child fed on a diet of stories, it is the *stories* of Mallow's words and deeds that are most important, especially as September struggles towards the Lonely Gaol in the latter half of her journey. These stories become particularly important after September accepts the Marquess's quest, because she is quite literally following in Mallow's footsteps. Like Mallow did, September confronts her death in the Worsted Wood to retrieve her mother's sword (Valente 148, 171); September, too, meets and learns from the wolf-eared sorcerer, once Mallow's husband, who now answers to the name Mr. Map (Valente 169); and she knows and loves Imogene, the Leopard of Little Storms, who was once Mallow's companion (Valente 18, 203, 240). Throughout her journey, Mallow's allies become September's, even if only for a short time, and September's memory of Mallow's words, passed to her through these allies, help to sustain September through some of the most difficult parts of her adventure. When she must use her dress as a sail for the raft she has built to circumnavigate Fairyland, body-shy September remembers Mallow's words (told to her by Lye), "Even if you've taken off every stitch of clothing, you still have your secrets, your history, your true name. It's hard to be really naked.... It's just showing skin" (Valente 174). Though it is this quote specifically that the novel shows September remembering, the scene in which Lye originally says this to September contains a second and arguably more important recitation of Mallow's beliefs, which resonates throughout the remainder of the text. According to Mallow, if you "give of yourself ... it will return to you as new as new can be," a maxim Lye offers to explain her ritual sacrifice of one of her soap fingers to September's bath (Valente 61). Following Lye's and Mallow's examples, September will give of herself throughout the novel, choosing, again and again, the hard and dangerous path over repeated offers of escape.

If there is anything troubling about the Green Wind's declaration that "little girls are terrible," it is that the Marquess and Maud appear to have more power than the adult Mallow. Mallow is presented in the painting as an adult "in the fullness of her strength," a phrase that becomes cruelly ironic when Maud tells her story (Valente 92). All of Mallow's strength is useless against the laws of a Fairyland that has finished with her; her expulsion from Fairyland kills the beautiful, armed adult woman and leaves the battered, hungry child in her place. However, as I noted above, it is often Mallow's example of selfless kindness that September follows, and, more importantly, even Maud herself (and thus the Marquess) can only return to Fairyland because of Mallow's magic. Maud tells September that she "*clawed* [her] way back" (Valente 226), but then acknowledges that it was her connection to Lye, Mallow's soap golem, that gave her enough of a foothold in Fairyland to force her way back. Without Lye turning back her clock, Maud would never have been able to return to Fairyland, and thus would never have unleashed the terrible power of the Marquess. And without Mallow, there would be no Lye.

Lye, like Pandemonium, is a physical embodiment of Mallow's strength of will, and her role in bringing Maud back to Fairyland is a pointed reminder that Maud and the Marquess *are* Mallow. The terrible power of the little girl matures with her body, and despite all of her struggling, Maud cannot fully break away from the woman she once was. Instead, as the Marquess, Maud deliberately warps the benevolent femininity that characterized Mallow, turning Mallow's gifts into the tools of oppression and manipulation. Where Mallow ruled with cherries for all, the Marquess tempts with them, offering September a devil's bargain in exchange for the material comfort Mallow once offered for kindness's sake. Indeed, much of the Marquess's self-definition is a careful inversion of Mallow's—where Mallow had the Leopard of Little Breezes, the Marquess has the Panther of Rough Storms and the Blue Lions. Where Mallow defined a city with wool and cloth, the Marquess wraps it in red tape and iron shoes, ruling with terror and cold efficiency in place of the safety, warmth and light that Mallow offered her erstwhile subjects.

Maud, now broken, can only define her newer self through a warped reconstruction of the woman she once was, and she fails in her quest because she can no longer understand that older self's power. Although Maud possesses a tremendous capacity for understanding and manipulating the fairy tale conventions she and September know so well, she fails to recognize that Mallow's story is one of those conventions, because she is too devastated by the loss of Mallow's autonomy to see that story *as* a story. Because of Mallow, Maud is fundamentally self-defeating: Mallow's example mentors September in the selfless heroism of kindness even as the Marquess mentors her through manipulation and cruelty.

"No one should have to go back": Maud Elizabeth Smythe

In "Follow the Yellow Brick Road: Katabasis and the Female Hero in *Alice in Wonderland*, *The Wizard of Oz*, and *The Nutcracker*," Valente observes that female heroes have traditionally diminished once they marry and especially after they have children. They fade into the background of the (male) heroic narrative, becoming mothers of heroic children or Penelope figures to questing husbands (para. 2). In some ways, Maud's journey as Mallow could be read as a disturbingly literal recapitulation of this narrative: she is "born" as Mallow through her adventures, courts and marries her sorcerer, and literally vanishes from Fairyland when she is pregnant (Valente 225). However, by shaping Maud's anger and the Marquess's villainy so clearly around Maud's forcible return to childhood, Valente uses Mallow's loss as a feminist critique of that story: rather than disappearing *into* wife- and motherhood, Maud disappears from adulthood into childhood. Unlike Carroll's Alice or Barrie's Wendy, whose maturations are painted with regret by their authors, Valente's Maud is most beautiful and appealing when she has reached physical, emotional, and sexual maturity, while the preservation of her childhood is wholly nightmarish.

Although Mallow was pregnant when she vanished, thus apparently fulfilling the troubling feminine destiny of disappearing into motherhood, she did not vanish—she was *banished*. Her disappearance is a trauma and an injustice; the novel makes it quite clear that Maud has not been rewarded by being given a second chance at youth. Once she is returned to the human world, Maud is not just a child again, but an impoverished child trapped with an abusive father—she has been cast back into the personal hell she believed she had escaped. Above all else, Fairyland gave her autonomy; it gave her the ability to pursue her intellectual interests and to devote herself to making things both beautiful and functional. Fairyland gave Maud a glimpse of childhood she might have had and let her grow into powerful adulthood, only to take it all away when she was supposed to have been "in the fullness of her strength" (Valente 92). Maud fights her way back to Fairyland and takes revenge upon it in large part because of the loss of her adulthood—an adulthood that includes a husband and a child as well as a throne, each of which represent not confinement or traditional domesticity, but a triumph of personal autonomy and freedom.

When Maud tells her story to September, she says that she "grew up a bit" in Fairyland well before she became queen (Valente 224), and in Valente's companion story to the novel, "The Girl Who Ruled Fairyland—For a Little While," Mallow is a young woman, not a child, when she comes to rule. Unlike the Pevensie children or Wendy Darling, Maud is not cast out of Fairyland because she grows up or because she becomes a sexually active woman, but in spite of these factors. Maud is thus stripped of the rewards of *both* the feminine hero's journey that Valente alludes to in "Follow the Yellow Brick Road," and the traditionally masculine hero's journey articulated by Joseph Campbell. Per Campbell, the monomyth ends with a return, but that return is the return of the fully realized hero, now master of two worlds. The (usually male) hero of Campbell's monomyth can choose between home and adventure, and initially it seems that Fairyland will allow Mallow to embrace both when she defeats the wicked king Goldmouth with her needle-shaped sword. However, Maud is denied even the illusion of choice when she is banished from one world and doomed to live out a horrific childhood in the other. Both home and adventure are stripped away from her.

At September's suggestion that Maud was brought to Fairyland only to fulfill a certain destiny, and returned home when her work was through (Valente 227), Maud, who initially made all of the correct heroic choices in her first visit to Fairyland, fiercely rejects that concept of heroic destiny and the abuse of a hero's free will that goes along with it:

> I am not a toy, September! Fairyland cannot just cast me aside when it's finished playing with me! ... I made Fairyland *nice* for the children who come over the gears, I made it *safe*. I did it for every child before me who had a life here, who was happy here! Don't you see, September? *No one should have to go back*" [Valente 227–8, emphasis in original].

When she forces her way back into Fairyland and becomes the Marquess, Maud sets out to systematically dismantle the fantasy-quest conventions that she once embraced. By "[dropping] the human world into theirs" and then attempting to sever Fairyland from the human world, Maud violently rejects any possibility of heroic return and the entire concept of being master of two worlds. Since her choices turned out to be false, Maud will eliminate the illusion of choice rather than be cast out again or allow other child-heroes to suffer the same fate, by eliminating the possibility of travel between worlds and thus undoing the very foundation of the tales she once believed in.

It is somewhat ironic, then, that in her final act, Maud returns to those stories to wrest control of her destiny away from September. As September struggles to restart Maud's clock and send her back to the human world, Maud steps back, and says:

> I know a secret you do not: I am not the villain. I am no dark lord. I am the princess in this tale.... And how may a princess remain safe and protected through centuries, no matter who may assail her? She sleeps.... Until her enemies have all perished and the sun rises over her perfect, innocent face once more [Valente 230].

When she finishes speaking, Maud immediately collapses, asleep—possibly forever. Although September restarts the clock, Maud's body remains comatose on the floor of the Lonely Gaol. Maud's panther companion, Iago, theorizes that she may be dreaming of "tomatoes and her father," but Maud's physical body remains in Fairyland (Valente 231–2); she has not been sent back.

While the Marquess exploits and Mallow expands the expectations of traditional femininity during their respective rules of Fairyland, Maud weaponizes it when she turns to the most passively feminized role in literature, the sleeping princess, to prevent her own defeat. Valente foreshadows Maud's final action by locating the Marquess's throne in the Briary—the palace surrounded by thorns—a narrative move that may validate that Maud's conviction that her story is unfinished. By embracing the role of the princess, Maud ensures that the Marquess's defeat is not the end of her story, but a hiatus, of sorts; in the fairy tales both September and Maud know, the princess sleeps in the middle of the story, not its end.

As I said above, Maud's tragic history and the visible desperation of her retreat elicit a powerful compassion in September and in the reader, and come perilously close to justifying the Marquess's actions. Even her endgame, the severing of Fairyland from the human world, is, in some way, as heroic as it is terrible. Although her actions towards Fairyland and its people are unquestionably vengeful, Maud clearly believes that she is acting in the best interests of children like September. Despite September's sympathy for Maud, however, through September, Valente resists absolving Maud of guilt for her cruelty. September wonders if she, too, could become as warped as Maud has, but she rejects Maud's actions, thinking, *"Even if it were me ... I could not chain Ell's wings like that"* (Valente 229, emphasis in original). In other words, September believes that she could not exact vengeance upon innocent beings, no matter how badly she herself has been hurt. Whether or not September is right about this is a different question; Mallow's parallel presence throughout September's adventure strongly indicates that September, *could* have become Maud, were her situation slightly altered. The primary difference between the two is that September, unlike Maud, can consciously choose Fairyland *and* home—because, unlike Maud, September has a home worth going to, and because she is given that choice by having been Ravished into Fairyland. Though the story depends upon the concept of heroic choice, the disturbing similarities between September and Maud suggest that the real difference between them is not a difference in kind, but in circumstance. Each represents what the other might have been, given a different set of beginning circumstances and a very slightly different set of choices.

In their first encounter, the Marquess tells September that September reminds her very much of herself, and she reaffirms this in their final meeting, saying, "What is it that villains always say at the end of stories? 'You and I are more alike than you think.' Well. ... We are. Oh, how alike we are!" (Valente 217). Though September naturally rejects this claim, as I noted above, Valente has clearly constructed the two girls as mirror images—and, like a reflection, they are inverted images of each other. This is made particularly apparent when we look at the few descriptions of Maud (as herself or as Mallow) next to the few descriptions of September.

On the first page, the narrator describes September: "she had been born in May, and ... she had a *mole on her left cheek*, and ... her feet were very large and ungainly" (Valente 1, my emphasis). Several chapters later, Lye recalls Mallow as "a beautiful young girl with hair like new soap and big green eyes and a *mole on her left cheek* and she was a Virgo ... and she always went barefoot" (Valente 55, my emphasis). They share the mole on their left cheeks, but blonde Maud's birthday is most likely in September, while dark-haired September's birthday is in May. Their personalities and lives, too, follow this pattern of reflection and refraction—both Maud and September are lonely children who prefer books to other children, and both have been marked, in some way, by parental absence, but September's family is the positive inverse of Maud's. Both girls are transformed and empowered by Fairyland; but Maud's story is ultimately further along in its plot than September's.

Each girl, then, represents what the other might have been, or might yet be, and the similarities between them serve to bring out the difference in their circumstances and their choices. Maud bargains on September's selfishness (love of adventure and of Fairyland) overcoming her compassion and ability to see beyond herself because she sees September as a version of herself. However, just as September, perhaps mistakenly, believes she would not behave as Maud has, whatever the circumstances, Maud cannot see why anyone would willingly return home. In this, they are alike: both hero and (anti-)villain are limited by their own experiences to such an extent that neither can fully understand nor predict the other's final actions. Despite her efforts to bring September to her side, Maud, frustrated by the self-defeating role she has adopted, remains antagonistic. Both characters bring to life the Green Wind's warning—"all little girls are terrible" (Valentine 3)—because the fates of two worlds lie in the hands of little girls.

In *The Girl Who Circumnavigated Fairyland in a Ship of Her Own Making*, Valente thus reinvents the role of the little girl in children's fantasy. When Maud tells September that she is not a toy, she is pushing back against the fantasy narrative that brings little girls to magical lands to serve others' ends and expects them to go quietly when their time, or their childhood, is through. Although Maud is neutralized at the end of the novel, her influence on Fairyland and especially upon September creates a powerful resonance that brings to life the Green Wind's warning: "all little girls are terrible." Given this terrible power, it seems unlikely that Valente will not return to the character.[10] In other words, we have not met Maud at the end of her story, but in its middle. It remains to be seen if Valente will restore the sleeping princess, and if she does, what role she might play in September's further adventures.

NOTES

1. Henceforth referred to as *GWCF*.

2. Though September consistently refers to her as "the Marquess," I will refer to her here as "Maud" unless I am specifically talking about actions taken when she is in the forms of the Marquess or Mallow. Though as Mallow she forgot about and as the Marquess sought to disavow the existence of Maud Elizabeth Smythe, and she reassumes the form of the Marquess immediately before her defeat, she also disavows the name Mallow and allows September to call her Maud. Furthermore, Maud's most important and haunting encounters with September take place when she is in her "original" human form, arguably marking that as her core identity.

3. *TV Tropes*, despite its rather misleading name, is dedicated to defining and unpacking the tropes used in multiple media forms, but its largely self-referential nature makes it difficult to use as a stand-alone source. The site's two-sentence explanation of how a "normal villain" becomes an anti-villain contains no fewer than seven hyperlinks to other tropes/pages within the site.

4. Further examples from popular culture might be Ra's Al Ghul, as depicted in Christopher Nolan's 2005 film *Batman Begins* or Severus Snape in Books 1–6 of J. K. Rowling's *Harry Potter* series. (Rowling's revelation in *Harry Potter and the Deathly Hallows* that Snape works as a triple agent makes him more properly an anti-hero, but his ambiguous behavior in the earlier novels is, by my definition, at least partially anti-villainous. Even when he is actively working against Harry, Snape engages in perverse mentorship by refusing to allow Harry to grow complacent with his own success.)

5. Diana Wynne Jones's description is particularly fitting here; Jones explains that this is how she understood heroism when she herself was a young girl who had been raised on heroic narratives.

6. In chapter XV ("The Island of the Nasnas,") one of the Nasnas offers to make September a pair of shoes that will return her home—"No worries, no faults, no blame"—and September refuses (Valente 187). Later, in chapter XVII ("One Hundred Years Old"), the Green Wind tells September he can return her to her home, and Fairyland will have been a dream, but she, again, refuses so that she can save her friends (Valente 204–5).

7. Half wyvern, half library, according to his mother (Valente 42).

8. See, for instance, David Emerson's "Innocence as a Super-Power: Little Girls on the Hero's Journey."

9. There are, obviously, unattractive female villains and attractive male villains, but the beauty and sexual desirability of female villains is a literary commonplace.

10. Maud's shadow is an important secondary character in this book's sequel, *The Girl Who Fell Beneath Fairyland and Led the Revels There* (2012) and part of Mallow's story is told in Valente's short story "The Girl Who Ruled Fairyland—For a Little While." It seems fairly clear that Valente has not finished with her, though she does not appear in the third novel, *The Girl Who Soared over Fairyland and Cut the Moon in Two* (2013).

WORKS CITED

"Anti-Villain." *TV Tropes.* TV Tropes Foundation, n.d. Web. 6 Jan. 2014.

Baum, L. Frank. *The Wonderful Wizard of Oz.* 1900. Introd. Ray Bradbury. New York: Modern Library-Random House, 2003. Print.

Campbell, Joseph. *The Hero with a Thousand Faces.* New York: MJF Books, 1949. Print.

Dorsey, Leroy G. "Re-reading *The X-Files*: The Trickster in Contemporary Conspiracy Myth." *Western Journal of Communication* 66.4 (2002): 448–468. Web. *Communication & Mass Media Complete*. 3 Feb. 2014.

Dove, Bryan. "Wanting the White Witch." *Vader, Voldemort, and Other Villains: Essays on Evil in Popular Media*. Ed. Jamey Heit. Jefferson, NC: McFarland, 2011. 113–124. Print.

Emerson, David. "Innocence as Super-Power: Little Girls on the Hero's Journey." *Mythlore* 28.107–8 (2009): 131–49. Web. *LiteratureOnline*. 26 Jul. 2013.

Jones, Diana Wynne. "The Heroic Ideal—A Personal Odyssey." *The Lion and the Unicorn* 13.1 (1989): 129–140. Web. *Project Muse*. 31 Jan. 2014.

Lewis, C. S. *The Lion, the Witch, and the Wardrobe*. 1950. New York: HarperTrophy, 1994. Print.

Nikolajeva, Maria. *The Rhetoric of Character in Children's Literature*. Lanham, MD: Scarecrow Press, 2003. Print.

Valente, Catherynne M. "Follow the Yellow-Brick Road: Katabasis and the Female Hero in *Alice in Wonderland, The Wizard of Oz*, and *The Nutcracker*." 2005. *Catherynne M. Valente*. Web. 18 July 2013.

_____. *The Girl Who Circumnavigated Fairyland in a Ship of Her Own Making*. 2011. New York: Feiwel and Friends, 2012. Print.

_____. *The Girl Who Fell Beneath Fairyland and Led the Revels There*. New York: Feiwel and Friends, 2012. Print.

_____. "The Girl Who Ruled Fairyland—For a Little While." 2011. Torwww. Web. 18 July 2013.

_____. *The Girl Who Soared Over Fairyland and Cut the Moon in Two*. New York: Feiwel and Friends, 2013. Print.

_____. "Questions for the Author." *The Girl Who Circumnavigated Fairyland in a Ship of Her Own Making*. 2011. New York: Feiwel and Friends, 2012. 248–65. Print.

The Unbreakable Vow:
Maternal Impulses and Narcissa Malfoy's Transformation from Villain to Hero in J. K. Rowling's *Harry Potter* Series

Sarah Margaret Kniesler

The villain-hero phenomenon is hardly incongruous to the *Harry Potter* series. To varying degrees, Severus Snape, Regulus Black, and even Draco Malfoy flirt with undermining or thwarting Lord Voldemort, the Dark Arts, and the pureblood prejudices they had spent years upholding. Yet, none of these characters provide the locus for the transformation that most influences the outcome of the final conflict of the series—that honor rests with Narcissa Malfoy. Unique in her classification as one of the few female villains of the *Harry Potter* saga, Narcissa's metamorphosis further emphasizes how essential she is to the resolution of the series; the infrequency of her appearances in the *Harry Potter* books becomes irrelevant in light of the potency of her final impact. Narcissa's transition from villain to hero encompasses more than her decision to undermine the contrivances of Voldemort: she challenges the oppressive patriarchal structure that is apparently commonplace within old, pureblood wizarding families, particularly those inclined toward the Dark Arts. Both of these major personal alterations appear to be the result of the, purportedly, hegemonic maternal instinct to protect and defend one's children. This essay examines Narcissa's transformation and what it means for maternal instinct to be the driving motivation behind Narcissa's character overhaul.

Joseph Campbell's later work, *The Power of Myth*, serves as the reference point for the definition of "the hero" that I work from in this essay. In an interview with Bill Moyers, Campbell defines a hero as "'someone who has given his *or her* life to something bigger than oneself'" (123, my emphasis). This basic, malleable definition aligns with our contemporary understanding of heroes. Since our society, particularly the media, relishes the opportunity to highlight someone's actions as "heroic" (I am specifically thinking of "everyday" or "ordinary" heroes), it is appropriate to invoke this definition that points to heroism as repeatedly acting in support of a cause. Such an understanding of the term also aligns with the overall messages in the *Harry Potter* series, namely that there is a spectrum of heroic deeds.

Turning specifically to the validity of identifying women as heroes, Campbell opens his definition to encompass both men and women. However, his thoughts on female heroes, particularly mothers, lack full development. Campbell claims that the term "hero" does not necessarily imply male, yet "the male usually has the more conspicuous role, just because of the conditions of life. He is out there in the world, and the woman is in the home'" (125). Here, he suggests that domesticity, and relegation to the home, inherently provides women with fewer opportunities to be heroic; yet, recent feminist scholarship works to undermine this implicit assumption. Exploring motherhood's place in contemporary feminist discussions, Andrea O'Reilly suggests that feminism is exploring and attempting to embrace "a view of mothering that is *empowering* to women as opposed to oppressive" (10). This particular "counternarrative of motherhood" expands the opportunities for and possibilities of heroic women by reclaiming the agency and decision-making of maternity (10). O'Reilly continues on to explain that "this new perspective [...] gave rise to the view of mothering as a socially engaged enterprise that seeks to effect cultural change in [...] the world at-large through political/social activism" (10). In this revisionist conception of maternity, motherhood's influence extends beyond the domestic and into the public realm. With the potential to enact change for both their children and the world at large, mothers have the potential to actualize Campbell's conception of the hero as someone who is selflessly devoted to a higher cause.

Returning to Campbell's passing ideas on "'the mother as hero,'" he pinpoints this concept as a distinct category of female heroes, one that he considers to be a "'wonderful image'" (125). Yet, he locates maternal heroism primarily, if not solely, in the act of giving birth. Campbell sees giving birth as the moment of transformation, when a woman successfully "'leav[es] one condition and find[s] the source of life to bring [her] forth into a richer or mature condition,'" a requirement he has for any "'hero's journey'" (126). Combining these thoughts on heroes and "the mother as hero," if a mother were compelled to metamorphose because of a threat to her child's safety or life, that change would make her heroic as well.

As the foundation of this essay, I am suggesting that maternal love, beyond the act of giving birth, *can* be heroic, but is not inherently so. J.K. Rowling, in particular, has encouraged this reading. Rowling not only has Lily Potter sacrifice herself "'to save [Harry],'" but also defines maternal love as so "'powerful'" that it "'leaves its own mark'" (*Sorcerer's Stone* 299). At the end of *Harry Potter and the Sorcerer's Stone*, to explain to Harry why he was able to survive Professor Quirrell's attack, Albus Dumbldore reveals these truths about Lily's death and the protective capabilities of maternal love. In offering her life for that of her son, Lily absolutely fulfills Campbell's description of the hero. Thus, early in the series, and in a critical plot device, Rowling positions maternal love as having the potential to be heroic.

For the purposes of facilitating a close reading of Narcissa, I will begin this essay by introducing some of the existing criticism on the *Harry Potter* series, focusing on the critiques of gender representations. Then, I will proceed to trace Narcissa's character through the *Harry Potter* books. In this second section, I focus primarily on presenting her character at face value and briefly delving into feminist, or anti-feminist, analyses of her actions and voice. The third section is dedicated to understanding Narcissa as a villain. Using counterexamples, Aunt Petunia and Bellatrix Lestrange, I attempt to determine whether Narcissa can be classified as a villain, or if she is simply an adversary. Following this, I will build upon my earlier introduction to reading maternal love as heroic in the *Harry Potter* series, briefly analyzing Molly Weasley, the prominently good, heroic mother, as a point of comparison to Narcissa. This final section dissects the heroics of Narcissa's lying to Voldemort as I attempt to locate a place for maternal urges and instincts within heroic deeds.

Gender Critiques of the *Harry Potter* Series

It is my intention in providing the following examples of the disparate arguments surrounding gender portrayals in the *Harry Potter* series to establish grounds for delving into the figure of the mother as represented by Narcissa Malfoy. Rowling has been widely criticized for narrowly and stereotypically portraying gender roles in the *Harry Potter* series, particularly in the first four books. In *Females and Harry Potter: Not All That Empowering*, Ruthann Mayes-Elma provides an overview of how gender is socially constructed, noting, "through literature, children learn how to act in accordance with their gender [...] Males are often shown as occupying diverse occupations and are usually portrayed as the problem solvers and the heroes, whereas females are often shown as housewives, secretaries, nurses, or teachers" (43). Essentially, Mayes-Elma argues that children's literature reinforces stereotypical patriarchal divisions of talents and labor. According to Mayes-Elma, with a few exceptions, Rowling's female characters appear to fall into these traditional categories.

Critics are largely divided as to whether Rowling's later books introduce characters with more dynamic and even transgressive conceptions of gender, or offer additional information that allow us to reinterpret early portrayals. In the second edition of *Critical Perspectives on Harry Potter*, Elizabeth Heilman and Trevor Donaldson revisit the piece that Heilman originally wrote for the first edition in which she argued that "it was clear that the Harry Potter books featured females in secondary positions of power and authority and replicated some of the most familiar cultural stereotypes for both males and females" (Heilman and Donaldson 139). Although the later, co-authored article concedes moments of female development like Hermione Granger's revelation of "personal ambition" or Professor McGonagall's leadership role during the Battle of Hogwarts (Heilman and Donaldson 144 and 143), Heilman and Donaldson maintain:

> Women are still marginalized, stereotyped, and even mocked [in the last three books]. The overall message related to power and gender still conforms to the stereotypical, hackneyed, and sexist patterns of the first four books, which reflect rather than challenge the worst elements of patriarchy [140].

Thus, Heilman and Donaldson echo Mayes-Elma's concern about literature replicating conventional gender divides. Allowing for the influx of, and increased attention to, female characters that begins in *Order of the Phoenix*, Heilman and Donaldson remain committed to the stance that Rowling's portrayals of women are problematic and concerning.

In contrast, Rowling has also been credited with presenting modern, even unconventional, gender roles. For example, scholars have suggested that characters like Hermione Granger are strong examples of contemporary feminist role models. Ximena Gallardo and C. Jason Smith have written two pieces arguing that Rowling's books contain "ample material to support feminist positions" (Gallardo and Smith 91). In *Reading Harry Potter,* which analyzes the first four books, Gallardo and Smith determine that "despite its rather stereotypical portrayal of female and male characters, the series challenge[s] standard constructions of gender and gender roles in significant ways" (91). A second piece they co-authored in 2009 for *Reading Harry Potter Again* encompasses all seven books and suggests "Rowling's creation actively troubles the culturally defined binaries that divide us all" (Gallardo and Smith 92). Narcissa is representative of how Rowling complicates and questions traditional gender roles. In Narcissa's transition from secondary citizen to controlling matriarch of the Malfoy family, Rowling's text reveals a critique of oppressive patriarchal constructs and highlights the subsequent move toward equality.

As will be evidenced, the majority of her appearances in the series show Narcissa to be conforming to traditionally stereotypical definitions of women and mothers. Yet, within these regressive representations, there is the possibility for progressive readings, as is acknowledged by all of the above critics in regard to Rowling's various portrayals of women. A deeper understanding of Narcissa's character, as it contributes to conversations about gender in the *Harry Potter* series, allows for a greater appreciation of her transition from female villain to female hero. Using a gender studies lens to analyze Narcissa and her fellow female characters allows us to complicate their actions, helping to define the nuances of the female hero archetype. Through close reading, actions that initially seem to be passive or subconscious become more intentional and meaningful, and these women can be seen for the heroes that they are.

A Voice of Her Own: Narcissa Malfoy's Journey from Villain to Hero

As she is largely a non-existent or peripheral character for the majority of the series, a broad examination of Narcissa's presence in the seven *Harry Potter* books will prove to be useful prior to analyzing her transformation and impact. Although she is mentioned in *Sorcerer's Stone*, readers are not actually introduced to Narcissa until the fourth book, *Harry Potter and the Goblet of Fire*. In the early installments, Narcissa is depicted simply as an extension of her husband. For example, Narcissa's first appearance, at the Quidditch World Cup in *Goblet of Fire*, is with her husband and son. While Rowling details how the two male Malfoys reach their seats, Narcissa's actions are only implied. After a terse greeting between the Malfoy and Weasley families, "[Mr. Malfoy] nod[s] sneeringly to Mr. Weasley and continue[s] down the line to his seats. Draco sho[ots] Harry, Ron, and Hermione a contemptuous look, then settle[s] himself between his mother and father" (*Goblet of Fire* 102). Narcissa is relegated to existing as an inference; we are asked to assume that her actions mirror those of her husband and son. Heilman and Donaldson see such discrepancies in characterization as part of the larger gender representation problem of the *Harry Potter* series. To their point, most of the narrative space of the series is devoted to male characters. Heilman and Donaldson suggest that the sudden inclusion and development of female characters that begins in *Order of the Phoenix* "reads as a willful attempt at gender inclusion" (142). Even though this drastic change appears to be contrived in order to appease critics, I would argue that the increasing revelation of details about Narcissa's character parallels the complication of the plot and Rowling's expanding word count.

In the sixth book, *Harry Potter and the Half-Blood Prince*, Rowling makes it much more apparent that Narcissa defers to her husband and his ilk, not due to a lack of attention paid to her characterization, but instead *because* of her characterization. The firm prejudices of the old wizarding family into which she was born, and the one into which she married, apparently extend beyond muggles and half-bloods, to pinpoint women as secondary citizens as well. Such prejudices help to define the social and political tensions inherent in wizarding culture, which is not an ideal society. The way in which Rowling aligns evil (primarily Voldemort and the Death Eaters) with sexism in the series suggests that she is problematizing traditional gender stereotypes. Just as Narcissa's individualization follows the trajectory of Rowling's expanding plot, so too her development mirrors her slow separation from the oppressive misogyny of the Death Eaters.

Even when she interacts with men outside of the pureblood ranks, Narcissa becomes meek and deferential. Of course, this only applies to men deemed worthy by Voldemort and his followers. It is important to note that Snape, although a half-blood, demands a certain amount of respect that vaults him closer to pureblood status because of the degree of intimacy he shares with Voldemort. For example, in the *Half-Blood Prince* scene in which Narcissa attempts to persuade Snape to protect Draco, the narrator describes:

> When Snape said nothing, Narcissa seemed to lose what little self-restraint she still possessed. Standing up, she staggered to Snape and seized the front of his robes. Her face close to his, her tears falling onto his chest, she gasped [...]. She crumpled, falling at his feet, sobbing and moaning on the floor [34–5].

The use of the word "self-restraint" here is telling: Narcissa is expected to be a demure, obedient woman, typically seen rather than heard, and when she does speak, she is supposed to be gracious and capitulating to her peers. When she breaks with normality and is in close proximity to Snape, she "staggers," indicating how emotionally distraught she is at this point in time and how unusual her actions are. After making her declaration, she prostrates herself on the ground in front of Snape, bodily acknowledging the shame that such a blatant display of emotion has caused, and how her actions have, despite her purer blood status, firmly given him the upper hand in their relations. Immediately following this, Narcissa fully breaks down, and Snape must take charge of this situation: "Snape stooped, seized her by the arms, lifted her up, and steered her back onto the sofa. He then poured her more wine and forced the glass into her hand" (*Half-Blood Prince* 35). For a man supposedly beneath her due to the status of his parents, Snape takes a very aggressive, authoritative stance with Narcissa. He takes charge of her, physically, and even controls her voice—she quiets her weeping only at his directive: "'Narcissa, that's enough. Drink this. Listen to me'" (*Half-Blood Prince* 35). At first glance, this simply appears to be one person trying to calm another. Underneath the seemingly well-intentioned statements, though, there are layers of implications regarding male power over female bodies—we cannot overlook the fact that these are *orders*.

Conventional iterations of patriarchy allow men to maintain control over women's actions and speech, as is seen in the above scene with Snape and Narcissa. With the interaction between Snape and Narcissa as indication, obedience is expected in interactions between Death Eaters and women. One of our first true glimpses into Narcissa's psyche is when she appeals to Snape to help Draco. It is important to note that the reason behind Narcissa's distress, the reason she appeals to Snape for help, is because her son is in danger. I will discuss this further in a later section. For now, it is important to recognize that this scene I have just described weighs heavily in an assessment of Narcissa's character, at least as it stands up until this point. Narcissa seems to actualize the image of the oppressed, secondary status of women in patriarchal society.

From the outset of the following and final book of the series, *Harry Potter and The Deathly Hallows*, Narcissa displays a new control over both her husband and son. This control extends beyond a traditional female dominance of the hearth and home. In *Deathly Hallows*, Narcissa appears to be in charge of the family's dealings with the Death Eaters and Voldemort himself. When Voldemort and his top tier of Death Eaters are gathered around the table, planning how to attack Harry on his birthday, Voldemort requests the use of Lucius Malfoy's wand. As the narrator describes, Lucius "glanced sideways at his wife. She was staring straight ahead quite as pale as he was [...] but beneath the table her slim fingers closed briefly on his wrist. At her touch, Malfoy put his hand into his robes, withdrew a wand, and passed it along" (*Deathly Hallows* 8). Despite having had a request made of him by Voldemort, a wizard known for brutally punishing or killing those who defy him, Lucius pauses to seek Narcissa's consent, perhaps even her instructions.

Draco, too, begins visibly taking directions from his mother, rather than his father: "[he] looked in terror at his father, who was staring down into his own lap, then caught his mother's eye. She shook her head almost imperceptibly, then resumed her own dead stare at the opposite wall" (*Deathly Hallows* 10). These actions starkly contrast Narcissa's persona in *Half-Blood Prince* when she pleads with Snape to take on Draco's task of murdering Dumbledore. In that scene, Narcissa seeks Snape's assistance without Lucius or Draco having any foreknowledge or approval, hinting at Narcissa's growing ability to take the initiative and act and think for herself. Yet, as I detailed earlier, Narcissa's strength falters and she emotionally crumbles and acts submissively to Snape. In *Deathly Hallows*, however, Narcissa's composure and confidence are absolute; both Lucius and Draco actively seek Narcissa's opinion of the situation at hand and allow her to guide their reactions. Furthermore, by the angles of their heads— Narcissa's raised and Lucius's lowered—the transfer of familial power and confidence is physically displayed. Since both Lucius and Draco are able to take and follow directions in silence, Rowling implies that, sometime between *Half-Blood Prince* and *Deathly Hallows*, Lucius and Draco both began deferring to Narcissa—her authority is now so ingrained that it can be communicated without vocalization.

Narcissa's transition from hyper-emotional and submissive to controlled and authoritative supports Heilman and Donaldson's finding that "in the later books, Rowling depicts women in positions of leadership in which they often control the actions or even the thoughts of male characters, as the very many females develop beyond the stereotypical femininity in which they have previously been cast" (143). Although Narcissa has taken on one of these "positions of leadership," I suggest that, rather than "develop[ing] beyond the stereotypical femininity," she, and her fellow mothers, work to redefine the maternal aspects of femininity. By this I mean that Narcissa and other mother figures, such as Molly Weasley, are prompted to action as a result of their maternity. Rather than moving "beyond," they more fully develop traits inherent in maternity, specifically the maternal impulse to protect, redefining this instinct to now include political, strategic, and militant actions that are not typically associated with women, especially not with mothers. In this expansion, Rowling's mothers are motivated to heroism in order to save their children and/or to make the world safer for their children. Ultimately, this incentive aligns with Campbell's understanding of the heroic deed as having "'the moral objective [of] of saving a people, or saving a person, or supporting an idea. The hero sacrifices himself for something'" (Campbell 127). Narcissa and Molly are overtly motivated by their need to protect their children. In the midst of a battle between two distinct sides, their decisions also align them with a specific idea and their actions impact more than their children; they are unquestionably heroic.

Building upon Narcissa's newly realized emotional control and authority, Rowling makes Narcissa's cool use of logic eminently apparent in *Deathly Hallows* as well. When Harry, Hermione, and Ron are brought to Malfoy Manor, Lucius's eagerness to alert Voldemort and earn forgiveness almost outweighs his thought to be careful by first confirming the captive's identities. Whereas Lucius is willing to quickly assume that he sees Harry's "'scar, stretched tight'" (*Deathly* Hallows 458–9), Narcissa is more cautious, calculating, and interested in sorting through the facts:

> "We had better be certain, Lucius," Narcissa called to her husband in her cold, clear voice. "Completely sure that it is Potter, before we summon the Dark Lord.... They say this is his"—she was looking closely at the blackthorn wand— "but it does not resemble Ollivander's description.... If we are mistaken, if we call the Dark Lord here for nothing.... Remember what he did to Rowle and Dolohov?" [*Deathly Hallows* 459].

Despite being excited to regain Voldemort's trust, Narcissa is unwilling to risk furthering their downfall by acting hastily, and perhaps mistakenly. During this scene, Draco seeks protection from his mother, staying as far away from his father and the captives as possible, as the narrator describes: "[Draco] walked away toward the fireplace where his mother stood watching" (*Deathly Hallows* 459). In the midst of the chaos that follows, Narcissa continues to think of Draco's safety first and foremost, "drag[ging] Draco out of the way of further

Dudley as the driving force behind her actions, Aunt Petunia should be
achieve heroic status through her maternal love. However, Aunt Petunia
her maternal love to the extreme, ultimately imploding any heroic under-
This is particularly true because she has been charged with being a sur-
mother to Harry, yet, in her quest to give everything to Dudley, she
ts and abuses Harry. Aunt Petunia is the exact opposite of a good mother
ry and, therefore, cannot be read as heroic through her maternal love.
ssa, on the other hand, takes Aunt Petunia's distaste for Harry to the
ne—for most of the series, she would certainly serve up Harry's life if it
o benefit her son. As such, it is difficult, if not impossible, to read Narcissa
rely "irritating," relegating her to the category of villain, at least for the
rity of the series.

Yet, when compared to Bellatrix, who is as "dark as her sister was fair"
f-Blood Prince 22), Narcissa's cold-hearted nature pales in comparison with
ister's deranged menace, echoing the dichotomy of their physical appear-
s. The enjoyment Bellatrix derives from watching other people suffer is
ing short of psychotic, although it is arguable that this extreme personality
esult of her stint in Azkaban. Regardless of how she came to be so ruthless,
willingness to torture and kill in the name of her recognized master is whole-
ted. For example, when the Death Eaters lure Harry and his friends to the
artment of Mysteries in *Order of the Phoenix*, Bellatrix is eager to begin
sically harming the *children*: "'You need more persuasion?' she said, her
st rising and falling rapidly. 'Very well—take the smallest one,' she ordered
Death Eaters beside her. 'Let him watch while we torture the little girl. I'll
it'" (783). Even Bellatrix's death emphasizes her extreme villainy: "Bellatrix
ghed [...] Molly's curse soared beneath Bellatrix's outstretched arm and hit
r squarely in the chest, directly over her heart. Bellatrix's gloating smile froze"
)eathly Hallows 736). Her laughter and "gloating smile" at the thought of
reaking further destruction on the Weasley family parallels the maniacal
havior of Voldemort who, for example, sets the Sorting Hat on fire after plac-
g it atop Neville Longbottom's head (*Deathly Hallows* 732). In comparison,
arcissa is not so openly brutal in her hostility and her actions in the series are
guably less villainous. Nevertheless, those same actions, and her words, suggest
hat Narcissa would willingly and without hesitation display her villainy, if
ressed.

We see this in Narcissa's reaction to Harry and Ron when they meet buying
obes in Madam Malkin's prior to returning to Hogwarts for the sixth year.
Narcissa is not above threatening Harry and Ron, and although she is not given
a chance to follow through, she demonstrates that she is willing to sacrifice
other lives—other *teenage* lives—for the sake of her family. In this moment,
sharp words are exchanged and wands are drawn: "'Put those away,' [Narcissa]
said coldly to Harry and Ron. 'If you attack my son again, I shall ensure that it

harm" (*Deathly Hallows* 474). It is this concern for I
newly acquired authority over the family's dealing wi
lesce and allow Narcissa to transition from a villain t

Shades of Evil: Female Villains of *Harry Potte*

Because there is a plethora of truly evil, ruthless (
Potter series, Narcissa does not necessarily stand out as
are very few memorable female villains in the series. V
characters dominate the *Harry Potter* series, as Heilman a
"among characters with some role [...] there are 115 fema
tioned in the series as a whole. Further, the more importa
dominantly male" (141). They go on to suggest that "th
frightening, evil, or suspected of evil, are overwhelmingly
books and primarily male in the later books. [...] Most of tl
evil) grown-ups are female" (142). While this assessment
rization of many female adults in the series as "irritating'
look when considering Narcissa as a villain. The dominan
the series are: Narcissa's sister, Bellatrix Lestrange; the M
Dolores Umbridge; and, slightly stretching the term "domina
Death Eater and temporary Hogwarts teacher, Alecto Carı
and Rita Skeeter, on the other hand, firmly occupy the categ
adult female. I imagine Bellatrix and Aunt Petunia to be repre
respective categories, and cursorily analyze some of their ac
determine a place for Narcissa on the spectrum of evil to irrita
acters: is Narcissa simply another Aunt Petunia, annoying and
Harry's life uncomfortable in order for her own son to benefit
more devious and underhanded, in the same vein as her sistei
gleefully kills Harry's godfather Sirius Black, and worships Volc
ately wanting to be his second-in-command?

Without a doubt, Aunt Petunia treats Harry in a terribly egre
Along with her husband, she forces Harry to sleep in a cupbo
stairs, treats him as some combination of household staff and intr
bally abuses him, to name a few. To Aunt Petunia, Harry is an i
and a reminder that her sister and her sister's husband were a pa
of which she was both envious and terrified (*Deathly Hallows* 66
of Harry's magical powers appears when Aunt Petunia attempts to
do something unpleasant, such as when she gives him a terrible hair
she tries to make him wear a horrid secondhand sweater (*Sorcerer'*
Aunt Petunia never says or does anything to indicate that she actu
Harry *dead*; she simply wants everything to be perfect for her sor

is the last thing you ever do.' [...] [She] smiled unpleasantly. [...] Dumbledore won't always be there to protect you'" (*Half-Blood Prince* 113). Note that Narcissa steps in to protect "'her son'" and that it is this, *specifically,* that drives her to issue death threats. By issuing her threats "coldly," Narcissa maintains her composure and, in doing so, becomes more convincing and menacing than she might have been otherwise.

Along with her authority, Narcissa's villainy (in order to protect her son) escalates as the series progresses. A prime example is her excitement in being able to identify Hermione Granger at Malfoy Manor in *Deathly Hallows*. Narcissa's reaction indicates that she would have no reservations about sending three teenagers to their supposedly unavoidable deaths in order to save her family: "'Wait,' said Narcissa sharply. 'Yes—yes, she was in Madam Malkin's shop with Potter! I saw her picture in the *Prophet*! Look, Draco, isn't it the Granger girl?'" (*Deathly Hallows* 459). She and Lucius never get the opportunity to summon Voldemort, however, because her sister intervenes to protect herself and to attempt to disguise her own mistakes (*Deathly Hallows* 461).

Between these two scenes, we see that Narcissa's villainy seems to exist in unrealized threats—she has the *potential* for causing great harm. As such, she is certainly far from being the most maniacal adversary that Harry faces. In fact, through her maternal instincts, Narcissa becomes more of a threat to Dumbledore than she ever is to Harry. Voldemort himself tasks Draco with killing Dumbledore. In her quest to protect her son, Narcissa becomes single-minded in her pursuit to locate someone who, unlike Draco, can almost certainly succeed in murdering Dumbledore. Narcissa's plea to Snape is desperate and heartfelt: "'You could do it. You could do it, instead of Draco, Severus. You would succeed, of course you would [...]' (*Half-Blood Prince* 34). Even when her sister, Bellatrix, attempts to stop her from seeking out Snape, Narcissa "dr[aws] a wand from beneath her cloak, holding it threateningly in [Bellatrix's] face [...] 'There is nothing I wouldn't do anymore!'" (*Half-Blood Prince* 21). Narcissa's desperation is evident and resisting her sister seems very out of character. Rereading this scene knowing that Narcissa submits to Bellatrix as she usurps the control of Malfoy Manor in *Deathly Hallows*, we see how distraught Narcissa must be in order to challenge her sister's authority by threatening her (*Deathly Hallows* 462). It is later revealed that Snape and Dumbledore had an agreement regarding the latter's death from the very beginning (*Deathly Hallows* 682–3). Since Narcissa was not privy to this arrangement, however, her efforts to facilitate Dumbledore's demise mark her as a true villain in *Half-Blood Prince*. As previously mentioned, however, the final two books of the series reveal a significant, ongoing transformation in Narcissa. In resisting her husband's control and acting of her own discretion in order to protect her son, Narcissa moves toward a resolution that finds her heroic, not just for Draco, but for the entire series.

Anything for Love: Heroic Mothers of *Harry Potter*

To better understand the transformation that Narcissa undergoes between *Half-Blood Prince* and *Deathly Hallows*, it is important to recognize that the maternal hero is a pervasive figure throughout the *Harry Potter* series. As I previously mentioned, Lily Potter's death establishes the concept of maternal love as heroic as foundational to the series. But, how does maternal love breach the divide between expected actualizations of femininity and heroism?

Until the final installments of the series, Rowling presents extremely conventional depictions of nuclear families: "the Weasleys and the Dursleys have stay-at-home mothers and employed, head-of-the-household type fathers. The mothers are bossy, and are so over-involved with their children they are stifling, spoiling, and inappropriate" (Heilman and Donaldson 152–3). Although Molly Weasley eventually moves beyond the domestic, taking an active role in the Order of the Phoenix, Heilman and Donaldson point out that she "leaves The Burrow to protect her children and duels to defend her daughter, making her aggressive assertions consistent with her mothering role" (Heilman and Donaldson 144). The way in which Heilman and Donaldson present Molly's participation in the Order of the Phoenix and the Battle of Hogwarts suggests that Molly's maternal motivation lessens her agency. And yet, Molly remains in control of her decision *to act* and the specific course of her action—maternal motivation does not overwrite a mother's freedom to make decisions. In her work on family structure, feminist literary theorist Nancy Chodorow writes that the mother suffers from "a sense of diffuse responsibility for everything connected to the welfare of her family and the happiness and success of her children" (59). As such, mothers are positioned as having *additional* concerns factor into their decision-making processes, but they are not stripped of their personhood, as implied by conservative readings of maternal heroes. Furthermore, in the turbulent world that Rowling creates, mothers have the additional challenge of working not only to keep their children "happ[y] and success[ful]," but also, more importantly, alive. If we deny Molly (or Narcissa) credit for their actions because they evolve out of maternal instinct, we are validating regressive readings of motherhood.

Does this make Molly and Narcissa's actions any less important than those of childless characters who act heroically? I argue that it should not impact how we see their actions as we are urged to see several parental figures as heroes, including both of the elder Potters. James, like Lily who dies to save Harry, sacrifices his life in order to protect his wife and child. Rowling emphasizes the elder Potter's heroism in flashback in *Prisoner of Azkaban*. When attempting to cast a spell, Harry is hit with a memory of his father shouting the night of his death: "'Lily, take Harry and go! It's Him! Go! Run! I'll hold him off—'"

(*Prisoner of Azkaban* 178). The manner in which James's death is discussed within the series characterizes these actions as heroic. Voldemort himself can see how impressive their bravery was in the face of imminent death: "'Yes, boy, your parents were brave...I killed your father first, and he put up a courageous fight ... but your mother needn't have died ... she was trying to protect you'" (*Sorcerer's Stone* 294). Voldemort's account of the night the Potters died is very telling: he describes James's willingness to sacrifice himself for his family as "courageous," yet Lily's actions were needless.

This motif of the heroic *paternal* figure is repeated again and again throughout the series. Sirius Black's heedless heroics are born out of the overwhelming desire to protect Harry, his godson; and readers are asked to forgive and understand Remus Lupin first when he attempts to abandon his pregnant wife for both her sake and that of their baby, and then again when he leaves them with his mother-in-law as he goes to fight in the Battle of Hogwarts (*Deathly Hallows* 624). Although it is frustrating that so many women of the *Harry Potter* series conform to the stereotypical roles of mother, educator, or evil aberrant, the actions of Molly and Narcissa are no less heroic because they are undertaken out of a desire to protect their respective children, particularly when viewed in conjunction with the heroic fathers (or father-figures) of the series.

In fact, returning to Molly and her critical departure from The Burrow in *Deathly Hallows*, I suggest that Molly is heroic *because* she is acting in defense of her daughter, specifically, and her family, in general. Yes, the moment when she engages Bellatrix in a duel in the Final Battle has its comical elements. When she cries out "'NOT MY DAUGHTER, YOU BITCH'" (*Deathly Hallows* 736), it is so incongruous to Molly's typical behavior that it is humorous. At the same time, this threat, so apparently incompatible with the character that Rowling has constructed until this point, serves a dual purpose. Firstly, it is a nod to how devoted Molly is to protecting her family, and how she is accessing and harnessing her latent aggressive capabilities in order to keep them safe. Secondly, this line, and Molly's ferocity in this final battle, suggest that there is more to her character than Rowling has been able to reveal—that Molly might not be as mild-mannered as she seems. Furthermore, in the midst of their duel, Molly verbally references the fact that her cause extends beyond her family to the wizarding world: "'You—will—never—touch—our—children—again'" (*Deathly Hallows* 736). The use of "our" is critical. Molly reveals that her motives are twofold: to protect her family and to help make the world safer for *all* children. Undeniably, in Molly, the maternal has become the heroic: maternal impulses have not only revealed a hidden side of her, but they have expanded to a type of global maternity.

In the same vein, Narcissa's transformation coincides with the increasing need to protect her son from harm. She begins to find her voice and cultivate her power when her son's safety demands it. Thus, when we arrive at the pivotal scene in *Deathly Hallows* that follows Harry's willing sacrifice to Voldemort, several powerful changes have coalesced within Narcissa causing her to lie to Voldemort about Harry being dead in a desperate hope to see her own son again. When Voldemort sends Narcissa to assess Harry's body and determine whether or not he is dead, she examines him with a touch "softer than he had been expecting" (*Deathly Hallows* 726). This gentle touch both hints at her compassionate side and suggests that she is finally drawing connections between Harry and Draco—she treats Harry with the care that she might show her son. The only words that Narcissa dares to utter to the supposedly-dead Harry are: "'*Is Draco alive? Is he in the castle?*'" (*Deathly Hallows* 726, emphasis in original). Narcissa risks both her own life and Harry's in order to hear her son's fate; once she has secured the hope of seeing Draco again, Narcissa decides to lie to Voldemort and place her family's future in Harry's hands. With that decision, Narcissa realigns her fate (and that of her family) with that of Harry, cementing her transition from villain to hero. Simultaneously, she reaches a defining point of self-reinvention as she takes the lead on family affairs instead of deferring to her husband's decisions—Lucius has absolutely no role in this scenario.

In this moment, Narcissa not only controls the fate of her family, but that of the entire wizarding world. In the Epilogue, Rowling introduces us to the next generation of Hogwarts students, a generation that would not have existed, or would have been inexplicably altered, had Narcissa made a different choice. Narcissa, even more so than Molly, inadvertently becomes the global maternal, and her heroics are undeniable. Writing on motherhood, Evelyn Nakaon Glenn argues, "[Mothers] are seen as all-powerful—holding the fate of their children and ultimately the future of society in their hands—and as powerless—subordinated to the dictates of nature, instinct and social forces beyond their ken" (11). Narcissa, for the early books, conforms to both parts of this concept, protecting Draco as much as she can while still acting properly according to the rules of the society in which she lives and operates. Only in the final book does she truly break away from this conventional notion, acting with Draco's fate in the forefront of her thoughts while simultaneously shedding the shackles of her oppressors and manipulating sociopolitical forces to achieve her own end. Since Narcissa dedicates her life, with awareness that she might have to sacrifice herself or others to protect Draco, the *Harry Potter* series ends with her firmly established as a female hero, through her maternal heroics. Rowling does assign many of her female characters very traditional roles, but in doing so, she also allows herself the space to reinvent and fully develop these roles for women in unconventional ways. In effect, through devising maternal heroes like Narcissa, Rowling adds her voice to the conversation about whether or not women can have it all and what exactly that means.

Works Cited

Campbell, Joseph, and Bill Moyers. *The Power of Myth.* New York: Doubleday, 1988.

Chodorow, Nancy. "Family Structure and Feminine Personality. " *Woman, Culture, & Society.* Ed. Michelle Zimbalist Rosaldo and Louise Lamphere. Stanford: Stanford University Press, 1974. 43–66.

Gallardo-C., X. and C. Jason Smith. "Happily Ever After: Harry Potter and the Quest for the Domestic. " *Reading Harry Potter Again.* Ed. Giselle Liza Anatol. Santa Barbara: Praeger, 2009. 91–108.

Glenn, Evelyn Nakano, Grace Chang, and Linda Rennie Forcey, eds. *Mothering, Ideology, Experience, and Agency.* New York: Routledge, 1994.

Heilman, Elizabeth E., and Trevor Donaldson. "From Sexist to (sort-of) Feminist: *Representations of Gender in the Harry Potter Series.* " *Critical Perspectives on Harry Potter.* Ed. Elizabeth E. Heilman. New York: Routledge, 2009. 139–161.

Mayes-Elma, Ruthann. *Females and Harry Potter: Not All That Empowering.* Lanham, MD: Rowman & Littlefield, 2006.

O'Reilly, Andrea, ed. *From Motherhood to Mothering: The Legacy of Adrienne Rich's Of Woman Born.* Albany: State University of New York Press, 2004.

Rowling, J. K. *Harry Potter and the Deathly Hallows.* New York: Arthur A. Levine, 2007.

_____. *Harry Potter and the Goblet of Fire.* New York: Scholastic Press, 2000.

_____. *Harry Potter and the Half-Blood Prince.* New York: Arthur A. Levine, 2005.

_____. *Harry Potter and the Order of the Phoenix.* New York: Scholastic Press, 2003.

_____. *Harry Potter and the Prisoner of Azkaban.* London: Bloomsbury, 1999.

_____. *Harry Potter and the Sorcerer's Stone.* New York: Scholastic Press, 1997.

Conclusion

Lori M. Campbell

The past fourteen chapters demonstrate that the female hero in modern fantasy is a subtle, complex, and formidable creature. While retaining the obvious and ubiquitous qualities (strength, courage, a willingness to self-sacrifice) that have long defined her male counterpart, the female hero performs these traits in her own way, both complicating and problematizing the tropes of heroism itself in the process. As this closing section is designed to inspire further thinking and research, it is perhaps more productive here to define her, based on the findings of the contributors, by using the shorter list of what she is *not* as a way of understanding who she is.

1. At first glance, she is not likely to succeed.

    I dedicate a grouping of essays to "Underestimated Overachievers," but to varying extents all of the heroes discussed in *A Quest of Her Own* fit the category of those whose "arête is concealed" (37), as W.H. Auden famously identifies. Diana Wynne Jones' view that "above all, heroes go into action when the odds are against them" (130) epitomizes the unlikely hero whose personal situation (lack of strength, finances, social status, etc.) leaves her (or him) at a disadvantage before they even face the actual tests of their quests. From medieval women such as Nyneve, who stretch the boundaries of a system that sorts women into binaries of angel or witch; to Neil Gaiman's Coraline, who transforms the relative powerlessness of childhood into heroism through her "ordinary" imagination; to Katniss Everdeen, the impoverished, half-orphaned breadwinner for her family in District 12, which had only placed two winners on the podium in seventy-four years of the Hunger Games' existence—all of these female heroes and the others discussed in this volume rise above their respective circumstances to claim power and commit acts of courage and self-sacrifice that resonate beyond themselves.

2. She is not overly burdened by gendered or other social expectations.

A major consideration of defining the female hero involves rescuing stereotypically feminine traits from the negative connotations that might have previously compromised perceptions of her heroism. Indeed, an important critical pattern that has emerged in the preceding essays is the interrogation of notions of "masculine" or "feminine" being rigidly applied to what are in reality *human* qualities. For example, in his essay "A New Kind of Hero: *A Song of Ice and Fire's* Brienne of Tarth," John D. Cameron ponders "Is compassion a mark of female heroism in a way that it is not for a male hero?" and similar questions are implicit in several other essays in this collection. I am particularly struck by Erin Wyble Newcomb's exploration of Ursula Le Guin's *Tehanu* in which care work is positioned as a trope of female heroism and a mark of strength such that Tenar as a middle-aged widow—certainly not the traditional guise of heroism, female or otherwise—out-powers all of the men who underestimate and threaten her.

In the same way, motherhood and maternal impulses emerge as a main point of contention, again being transformed from potentially limiting, purely female provinces into heroic acts that are not necessarily restricted to biology. As Cothran illustrates in her essay, Tenar's mothering in *Tehanu* takes diverse forms and touches several people, none of whom are her own flesh-and-blood, including Ogion and even Ged. Both Phillip Pullman's Mrs. Coulter (*His Dark Materials*) and J.K. Rowling's Narcissa Malfoy (*Harry Potter*) achieve heroism and redemption through maternal love, and the hero journey of Nix's Arthur Penhaligon in *Keys to the Kingdom* is entirely motivated by his unresolved feelings of maternal loss. As Carol Pearson and Katherine Pope assert, "Freeing the heroic journey from the limiting assumptions about appropriate female and male behavior, then, is an important step in defining a truly human—and truly humane—pattern of heroic action" (5). Examples such as these and those explored throughout this book free the female hero to exert her particular talents in powerful ways and in the process to overturn any possible negative associations that might have previously undermined femininity and the value of woman as a woman.

3. She is not a superhero (but she can be a *super* hero.)

In other words, the female hero in modern fantasy need not (and generally is not, given her unlikeliness) a figure of idealized perfection or masculinesque power. Like her male counterpart, she has flaws; she shows fear, she makes mistakes or misreads situations, and in the case of the villain-heroes discussed in section IV, she does not always have good intentions. Despite these flaws, however, she is extraordinary in her ability to enable positive change and shows superior bravery, assertiveness, and intelligence in the face of seemingly insurmountable obstacles.

In "What Is a Female Superhero?" Jennifer K. Stuller explains, "according to the most basic definition, a superhero might or might not have powers and might or might not wear a costume, but he or she must be committed to working for the greater good" (19). While I maintain the distinctions between the female hero in modern fantasy and the female super-heroine, Stuller's notion of the contemporary superhero neatly applies here. In similar terms, the female hero in modern fantasy is often disinterested in flashy appearances, as illustrated by the women struggling to negotiate the public gaze in the terms suggested in Casey A. Cothran's essay. She is sometimes but not always a magic user, but when she is, like Garth Nix's Lirael and Diana Wynne Jones's Roddy (*The Merlin Conspiracy*), her magic meaningfully links her to a tradition of female power being used to create or rescue—while retaining the potential to destroy. Ultimately, then, the female hero in modern fantasy is "super" in her ability to carve an identity for herself, to rise above her circumstances, and to remake her surroundings as well as the world at large.

4. She is not going away.

When in the early 1970s, Alison Lurie and Marcia R. Lieberman debated the power and assertiveness of female characters in fairy tales; and in 1981, when Carol Pearson and Katherine Pope sought to define *The Female Hero in American and British Literature,* few if any characters existed who could adequately represent the category as described in *A Quest of Her Own.* The fact that in 2014 there are enough to fill fourteen chapters—and indeed, there are easily enough for several more such books—proves that the female hero has truly achieved the status of a modern fantasy archetype. As fantasy continues to evolve along with the culture that it continually engages, so too will the female hero, until one day—perhaps in the not-too-distant future—there will be only one word, "hero," to describe the character who demonstrates such qualities, whether female or male.

WORKS CITED

Auden, W.H. "The Quest Hero." *Understanding* The Lord of the Rings: *The Best of Tolkien Criticism.* Rose A. Zimbardo and Neil D. Isaacs, eds. New York: Houghton Mifflin, 2004. 31–51,

Jones, Diana Wynne. "The Heroic Ideal: A Personal Odyssey." *The Lion and the Unicorn* 13.1 (June 1989): 129–40.

Pearson, Carol, and Katherine Pope. *The Female Hero in American and British Literature.* New York: R.R. Bowker, 1981.

Stuller, Jennifer K. "What Is a Female Superhero?" *What Is a Superhero?* Robin S. Rosenberg and Peter Coogan, eds. New York: Oxford University Press, 2013.

About the Contributors

Kristin **Bovaird-Abbo** is an assistant professor of English at the University of Northern Colorado, where she teaches courses on Old English, Middle English, linguistics, mythology, Tolkien and the Arthurian legend. She is at work on a book project exploring the effects of gender and class on depictions of Gawain in fifteenth-century Middle English romances.

John H. **Cameron** teaches English literature at Saint Mary's University. His field is Shakespeare and early modern drama, but he has also published on film and television, postcolonial literature, the detective story and the works of Tom Stoppard and Robert Louis Stevenson. He is working on a monograph dealing with critical readings of Hamlet and what these readings may suggest about the nature of literary criticism.

Lori M. **Campbell** is a lecturer in the Department of English at University of Pittsburgh, where she teaches courses in fantasy, myth and folktale, and children's literature. Her book *Portals of Power* was published by McFarland in 2010. Other publications include articles on J.R.R. Tolkien, J.K. Rowling, Frances Hodgson Burnett, J.M. Barrie, Thomas Hardy and William Morris.

Casey A. **Cothran** is an assistant professor of English at Winthrop University. She has published articles on Wilkie Collins, New Woman writers and J.K. Rowling's *Harry Potter* series.

Jack M. **Downs** is an independent scholar and researcher specializing in the history of English studies and Victorian literary culture. In his most recent academic appointment, he was a visiting assistant professor of English and Writing Center director at Whitworth University.

Amanda M. **Greenwell** teaches courses in literature for young adults, English teacher education and composition at Central Connecticut State University and the University of Saint Joseph. She also facilitates workshops in writing and academic success in the Center for Academic Excellence at USJ.

Zoe **Jaques** is a research fellow at Anglia Ruskin University and a by-fellow at Homerton College, University of Cambridge. Her co-authored Ashgate book on the publishing history of Lewis Carroll's *Alice* books led to fellowships at Harvard University and the University of Texas at Austin. Her second book, *Children's Literature and the Posthuman*, is forthcoming.

Jeana **Jorgensen** teaches courses in the departments of anthropology and history as well as gender, women's and sexuality studies at Butler University. Her research interests include fairy tales, feminist theory, fantasy literature, digital humanities, dance and body art.

Sarah Margaret **Kniesler** is a Ph.D. student in English at the University of Florida. Her primary research focus is on maternity in British sensation novels. She has published on Hermione Granger as a contemporary feminist role model, an ecofeminist reading of the *Hunger Games* trilogy, and complicating the roles of maternal figures in both contemporary crime fiction and children's literature.

Apolline **Lucyk** is a graduate student and freelance writer from Saskatchewan, Canada. Her research interests include fantasy literature, women's literature, adaptation studies and the works of the twentieth-century Dutch writer and thinker Etty Hillesum. Her master's thesis is on postmodern identity in the fantastical works of Diana Wynne Jones.

Erin Wyble **Newcomb** teaches in the Department of English at the State University of New York at New Paltz. Her courses include young adult literature, American literature and American women's literature, as well as various composition courses.

Jill Marie **Treftz** is an assistant professor of English at Marshall University. She specializes in nineteenth-century British literature, with a particular emphasis in women's poetry, and she also teaches courses on fantasy literature and on Harry Potter.

Melissa **Wehler** is an associate professor of English at Central Penn College, where she teaches courses on writing, the gothic, film and popular culture. She has contributed essays to *Demons of the Body and Mind* (McFarland, 2010), *Transnational Gothic* (Ashgate, 2013), and a forthcoming collection on *Downton Abbey* (McFarland).

Sarah **Workman** is a Ph.D. candidate in the Department of English and Comparative Literature at the University of North Carolina Chapel Hill, where she studies twentieth and twenty-first century American and multi-ethnic literatures.

Index